Microsoft® Expression® Web 4 Step by Step

Chris Leeds

Acquisitions and Developmental Editor: Russell Jones
Production Editor: Teresa Elsey
Editorial Production: Online Training Solutions, Inc.
Technical Reviewers: Kathleen Anderson and Gerry Tiegrob
Illustrator: Robert Romano
Indexer: Ellen Troutman Zaig
Cover: Karen Montgomery

978-0-735-63902-7

Contents at a Glance

Table of Contents

What do you think of this book? We want to hear from you!

Microsoft is interested in hearing your feedback so we can continually improve our books and learning resources for you. To participate in a brief online survey, please visit:

www.microsoft.com/learning/booksurvey

Acknowledgments

I want to thank the readers of my previous edition of this book, and the visitors to my support site (www.expressionwebstepbystep.com). I'd like to include a special thanks to Russell Jones (O'Reilly Media, project editor), Kathleen Anderson and Gerry Tiegrob (technical reviewers), and all the people at Microsoft Press and O'Reilly Media who really had more to do with the physical manifestation of this book than I did. Last but not least, I'd like to thank the people on the Expression Web product team for their commitment to deliver a truly technology-agnostic Web design tool that makes modern, standards-based Web authoring so much easier than it used to be. Thank you all!

—Chris Leeds

Introduction

Microsoft Expression Web 4 is the newest Web editing and management application from Microsoft. It is a professional design tool used to create modern, standards-based sites that deliver superior quality on the Web.

From the perspective of a designer or developer, the modern Web bears only a slight resemblance to the Web of even as little as five years ago. Expression Web 4 is an effort by Microsoft to provide a tool that helps designers attain modern Web design standards and practices.

Expression Web 4 includes features that help ensure your output adheres to World Wide Web Consortium (W3C) validity standards, and that help you to cleanly separate content from presentation by taking advantage of the functionality and capabilities of cascading style sheets (CSS).

As you drill deeper into Expression Web 4, you will find tools to make working with Microsoft ASP.NET much more comfortable than ever before, such as the ASP.NET Development Server that installs with Expression Web and the ASP.NET Controls group in the Toolbox panel.

In addition, Expression Web helps you to easily use some of the features that ASP.NET offers, specifically, ASP.NET Master Pages, Navigation Controls, and Data Controls. It's refreshing that tools with this type of power are available in a user-friendly designer-centric application like Expression Web 4 as opposed to being limited to programmer-oriented tools such as Microsoft Visual Web Developer or Microsoft Visual Studio.

System Requirements

To perform the exercises in this book, your computer should meet the following requirements:

- Windows XP with Service Pack 3, Windows Vista, Windows 7, or Windows Server 2008 operating system
- PC with 1 GHz or faster processor
- 1 GB of RAM or more
- 2 GB or more of available hard disk space
- Microsoft .NET Framework 4
- Microsoft Silverlight 4
- A monitor capable of 1024×768 or higher resolution with 24-bit color

- Support for Microsoft DirectX 9 graphics with Windows Vista Display Driver Model (WDDM), 128 MB of graphics RAM or more, Pixel Shader 3.0 in hardware, 32 bits per pixel

- Internet access (additional fees may apply)

- Some product features require Firefox 3.0 or later and Internet Explorer 8

Actual requirements and product functionality may vary based on your system configuration and operating system.

Information for Readers Running Windows XP or Vista

The graphics and the operating system-related instructions in this book reflect the Windows 7 user interface, but you can also use a computer running Windows Vista or Windows XP with Service Pack 3 (SP3) installed.

Most of the differences you will encounter when working through the exercises in this book on a computer running Windows Vista or Windows XP relate to appearance rather than functionality. For example, the Windows 7 and Windows Vista Start buttons are round rather than rectangular and are not labeled with the word Start; window frames and window-management buttons look different; and if your system supports Windows Aero, the window frames might be transparent.

For the most part, differences in navigating to or through menus and dialog boxes in Windows Vista or Windows XP are small enough that you will have no difficulty in completing the exercises.

Who Is This Book For?

This book is intended for existing or new Web designers. Although the book intends to provide lessons to new Web designers, experienced practitioners will be able to quickly gain familiarity with the Expression Web 4 user interface and features. Former Microsoft FrontPage users should also find this book helpful in making a transition from FrontPage to Expression Web.

Assumptions

This book expects that you have at least a minimal understanding of basic computer use and file operations with your chosen operating system. No experience in Web design or development is required.

What's New in Expression Web 4

- **SuperPreview Online Service** The Microsoft Expression Web SuperPreview online service is a beta service that extends the capability of SuperPreview to include support for additional browsers and operating systems. For example, you can preview your pages in Apple Safari running on an OSX system "in the cloud."

- **SEO Checker** The SEO Checker feature of Expression Web analyzes your site against the best practices for getting the highest possible search engine rankings for your site. You can choose SEO options, display an SEO report, filter the results in the SEO report, and step forward and back through the list of results in the SEO report to see more detail for individual list items.

Acquiring Expression Web 4

You can purchase Expression Web 4 as part of Microsoft Expression Studio 4 Web Professional, which is an integrated group of applications that includes:

- **Expression Web 4 and SuperPreview** Expression Web is a professional design tool used to create engaging, Web-connected multimedia experiences for Windows. SuperPreview speeds browser compatibility testing by not only showing a high-fidelity rendering of how pages will look on different browsers, but it also identifies the element's tag, size, and position; applied styles; and location in the Document Object Model (DOM) tree so you can quickly fix the error.

- **Expression Design 4** Microsoft Expression Design 4 is the perfect companion to Microsoft Expression Blend or Expression Web. Use existing artwork or intuitive vector drawing tools to quickly build sophisticated vector and image assets. Seamlessly transfer them to your Expression Blend or Expression Web projects knowing that their fidelity and live effects will be maintained throughout the entire designer-developer workflow.

- **Expression Encoder 4** Microsoft Expression Encoder simplifies publishing video to Silverlight. Encode a wide array of video file formats, stream live from Web cams and camcorders, and screen capture on your computer. Make simple edits to video files and enhance your media with overlays and advertising. Choose encoding settings, select from a range of player templates, and publish rich media experiences with Silverlight.

You can also purchase Expression Web 4 as a component of Microsoft Expression Studio 4 Ultimate, which includes all that the professional version contains, plus these additional products:

- **Expression Blend 4** Utilizing the industry-proven technologies in Silverlight, WPF, XAML, Microsoft Visual C# and Microsoft Visual Basic, Expression Blend enables you to deliver applications that are stable, scalable, accessible, reliable, and highly secure, while maintaining optimum performance. SketchFlow, a feature of Expression Studio Ultimate, revolutionizes how quickly and efficiently you can demonstrate your vision for an application. It provides an informal and quick way to explore, iterate, and prototype user interface scenarios, allowing you to evolve your concepts from a series of rough ideas into a living and breathing prototype that can be made as real as a particular client or project demands.

- **Expression Encoder 4 Professional** The professional version of Expression Encoder contains more import and export codecs and unlimited screen recording duration, whereas the basic version of Expression Encoder is limited to 10-minute screen recordings.

Additionally, you can purchase both versions of Expression Studio as an upgrade—and the upgrade isn't limited to users of just Expression Web 3, but is available to owners of any previous Microsoft Expression product as well as any version of Adobe Creative Suite or Microsoft Visual Studio 2005 or later.

Beyond that, you can get Expression Studio as part of the Microsoft Partner program, at *https://partner.microsoft.com/40043420*, and through the Microsoft WebsiteSpark program at *http://websitespark.com*.

Finally, if you're a student, you can get Expression Studio 4 and a huge collection of other Microsoft development software through Microsoft DreamSpark, at *http://www.dreamspark .com*. With DreamSpark, students can download Microsoft developer and design tools at no charge, making it easier for them to learn the skills they need to excel both during school and after graduation.

Code Samples

Most of the chapters in this book include exercises that let you interactively try out new material learned in the main text. All sample projects are available for download from the book's page on the Web site for the Microsoft publishing partner, O'Reilly Media:

http://oreilly.com/catalog/9780735639027

Click the Companion Content link on that page under the book cover image. When a list of files appears, locate and download the examples.zip file.

Installing the Code Samples

Unzip the examples.zip file that you downloaded from the book's Web site to a location on your hard drive. In order for your screen to match the images in this book, we recommend that you unzip the folder to \User\Documents\Microsoft Press\Expression Web 4 SBS\.

What's in the Sample Code?

This book's sample code contains the main site called "SampleSite" with a page for each chapter of this book, several Deep Zoom Composer projects, videos, an Expression Design graphics template, and all the other assets required to complete the chapter exercises you will encounter.

Organization of This Book

- Chapter 1, Understanding How Expression Web 4 Works
  - ❏ Identify and use the Expression Web 4 user interface elements
  - ❏ Open a site
  - ❏ Use Site Views
  - ❏ Open a page
  - ❏ Use page views
  - ❏ Use the Snapshot Panel
  - ❏ Use Visual Aids
  - ❏ Use browser preview
  - ❏ Use SuperPreview
- Chapter 2, Capitalizing on Expression Web 4 Functionality
  - ❏ Change site settings
  - ❏ Change Application Options
  - ❏ Change Page Editor Options
  - ❏ Use the Expression Development Server
  - ❏ Use PHP with the Expression Development Server
  - ❏ Create a new site with Expression Web
  - ❏ Use the Import Site Wizard
  - ❏ Configure add-ins

- Chapter 3, Capitalizing on the Template Options in Expression Web 4
  - ❏ Understand template concepts
  - ❏ Use Dynamic Web Templates
  - ❏ Use the Include Page feature
  - ❏ Use ASP.NET master pages
  - ❏ Use ASP.NET Web user controls
  - ❏ Use PHP include files
- Chapter 4, It's All About Content
  - ❏ Use tables properly
  - ❏ Use lists to group information
  - ❏ Use semantic markup
  - ❏ Style the presentation of your content
  - ❏ Add images to a Web page
  - ❏ Edit images with Expression Design
  - ❏ Use Photoshop files in a Web page
  - ❏ Use Silverlight Video in a Web page
  - ❏ Use Deep Zoom Composer projects in a Web page
- Chapter 5, Understanding Validity and Accessibility
  - ❏ Understand and change a DOCTYPE
  - ❏ Verify and address W3C validity
  - ❏ Verify and address accessibility
  - ❏ Address problems within HTML/XHTML code
  - ❏ Style text with cascading style sheets
- Chapter 6, Creating a Web Site from Scratch
  - ❏ Work with a graphics template
  - ❏ Create an HTML layout
  - ❏ Style major HTML elements
  - ❏ Design the site architecture and navigation
  - ❏ Style for alternative media

- Chapter 7, Adding Client-Side Functionality
    - Understand server-side versus client-side scripting
    - Use layers and behaviors
    - Use Data View in an HTML page
    - Create and use HTML forms
- Chapter 8, Adding Functionality with jQuery and PHP
    - Use jQuery in Expression Web
    - Use the Expression Web PHP tools
- Chapter 9, Adding Functionality with ASP.NET and AJAX
    - Use ASP.NET tools in Expression Web
    - Convert a DWT to a master page
    - Use site navigation controls
    - Use the AdRotator control
    - Link to data sources and use data controls
    - Use ASP.NET Ajax features
- Chapter 10, Managing and Publishing Your Work
    - Understand hosting requirements and publishing protocols
    - Find and register a domain name
    - Use Microsoft Office Live Small Business
    - Understand the publishing protocols available in Expression Web
    - Understand and evaluate security requirements
    - Publish with FTP, HTTP, or File System
    - Create a subsite
    - Import and export Web packages
    - Use SEO reports

Conventions and Features in This Book

This book has been designed to lead you step by step through all the tasks you are most likely to want to perform in Microsoft Expression Web 4. If you start at the beginning and work your way through all the exercises, you will gain enough proficiency to be able to create complex Web sites and pages. However, each topic is self-contained. If you have worked with another HTML or Web page editor, such as FrontPage, and simply need a quick guide to performing a task in Expression Web, or if after you complete all the exercises, you need a fast way to find the information to perform a procedure, the following features of this book will help you locate specific information:

- **Detailed table of contents**   Scan this listing of the topics and sidebars within each chapter to quickly find the information you want.

- **Detailed index**   Look up specific tasks, features, and general concepts in the index, which has been carefully crafted with the reader in mind.

- **Companion content**   Install the practice files needed for the step-by-step exercises through this book's Web site. See the "Code Samples" section of this Introduction for instructions on getting and installing the practice files.

In addition, this book presents information using conventions designed to make the information readable and easy to follow.

- Most chapters include step-by-step exercises that you can follow to get guided exposure and practice to completing tasks.

- Each exercise consists of a series of tasks, presented as numbered steps (1, 2, and so on) listing each action you must take to complete the exercise.

- Boxed elements with labels such as "Note," "Tip," "Important," and so on provide additional information, directions for starting or ending the step-by-step exercises, or alternative methods for completing a step successfully.

- Text that you are supposed to type (apart from code blocks) appears in bold.

- A plus sign (+) between two key names means that you must press those keys at the same time. For example, "Press Alt+Tab" means that you hold down the Alt key while pressing Tab.

Errata and Book Support

We've made every effort to ensure the accuracy of this book and its companion content. If you do find an error, please report it on our Microsoft Press site at *oreilly.com*:

1. Go to *http://microsoftpress.oreilly.com*.

2. In the Search box, enter the book's ISBN or title.

3. Select your book from the search results.

4. On your book's catalog page, under the cover image, you'll see a list of links.

5. Click View/Submit Errata.

You'll find additional information and services for your book on its catalog page. If you need additional support, please email Microsoft Press Book Support at *mspinput@microsoft.com*.

Please note that product support for Microsoft software is not offered through the addresses above.

The author also maintains a support site for this book and Expression Web in general. Visit *www.expressionwebstepbystep.com*. Visit the site for links to this book's Facebook Fan Page, Live.com group, additional content, and contact information for the author. As a long-term member of the Microsoft MVP Community, Chris has been personally helping users with Microsoft Web design and development software for more than 10 years.

We Want to Hear from You

At Microsoft Press, your satisfaction is our top priority, and your feedback is our most valuable asset. Please tell us what you think of this book at:

http://www.microsoft.com/learning/booksurvey

The survey is short, and we read every one of your comments and ideas. Thanks in advance for your input!

Stay in Touch

Let's keep the conversation going! We're on Twitter: *http://twitter.com/MicrosoftPress*

Chapter 1
Understanding How Expression Web 4 Works

After completing this chapter, you will be able to:

- Identify and use the Expression Web 4 user interface elements
- Open a site
- Use Site Views
- Open a page
- Use page views
- Use the Snapshot Panel
- Use Visual Aids
- Use browser preview
- Use SuperPreview

Microsoft Expression Web is an incredibly versatile tool. Almost anything you could imagine doing with a Web page or Web site is possible with Expression Web 4. Due to its broad versatility, there are hundreds of menu items, buttons, and other interface objects.

The Expression Web software developers have grouped all these interface objects into three basic types, which are *menus*, *toolbars*, and *panels*.

Menus are logical groupings of commands; there are 12 menus on the menu bar and they are always present in the Expression Web 4 interface.

Toolbars are composed of button elements. There are 11 different toolbars available in the interface. Some toolbars, such as the Common or Standard toolbars, are appropriate for almost any working scenario, whereas some are intended for very specific tasks such as the Dynamic Web Template or Master Page toolbars.

Panels are interface objects for which neither a button nor a menu would be sufficient. There are no less than 20 different panels available in Expression Web 4.

In addition, you can apply several Views to either a page or a site. Finally, there are also more than 100 keyboard shortcuts available!

To use an application with such broad use scenarios and such a vast collection of interface elements effectively, it is imperative that you learn not only what features are available but where to find the tools to deploy those features from within Expression Web 4. After you understand the logic behind how Expression Web groups these various interface objects, you'll be able to find what you are looking for quickly. In addition, your comfort level will improve with much less effort than if you tried to memorize the interface objects' locations.

This chapter focuses on how to adjust the Expression Web user interface (UI) to suit your personal preferences and to simplify how you perform specific tasks. Expression Web 4 has a default layout that appeals to a maximum number of users in the widest range of work scenarios. This type of generalized layout means that it'll most likely work for you no matter what type of task you're performing. However, when you customize the interface to your workflow processes, you'll increase your efficiency, speed, and comfort.

 Important Before you can use the practice files in this chapter, you need to download and install them from the book's companion content Web site to their default location. For more information about downloading and installing the practice files, see the "Code Samples" section at the beginning of this book.

 Troubleshooting Graphics and operating system-related instructions in this book reflect the Windows 7 user interface. If your computer is running Windows XP or Windows Vista and you experience trouble following the instructions as written, please refer to the "Information for Readers Running Windows XP or Vista" section at the beginning of this book.

Understanding the Expression Web 4 Interface

This section walks you through the Expression Web 4 default screen layouts so you can familiarize yourself with the various parts of the user interface.

 Important Be sure to install Expression Web 4 before beginning this exercise.

Take a clockwise tour of the Expression Web 4 default layout

1. Click the Start button, click All Programs, click Microsoft Expression, and then click Microsoft Expression Web 4.

   A page named *Untitled_1.htm* opens when you start Expression Web 4 for the first time. You may also be prompted as to whether you want to make Expression Web 4 your default HTML editor.

Troubleshooting By default, Expression Web will automatically display the last site you opened. To close that site and open another site, select Close from the Site menu, choose Exit from the File menu, and then restart Expression Web 4.

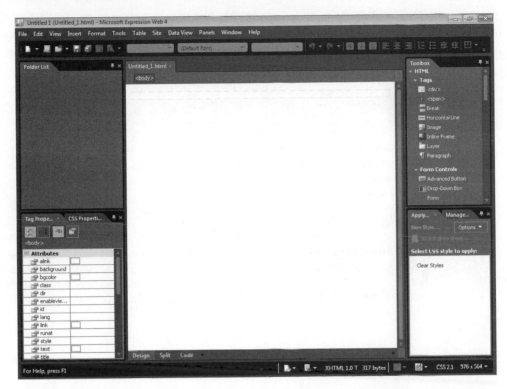

At this point, Expression Web 4 is open and a page is displayed without a site. It's actually a rare instance that you'll use the interface in this way. Think about it. What's a Web page without a "site," or at the very least without folders containing images and other assets that the page uses? Such an arrangement would be considered a "one-page site."

Tip This topic of an open page without a site or an open page that is part of a site is very important. Not understanding the page/site concept will result in unnecessary confusion.

Even without an open site, take the opportunity to explore the default workspace layout.

In the center of the user interface is the editing window. This is where you will do most of your work. The editing window can display a page, or it can display information about a Web site, as you will see later in this chapter.

The menus and toolbars ❶ let you perform tasks such as saving files and sites, generating reports, and changing how you view a page. Panels ❷ let you perform common tasks, such as managing files in a site, adding tags to a page, and managing styles. The editing window ❸ lets you visually edit pages or directly edit page markup. The status bar ❹ shows you important information about sites and pages.

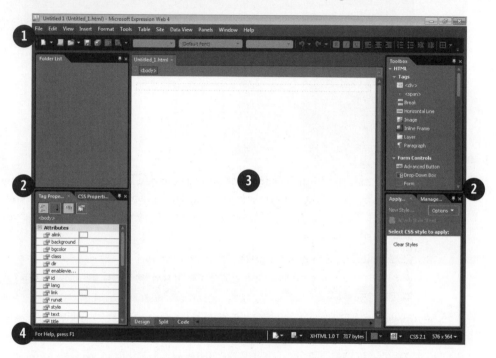

Across the top of the workspace is the menus and toolbars area. It's probably the most important part of the interface for many reasons.

The menu bar interacts with Expression Web 4, individual files in Expression Web, and Web sites as collections of files. Having an idea of where to find things on this bar is helpful for building familiarity before frustration occurs. Fortunately, commands are grouped logically.

2. Click File. The File menu opens. You can see that all the available menu entries are related to creating, saving, opening, or previewing a file.

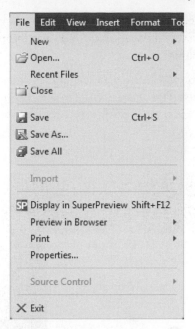

Notice that the Import menu option is unavailable. Because you don't have a site open, you can't import anything into it. The reason for this is due to the site/page concept. There's a huge difference between having an open page, as you do now, and an open site.

3. Click Edit. The Edit menu opens. Similar to the logical arrangement of the File menu, the Edit menu has entries for cutting, pasting, searching, and other operations related to editing a file.

4. Click View. The View menu is full of options that affect the editing window and what you see in the user interface. You'll find options for every aspect and feature available for viewing work in the editing window.

5. Click Insert. The Insert menu items are associated with elements such as HTML, ASP.NET, or PHP code as well as images and media that a designer may want to insert into a page.

6. From the Insert menu, choose Media. The Media menu expands. From the Media menu, you can insert Flash movies, Microsoft Silverlight applications, Silverlight videos, Deep Zoom Composer images, and also a Windows Media Player file.

Note A right-pointing navigational arrow on a menu item in Expression Web indicates that multiple submenu items are associated with that menu entry.

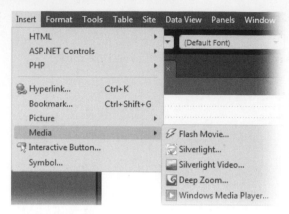

7. Continue exploring the menu items in each of the Format, Tools, Table, and Site menus. Notice that each menu contains items grouped logically as tasks associated with their parent menu label.

8. Click Data View. Because you don't have a Web site open, all the Data View menu items are unavailable.

    The Data View menu is an important and powerful part of Expression Web 4 because it displays data from XML data sources such as RSS feeds, and makes it easy for designers to style them in both HTML and ASP.NET pages. You will learn more about Data View in Chapter 7, "Adding Client-Side Functionality," and Chapter 9, "Adding Functionality with ASP.NET and AJAX."

9. Click Panels. The Panels menu opens.

    Because panels are so important in the UI, take a moment to look at the various panels available. Expression Web 4 contains 20 separate panels.

10. Complete your exploration of the menu bar by clicking and examining the Window and Help menus.

11. Below the menu bar, you will find the Common toolbar. Point to each button on the Common toolbar to reveal its tooltip. Each toolbar will show you tooltips for its buttons and interface elements.

    Whereas the Common toolbar is the only toolbar visible by default in Expression Web 4, there are a total of 11 toolbars available in Expression Web.

12. From the View menu, choose Toolbars. You will see all the toolbars that you can use.

    Notice that Common has a check mark beside it. That's because it is currently active. By clicking a toolbar with a check mark, you remove it from the interface. By clicking a toolbar without a check mark, it is added to the interface and will have a check mark beside it when you revisit the Toolbars menu. A user can have as many toolbars open simultaneously as they like.

13. On the upper-right side of the UI, you will find the Toolbox panel.

The Toolbox panel contains HTML tags, Form Controls, Media Elements, and ASP.NET Controls. The designer can drag items from this panel onto the page.

14. Click the thumbtack icon on the upper-right corner of the Toolbox panel to enable AutoHide. When you apply AutoHide to a panel, it minimizes off the screen, but when you hold your cursor over the panel's tab it reappears.

AutoHide is a great way to get more screen space for your work area, yet you don't lose quick access to the panels you use most often.

The Apply Styles panel now uses all the space to the right of the editing window that it previously shared with the Toolbox panel.

Notice the tab to the right of the active tab.

15. Click the Manage Styles tab. The Manage Styles panel now becomes the active panel in this workspace area. The panels are grouped together because they both pertain to cascading style sheets.

16. Drag the Manage Styles tab to the left of the Apply Styles tab. In this way, you can order the panels within a group to suit your preference.

17. Click the thumbtack icon on the upper-right corner of the panel to enable AutoHide.

18. You will find the status bar across the bottom of the user interface. Hold your cursor over each item on the status bar to see its associated tooltip.

The status bar contains context-sensitive messages on the left, such as line and column numbers when the cursor is in Code view. On the right side, it contains warnings and tools for Compatibility issues and HTML errors based on the DOCTYPE of the active page in the editing window as well as information about the page's file size, Style Application Mode, Visual Aids, CSS Schema, and lastly, the size of the editing window. The status bar is a useful tool and shouldn't be overlooked. Consider it as a quick visual overview of the technical aspects of the active document.

Above the status bar on the lower-left side of the UI, you will find the Tag Properties panel. Through the tag properties panel, the designer can quickly change the attributes of any selected tag in the Design or Code view. Like the Apply Styles and Manage Styles panels, this user interface area contains an additional panel as well—the CSS Properties panel, which works similarly to the Tag Properties panel, except it allows for quick modification of the CSS properties applied to the selected tag.

> **Tip** Notice that of the six default panels, three are CSS-oriented. That's not a coincidence. Expression Web 4 leans toward modern Web design using cascading style sheets for text appearance as well as structural page layout.

19. Click the thumbtack icon on the upper-right corner of the Tag Properties panel to enable AutoHide.

20. The final panel on the left side of the editing window is the Folder List. Click and drag the Folder List tab to the center of the editing window. Any panel can be undocked and either floated over the workspace or docked to another area.

21. Click the close icon on the right side of the floating Folder List panel. The Folder List panel closes.

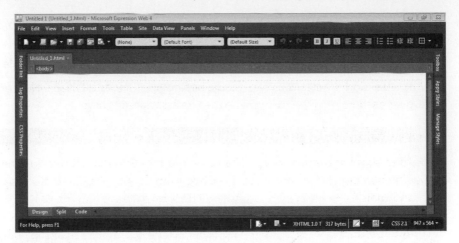

22. From the Panels menu, select Reset Workspace Layout. The workspace returns to its default state.

23. From the File menu, select Exit. Expression Web 4 closes.

You've completed a brief overview of the default Expression Web 4 layout. You will use most, if not all, of the interface objects you viewed during this exercise throughout the remainder of this book. As you become more familiar with Expression Web 4, you will develop your own preferences for which elements of the user interface you prefer to use and how you like your workspace laid out. Knowing the tools that are available to you and how you can customize the user interface is a necessary step in mastering Expression Web 4.

> **Note** Leave the SampleSite site open if you are proceeding directly to the next section.

Opening a Site

An Expression Web 4 site consists of a logical grouping of folders that contain all the pages, images, and other files that make up the site. In most cases, the site also contains metadata that Expression Web uses to recognize when files were changed, to update references to files you might have renamed or replaced, the locations to which the site has been published, and an array of other data the program can use for behind-the-scenes management.

Troubleshooting There is a significant difference between choosing Open from the File menu and selecting Open Site from the Site menu. Open Site opens an entire Web site within Expression Web 4, thereby enabling automatic hyperlink updates, publishing capabilities, and so forth. In contrast, choosing Open on the File menu opens only a single page or file. Any changes made to this file do not affect any other files. In most cases, clicking Open Site will be the preferred action.

Open and examine an entire site

Note For this exercise, use the sample site located at Documents\Microsoft Press\Expression Web 4 SBS.

1. Click the Start button, click All Programs, click Microsoft Expression, and then click Microsoft Expression Web 4.

   When you start Expression Web 4 without a site open, it creates a page named *Untitled_1.htm*. When you open a site, though, that page closes automatically. Expression Web 4 may also prompt you as to whether you want to make Expression Web 4 your default HTML editor.

Troubleshooting If you previously had a site open with Expression Web 4, that site will open automatically by default when you launch Expression Web 4. If that's the case, choose Close from the Site menu.

2. From the Site menu, select Open Site. In the Open Site dialog box, browse to Documents\Microsoft Press\Expression Web 4 SBS, click SampleSite, and then click Open.

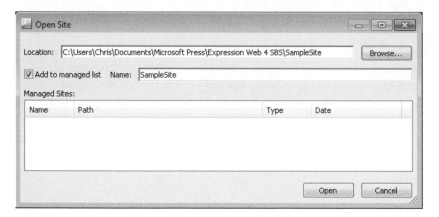

3. From the Open Site dialog box, select the Add To Managed List check box, type **Expression Web 4 Step by Step Examples** in the Name field, and then click Open to open the site in Expression Web 4.

> **Tip** If the check box beside Add To Managed List in the Open Site dialog box is selected, the site you open will be added to Expression Web's Managed Sites List and will appear in the Open Site dialog box. You can also add and remove sites from the Managed Sites List by selecting Manage Sites List from the Site menu.

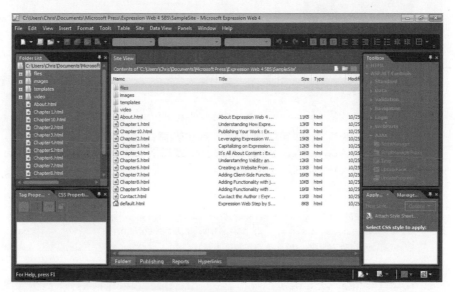

Notice that the workspace with an open site in Folders view looks very different compared to the Folders view in the previous exercise where you examined the user interface with only a page opened.

> **Troubleshooting** It is possible for Expression Web 4 to automatically open the default page of a site during the Open Site process. If this is the case, close the page by clicking the close icon on its tab at the top of the editing window.

4. In the Folder List panel, click Images. The entire content of the Images folder now appears in the editing window.

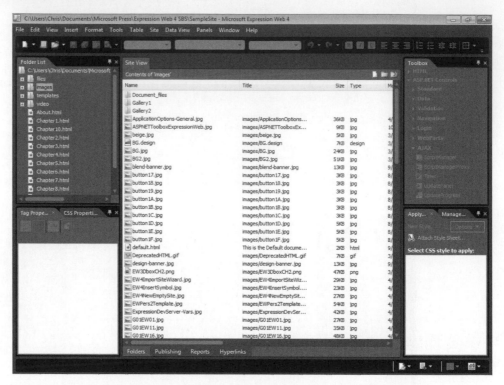

5. Click each of the folders in the Folder List panel to see the content in the editing window, and then click the root folder (SampleSite) at the top of the Folder List panel to return the editing window to its default view of the Site's root folder.

6. Right-click Chapter1.html in the editing window to open the context menu. The menu items you'll see are identical, whether you right-click a file in the Folder List panel or the editing window.

Through the Folder List panel and the editing window, you can quickly view all the folders and files in a site in a hierarchical view. You can also copy, paste, rename, and otherwise modify them through the context menu. This is a useful way to work with the files and folders of a site as opposed to editing individual pages.

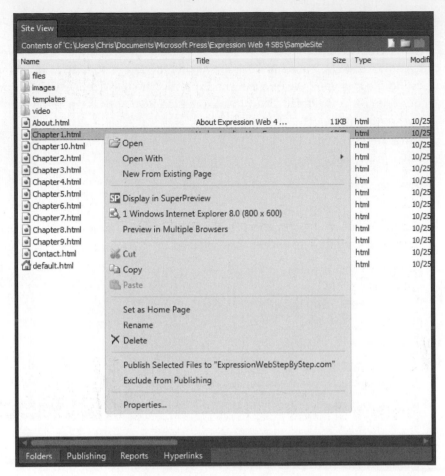

 Warning When you delete a file or folder in Expression Web 4, that file is not sent to your computer's Recycle Bin. It's deleted permanently. You should also consider this warning in conjunction with the fact that if you select Open from the File menu, the default Expression Web 4 behavior opens the file along with the entire contents of its containing folder. For example, if you wanted to edit an HTML file in My Documents, and you select Open from the File menu, browse to the file and open it, the entire contents of your My Documents folder would be visible in the Folder List panel and the editing window—and could then be permanently deleted.

 Note Leave the SampleSite site open if you are proceeding directly to the next section.

Using Site Views

Expression Web 4 provides four basic views of a site. They're designed to help you work with a site in efficient ways. These site views are helpful for designing a new site or understanding an existing site that you have opened with Expression Web. Folders view, the view used in the previous exercise, is the default view that Expression Web applies when the user opens a site.

Use Site Views

> **Note** Open the SampleSite if it isn't already open.

1. Open the Site menu, and select Site Settings. Make sure the Maintain The Site Using Hidden Metadata Files check box is selected.

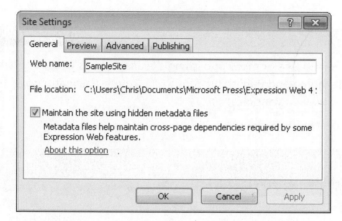

   Expression Web uses these hidden metadata files to manage the site. For many of Expression Web's site management features to work, this metadata setting must be enabled. You will learn more about the Site Settings and Expression Web's site management features in Chapter 2, "Capitalizing on Expression Web 4 Functionality."

2. Click OK on the Site Settings dialog box.

   Expression Web will open an alert that it needs to add hidden files and folders. This is necessary for the metadata to be added to your site. Click OK on the Alert to allow Expression Web to add the required metadata.

3. At the bottom of the editing window, you will see four views listed: Folders (which is the default view), Publishing, Reports, and Hyperlinks. Click Publishing.

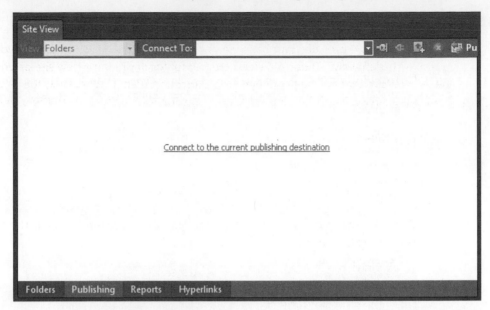

After you have set up one or more publishing destinations, as you will learn about in Chapter 10, "Managing and Publishing Your Work," these destinations will be available in the Publishing view of your local site.

4. At the bottom of the editing window, click Reports.

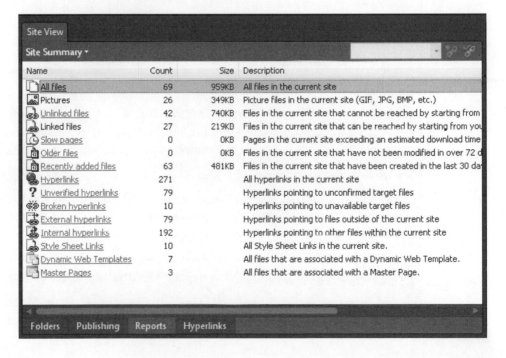

Reports view, by default, shows the Site Summary. Each item in the list of reports is hyperlinked to its respective report.

> **Troubleshooting** The images in this section are intended to illustrate the general appearance of specific reports and views. Your results will be different from those pictured here.

5. In the Site Summary report, click the link for Unlinked Files. A full list of all the unlinked files in the site is shown.

Although they're in the Problems menu of the reports, unlinked files aren't necessarily a problem. In many cases, designers may keep files that they either used or will use in the future within the Web site folder structure.

6. Click the Type column heading. The unlinked files list groups the files by item type.

By clicking the column headings, users can sort the file list by file name, folder name, file type, last modified date, or by the user who modified them.

7. At the top of the editing window, click the Unlinked Files tab, point to Files, and then click All Files to view the All Files report.

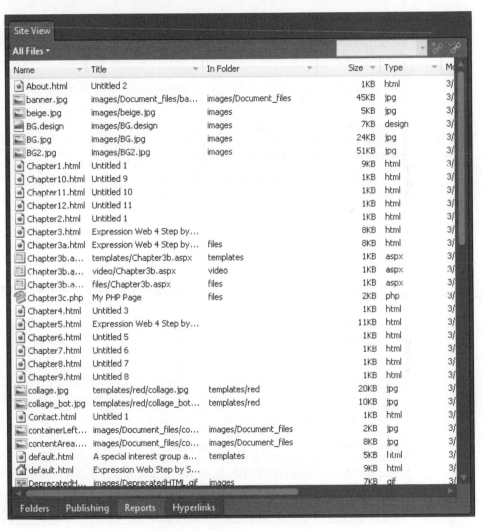

Similar sort options are available in this report as well.

8. At the top of the editing window, click the All Files tab, and then click Site Summary to return to the original summary view of the site.

    The Reports view options cover a very broad scope of site information, and they can greatly ease Web site maintenance and management.

9. At the bottom of the editing window, click the Hyperlinks tab, and then click the default.html file in the Folder List panel to select the sample site's home page.

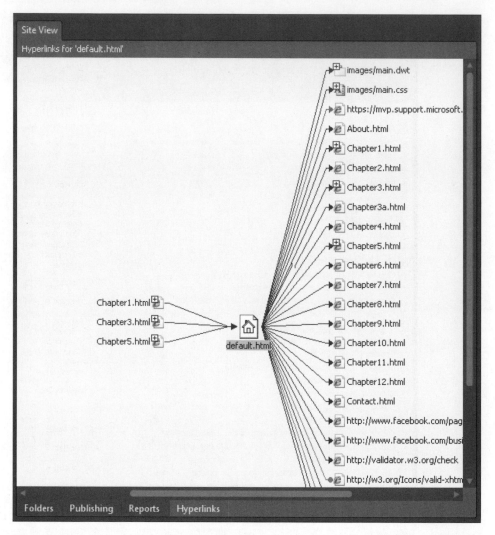

Hyperlinks view provides a diagram of all files that link to or from a selected file and helps you verify and identify broken hyperlinks.

10. Click the plus (+) sign on one of the pages linked to default.html to expand it.

When expanded, the diagram shows all the pages that link to the expanded page, which links to the default.html file.

11. Right-click the workspace and select Show Page Titles from the context menu. The diagram now contains titles to each page, which is often more helpful than only seeing the page's file name.

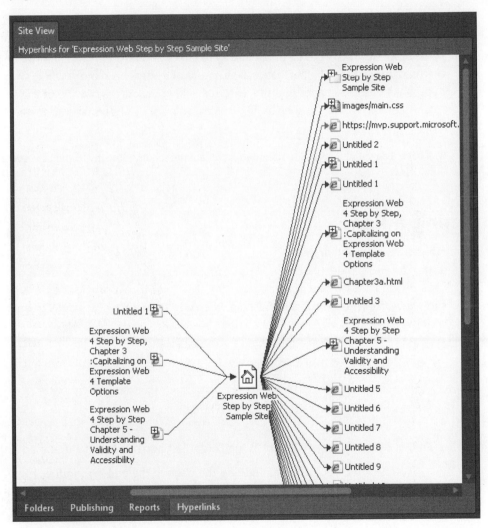

The diagram represents broken hyperlinks and file references by an arrow with a broken shaft, and links that aren't broken by an arrow with a solid shaft.

12. In the diagram, right-click the page you expanded, and select Move To Center from the context menu. The page becomes the focus of the Hyperlinks view.

   By focusing individual pages in the Hyperlinks view, the user can check and address broken links.

13. In the Folder List panel, click default.html to focus the home page of the site in the Hyperlinks view.

   Take a few minutes to click some of the files in the Folder List panel to see their file associations and incoming and outgoing hyperlinks.

Hyperlinks view provides an efficient way to check and address links in a site and can help the user understand the navigational structure of a site. This feature works with internal hyperlinks between pages of a site, external links to resources outside of the site, and file references within the site such as links to cascading style sheets, and so forth.

 Note Leave the SampleSite site open if you are proceeding directly to the next section.

Opening a Page

No matter how well or in how many ways Expression Web 4 helps you view the structure of a site, the site is made up of the files it contains. Expression Web provides a number of views for individual files within a site in much the same way that it provides different views of the site structure. These views are available when you have a page or pages open in the editing window.

Open pages in various ways

 Note Open the SampleSite if it isn't already open.

1. Double-click Chapter1.html in the Folder List panel to open it in the editing window.

   At this point, you can begin editing the page in the editing window, but you can also open multiple pages at once and edit, save, and publish them as a group.

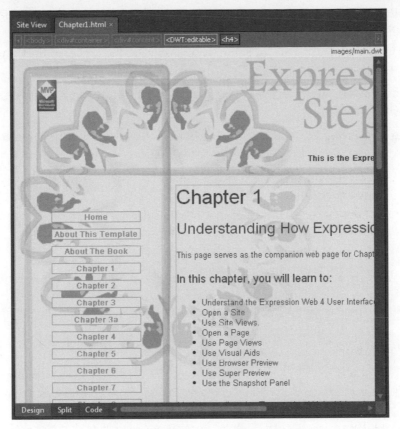

2. At the top of the editing window, click the Site tab to return to Site view, and then click the Folders tab at the lower left of the editing window.

3. In the editing window, hold down the ~~Shift~~ *control* key and click the Contact.html, About. html, and default.html files. Then press Enter on your keyboard. All three pages open in the editing window.

4. Press Ctrl+Tab on your keyboard to cycle through each of the open pages.

 Tip Because functionality such as searching, accessibility, and compatibility reporting can be performed on "open pages," you can gain efficiency by working on groups of pages.

5. Open the Window menu and select Close All Pages. All the open pages close and the user interface switches to Site view. Expression Web enables you to open and work with groups of pages simultaneously. You can also switch between them by clicking their tabs

at the top of the editing window or by pressing Ctrl+Tab. Expression Web provides convenient group operations with the open pages.

 Note Leave the SampleSite site open if you are proceeding directly to the next section.

Using Page Views

Expression Web lets you view individual pages in a number of ways. This provides visual options that work well across a range of editing scenarios and for users of varying skill levels.

Explore page view functionality

 Note Open the SampleSite if it isn't already open.

1. In the Folder List panel, double-click Chapter1.html to open it in the editing window.

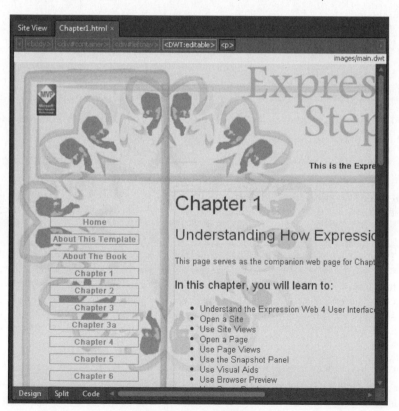

The default view of an HTML file is Design view.

2. At the bottom left of the editing window, you will see three tab options: Design, Split, and Code. Click Split.

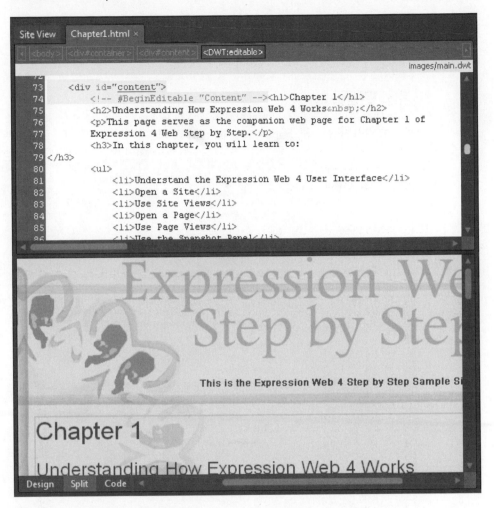

 Tip Split view is helpful to both beginners and experts alike. An expert can quickly work in the Code pane and see a visual representation in the Design pane. A beginner can work in the Design pane and because the Design and Code panes are synchronized, a user can become more familiar with the coding of Web pages simply by working in the Design pane and looking at the corresponding HTML elements in the Code pane.

3. In the Design pane of the editing window, set your cursor inside of the first *h1*, which reads "Chapter 1."

Notice the relationship between the Design and Code panes. Your cursor in the Design pane matches the cursor in the Code pane.

Notice the tab in the Design pane just above the *h1* element where your cursor is. It is called a Block Selection label and is part of the visual aids you will learn about in the next exercise.

4. Click the Block Selection label and notice how the entire *h1* element is selected in both the Design and Code pane of the editing window.

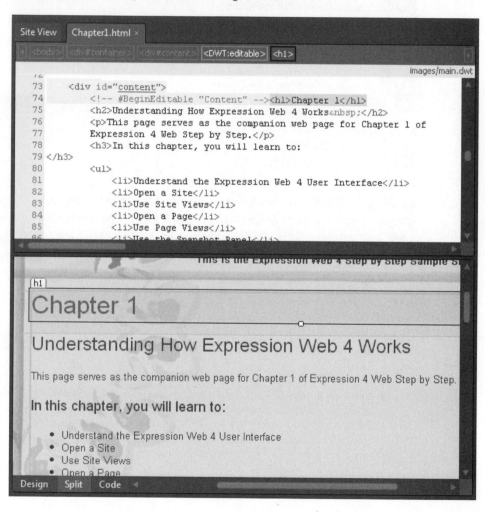

That's the idea of block selection. It selects the entire tag and its contents.

> **Troubleshooting** If you're not seeing the Block Selection labels, click Block Selection on the Visual Aids submenu of the View menu.

5. With the page's first *h1* element still selected, look at the Quick Tag Selector at the top of the Code pane. Point to the *h1* tab on the Quick Tag Selector, and then click its drop-down arrow. The Quick Tag Selector's options appear.

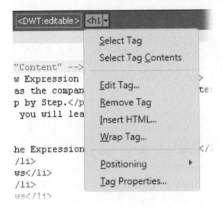

By using the Quick Tag Selector and its options, a designer can easily navigate a very complex page and edit specific areas simply by selecting an element in the Design pane, and then using the Quick Tag Selector's options, which are Select Tag, Select Tag Contents, Edit Tag, Remove Tag, Wrap Tag, Positioning, and Tag Properties.

6. At the bottom of the editing window, click Code. The interface switches to Code view.

```
Site View    Chapter1.html ×

<body>  <div#container>  <div#content>  <DWT:editable>  <h1>

                                                    images/main.dwt
72
73      <div id="content">
74          <!-- #BeginEditable "Content" --><h1>Chapter 1</h1>
75          <h2>Understanding How Expression Web 4 Works </h2>
76          <p>This page serves as the companion web page for Chapter 1 of
77          Expression 4 Web Step by Step.</p>
78          <h3>In this chapter, you will learn to:
79  </h3>
80          <ul>
81              <li>Understand the Expression Web 4 User Interface</li>
82              <li>Open a Site</li>
83              <li>Use Site Views</li>
84              <li>Open a Page</li>
85              <li>Use Page Views</li>
86              <li>Use the Snapshot Panel</li>
87              <li>Use Visual Aids</li>
88              <li>Use Browser Preview</li>
89              <li>Use Super Preview</li>
90          </ul>
91          <h4>Understanding the Expression Web 4 User Interface</h4>
92          <p>In this chapter segment you will start Expression Web 4, take a
93          clockwise tour of the default User Interface layout, and then exit
94          Expression Web 4. </p>
95          <h4>Opening a Site</h4>
96          <p>In this chapter segment you will start Expression Web 4, open, and
97          examine an entire site.</p>
98          <h4>Using Site Views</h4>
99          <p>In this chapter segment you will use Site views to examine the sam
100         site</p>
101         <h4>Opening a Page</h4>
102         <p>
103         In this chapter segment you will open several pages in different ways
104         <h4>Using Page Views</h4>
105         <p>
106         In this chapter segment you will use each type of page view within th

Design    Split    Code
```

Code view is helpful when working specifically with the code of HTML pages and on pages that don't render HTML visually like some PHP or ASP.NET files. Whereas Code view may at first look like a simple text editor such as Notepad, you will see in the next few steps that it has many tools to offer a designer.

7. From the View menu, select Toolbars, and then choose Code View. The Code View tool-bar opens.

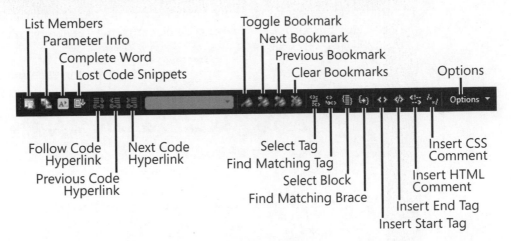

The Code View toolbar provides you with buttons to access the most often used com-mands from the Code View and IntelliSense submenus on the Edit menu, as well as the options such as Word Wrap, HTML Incompatibility, and Error Highlighting. You will learn about IntelliSense for PHP and ASP.NET code beginning in Chapter 8, "Adding Functionality with jQuery and PHP."

8. Hold your cursor over each of the buttons on the Code View toolbar to see its associ-ated tooltip.

Suppose you were working in Code view on this HTML file, and your task was to make sure that the list items in the bulleted list match the *h4* headings in the body of the page. In the following steps, you will use several tools from the Expression Web's Code view to make that task easier.

9. In Code view, set your cursor just after the *<ul>* tag and press Enter on your keyboard to break to a new line. On the Code View toolbar, click the Insert HTML Comment but-ton. Expression Web inserts an HTML comment into the page and positions your cursor within the comment.

10. Type **Match this list to the h4 elements**.

11. Set your cursor just before the first *h4* element in the code: *<h4>*Understanding the Expression Web 4 user interface*</h4>* and then click the Toggle Bookmarks button on the Code View toolbar. A Code Bookmark is placed by the line number on the left side of the Code view.

12. Set your cursor before each of the remaining *h4* elements in the page and use the Toggle Bookmarks button to set a bookmark on each of them.

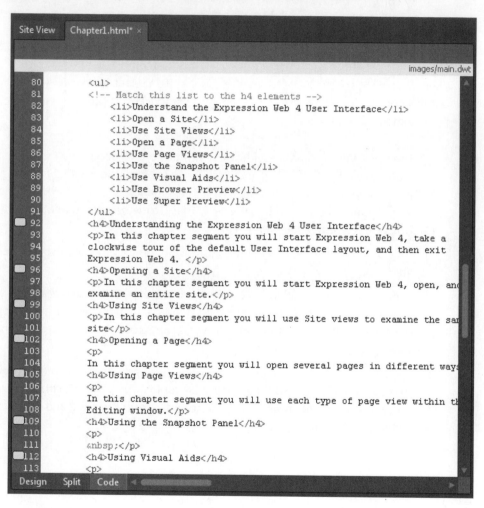

Now you have a bookmark beside each of the *h4* elements you are matching to each of the list item elements. This will make it easy for you to cycle through the bookmarks to verify their text against the list items.

13. Set your cursor just before the HTML comment you inserted in step 9.

14. On the Code View toolbar, click the Next Bookmark button. The cursor moves to the first column of the appropriate line. Check the first list item's text against the *h4* text.

    By continuing the process of verifying the list item text against the *h4* text, using the Next Bookmark button, you can more easily focus on the task rather than struggling through the HTML code.

15. Click Save on the Common toolbar.

There are many tools available to a user in Code view. You will learn more about them throughout this book. If you found it uncomfortable to work strictly in Code view, despite the availability of numerous Code View tools, the next section will be of interest to you.

 Note Leave the SampleSite site open if you are proceeding directly to the next section.

Using the Snapshot Panel

The Snapshot panel offers a true browser view of a Web page within the Expression Web user interface. Designers will find it much more convenient than previewing a page in a browser that requires them to exit and return to the Expression Web interface. Besides seeing a browser rendering within the workspace, the user can view the browser rendering in multiple versions of Internet Explorer and any number of browsers they have installed on their computers.

Use the Snapshot panel

> **Note** Open the SampleSite and Chapter1.html, if they aren't already open.

1. From the Panels menu, select AutoHide All Panels. All of the panels disappear, and the Code view expands to fill the interface.

2. From the Panels menu, choose Snapshot. The Snapshot panel appears.

By default, the Snapshot panel appears below the Code view of the editing window.

3. Click the Snapshot tab and drag the Snapshot panel to the right side of the user interface just below the Manage Styles tab, so that the Code pane and Snapshot panels are side by side. Click and drag the separator between the Code view and Snapshot panel to divide the available space evenly between each view.

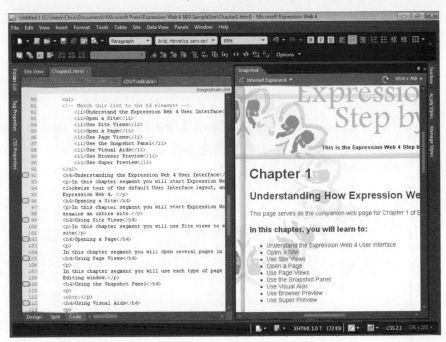

4. Make a simple edit in the Code view by putting an exclamation point at the end of the first list item, which reads, "Understand the Expression Web 4 User Interface," and then click Save on the Common toolbar.

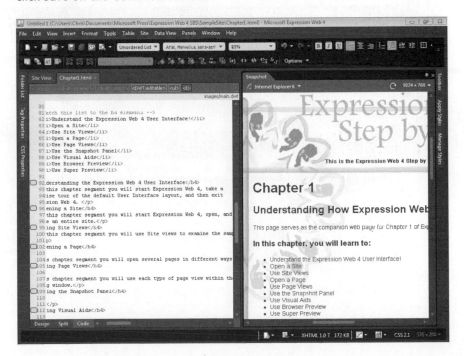

Notice that the Snapshot panel automatically shows the text revision when the page was saved. If necessary, scroll or drag the Snapshot panel to see your change.

5. At the top of the Snapshot panel, click the drop-down arrow and then click Internet Explorer 7. The panel redraws the results of the Code pane based on the rendering of Internet Explorer 7.

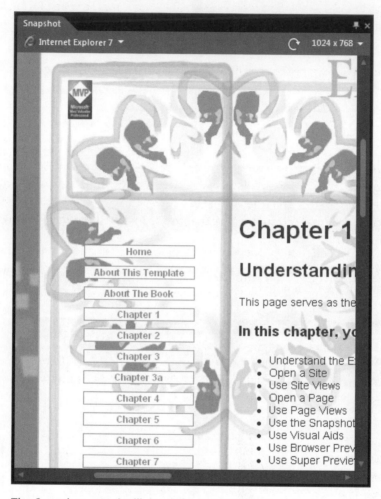

The Snapshot panel will, by default, show multiple versions of Internet Explorer, but it will also show previews from other browsers you have installed on your system. You will learn how to add alternative browsers to Expression Web later in this chapter, in the section "Using Browser Preview."

6. From the Panels menu, choose Reset Workspace Layout. Expression Web returns to its default workspace layout.

7. At the bottom of the editing window, click Design to return the page to Design view, choose Toolbars from the View menu, and then click Code View to close the Code View toolbar.

Besides showing you several available features in the Snapshot panel, this exercise should give you an indication of just how flexible the Expression Web 4 user interface is. Although it's early in this book, you will find tools like the Snapshot panel very helpful in cross-browser verification of your pages as you progress through the remaining chapters.

 Note Leave the SampleSite site open if you are proceeding directly to the next section.

Using Visual Aids

Expression Web 4 provides a vast array of visual aids. Even though a WYSIWYG ("what you see is what you get") editor is helpful, true WYSIWYG isn't the best way to look at Web pages when you're editing them. For a true WYSIWYG preview, you can view your page in a browser or by using another method such as the Snapshot panel or SuperPreview, which you will see later in this chapter.

Use Visual Aids in the editing window in Design view

 Note Open the SampleSite and Chapter1.html if they aren't already open.

1. Open the Chapter1.html file if it isn't still open from the previous exercise, and then on the status bar below the editing window, click the Visual Aids button. The Visual Aids options appear.

Tip The Visual Aids button provides convenient access to commonly used visual aids. To access all visual aids, select Visual Aids from the View menu, and then click the individual options you want to turn off or on.

2. Click Show to turn off Visual Aids completely. The Design view changes to as much of a WYSIWYG presentation as is possible. Click the Visual Aids button again and then click Show once more to bring the Visual Aids back.

3. Click the Visual Aids button on the status bar and then click Margins And Padding.

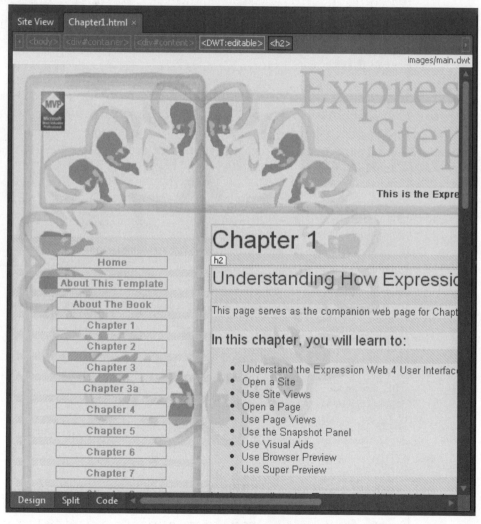

Notice how every page element has a pattern design around it, which indicates padding. Sometimes eliminating a visual aid will give you a more realistic and clear view of the page, and in other editing scenarios, it's more helpful to turn them on.

4. From the Visual Aids menu, select Margins And Padding again to turn it off. Continue to experiment with the visual aids and toggle each option off and on to see their effects in the Design pane.

Although not included in the Visual Aids menu, formatting marks are a type of visual aid that some designers like. It's especially useful for text entry in the Design pane.

5. Open the View menu and select Formatting Marks, and then choose Show. Formatting marks appear within the Design pane.

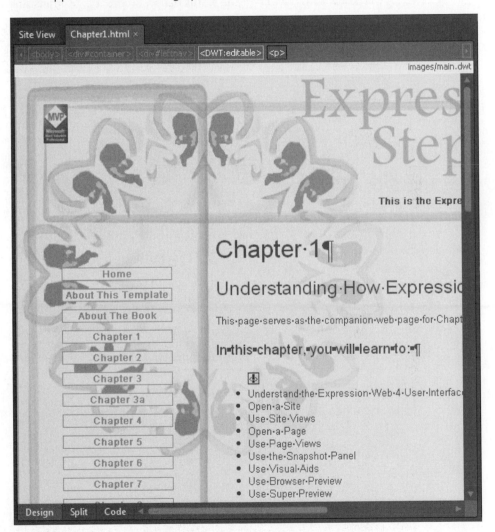

You may not want to have the formatting marks turned on all the time when you work, however, they're helpful for authoring text. You can see spaces between words more easily, and you can identify errant spaces before line returns and so on. You can also see a visual representation in the Design pane of the JavaScript comment you inserted in the Code view exercise.

6. Open the View menu, select Formatting Marks, and—as you did with the visual aids— experiment with turning some of the options on and off to see what their effects look like in the Design pane.

7. Open the View menu, select Formatting Marks, and then choose Show again to turn off the formatting marks.

Visual Aids and Formatting Marks are there for designers to take advantage of. WYSIWYG isn't always what you want. Experiment with these visual treatments in the Design pane and see what works best for you. You can definitely use these tools to speed your work and improve your accuracy.

> **Note** Leave the SampleSite site and Chapter1.html open if you are proceeding directly to the next section.

Using Browser Preview

No matter how good the various page views look in Expression Web, they serve only to give the designer an idea of what their pages will look like in a browser. To that end, Expression Web contains a number of tools that allow you to view your page in a browser, at multiple sizes, and even in multiple browsers simultaneously.

View pages with browser preview and alternative browsers using Expression Web

> **Note** Open the SampleSite and Chapter1.html if it they aren't already open.

1. Open the Chapter1.html file in the SampleSite if it isn't still open from the previous exercise, and then click Preview on the Common toolbar. The page opens in a browser.

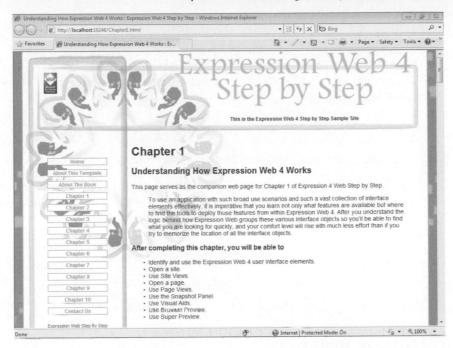

Clicking Preview in a browser opens the page with the last browser that you used when viewing a page from within Expression Web. For example, if you previewed a page in a browser that wasn't your system default browser, clicking the Preview button will open the page in that browser instead of the default browser.

2. Close the open browser and return to Expression Web.

3. Click the Preview button on the Common toolbar, and then click the drop-down arrow beside it.

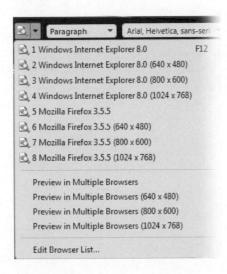

You will see a number of options for browser sizes, which is helpful when you're designing a page and need to see what it looks like in browsers of varying sizes. What's even better is the ability to preview the page in multiple browsers. In the next steps, you will add one or more alternate browsers to your system and then enable them in Expression Web.

4. Download and install one or more of the following browsers:

 Warning Download and install as many of these browsers as you like. However, when you install them, pay attention to the installation dialog boxes. You don't want to install extra toolbars and you don't want to make changes to your system, such as modifying your default search engine or your default browser. If you do want to make these changes, make them manually after you complete this chapter.

- Firefox: *http://www.mozilla.com/en-US/firefox/all.html*

- Opera: *http://www.opera.com/browser/download/*

- Safari: *http://www.apple.com/safari/download/*

- Chrome: *http://www.google.com/chrome/*

 Tip Links to each of these browsers are included in the Chapter1.html file. Preview that page in a browser and use the links to navigate to each of the download locations.

5. Once you have at least one of the alternative browsers installed, select Preview In Browser from the File menu, and then click Edit Browser List. The Edit Browser List dialog box opens.

The Edit Browser List dialog box is not only where you can add and remove the browsers that open when you click Preview In Multiple Browsers, but it also includes the window sizes that will open as well.

6. In the Edit Browser List dialog box, click Add. In the Add Browser dialog box, type the name of the browser you want to add in the Name field, and then click Browse, beside the Command field.

7. In the Add Browser dialog box, browse to the browser's installation location. For example, the default location for Mozilla Firefox is C:\Program Files\Mozilla Firefox\Firefox.exe. Click the executable program file, and then click Open.

When you return to Expression Web, you will see the browser's folder location in the command field.

Troubleshooting If you're having trouble finding the location of a browser you've installed, click the Windows Start button, find the browser in question, right-click the particular browser, and then in the Context menu, click Open File Location. Then copy the address from the Windows Explorer address bar. Using this method, you can paste the address of the folder into the address bar of the Add Browser dialog box to make it much easier to locate the executable file you want to add.

8. Click OK in the Add Browser dialog box. Repeat this process for each browser you want to add to the list.

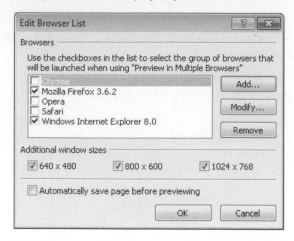

In this image, all the browsers mentioned have been added.

9. When you've finished adding the additional browsers, select the check box beside each browser you want to open when you click Preview In Multiple Browsers. You don't have to use all of them if you don't want to.

10. Beneath Additional Window Sizes, clear the check box next to 640×480, because that particular size isn't much use in modern design, and then click OK.

11. Click the drop-down arrow on the Preview button, and then click Preview In Multiple Browsers. The page opens in all the browsers you added to the Edit Browser List dialog box.

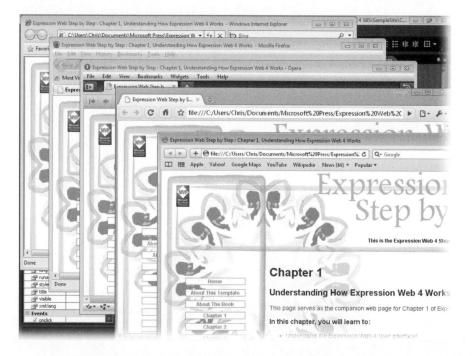

12. Close all the open browser windows and return to Expression Web.

It's a good design practice to consistently check your pages in multiple browsers. Expression Web makes it easy to do that with the Browser List dialog box, and you also have handy commands to preview pages in multiple browsers and at multiple window sizes.

> **Note** Leave the SampleSite and Chapter1.html open if you are proceeding directly to the next section.

Using SuperPreview

SuperPreview can be one of a designer's most powerful tools because it simplifies the process of debugging and verifying cross-browser rendering of Web pages. With it, you can preview your pages in multiple browsers simultaneously. You can also compare a browser rendering to a composite mock-up image of the page, both side-by-side or in an overlay. It also provides tools to help diagnose the cause of cross-browser inconsistencies.

In Expression Web 4, SuperPreview includes SuperPreview Remote, which enables SuperPreview to show the designer a rendering of their page in a Safari browser running on a Macintosh operating system.

Compare Web pages in multiple browsers with SuperPreview

> **Note** Open the SampleSite and Chapter1.html if they aren't already open.

1. Open the Chapter1.html file if it isn't open from the previous exercise, and then click SuperPreview on the Common toolbar. Expression SuperPreview opens in a new window outside of Expression Web.

The Baseline Pane ❶ will display your page in your development browser. The Comparison Pane ❷ will display your page as it renders in your comparison browser. The toolbar ❸ contains all of the tools in SuperPreview. There is no Menu in this application. The Baseline browser selector ❹ enables you to choose your development browser as the baseline browser. The Comparison browser selector ❺ enables you to choose the browser you will use for the comparison rendering of your page. The Compositions segment ❻ enables you to use a graphic as either the baseline or comparison rendering of your page.

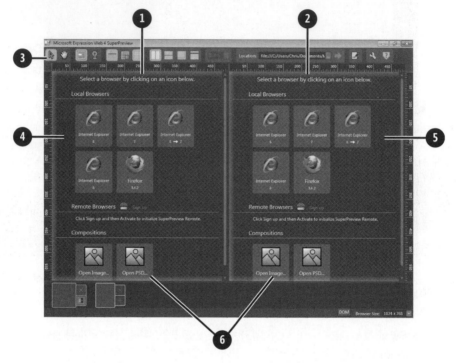

The SuperPreview window is divided into two panes. On the left is the Baseline browser and on the right is the Comparison browser.

> **Tip** You will see a Sign Up link in each pane for Remote Browsers. Sign up for this service to take advantage of features such as checking your page in the Safari browser on a Macintosh operating system without actually needing to set up a Mac locally.

2. In the left pane, click Internet Explorer 8, and then on the right, click one of the alternate browsers you installed in the previous steps. The screenshot in the next step compares Internet Explorer 8 to Firefox 3.6.2.

3. Click the green arrow beside the Location field at the top of the SuperPreview interface. Both panes show their respective browser views.

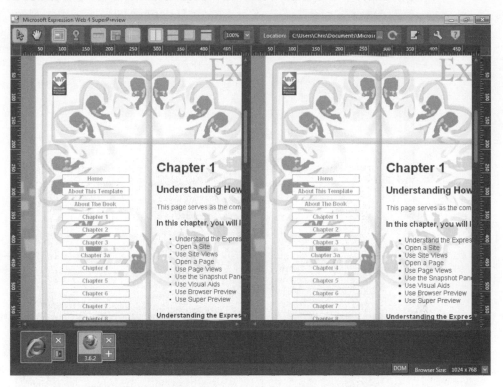

One of the first things you might notice about SuperPreview is the lack of a menu bar at the top of the interface. All SuperPreview's functions are available from the buttons above the browser view panes.

4. Hold your cursor over each of the buttons on the SuperPreview toolbar to see corresponding tooltips.

5. Hold your cursor over page elements in the Baseline pane. Then watch how the same element is highlighted in the Comparison pane and how its dimensions are shown in the status bar at the bottom of the interface.

When you select a page element where an inconsistency is found, the dimensional difference is shown on the preview pane in red.

6. Click the Overlay Layout button. The SuperPreview interface switches to overlay mode.

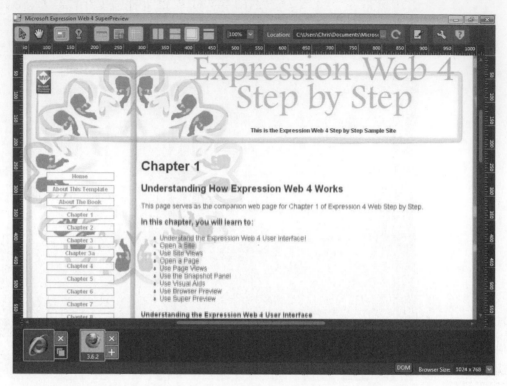

In Overlay, the Baseline browser is always beneath the Comparison browser.

7. Click the Vertical Split Layout button. The interface switches to the default Vertical Split Layout display.

8. On the status bar, click the DOM (Document Object Model) tab. The DOM Tree View opens. Click an element in the Baseline pane, such as the *h1* element that says "Chapter 1." The *h1* element is highlighted in both the Baseline and Comparison panes, and the DOM node in the DOM Tree View is highlighted.

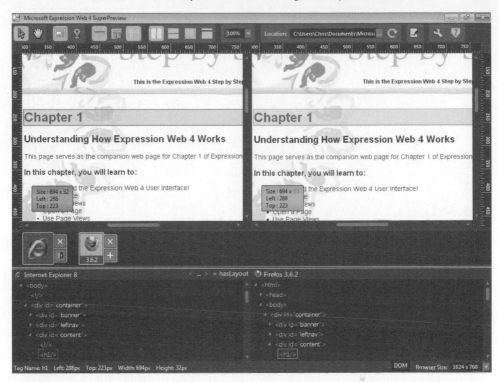

DOM is the structural map of the document. Take a few minutes to expand each entry in the DOM Tree View and watch the effect on the Baseline and Comparison panes. If you're interested in learning HTML/XHTML, this DOM Tree View and SuperPreview might actually be even better teaching tools than Split view in the Expression Web interface.

9. Close SuperPreview and return to Expression Web.

SuperPreview is an incredibly useful tool. One interesting feature is that you can open SuperPreview independently of Expression Web, by selecting SuperPreview from the Windows Start menu. You can then enter a URL into the Location field, which enables you to check any Web page on the Internet. You'll find this particularly helpful both when someone reports a cross-browser issue with a page that you've already published to the Internet, and as a learning tool, because you can use it to dissect and examine existing Web pages from popular Web sites.

Note Close the SampleSite and exit Expression Web 4.

Throughout this chapter, you have seen various ways that Expression Web enables you to view a Web site or a Web page. In addition, you examined several tools that Expression Web provides so that you can edit pages and sites. All these tools are there to help you take control of your work and work the way you feel most comfortable. Don't feel like you need to leave this chapter as an expert in Expression Web, because that's not the intention. Recognizing how Expression Web works with sites and pages, how the user interface works, and knowing about the tools that are available to you is all that's required at this point. You will use many, if not all, of these tools and concepts as you progress through the rest of this book.

Key Points

- Opening a page is a completely different operation than opening a site and then opening a page within that site.

- Expression Web uses metadata to enable many of its site management features.

- Expression Web provides a number of site views to assist you in working with a site.

- Expression Web provides a variety of page views and visual aids to assist you in working with Web pages.

- Flexible browser preview options help you continually check your work in multiple browsers.

- The Expression Web user interface is highly customizable and can be modified by the user to provide a layout that suits the specific editing task at hand.

- SuperPreview helps diagnose cross-browser inconsistencies in ways that were previously not possible.

- With SuperPreview's Remote Preview, you can check the rendering of your pages in the Safari browser running on a Macintosh operating system.

Chapter 2
Capitalizing on Expression Web 4 Functionality

After completing this chapter, you will be able to:

- Change site settings
- Change Application Options
- Change Page Editor Options
- Use the Expression Development Server
- Use PHP with the Expression Development Server
- Create a new site with Expression Web
- Use the Import Site Wizard
- Configure add-ins

The previous chapter emphasized how Microsoft Expression Web displays a Web site or a page. This chapter focuses on how Expression Web performs its tasks and how you can work with Expression Web as the Integrated Development Environment (IDE) that it really is.

By taking advantage of the potential available in Expression Web 4, designers can gain efficiency and speed, while at the same time improving accuracy and personal convenience.

Expression Web 4 is not just a Hypertext Markup Language (HTML) editor, it's also a top-notch Web site management tool and an IDE in the same way that Microsoft Visual Studio is an IDE for programmers, but built with Web professionals in mind.

Important Before you can use the practice files in this chapter, you need to download and install them from the book's companion content Web site to their default location. For more information about downloading and installing the practice files, see the "Code Samples" section at the beginning of this book.

Troubleshooting Graphics and operating system-related instructions in this book reflect the Windows 7 user interface. If your computer is running Windows XP or Windows Vista and you experience trouble following the instructions as written, please refer to the "Information for Readers Running Windows XP or Vista" section at the beginning of this book.

Changing Site Settings

To build on one of the most important concepts introduced in the previous chapter, you will begin this chapter by capitalizing on how Expression Web 4 works with sites.

Explore site settings

 Note Use the sample site located at Documents\Microsoft Press\Expression Web 4 SBS.

1. With Expression Web 4 open, select Open Site from the Site menu. In the Open Site dialog box, click Browse, and then browse to the location where you installed the sample files from this book's CD. Click the SampleSite folder, click Open, and then click the Open button in the Open Site dialog box. The sample site opens in Expression Web 4.

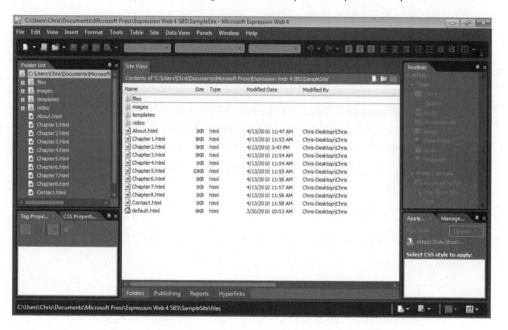

 Tip To take full advantage of Expression Web and all its features, you must begin with an open *site*—and opening a site is different than opening a file or a folder.

2. With the book's SampleSite site open in Expression Web, select Site Settings from the Site menu to open the Site Settings dialog box.

This simple dialog box is incredibly important, because it is the access point into the settings of each site that users work with in Expression Web.

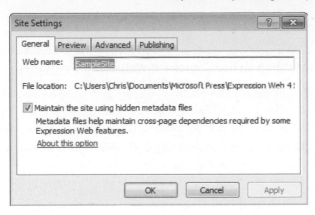

The Site Settings dialog box has four tabs. You will explore each of these and their potential effects on a site in the following steps.

3. The General tab of the Site Settings dialog box contains two items of note. For this exercise, accept the Web Name field's default, *SampleSite*, and make sure that the check box beside Maintain The Site Using Hidden Metadata Files is selected. If it's not selected, be sure to select it before moving on to the next steps.

   The Web Name field in the Site Settings dialog box is the *only place to safely change the name of a site*. Changes in this field will be reflected in the site name in Windows Explorer as well as within Expression Web. To use Expression Web's site management features fully, you must enable hidden metadata. If you can't enable metadata in a production site for some reason, you can remove it by clearing the check box when your work is done.

4. Click the Preview tab at the top of the Site Settings dialog box.

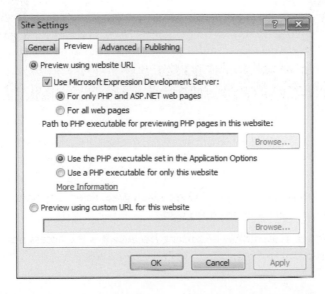

The Preview tab has two groups of options:

- Preview Using Website URL
- Preview Using Custom URL For This Website

By default, the check box beside Use Microsoft Expression Development Server is selected, so the feature is enabled. The two options for this feature are For Only PHP And ASP.NET Web Pages, and For All Web Pages. You might select the For All Web Pages option if, for instance, you are designing an HTML Web site but the navigation links are links to folders, not to specific files. If you set up the navigation links as folder links and preview the site, Windows Internet Explorer will show the contents of the *folder* and not the default document within the folder. You can solve that problem by setting the option to use the Expression Development Server to preview all pages.

The next options are:

- Use The PHP Executable Set In The Application Options
- Use A PHP Executable For Only This Website

If you select the second option, the Browse button will become enabled and you can browse to the PHP executable file that you want to use specifically for this Web site. One reason you might want to specify a path to a PHP executable file would be to test the Web site with different versions of PHP. For instance, if you need to know whether the site will function in PHP 4, but your application options are set to test with PHP 5, you can enter the specific path to a PHP 4 installation and test against that version, which can be very helpful.

The last option on this tab is Preview Using Custom URL For This Website. This option is most useful if you have a Web site open through file transfer protocol (FTP). By using this option, you can open a site on an FTP server, but when you preview it, you can substitute an http:// path so that the pages will render properly in your browser. Another possible use is if you have a local server set up but have opened it by its folder path (such as c:\inetpub\www\SampleSite), and you want to preview it from within Expression Web from *http://localhost/SampleSite*. This option is particularly convenient in a corporate setting, where the site you're working on isn't necessarily on your local computer.

5. Click the Advanced tab at the top of the Site Settings dialog box.

On the Advanced tab, under Options, note the Hide Files And Folders That Begin With An Underscore Character ('_') check box. By using this option, designers and developers can hide special files and folders from other users and editors of the site.

Under Language Settings, there are three options. With the Server Message Language setting, you can designate the language for messages, such as errors. With the Default Page Encoding setting, you can specify the default encoding, which is useful when you are creating non-English pages. Finally, the Ignore The Keyboard When Deciding The Encoding Of New Pages option is useful when a designer is creating foreign-language pages and the language of those pages doesn't match the designer's keyboard setting. One example is the designer who has an English keyboard but needs to author pages in Arabic or another language.

At the bottom of this dialog box is a button for deleting temporary files. Expression Web uses temporary files for many of its operations. If Expression Web begins to act strangely when you are viewing or previewing pages, this should be your first stop for a remedy. Occasionally the temporary files can become corrupted, and you'll need to delete them to restore normal behavior.

6. Click the Publishing tab at the top of the Site Settings dialog box.

In the first section on this tab, designers can add, edit, and delete publishing destinations, as well as set a default publishing destination. This is a convenient way to access the publishing settings of a Web site. For instance, you might have one publishing destination that you use for site backup, another on a Hypertext Transfer Protocol (HTTP) server used as a testing location, and still another as the location of the publically visible production site. There is no limit to the number of locations you can set up for a Web site. The ability to configure and control these locations can be a tremendous efficiency boost.

The next section of the Publishing tab, Options, contains a check box for including subsites when publishing, which isn't selected by default. You will learn about subsites later in this chapter.

7. Select the Optimize HTML During Publishing check box, and then click the Customize button. The HTML Optimization Settings dialog box appears.

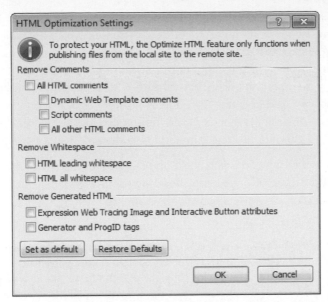

This dialog box contains options you can use to modify the HTML in your pages during the publishing operation to remove HTML comments and whitespace and manipulate the HTML code in several ways. This is helpful because it leaves you free to comment your HTML however you like locally, yet not expose those comments to visitors who view the page's source code.

These options fall into three distinct groups:

■ **Remove Comments**   You can remove all HTML comments or selectively remove any of the following: Dynamic Web Template comments, script comments, or all other HTML comments—which means any HTML comments other than Dynamic Web Template or script comments.

■ **Remove Whitespace**   With these options, you can remove leading whitespace, which is the space before the HTML code begins on each line in a page's source code. You can also elect to remove all whitespace, which literally removes all the whitespace in an HTML document. Some designers like to remove all the whitespace because doing so reduces file size, but it's of questionable value since whitespace doesn't add that much file size and an HTML file with no whitespace is very difficult to read. Another reason you might want to remove the whitespace is to simply make the document's source code more difficult for a visitor to read, making it more difficult for others to copy your design methods.

- **Remove Generated HTML**   With these options, you can remove Expression Web Tracing Image and Interactive Button attributes, which are features that Expression Web uses to manage the site as it pertains to Tracing Images and Interactive Buttons. The second option lets you remove Generator and ProgID tags, which are meta tag entries in the head of a document that indicate which application was used to create the page. This option is useful only when you are working with documents built in other applications, because Expression Web 4 doesn't add Generator or ProgID meta tags to documents.

After making whatever selections you want, you can opt to make your selections the default optimization options, or you can choose to remove your selections and restore the original application defaults, which change nothing.

> **Tip** Be careful with your selections if you choose to use these options. Consider what you would be faced with if you were to strip all of this content during publishing—and then lose the local copy of the site. Your online copy of the Web site will not include any of the comments and attributes that you would need if you downloaded the server-based copy of the Web site to restore your damaged or deleted local copy.

8. Click Cancel to close the HTML Optimization Settings dialog box, and then clear the Optimize HTML During Publishing check box.

   Back on the Publishing tab of the Site Settings dialog box, the last check box lets you choose whether to log changes during publishing. This option is selected by default. There's also a button you can click to view the log file. You will learn more about the publishing log in Chapter 10, "Managing and Publishing Your Work."

9. Click OK to close the Site Settings dialog box.

Keep the features and functions contained in this dialog box in mind as you work with Expression Web. Because the key concept for understanding how Expression Web deals with collections of folders and files is the Expression Web "site," it's important to be familiar with the access methods that Expression Web provides for these important settings.

Changing Application Options

In the previous exercise, you learned how Expression Web uses site settings for an individual site. This exercise is similar, except that the settings described in this section dictate how Expression Web 4 behaves as an *application*, with every site and page. Consider this the broadest point of access to the inner workings of Expression Web 4.

Explore Application Options settings

 Note Open the sample site located at Documents\Microsoft Press\Expression Web 4 SBS if it isn't still open from the preceding exercise.

1. Select Application Options from the Tools menu to open the Application Options dialog box.

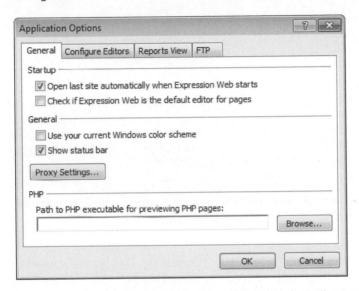

The layout of the Application Options dialog box is similar to that of the Site Settings dialog box; it's organized into four tabs. The General tab is visible by default when you open it.

The Startup option group provides options for Expression Web to open the last Web site you were working with when you start the application, and to check whether Expression Web is the default editor for pages.

2. Clear the Check If Expression Web Is The Default Editor For Pages check box.

In the middle of the General tab, the General group contains two options and a Proxy Settings button. The first option lets you use your current Windows color scheme, which is a helpful feature for users who have a difficult time with the default Expression Dark color scheme. The second is a Show Status Bar option, which hides or shows the status bar at the bottom of the workspace.

3. Click the Proxy Settings button to open the Internet Properties dialog box.

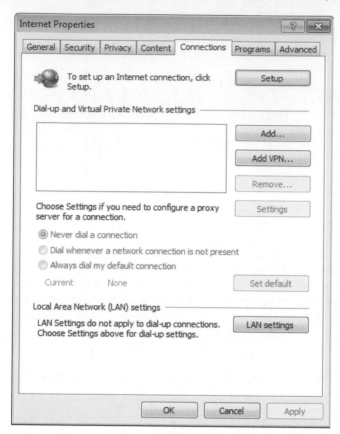

In the Internet Properties dialog box, you can choose to display or change the settings for connecting your computer to a network or to the Internet. You can also set up a new connection to a network or the Internet here. Note that this dialog box and these options work within the Windows system and are not directly part of Expression Web.

4. Click Cancel to close the Internet Properties dialog box.

Back in the Application Options dialog box, in the PHP group, you'll find the Path To PHP Executable For Previewing PHP Pages field. You can set the default path to PHP for *all sites* from this field. In the previous exercise, you saw this path at the *site* level. You will revisit this field later in this chapter, when you set up PHP for your installation of Expression Web.

5. Click the Configure Editors tab at the top of the Application Options dialog box.

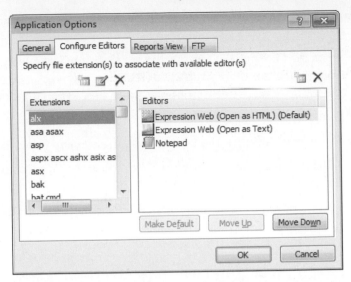

On this tab of the dialog box, you can designate which application opens a particular file type for editing when you open a file of that type from within Expression Web. The dialog box provides an initial list of common file extensions, but you can add more file extensions. You can associate any file extension with a specific application. In the next few steps you will add a file type and configure the editor for it, and you will designate an editor for an existing file type.

6. Click the New Extension button above the Extensions pane to open the Open With dialog box.

7. In the Open With dialog box, type **tpl** in the Extension field, click Expression Web (Open As HTML), and then click OK.

   As you can see on the Configure Editors tab, the .tpl extension you added is now configured to be opened by Expression Web as an HTML file. This is actually a useful addition, because many open-source PHP scripts use the .tpl file extension for templates.

8. In the Extensions pane, click Jpg Jpeg Gif Png.

   You can see that the default application for opening these image files is Paint.

9. Click the New Editor button above the Editors pane, and in the Open With dialog box, click Browse For More.

10. In the Browse dialog box, browse to C:\Program Files\Microsoft Expression\Design 4, and double-click the Design.exe file in that folder.

> **Tip** Some systems are set up to hide the file extensions for known file types. If this is the case, you will see just *Design* (without the *.exe* file extension).

You will learn more about Microsoft Expression Design in Chapter 4, "It's All About Content" and Chapter 6, "Creating a Web Site from Scratch."

11. On the Configure Editors tab, click Microsoft Expression Design, and then click Make Default.

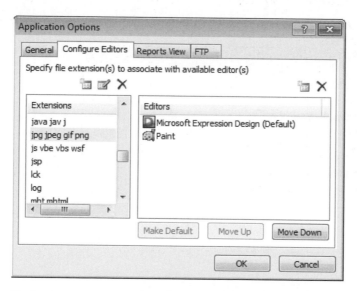

You've just set up your installation of Expression Web 4 so it will open .jpg, .jpeg, .gif, and .png files with Expression Design. You can substitute your favorite graphics editor in place of Expression Design if you want. In the next step, you'll add the native file type for Expression Design.

12. Click the New Extension button above the Extensions pane. Then in the Open With dialog box, type **design** in the Extension field. In the Programs pane, click Microsoft Expression Design, and then click OK.

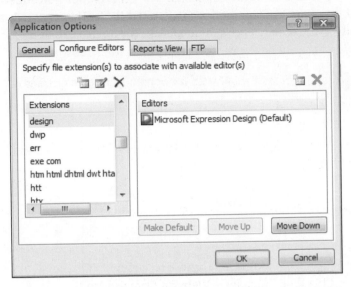

You can see that the .design file extension is now associated with Expression Design. If you open a .design file in Expression Web, Expression Design will automatically open with the file active in its workspace.

13. At the top of the Application Options dialog box, click the Reports View tab.

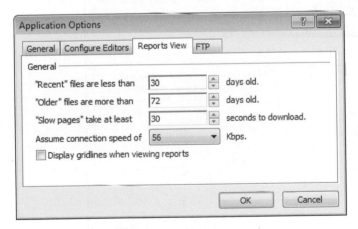

All of the options on this tab are related to the time increments Expression Web uses when building reports. By changing the values here, you can modify the reports to match your particular work scenario.

14. Change the "Recent" Files Are Less Than field to **15** days. Change the "Older" Files Are More Than field to **60** days. Change the "Slow Pages" Take At Least field to **10** seconds. Finally, change the Assume Connection Speed Of field to 128 Kbps.

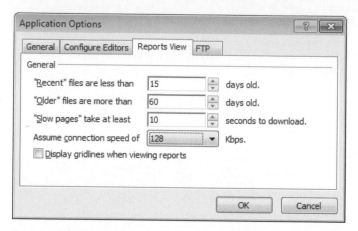

These changes will be reflected in the Reports view of your sites. By changing these values, you can generate reports based on your needs or the site owner's needs.

15. At the top of the Application Options dialog box, click the FTP tab.

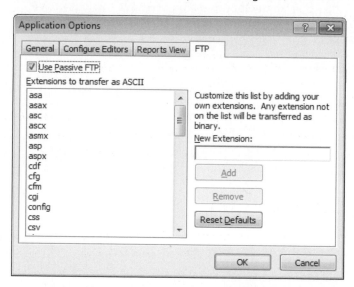

With the options on this tab, you can specify which file types are uploaded as binary and which as ASCII files. Generally, you would consider text-based files to be ASCII, and binaries would be everything else, from images to compressed files.

You can also set whether Expression Web 4 uses passive FTP by selecting or clearing the Use Passive FTP check box.

> **Tip** Some network configurations will work only with passive FTP enabled; others will work only with it disabled. If you have publishing failures, try changing the FTP mode here. Under most circumstances, passive FTP is the preferred choice.

16. Enter **tpl** in the New Extension field, and then click the Add button.

    Because the .tpl extension used for templates is a type of text file, this choice (ASCII) is the preferred upload method.

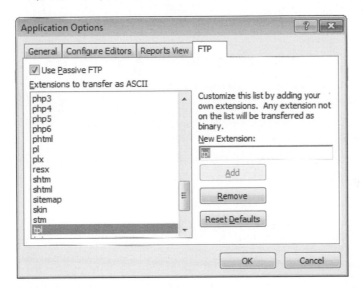

17. Click OK to close the Application Options dialog box and save your changes.

The settings you've just viewed and modified are made at the *application* level, and are applied no matter what site you have open in Expression Web. In contrast, the settings in the preceding exercise were made at the *site* level, and can be made on a per-site basis.

Changing Page Editor Options

In the previous exercise, you learned how to modify application settings to change the behavior of Expression Web at the application level. In this exercise, you will learn about Expression Web's Page Editor Options dialog box. From the Page Editor Options dialog box, the user can change many of the default settings for Expression Web.

Explore the Page Editor Options dialog box

 Note Open the sample site located at Documents\Microsoft Press\Expression Web 4 SBS if it isn't still open from the previous exercise.

1. From the Tools menu, select Page Editor Options.

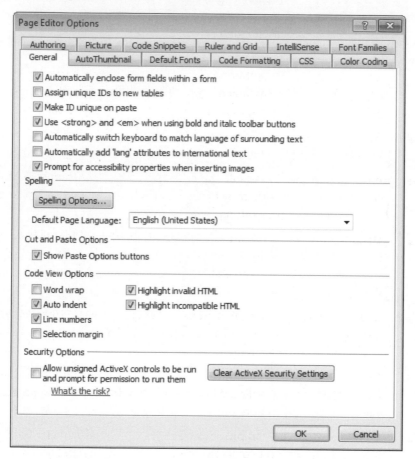

The Page Editor Options dialog box is divided into 12 tabs.

- **Authoring**   This tab provides options that control how Expression Web behaves when you are authoring pages. You can change the default file type that Expression Web creates, as well as control technical aspects such as the DOCTYPE, cascading style sheets schema, and Byte Order Marks.

- **Picture**   This tab provides optional configurations for how Expression Web works with pictures in your pages with regard to file type conversion, quality settings, and so on.

- **Code Snippets**   This tab provides control over the existing snippets in the code snippet library and enables the designer to add new snippets to the library.

- **Ruler and Grid**   This tab provides control over style, color, size, and spacing when Expression Web displays the Ruler and Grid in Design view.

- **IntelliSense**   IntelliSense has been available in Visual Studio for quite a while. It provides autocompletion, context-sensitive pop-ups, and code hyperlinks when you are authoring in code view. You can control this behavior for HTML, cascading style sheets, ASP.NET, and PHP code here.

- **Font Families**   This tab provides control over the fonts that are included in a font family when you are authoring cascading style sheets. If you want to add or remove a font from a cascading style sheets font family, such as Ariel, Helvetica, or sans-serif, or if you want to create your own families, you can do that here.

- **General**   This tab provides control over broad aspects of the default Expression Web page authoring behavior, such as language, spelling, code view, and security.

- **AutoThumbnail**   By default, the Expression Web AutoThumbnail feature is set to create a 100-pixel-wide copy of the main image and apply a 2-pixel border to it. You can change those settings here.

- **Default Fonts**   This tab provides access to the default font that Expression Web uses in Code and Design views on a per-language basis. These changes appear within the Expression Web editing window, not on pages made with Expression Web.

- **Code Formatting**   This tab provides access to the way Expression Web uses new lines and whitespace, as well as tag case, in Code view with specific HTML and cascading style sheets tags.

- **CSS**   This tab provides control over whether Expression Web manually or automatically applies cascading style sheets styles, as well as how it applies the styles to various page elements.

- **Color Coding**   This tab provides options for both Design and Code view regarding the fonts and font colors Expression Web uses. As on the Default Fonts tab, these changes appear within the Expression Web editing window, not on pages made with Expression Web.

For the most part, these settings can generally be left at their defaults. In the next few steps, you will make a worthwhile change to the Byte Order Mark (BOM) application setting.

Tip Many designers use the validation service at *http://validator.w3.org/* to check the validity of their pages. The validator will show warnings when it encounters a BOM. When you combine these validity warnings with the fact that the BOM can render in browsers when viewed from some servers and that it can also potentially cause PHP errors, you can see why some designers prefer to turn the BOM off all together.

2. Click the Authoring tab at the top of the Page Editor Options dialog box.

3. Clear the check box beside all eight file types that appear beneath the Add A Byte Order Mark (BOM)... label.

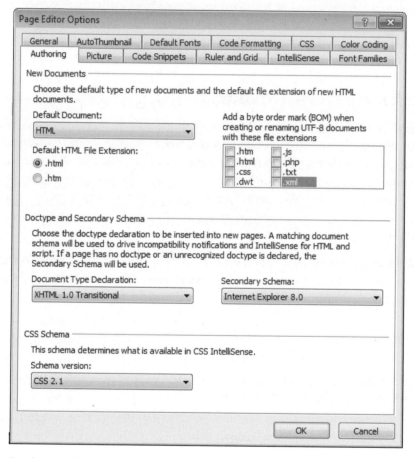

By clearing these check boxes, you ensure that Expression Web will no longer insert a BOM into any of the listed file types.

4. Click OK to save your setting changes and close the Page Editor Options dialog box.

   Because you have set Expression Web 4 to Manual Style Application mode, the Style Application toolbar appears.

5. From the View menu, select Toolbars | Style Application to hide the Style Application toolbar.

Take a few minutes to check out all the tabs in the Page Editor Options dialog box. You can modify virtually every aspect of how Expression Web works with your pages via the selections available in this dialog box. The change you made to the BOM setting is recommended for greater control of page source code.

Using the Expression Development Server

The Expression Development Server is a tremendously useful feature for designers. In the past, Web designers had to set up a local server or publish every change to an external server just to author and test dynamic pages such as ASP.NET or PHP. The Expression Development Server is also unique because it lets you store sites in any common folder location, such as your My Documents folder, your desktop, or even a folder on an external drive. The Expression Development Server will process these pages no matter where they reside; it does not require them to be in a special folder on a server.

In the following steps, you will preview a dynamic page through the Expression Development Server and change the site options to use the Expression Development Server to preview HTML pages.

Use the Expression Development Server

> **Note** Open the SampleSite located at Documents\Microsoft Press\Expression Web 4 SBS if it isn't still open from the preceding exercise.

1. Click the arrow on the New Document button, and then click ASPX to create a new ASP.NET file.

2. In the Folder List panel, expand the /files folder to view its contents.

3. Drag the ServerVars.ascx file from the Folder List panel and drop it onto the Design view of your new ASP.NET page.

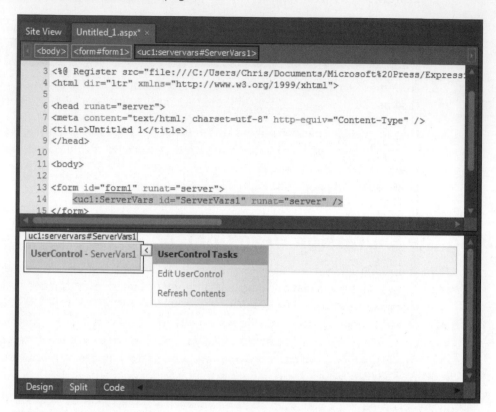

This file is an ASP.NET Web user control that contains some simple server-side code to display the variables of the server that processes the file. You'll learn more about the Web user control in Chapter 3, "Capitalizing on the Template Options in Expression Web 4."

4. Click the Save button on the Common toolbar. In the Save As dialog box, type **ServerVars.aspx** into the File Name field, and then click Save.

5. Click the Preview button on the Common toolbar.

The Expression Development Server starts, processes your page, and then passes it to a browser.

6. Scroll the browser view down to the row labeled SERVER_SOFTWARE, and you will see ExpressionDevServer listed.

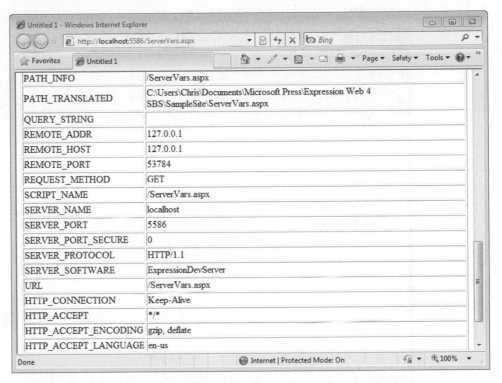

In addition to the address bar in the browser showing the page originating from *http://localhost*, you can see that the Expression Development Server has executed the code in the Web user control and is displaying the server variables. This simply wouldn't be possible without a server to process the Microsoft Visual C# code in the user control.

7. Close the browser and return to Expression Web.

In addition to executing server-side code, the Expression Development Server can be useful when you're creating a simple HTML site. In the next few steps, you will see the difference between previewing from a folder and previewing through the Expression Development Server.

8. Click the arrow on the New Document button on the Common toolbar, and select the HTML option to create a new HTML page.

9. Click in the Design pane of your new file and type **This is the default document in the Images folder.**

10. On the Common toolbar, click the Save button. In the Save As dialog box, double-click the site's Images folder, type **default.html** in the File Name field, and then click Save to save it in the site's Images folder.

11. In the Folder List panel, double-click the Chapter2.html file to open it in the Editing window, and then click the Preview button on the Common toolbar.

Notice that the browser's address bar displays this page's source location as folder based—in other words, the address doesn't display *http://localhost* as it did when you previewed the ASP.NET page.

12. In the browser, scroll down the page and click the image of the ServerVars.aspx page below the Using The Expression Development Server heading. This image is linked to the Images *folder*, not to a specific file within the folder.

Notice that instead of a page, you're seeing a Windows Explorer view of the Images folder. Because you weren't viewing the Chapter2.html file through a server, there's no mechanism to pass the default file you created in the previous step.

13. Close the browser and return to Expression Web.

Tip Designers often prefer to create site navigation that points to folder locations instead of specific pages. This provides shorter, more intuitive URLs for their pages, but it also gives designers the ability to change the default page in a folder without having to update the site's navigation structure.

14. From the Site menu, select Site Settings to open the Site Settings dialog box, and then click the Preview tab.

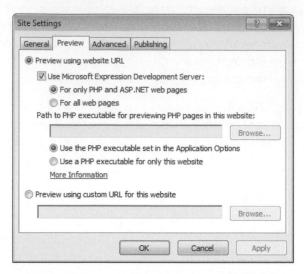

15. Beneath the Use Microsoft Expression Development Server check box, select For All Web Pages to make Expression Web display all pages through the Expression Development Server, and then click OK to save the change and close the Site Settings dialog box.

16. Click the Preview button on the Common toolbar to preview Chapter2.html in a browser.

Notice that you can see the *http://localhost* address in the browser's address bar, meaning that the Expression Development Server is serving this page to the browser.

17. Click the link to the Images folder again.

Notice that the default file you created is now shown in the browser. The address bar shows the folder name only, not the file name.

18. Close the browser and return to Expression Web.

In addition to processing ASP.NET pages and enabling designers to save their sites to any location while still providing server emulation, the Expression Development Server makes creating HTML sites with folder-based navigation structure a much more comfortable local preview workflow.

Using PHP with the Expression Development Server

PHP is a very popular and powerful open source Web development and programming platform. You will even find open source PHP applications in the Windows Web Application Gallery (*http://www.microsoft.com/web/gallery/*), which is a collection of Web applications you can install through the Microsoft Web Platform Installer. This is all part of the Microsoft Web Platform initiative. You can find out more at *http://microsoft.com/web*.

The days of PHP as a technology primarily for programs that are not based on Windows are over. In addition to the fact that the Microsoft Web Platform has obviously embraced PHP, Expression Web also recognizes the importance of PHP and makes it much easier to use, via the common PHP code blocks item on the Insert menu, IntelliSense for PHP in Code view, and so on.

> **Install and configure PHP for the Expression Development Server at both application and site levels**

> **Note** Open the sample site located at Documents\Microsoft Press\Expression Web 4 SBS if it isn't still open from the previous exercise.

1. Visit *http://windows.php.net/download/* and download the latest "thread safe" version packaged in the Windows Installer. At the time of this writing, the latest version was 5.3.2.

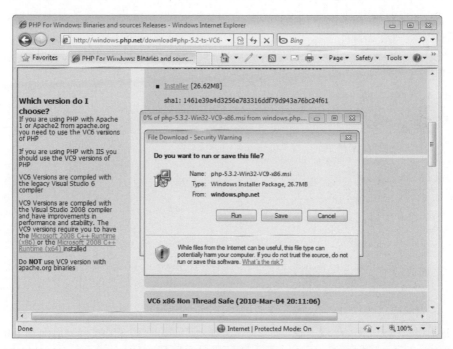

Tip Because PHP is constantly evolving, you might have downloaded a different version number. For this exercise, you can simply substitute your version for the one used in this exercise. If you need to test with very old versions, those are often available only as binary files from *http://www.php.net/releases/*.

2. Run the PHP installer, and in the Destination Folder field, append its default installation folder location (\PHP) by typing the version number into the folder field to append a folder name similar to **PHP532**.

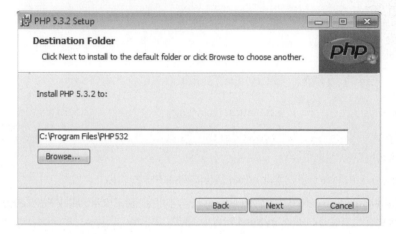

 Tip Adding the version number to the default installation folder location will simplify some steps that you'll see later in this exercise.

3. Click Next, and then choose Other CGI as the installation type.

4. Leave all other defaults as they are, and proceed through the remaining installation steps.

5. Click Finish on the final installation wizard page to finalize the installation process.

6. Using Windows Explorer, browse to the installation folder you specified in this example, C:\Program Files\PHP532.

7. Right-click the new PHP folder, and then click Properties.

8. In the Properties dialog box, click the Security tab, and then click Edit. Give full permissions to the Users group by selecting it and then selecting each unmarked check box under the Allow label.

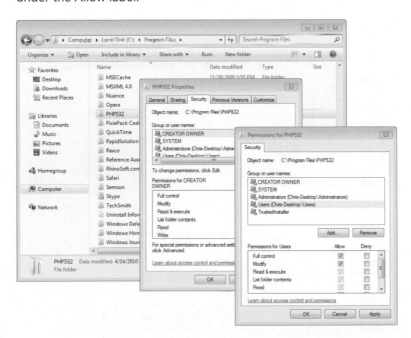

9. Click OK in the Permissions dialog box, and then click OK in the Properties dialog box.

> **Tip** The reason for this extra step is that Expression Web will attempt to edit the PHP .ini file to its own specifications. If the permissions aren't appropriate, it won't work, so taking this step now makes the next few steps much easier.

10. Close Windows Explorer and start Expression Web. If this book's sample site doesn't open with Expression Web, choose Open Site from the Site menu and open the sample site.

> **Tip** Select Recent Sites from the Site menu. You'll see that Expression Web maintains a list of the sites you worked with most recently.

11. From the Tools menu, select Application Options. In the PHP section at the bottom of the General tab, click Browse. Browse to the PHP directory for which you set permissions in the previous step, select the php-cgi.exe file, and then click Open.

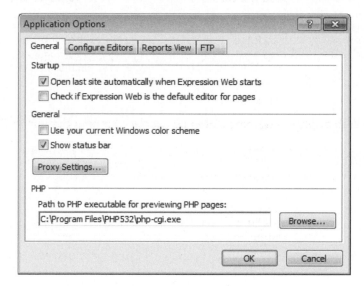

12. Click OK in the Application Options dialog box to save your change.

13. On the Common toolbar, click the arrow on the New Document button, and then click PHP.

Expression Web creates a new PHP file in your workspace.

14. At the bottom of the editing window, click Split to view the PHP page in Split view.

15. In the Code pane, set your cursor between the body tags and type
<?php (phpinfo()) ?>.

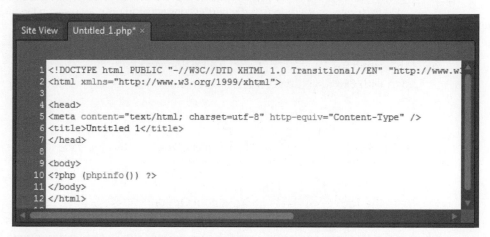

```
 1 <!DOCTYPE html PUBLIC "-//W3C//DTD XHTML 1.0 Transitional//EN" "http://www.w3
 2 <html xmlns="http://www.w3.org/1999/xhtml">
 3
 4 <head>
 5 <meta content="text/html; charset=utf-8" http-equiv="Content-Type" />
 6 <title>Untitled 1</title>
 7 </head>
 8
 9 <body>
10 <?php (phpinfo()) ?>
11 </body>
12 </html>
```

That simple line of PHP code will cause the server to write its variables into the page
that it returns to the browser.

16. On the Common toolbar, click the Save button. In the Save As dialog box, type
ServerVars.php into the File Name field. Then click Save to save your new PHP file
in the root of the site.

17. On the Common toolbar, click the Preview button.

18. Expression Web displays a warning dialog box about changing the .ini file. Click Yes.

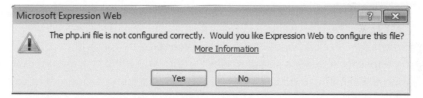

The Expression Development Server processes your page and passes it to the browser.

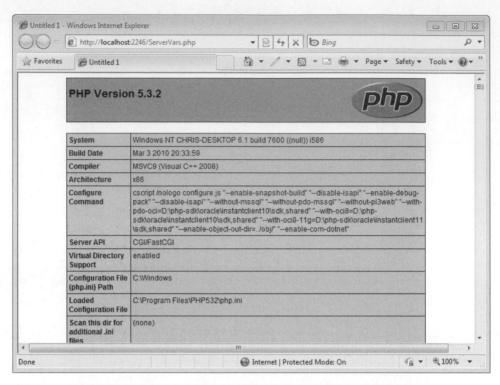

There is a tremendous amount of information on this page. For the purposes of this exercise, just take note of the PHP version at the top of the page (5.3.2 in this case).

19. Close the browser and return to Expression Web.

In this exercise, you have installed PHP and configured the application options so that Expression Web will use it. By default, every PHP page you preview through the Expression Development Server will be processed by the PHP executable file set in the application options. In the next few steps, you will install an older version of PHP, using the same method you used previously, and then configure that to be used by the Expression Development Server in the Site Settings dialog box.

> **Tip** If there is no specific path to PHP in the Site Settings dialog box, the Expression Development Server defaults to the version specified in the Application Settings dialog box.

20. Select File | Exit to close Expression Web.

21. Visit *http://windows.php.net/download/* and download the 5.2 Thread Safe version of PHP packaged in the Windows Installer.

22. Run the PHP installer. On the Destination Folder page, append its default installation folder location (\PHP) by typing the version number into the folder field to append the folder name: **\PHP5213**.

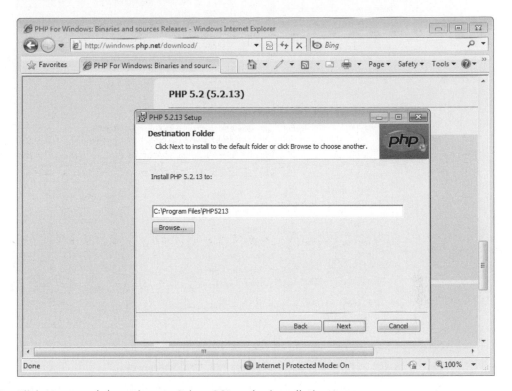

23. Click Next, and then choose Other CGI as the installation type.

Leave all other defaults as they are, and proceed through the remaining installation steps.

24. Click Finish on the final page to finalize the installation process.

25. Using Windows Explorer, browse to the installation folder you specified, which in this example is C:\Program Files\PHP5213.

26. Right-click the new PHP folder, and then click Properties.

27. In the Properties dialog box, click the Security tab, and then click Edit. Give full permission to the Users group by selecting each unmarked check box under the Allow label.

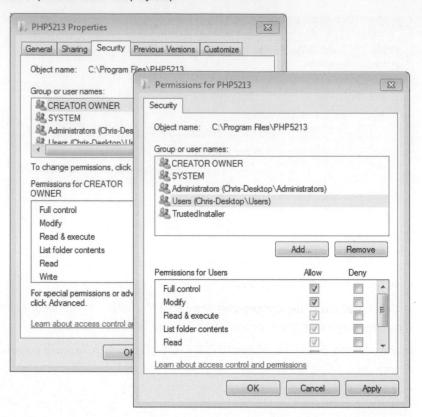

28. Click OK in the Permissions dialog box, and then click OK in the Properties dialog box.

29. Close Windows Explorer, and start Expression Web. If this book's sample site doesn't open with Expression Web, select Open Site from the Site menu and open the sample site.

30. Select Site | Site Settings, and then in the Site Settings dialog box, click the Preview tab.

 Tip Using the Site Settings dialog box, you can explicitly use different versions of PHP in the Expression Development Server for any site.

31. Select Use A PHP Executable For Only This Website. The Browse button becomes active.

32. Click the Browse button and browse to the installation location for the alternative PHP version—in this case, C:/Program Files/PHP5213. Double-click the php-cgi.exe file within this folder to select it.

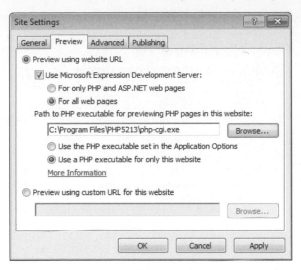

33. Click OK in the Site Settings dialog box to save your change.

34. In the Folder List pane, double-click the ServerVars.php file you created in the previous steps, and then click the Preview button on the Common toolbar.

35. In the warning dialog box about the php.ini file, click Yes to allow Expression Web to configure it.

The Expression Development Server starts, processes the page, and then passes it to your browser.

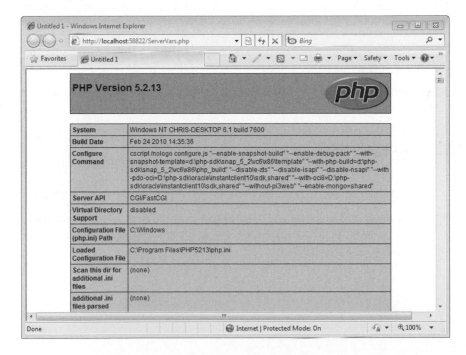

Notice that, this time, the very top of the browser view shows the alternative version of PHP. Although these two versions' release dates are very close, you can download any available version of PHP and use it for testing. These other versions are often not available as Windows Installer packages but are still viable options.

36. Close any open browser windows and return to Expression Web.

The ability to specify different versions of PHP within the Expression Development Server is a very helpful feature when you need to test your applications against different versions of PHP, or to match the PHP version on a production server to the PHP version you're testing with locally. When you couple that with the fact that you can store the files anywhere you like instead of having to keep them on a running server, you can easily see how the Expression Development Server's integration with Expression Web provides significant workflow improvement.

Creating a New Site with Expression Web

The last few exercises highlighted the importance of working within an Expression Web site. By using the site concept to your advantage, you can apply specific and unique settings on a site-by-site basis. In addition to the site settings you've encountered so far, Expression Web offers other site-by-site features such as the Remote Website List. Even Expression Web's inherent behaviors—publishing, opening, searching, and providing reporting options—are configurable on a site-by-site basis. Because so much of how Expression Web works hinges on the site concept, the next section of this chapter will show you how to create new sites so you can segregate your projects and apply Expression Web's site-specific capabilities.

Creating a New Site from an Expression Web Template

Expression Web 4 comes with 19 different Web site templates divided into three categories: Personal, Organization, and Small Business. Each of these site templates is based on a Dynamic Web Template, which you will learn about in Chapter 3. Each template also contains three different cascading style sheets, which also control the site's visual properties. Because there are 19 templates, each with at least three different style sheets, there are at least 57 different appearances available that require little or no custom design work.

> ### Create a new site by using a site template

> **Note** Open the sample site located at Documents\Microsoft Press\Expression Web 4 SBS if it isn't still open from the previous exercise.

1. From the Site menu, select New Site.

   By default, the New dialog box opens with the General category displayed. This category contains Empty Site, One Page Site, and Import Site Wizard. You will be using these options later in this chapter.

2. In the New dialog box, click the Templates category on the left.

   Expression Web displays all 19 stock templates in the center pane of the dialog box. When you select one, you will see a description and a preview of that template on the right side of the dialog box.

3. Click Personal 2 to select it.

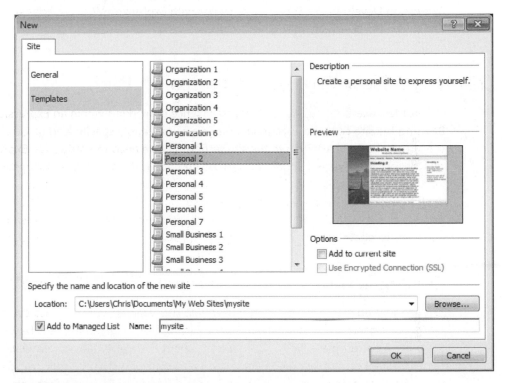

   You can pick any template you like, but for the purposes of this exercise and to make sure that the screenshots match what you see on your screen, use the Personal 2 template.

4. Click the Browse button beside the Location field.

   By default, Expression Web 4 sets the Location field to the user's My Web Sites folder. To segregate this book's exercise files, you will create the site in the book's installation folder.

5. In the New Site Location dialog box, browse to this book's CD installation folder (Documents/Microsoft Press/Expression Web 4 SBS).

6. Click Open to select the location.

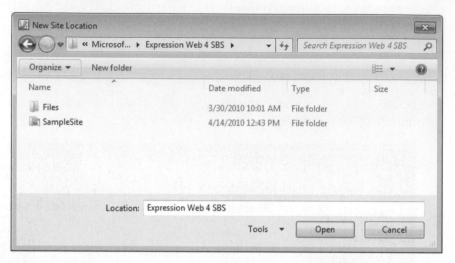

7. Type **Personal2** at the end of the file name in the Location field.

Because you have added Personal2 to the end of the file name in the Location field, Expression Web will create a site with that name.

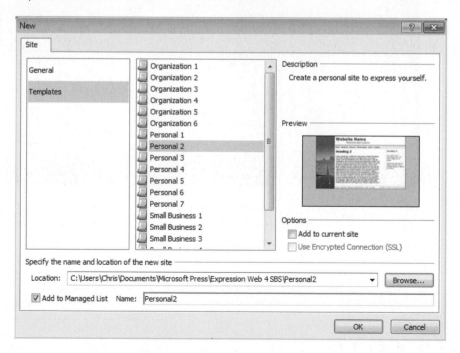

8. Clear the Add To Managed List check box, and then click OK.

> **Tip** Expression Web can keep sites in a managed site list. Although this makes it easier to keep track of production sites, this is just an example exercise, and there's no need to crowd your managed sites list with it at this point.

Expression Web creates all of the necessary files and folders for the template you chose, closes the currently opened site, and opens the new site you just created.

9. Double-click default.html in the Editing window's Site view to open it. Click Split at the bottom of your workspace if the page isn't already in Split view.

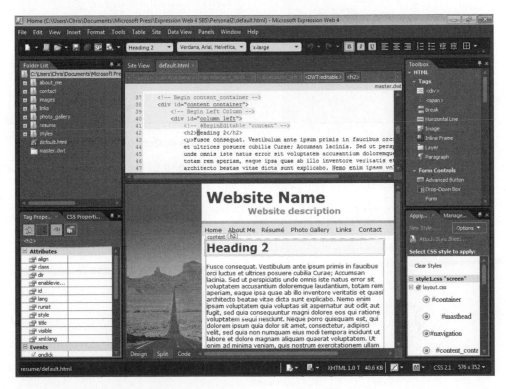

You can follow the same procedure to create a new site based on any template that comes with Expression Web 4. Each site is composed of World Wide Web Consortium–valid (W3C-valid) HTML code and can be modified easily to suit your needs.

> **Tip** To see each of the templates included with Expression Web 4 without having to create the sites locally, visit *http://ExpressionWebStepByStep.com/V4StockTemplates*.

10. On the Common toolbar, click the Preview button.

Your newly created site's default page opens in a browser.

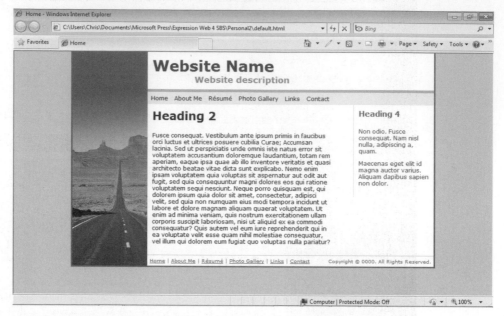

11. Click some of the links and navigate around the site template.

Each template is similar in construction, although the templates have different appearances and navigational structures.

12. Close the browser and return to Expression Web.

This section is about how to create sites. You will learn how to customize sites in many ways in later chapters. But because each of the templates that come with Expression Web has multiple style sheets that define its appearance, you will learn how to change the style sheet in the next few steps.

13. At the top of your workspace, click the Close icon on the default.html page tab, and then double-click the master.dwt file in the Folder List panel to open it for editing.

Every site template that ships with Expression Web is based on a Dynamic Web Template (DWT). Because each page gets its layout from the DWT, this is where you will change your style sheet link. All the pages in the site will reflect the style sheet change automatically.

14. From the Format menu, select CSS Styles | Manage Style Sheet Links.

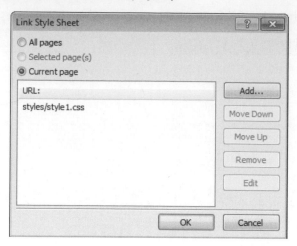

You can see that the DWT for this site is linked to styles/style1.css. In the next steps, you will change the style sheet that's attached to the DWT.

15. Click the entry for styles/style1.css, click the Remove button, and then click Add.

16. In the Select Style Sheet dialog box, double-click the site's /styles folder to open it.

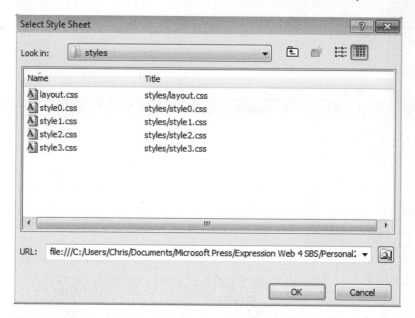

Each template supplied with Expression Web has a /styles folder where all of the site's style sheets are kept.

17. Click style2.css, and then click OK.

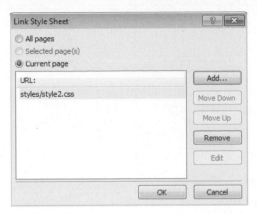

18. Click OK in the Link Style Sheet dialog box to complete your style sheet change.

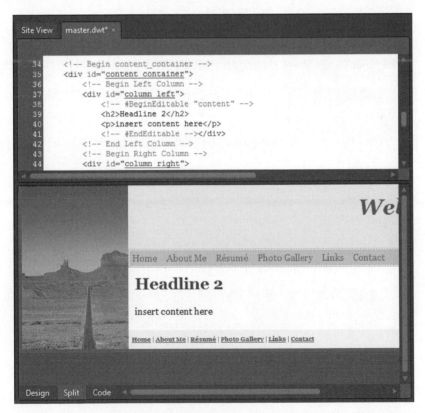

You can see in the editing window that the colors and fonts on the Dynamic Web Template have changed because of the new style sheet.

19. Click Save on the Common toolbar. In the Update Files dialog box, click Yes to allow Expression Web to update all of the pages attached to this DWT, and then click Close on the confirmation alert.

20. In the Folder List panel, click default.html, and then click the Preview button on the Common toolbar.

The default page appears in a browser. Be sure to click the navigation links and look around on the site. You will notice that every page in the site now has a different appearance based on the style sheet you're using.

21. Close your browser and return to Expression Web.

22. From the Format menu, select CSS Styles | Manage Style Sheet Links.

23. Click the entry for styles/style2.css, click the Remove button, and then click Add.

24. In the Select Style Sheet dialog box, double-click style3.css in the site's /styles folder to select it, and then click OK in the Link Style Sheet dialog box.

25. Click Save on the Common toolbar. In the Update Files dialog box, click Yes to allow Expression Web to update all of the pages attached to this DWT, and then click Close on the confirmation alert.

26. In the Folder List panel, click default.html, and then click the Preview button on the Common toolbar.

You've now seen three different versions of the same template just by changing the style sheet link. Each template supplied with Expression Web contains multiple style sheets that provide different appearances. As you work with the templates supplied with Expression Web, take a few minutes to check out each of the alternative style sheets that are included.

27. Close your browser and return to Expression Web.

To wrap up this section, you will attach the original style sheet to the site's Dynamic Web Template.

28. From the Format menu, select CSS Styles | Manage Style Sheet Links.

29. Click the entry for styles/style3.css, click the Remove button, and then click Add.

30. In the Select Style Sheet dialog box, double-click style1.css in the site's /styles folder to select it, and then click OK in the Link Style Sheet dialog box.

31. Click Save on the Common toolbar, in the Update Files dialog box click Yes, and then click Close on the confirmation alert.

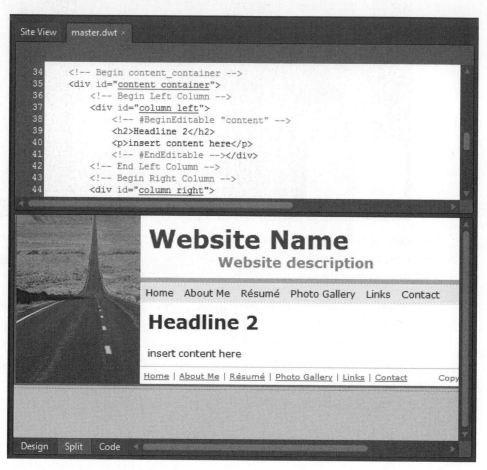

As you can see, the Dynamic Web Template looks like it did when you first created the site, because you've attached the original style sheet to it.

32. On the Site menu, click Close to close the site you've been working with.

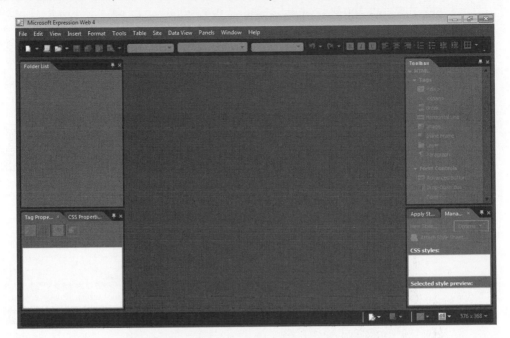

The ability to create a Web site with a design layout, font formatting, and a navigation structure already in place is a powerful feature. It's even more powerful when you can also change the appearance of the template by changing which style sheet the site uses.

In some cases, using one of Expression Web's stock templates will yield the result you need. Sometimes, a stock template along with some customization will work. You'll learn more about customizing and modifying Dynamic Web Templates in Chapter 3.

For this section, all you really need to know is that there are many stock templates available in Expression Web and that each has several different style sheets you can attach to change the template's general appearance.

Creating an Empty Site and Importing Files and Folders

No matter how many templates come with Expression Web or how many style sheets you can attach, in some cases only a custom site will do. In such cases, you will start with an empty site, import the graphics and other files you need, and then start building the custom site.

To use Expression Web to manage the site, you must know how Expression Web recognizes individual sites and their files. Basically, Expression Web needs to know the beginning and end point of the folder structure that it considers a "site." You must also have metadata enabled within the site to make Expression Web's advanced management features available.

Create an empty site and import files and folders

 Note Open Expression Web 4, if it isn't still open from the previous exercise.

1. From the Site menu, select New Site, and then in the General category, click Empty Site.

2. In the Location field, change Personal3 to **MyCustomSite**.

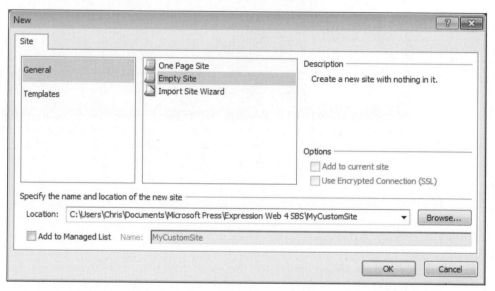

Expression Web remembers the name of the last site you created and the location where you created it. Because the last site you created was in the /Expression Web 4 SBS folder and was named Personal2, Expression Web's default behavior is to set up a save location in that same folder and name the site Personal3.

 Tip If you haven't been creating the Web sites in this chapter's exercises, the last site you created will appear in the Location field.

3. Click OK in the New dialog box.

Expression Web creates a new site named MyCustomSite in this book's companion media installation folder and then opens it.

You can see that even though there aren't any files or folders yet, the Expression Web interface is showing you a "site" view and the Folder List panel, with the root folder visible.

> **Tip** The only difference between the options for the empty site and the one-page site is that the one-page site has a default.html file. Considering the scope of work involved in creating a custom site, having a blank default.html file will be of little consequence.

Now that you have an empty site with which to start your custom project, one of the first things you will need to do is import the graphics, HTML, cascading style sheets, and any other files you need to accomplish the basic layout. Designers will often import some files and folders initially, and then import additional files individually as the need arises.

4. From the File menu, choose Import, and then click File.

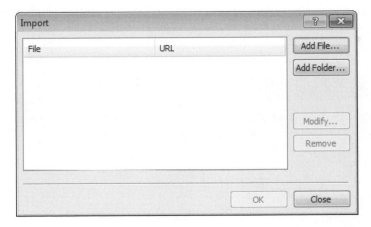

5. Click Add Folder in the Import dialog box.

6. In the File Open dialog box, browse to the \Files folder in this book's companion media installation location (Documents\Microsoft Press\Expression Web 4 SBS), and click the GenericSiteTemplate folder.

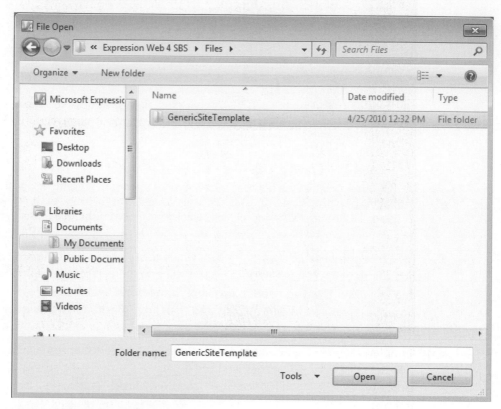

7. Click Open, and then in the Import dialog box, click OK.

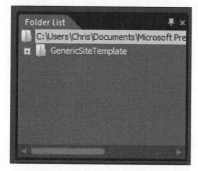

You can see in the Folder List pane that the GenericSiteTemplate folder is now within your site.

8. Expand the GenericSiteTemplate folder in the Folder List panel, and then double-click the default.html file within it to open it in your workspace.

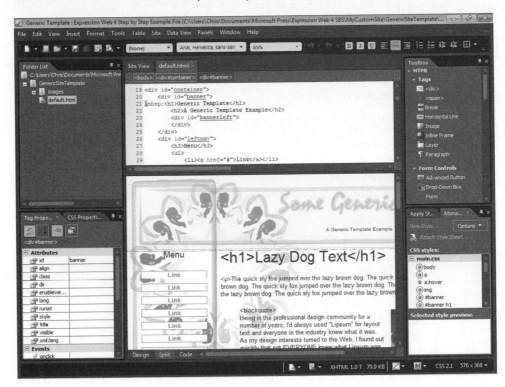

Templates for the Web come in a variety of different formats; some are created as full sites with individual pages, and some are made for specific editors such as Adobe Dreamweaver, Microsoft Office FrontPage, or even Expression Web. But the most basic templates are little more than a single page along with the required images. For this exercise, I've set up the most generic template possible. After importing a template such as this, you would go about the process of modifying it, creating a template for your pages, and so on. You'll learn about Expression Web's template options in Chapter 3.

Tip To see a continuously updated list of templates from all over the Web, visit *http://ExpressionWebStepByStep.com/Templates.*

9. From the Site menu, choose Close to close your newly created site.

Regardless of how you build your sites, using the Import dialog box ensures that Expression Web is aware of the files and folders that you've brought into the folder structure and can help you control and monitor the entire site during the development process.

Using the Import Site Wizard

The Import Site Wizard is a powerful and helpful tool. With it you can import a site from any location, regardless of whether the site is based on a local disk or located on a server. The benefit of using the Import Site Wizard is that the wizard will import all of the files and folders from an existing location into a new site, thereby protecting the original site from any accidental damage. You can work on the imported site without worrying about the original site and its files and folders.

Use the Import Site Wizard

Note Open Expression Web 4 if it isn't still open from the previous exercise. If a site opens within Expression Web, choose Close from the Site menu to close it.

1. From the Site menu, select Import | Import Site Wizard.

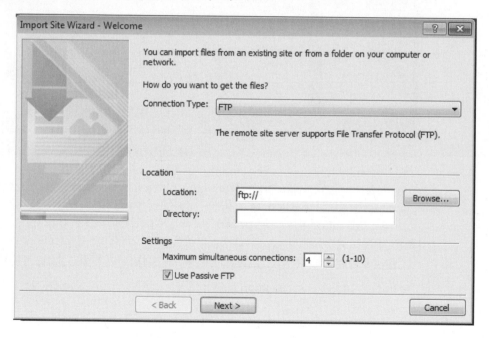

> **Tip** If you have a site on the Internet and need to get a copy of it to your local computer, the Import Site Wizard is perfect. It will connect to virtually any server via FTP, FTPS, SFTP, or HTTP; create a local site; and then import every file and folder from the server into the local site. All you need is the site's URL and the appropriate user name and password.

2. Select File System from the Connection Type list.

3. Click the Browse button beside the Location field.

4. In the Choose Import Location dialog box, browse into this book's CD installation folder (Documents/Microsoft Press/Expression Web 4 SBS).

5. Click SampleSite to select this book's sample site (which you're about to import), and then click Select.

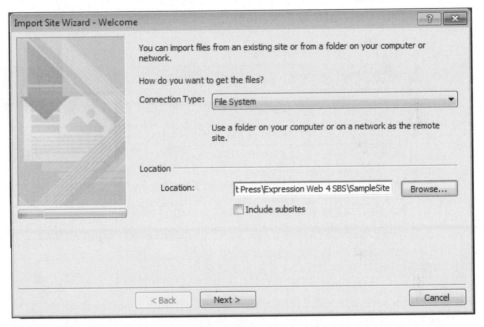

The Import Site Wizard Location field now shows this book's sample site location.

6. Click Next, and then click Browse beside the Local Copy Location field.

7. In the New Publish Location dialog box, browse to this book's CD installation folder and click New Folder.

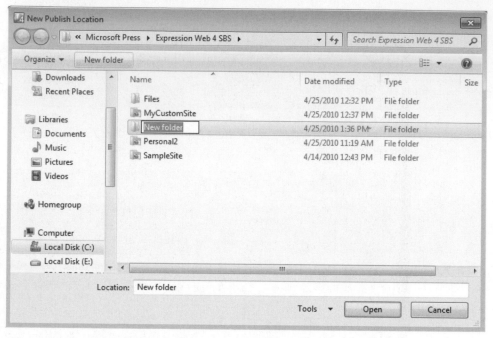

8. Name the folder **MyImportedSite** and click Open.

9. Click Next in the Import Site Wizard, and then click Finish.

Expression Web creates a new site in the location you specified, and opens the site you're importing in the remote site pane.

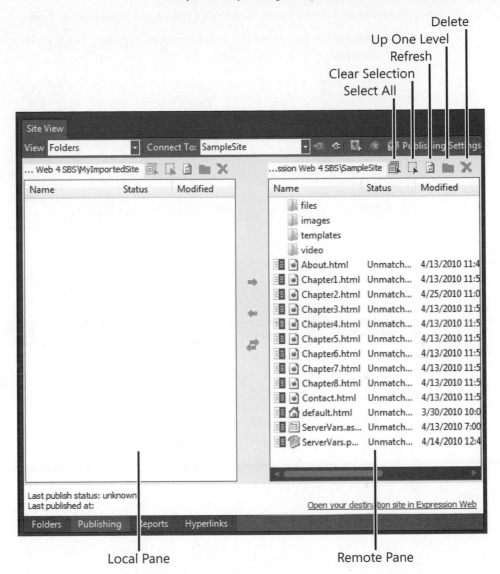

10. Click the Select All button above the remote site, and then click the Get Files From Remote Site button between the remote and local panes.

The Publishing Status pane opens at the bottom of your workspace, and Expression Web publishes all the files from the remote site to the local site.

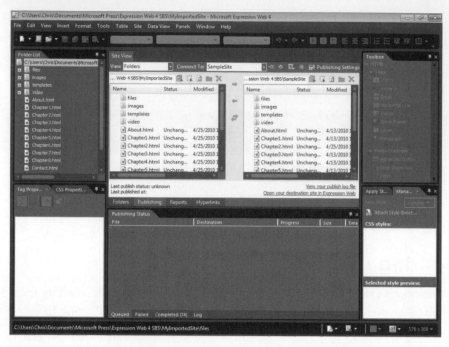

11. Close the Publishing Status pane, and then in the Folder List pane, double-click the Chapter2.html file to open it in your workspace.

12. Click the Preview button on the Common toolbar to open Chapter2.html in a browser.

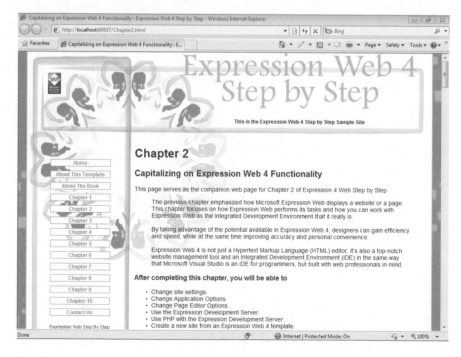

Click some of the links in the browser preview. Notice that the site is identical to the original sample site that was installed with this book's companion files.

13. Close the browser and return to Expression Web. From the Site menu, select Close to close your newly imported site.

By using the Import Site Wizard, you can work on a local copy of any Web site, whether the original Web site resides in a folder location as it did in this example, or on a server. Regardless of the original site's location, you can use the Import Site Wizard to create a local copy of the site and thereby protect the original site from potential damage.

Note Be sure to close your imported site.

Configuring Add-ins

Because this chapter has dealt primarily with how Expression Web works as an application and how you can control some of its default behavior, it seems fitting to end the chapter with the apex of application control: add-ins.

An add-in is a small program that extends the functionality of an application. Expression Web 4 contains a whole new add-in platform. In the past, add-ins were generally made by programmers in Microsoft Visual C++ and were fairly complicated. In Expression Web 4, each add-in consists of an XML manifest file that describes the add-in to Expression Web, an HTML file for the add-in's interface, and any necessary cascading style sheets or JavaScript files. In Expression Web 4, add-ins for the application can actually be created within Expression Web itself.

Add-ins fall into three basic categories: Panels, Dialog boxes, and Commands. Users can access the add-ins via menu commands, the Panels menu, and the Toolbar.

With that kind of ease of access, we can expect developers to create add-ins that provide extended functionality for Expression Web that would otherwise be unavailable except through significant manual work.

Tip A list of Expression Web add-ins, as well as documentation about creating add-ins, can be found at *http://expressionaddins.com/*.

View, enable, and disable add-in-based components

> **Note** Open the sample site located at Documents\Microsoft Press\Expression Web 4 SBS.

1. In the Folder List panel, double-click Chapter2.html to open it in your workspace.

2. Scroll the Design pane down to the paragraph that contains Insert Symbol Here:, and set your cursor at the end of that text.

3. On the Insert menu, click Symbol.

The Expression Web product team built the Insert Symbol dialog box by using the Expression Web 4 add-in model. Their willingness to use their add-in model for an integral part of the application interface speaks volumes about how serious they are about this new add-in model.

4. Click the ® symbol, click the Insert button, and then click Close.

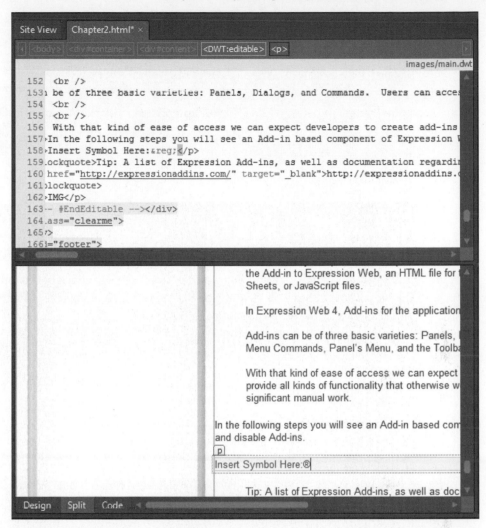

You can see that the Symbol dialog box inserted *®* into the Code pane, which results in the insertion of the registered trademark symbol, ®, in the Design pane.

5. On the Tools menu, click Add-in.

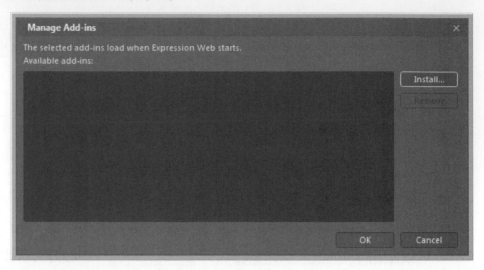

In the Manage Add-ins dialog box, you can select or clear check boxes for the add-ins that you want to start when Expression Web starts up, and you can install and remove add-ins by using the Install and Remove buttons.

6. Click Cancel in the Manage Add-ins dialog box.

> **Tip** Although you can add or remove add-ins while Expression Web is running, you need to restart Expression Web to finalize the process.

7. On the Common toolbar, click Save to save the change to your Chapter2.html file, and then, on the Site menu, click Close.

Because the new add-in model in Expression Web 4 was designed to provide programmers of all skill levels a chance to create add-ins, while at the same time exposing as much of the application functionality as possible, we can expect the Expression Web add-in ecosystem to grow rapidly. For more information, see *http://ExpressionAddins.com/*.

> **Note** Be sure to close Expression Web if you're not continuing directly to the next chapter.

Key Points

- Expression Web allows tremendous customization in default application behavior.

- The Expression Development Server processes files from any folder location and doesn't require the designer to install a separate server.

- The Expression Development Server's path to PHP can be set at an application level as well as on a site-by-site basis.

- By specifying a path to the PHP executable file in the Site Settings dialog box, the designer can test his or her PHP pages with various versions of PHP.

- Expression Web contains 19 site templates, each of which contains multiple cascading style sheets with which you can alter their appearance.

- With the Import Site Wizard, designers can create a copy of a site from a local folder location or a Web server–based location so they can work on the copy without the possibility of damaging the original site.

- Expression Web 4 contains an all-new add-in model designed to simplify the process of creating and using add-ins.

Chapter 3
Capitalizing on the Template Options in Expression Web 4

After completing this chapter, you will be able to:

- Understand template concepts
- Use Dynamic Web Templates
- Use the Include Page feature
- Use ASP.NET master pages
- Use ASP.NET Web user controls
- Use PHP include files

The term *template* has more than one definition. Even within the confines of Web design and development, the term can mean different things to different people. For instance, Microsoft Expression Web has several Web site templates. These are basically generic sites, complete with navigation and uniform page layout. The individual pages of these site templates are also based on templates; in this case, Dynamic Web Templates (DWTs).

In addition to the Web site templates and DWTs, Expression Web users can easily make use of a template system inherent to Microsoft ASP.NET called ASP.NET master pages.

Expression Web also provides the ability to make a template from just a part of a page. For example, to put a news box, Really Simple Syndication (RSS) feed, advertising content, or some other content on some pages but not all, a designer can create either an ASP.NET Web user control or a file that Expression Web will include on pages as a PHP include file. Expression Web even has an include file method that happens locally, like the DWT does, so that designers can use the Include Page feature without having to consider the server environment.

All this template functionality serves a larger purpose: maintaining uniformity across multiple pages. Prominent side benefits of templates include greatly easing the work of maintaining, managing, and even designing a site.

In this chapter, you will gain exposure to each of the different template options available in Expression Web 4.

 Important Before you can use the practice files in this chapter, you need to download and install them from the book's companion content Web site to their default location. For more information about downloading and installing the practice files, see the "Code Samples" section at the beginning of this book.

 Troubleshooting Graphics and operating system-related instructions in this book reflect the Windows 7 user interface. If your computer is running Windows XP or Windows Vista and you experience trouble following the instructions as written, please refer to the "Information for Readers Running Windows XP or Vista" section at the beginning of this book.

Understanding Template Concepts

Before you incorporate template techniques into your work, you should see them in action and understand how each kind of template yields tangible results in your design and development workflow. In Expression Web, the template methods can be divided into two categories: run-time and design-time.

Expression Web's design-time template functionality, which includes DWTs and the Include page, takes place on a local computer inside the Expression Web environment, and results in complete files that are published to a server. These design-time methods are handy because they are totally independent of server requirements. If the server can pass HTM/HTML files to a browser, Expression Web's design-time features will work.

In contrast, run-time template features, such as ASP.NET master pages, ASP.NET Web user controls, PHP include files, and other server-side include methods all have special requirements that the server must meet—or they won't work.

In Expression Web 4, you work with run-time features through the Expression Development Server. If you have designed a page that takes advantage of server-side features such as ASP.NET or PHP, Expression Web will display the files in WYSIWYG format, and even run those pages in the Expression Development Server when you preview them from within Expression Web—regardless of where the files are located on your computer.

Using Dynamic Web Templates

A DWT is a good way to template a Web site, because all the work of combining the template file and the content files occurs locally, on your computer, while still letting you see many of the same results produced by the server. DWTs let you control the layout and global elements of multiple pages from one centralized template file.

A DWT also enforces your layout on all the pages to which it is attached. This results in a more convenient workflow when someone other than the designer edits the page content.

You can also change the layout and format of every page attached to the template by modifying the DWT. Site mockup, redesign, and maintenance become much more manageable when you use a template or set of templates.

Use a Dynamic Web Template

> **Note** Start Expression Web 4 before beginning this exercise. Open the SampleSite site by selecting Open Site from the Site menu, browsing to the CD's default installation page, and double-clicking the SampleSite folder. With the sample site opened in Expression Web, double-click the Chapter3.html page in the Folder List panel.

1. If your editing window didn't open Chapter3.html in Split view, click Split at the bottom of your workspace. Notice that the banner, left margin, and footer of the Chapter3.html page are rendered in half color. In the Code pane, you can see these areas with a yellow background, indicating that they're coming from the DWT. Hold your cursor over one of these areas. The cursor changes to a no-insertion cursor. All these areas are controlled by the sample site's DWT.

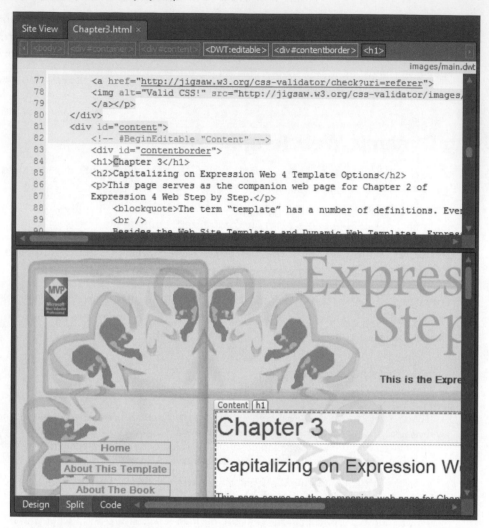

The only part of the Chapter3.html page that *isn't* part of the Dynamic Web Template is the center content area, which has a dashed border in this exercise, for emphasis.

In the upper-right corner of the workspace, you can see a DWT status message that shows images/main.dwt. All the pages of this sample site are attached to that Dynamic Web Template (main.dwt).

2. On the Common toolbar, click the arrow on the New Document button, and then click Create From Dynamic Web Template. The Attach Dynamic Web Template dialog box opens.

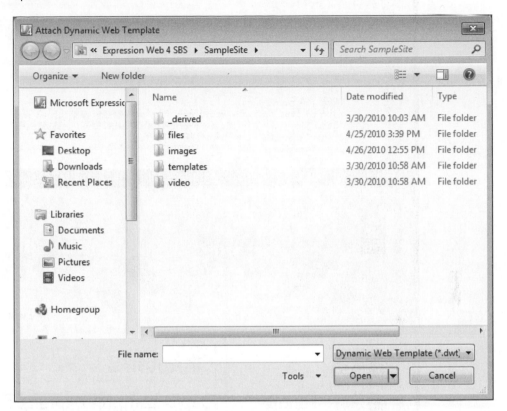

3. In the Attach Dynamic Web Template dialog box, double-click the Images folder, and then double-click main.dwt.

4. A new page named Untitled_1.html opens in your workspace. Click Close on the File Update Confirmation alert that opens on top of the new page.

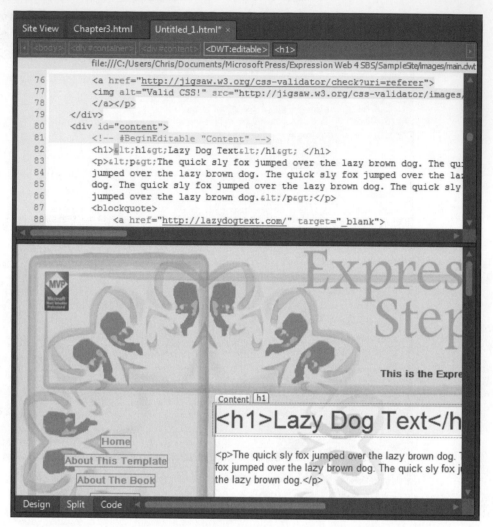

Now you have a new page that's an exact layout duplicate of all the other pages in the site because of the Dynamic Web Template.

5. Click Save. The Save As dialog box opens. Type **Chapter3a.html** into the File Name field, and then click Change Title. The Set Page Title dialog box opens. Type **My New Page** in the Page Title field, and click OK to close the dialog box. In the Save As dialog box, click Save.

6. In the Folder List panel, expand the Images folder, and then double-click the main.dwt file. The DWT for this sample site opens in Expression Web.

Because your new page isn't listed in the sample site's navigation, you will add it now.

> **Tip** Split view is a good HTML instructor. As you select elements in the Design pane, Expression Web selects the corresponding HTML code automatically in the Code pane. Split view also lets you see a map of the HTML code involved in that element in the Quick Tag Selector.

7. In the Design pane, locate the link for Chapter 3 in the navigation list on the left side of the pane. Set your cursor at the end of the text in the link for Chapter 3, and then press Enter on your keyboard to add a new line.

Now look at the Code pane. More than just adding a new line, Expression Web has added a new list item. The existing menu is an unordered list with cascading style sheet styling.

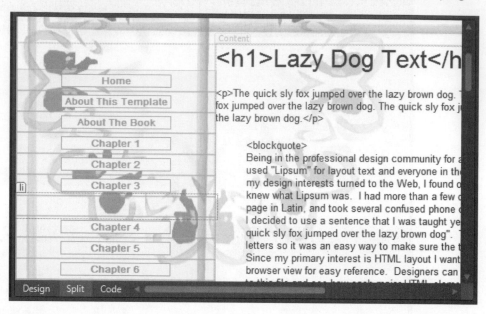

8. Type **Chapter 3a** in the new list item, and then highlight the text in the Design pane and right-click it. From the context menu, choose Hyperlink. The Insert Hyperlink dialog box opens.

> 💡 **Tip** Triple-clicking in the Design pane will select the complete content of a parent element.

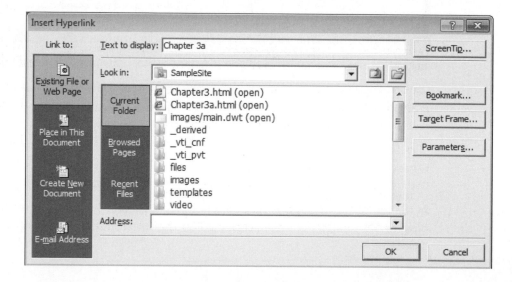

9. Locate the entry for Chapter3a.html and double-click it.

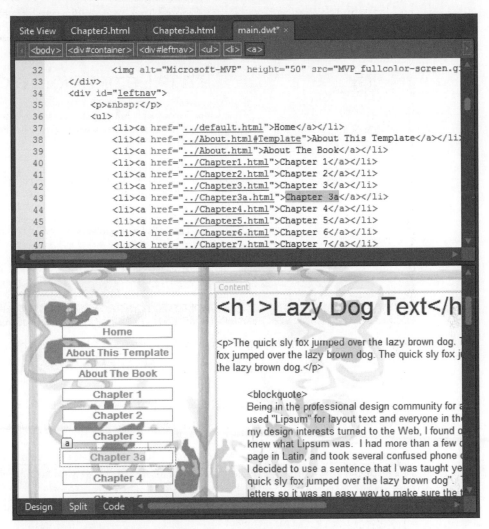

Look at the Design pane. You can see that the visual representation of your new link is identical to the others. And when you look in the Code pane, you can see that the HTML code added is identical to the adjacent code.

10. Click Save on the Common toolbar. In the Update Files alert that appears, click Yes. Expression Web updates all the attached pages with the changes you made to the DWT. When the Update Confirmation alert appears, click Close.

11. At the top of the workspace, click the Chapter3a.html tab. On the Common toolbar, click the Save button, and then click the Preview button. The new page opens in a browser.

Troubleshooting Open pages that are attached to a DWT don't automatically save as unopened pages do. You'll need to save them by either clicking the Save button or by choosing Save All from the File menu.

Click some of the links in the menu you modified. Notice that the additional link you added is now present on every page. Close the browser window and return to Expression Web.

 Tip From the View menu, select Toolbars, and then click Dynamic Web Template. A small toolbar for working with DWTs will appear at the top of your workspace.

12. Click the main.dwt tab at the top of your workspace. The DWT becomes the active document. In the Design pane, below the menu you worked on, click the Facebook fan page badge.

Look at the Quick Tag Selector at the top of the Code pane. You can see that the image you selected is inside an anchor tag, which itself is inside a paragraph tag.

13. On the Quick Tag Selector, click the <p> tab to select the paragraph tag that contains the Facebook badge, along with all its contents.

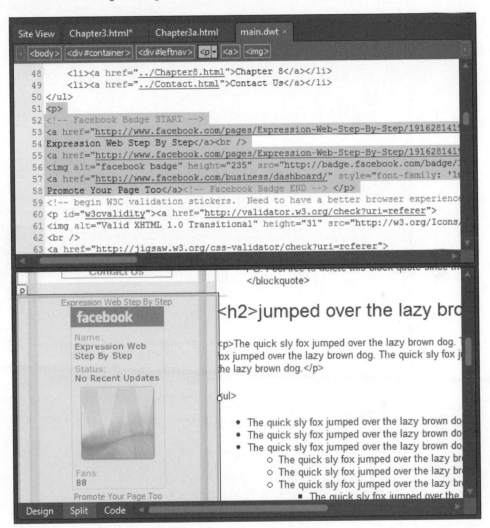

You can see in both the Design pane and Code pane that the paragraph tag is selected, along with all the elements that it contains.

14. From the Format menu, select Dynamic Web Template, and then choose Manage Editable Regions. The Editable Regions dialog box opens.

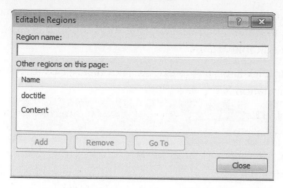

15. In the Region Name field, type **LeftBelowMenu**. Click Add, and then click Close. The Editable Regions dialog box closes.

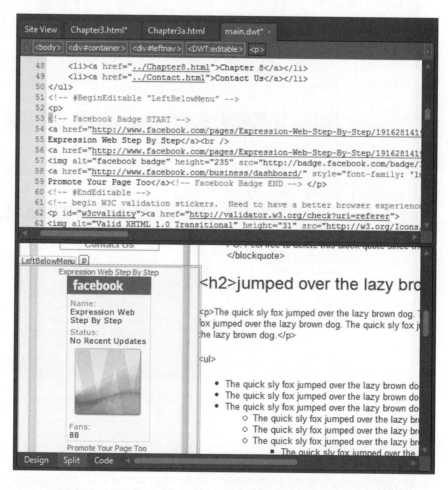

In the Design pane, you'll see a tag for the LeftBelowMenu editable region, and in the Code pane, you can see that the paragraph tag that surrounded the Facebook badge is now also inside the new editable region.

16. On the Common toolbar, click Save. In the Update Files dialog box, click Yes, and then in the Update Files confirmation alert, click Close.

17. Click the Chapter3a.html tab at the top of your workspace to make that page the active document, and then click Save on the Common toolbar.

18. In the Design pane, click the Facebook badge image, and on the Quick Tag Selector, point to the <p> tag inside the editable region. Click the arrow, and then click Select Tag Contents. Expression Web selects the paragraph's contents.

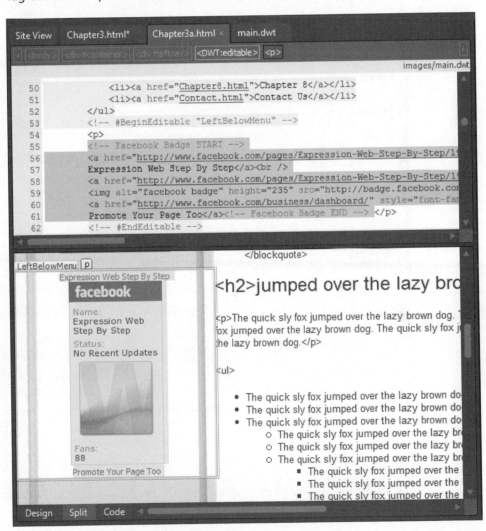

19. Press Delete on your keyboard, click Save on the Common toolbar, and then click Preview. The page opens in a browser. Click a few of the navigation links to the other chapter pages.

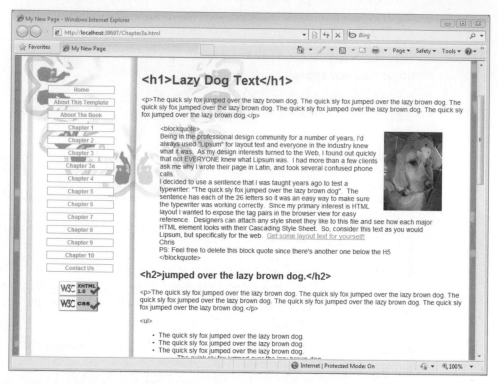

Notice that the Facebook badge has now been removed from the Chapter3a.html page that you made, but it's present on all the other pages. By using this method, you can selectively include or exclude elements from the DWT on a page-by-page basis.

20. Close your browser and return to Expression Web. Click the main.dwt tab at the top of the workspace to make main.dwt the active document.

Consider the flexibility of the Dynamic Web Template. You can employ DWT techniques to control pages or groups of pages with one or more templates. In the next steps, you will create a new DWT and transfer a layout onto it. You can then use this new template to provide a different appearance to any page you choose.

21. Point to the New Document icon on the Common toolbar, click the arrow, and then click Page. The New dialog box opens.

22. In the General category, click Dynamic Web Template, and then click OK. A new master page named untitled_1.dwt opens in your workspace.

23. Click Save. The Save As dialog box opens. Double-click the sample site's templates folder, type **red.dwt** into the File Name field, and then click Change Title. The Set Page Title dialog box appears. Type **My Template** into the Page Title field, and then click OK to close the dialog box. In the Save As dialog box, click Save. Expression Web saves the new DWT as red.dwt in the site's templates folder.

> **Note** Although this is only the third chapter of this book, and we haven't yet discussed how to create a layout from scratch by using cascading style sheets, there is still value in becoming comfortable with templates. For example, it's important to be able to transfer a design from an HTML file to a DWT. Many designers make use of third-party page templates. These pre-made templates are usually provided in HTML form; vendors assume that designers will be able to use the template layouts in their preferred template systems.

24. In the Folder List panel, expand the templates folder, and then double-click the red.html file to open it for editing. Click in the body of the page in the Design pane, and then on the Quick Tag Selector, point to the <body> tag, click the arrow, and then click Select Tag Contents.

25. In the Code pane, right-click the selected body tag contents, and select Copy from the shortcut menu.

26. At the top of the workspace, click the red.dwt tab to make red.dwt the active document in the workspace. Click in the Design pane, and on the Quick Tag Selector, point to the <body> tag, click the arrow, and then click Select Tag Contents.

27. Right-click the selected body tag contents in the Code pane, and select Paste from the shortcut menu. Expression Web pastes all the content from red.html into your new Dynamic Web Template.

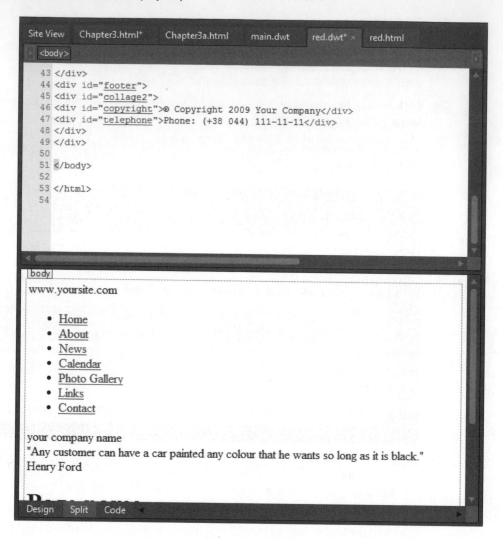

 Troubleshooting Press F5 on your keyboard or select Refresh from the View menu if you have made a change to a page and it isn't reflected in the Design pane.

Although you can see that the body contents of red.html have been pasted into the newly created DWT, the new page doesn't look anything like the original. That's because the original page's cascading style sheet isn't attached to this DWT. In the next steps, you will remedy that situation.

> **Tip** Whenever you're transferring the contents of an HTML file to a new DWT file, you should check the <*head*> section of the original file for cascading style sheet links, JavaScript, and special metadata.

28. Click the red.html tab at the top of your workspace to make that page the active document. In the Code pane, scroll up to the head section of the page's source code.

29. In the head section of red.html, you will see a style sheet link and two JavaScript links. Highlight all three entries.

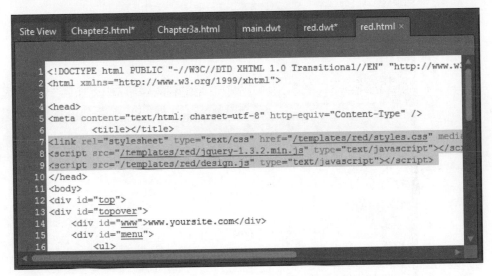

30. Right-click the highlighted lines of code in the Code pane, and from the context menu, select Copy.

31. Click the red.dwt tab at the top of your workspace to make that page the active document.

32. In the Code pane, scroll up to the head section of red.dwt. Set your cursor just before the <*!-- #BeginEditable "doctitle" -->* editable region tag, and press Enter to insert an empty line. Set your cursor in this new empty line, right-click, and select Paste from the context menu. Expression Web pastes the style sheet and JavaScript links into your Dynamic Web Template.

33. On the Common toolbar, click Save.

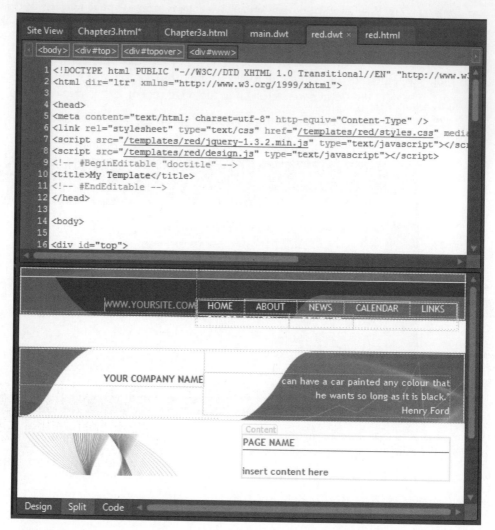

34. In the Design pane, set your cursor in the *h1* element that contains the words *PAGE NAME*. On the Quick Tag Selector, click the div#content tab to select the *div* and all its contents.

35. On the Format menu, point to Dynamic Web Template, and then click Manage Editable Regions. The Editable Regions dialog box opens.

36. Type **Content** into the Region Name field, click Add, and then click Close. Expression Web wraps the selected *div* in an editable region named *Content*.

Tip Adding an optional editable region makes for easier page-by-page editing because it puts contents from unnamed editable regions into an area outside the design.

37. Scroll the Design pane to the bottom and click below the page's footer.

38. From the Format menu, select Dynamic Web Template and then select Manage Editable Regions. Type **CatchAll** in the Region Name field, click Add, and then click Close. An editable region named *CatchAll* is placed in the page.

Notice the default text (CatchAll) that Expression Web provided in the newly placed editable region.

39. Select the paragraph tag and the text it contains (CatchAll), and then press the Delete key.

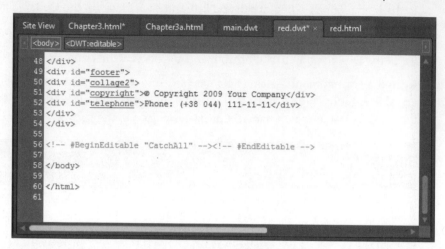

When a content page is attached to this DWT and there are no stray content regions, this area will stay empty. Conversely, if there is stray content, the designer can decide what to do with it on a page-by-page basis.

40. Click Save on the Common toolbar.

41. Click the chapter3a.html tab at the top of your workspace to make that page the active document. From the Format menu, select Dynamic Web Template, and then choose Attach Dynamic Web Template.

42. In the Attach Dynamic Web Template dialog box, navigate to the /templates folder, click red.dwt, and then click Open. The Match Editable Regions dialog box opens.

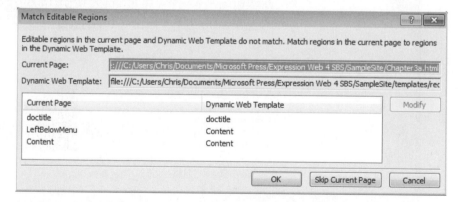

In this dialog box, you determine which editable regions of a Dynamic Web Template are associated with the editable regions on a content page.

43. Click the entry for LeftBelowMenu, and then click Modify. The Choose Editable Region For Content dialog box opens.

44. Click the arrow beside the New Region field, click CatchAll, and then click OK. Click OK in the Match Editable Regions dialog box and click Close on the Updated Files alert.

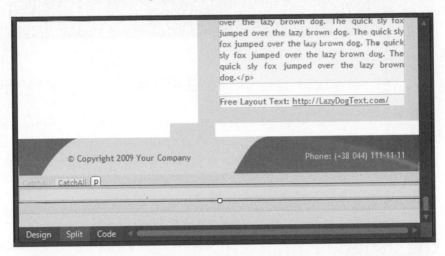

Scroll the Design pane all the way to the bottom. Notice that the empty paragraph tag where you deleted the Facebook badge is now located outside the page design.

45. Click Save on the Common toolbar, and then click Preview. The page opens in a browser.

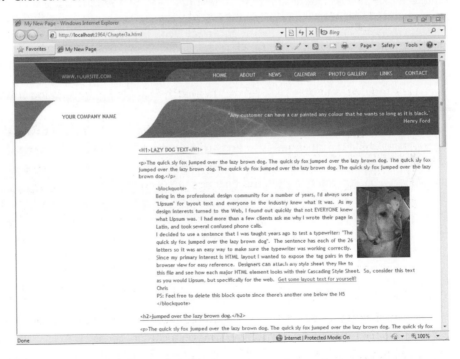

Consider the efficiency of redesigning a site and only modifying a single DWT, or the convenience of adding a new link to a menu and only adding the link to a single file, yet automatically modifying every menu in the site.

46. On the File menu, click Save All, and then on the Window menu, click Close All Pages.

> **Note** Leave the SampleSite site open if you are proceeding directly to the next section.

In this exercise, you created a new page and attached it to a DWT, edited the DWT, added editable regions, created a new DWT, and switched the DWT to which your content page was attached. By combining these techniques and methods, using multiple DWT files, and so on, you can use Expression Web to create an enforceable design with the flexibility required to work efficiently in a frequently changing Web site.

Using the Include Page Feature

Although Dynamic Web Templates are obviously designed to be used as page layout tools, sometimes a designer should use an include file. Because the Expression Web include page functions like the DWT, at design time, a designer can use it regardless of his or her server environment.

If you want to put advertising code, RSS feeds code, or any other piece of content on multiple pages, yet not be locked into having it on all pages as you would with a DWT, you'll find that the Include Page is a good choice.

Consider this example: a designer has 30 pages in a site; 20 pages have advertising code in them provided by the Expression Web include page. The site affiliates with another advertising vendor. All the designer needs to do is change the advertising code in the single file used as an include page, and that change will be updated into every page that the include page is present on. This is so much faster and flexible than changing the code in all 20 pages manually, and yet it allows the designer the flexibility of using the feature only where appropriate, as opposed to having it on every page, as would be the case with a Dynamic Web Template. In this exercise, you will move code out of the DWT you've worked with previously and put it into a file that you can use as an Expression Web include page.

Include a page

> **Note** Use the Chapter3.html page of the SampleSite site you opened in the previous exercise. Open this book's sample site and Chapter3.html page, if they aren't already open.

1. From the Format menu, select Dynamic Web Template, and then choose Open Attached Dynamic Web Template. The site's Dynamic Web Template opens in your workspace.

2. In the Design pane, scroll down so that you can see the content below the Facebook badge that you wrapped with an editable region in the previous exercise. Click the W3C Valid Code image to select it.

   The Quick Tag Selector above the Code pane shows that the image is inside a hyperlink, which itself is contained in a paragraph tag with an ID of "w3cvalidity", along with another hyperlinked image.

3. Click the <p#w3cvalidity> tag on the Quick Tag Selector to select the paragraph tag and its content.

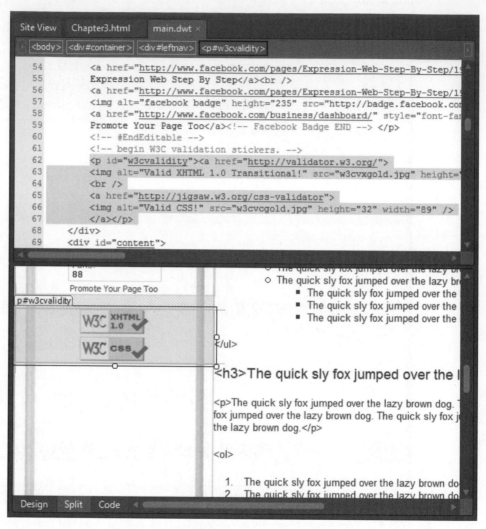

4. Right-click the highlighted content in the Design pane, and select Cut from the context menu. Expression Web cuts the content from the page.

5. On the Common toolbar, click Save. Click Yes in the File Update dialog box, and then click Close on the Update Confirmation alert.

Because these links are more appropriately used on pages that are under development rather than as a fixed part of a template, you will add this content to a new HTML page and then include it on a page-by-page basis.

6. Point to the New Document button on the Common toolbar, click the arrow, and then click HTML to create a new HTML file named Untitled_1.html.

7. Click the page in the Design pane to set your cursor. Right-click and select Paste from the context menu. Expression Web pastes the content you cut from the DWT into the new page.

8. Click Save on the Common toolbar. The Save As dialog box opens. Navigate into the templates folder, and then type **ValidationLinks.html** into the File Name field. Click Change Title. The Set Page Title dialog box appears. Type **W3C Validation Links** in the Page Title field, and then click OK. In the Save As dialog box, click Save.

Tip The HTML file that you will use as an Expression Web include page can contain any content you like; however, if the page contains JavaScript or any content outside the <body> tags, you will have to move that content inside the <body> tags. The only content that gets written into the receiving page is that which falls between <body> and </body>.

9. From the View menu, select Toolbars, and then choose Standard. The Standard toolbar opens above your workspace.

10. Click the chapter3.html tab at the top of your workspace to make that page the active document. In the Code pane, set your cursor at the end of the *h4* element that contains the text *Using the Include Page Feature,* and then press Enter on your keyboard to break to a new line.

11. Click the Include Page button on the Standard toolbar. The Include Page Properties dialog box opens. Click Browse, browse to the templates folder, and double-click ValidationLinks.html. Click OK in the Include Page Properties dialog box.

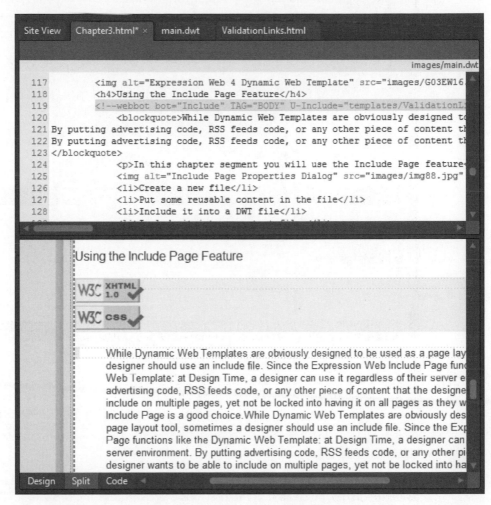

Expression Web inserted the body contents of ValidationLinks.html into the page.

12. In the Folder List panel, double-click the Chapter3a.html file that you created. Click inside the CatchAll editable region, and on the Standard toolbar, click the Include Page button.

13. Browse to the templates folder, double-click ValidationLinks.html, and then click OK in the Include Page Properties dialog box.

14. Click the Chapter3.html tab at the top of your workspace to make that page the active document, click the Save All button, and then click the Preview button. Chapter3.html opens in a browser. Scroll down to the area where you used the include page.

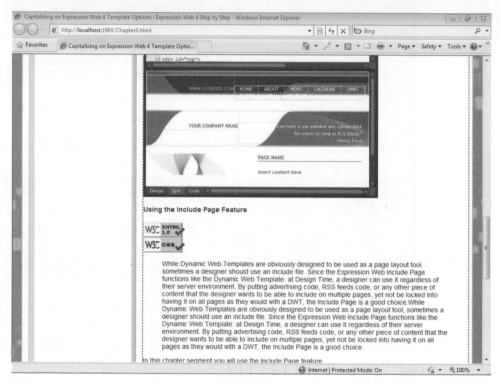

15. Click the menu item for Chapter3a.html. Scroll down to the bottom to see the include page you inserted into this page as well.

Notice that the validation icons are present on the original Chapter3.html page, as well as on the page you created in the previous exercise. Close the browser and return to Expression Web.

16. Double-click the Templates\ValidationLinks.html page in the Folder List panel to make it the active document, and then—using the page tabs at the top of your workspace—close all the other open documents.

Tip From the Window menu, select Close All Pages to close all your open pages at once.

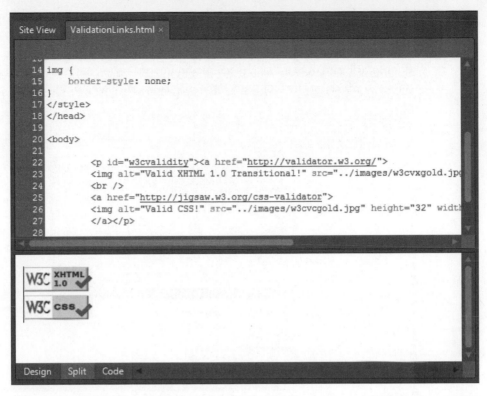

17. Right-click the XHTML validation image in the Design pane, and then, in the context menu, click Picture Properties.

18. In the Picture Properties dialog box, click the Browse button beside the Picture field, and in the Picture dialog box, double-click w3cvxblue.jpg in the site's Images folder. Click OK to close the Picture Properties dialog box.

19. Right-click the CSS validation image in the Design pane, then select Picture Properties from the shortcut menu.

20. In the Picture Properties dialog box, click the Browse button beside the Picture field, and in the Picture dialog box, double-click w3cvcblue.jpg in the site's Images folder. Then click OK in the Picture Properties dialog box.

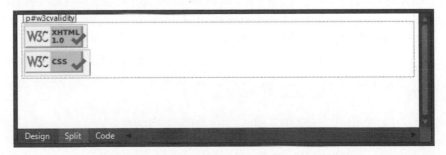

21. Click Save on the Common toolbar. In the Folder List panel, click the Chapter3.
html file, and then click Preview on the Common toolbar. Chapter3.html opens in
a browser. Notice that the validation link images are now blue. Click the link for
Chapter 3a, and notice that the validation images have changed in both of the
pages in which you included the ValidationLinks.html file contents.

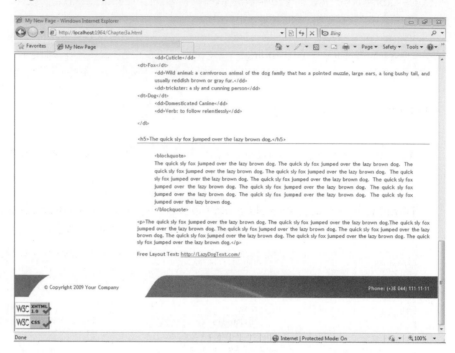

22. Close the browser and return to Expression Web. Select Toolbars from the View menu,
choose Standard to close the Standard toolbar, and then close the ValidationLinks.html file.

> **Note** Leave the SampleSite open if you are proceeding directly to the next section.

Consider the efficiency benefits of using the design-time include page in a complex site. It provides an easy way to use content selectively, on a page-by-page basis, yet retains the benefit
of enabling the designer to make changes in just one file and ensuring uniformity across all the
pages that receive the content. Also consider how these benefits are compounded if the designer has multiple pieces of content that he or she can include where necessary.

Using ASP.NET Master Pages

Unlike Dynamic Web Templates, which you explored in the previous exercise, the ASP.NET
master page template system requires a server to combine the content from the content
page and the content of the master page into one file and pass it off to the browser.

ASP.NET must be running on the server where you intend to host your site(s). The ASP.NET master page system is an example of a run-time feature.

Even though ASP.NET must be running on the server where you'll publish your production Web site, you don't need to do anything to get ASP.NET running on your local computer. Because Expression Web 4 includes the Expression Development Server, you can build and browse most ASP.NET files locally without taking any extra measures. Expression Web also displays the combined files in the workspace so you'll have a better feel for how your final layout is going to look. The combined view generally simplifies the design process in the ASP.NET workflow as well.

Use an ASP.NET master page

Note Use the SampleSite site you opened in the previous exercise. Open this book's sample site if it isn't already open.

1. From the File menu, select New, and then click Page. The New dialog box opens. Click the ASP.NET category on the left side, and then click Master Page.

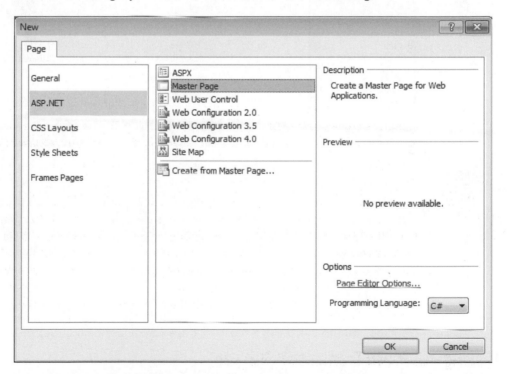

Notice the Programming Language field. Expression Web uses Microsoft Visual C# by default, but you can also choose to use Microsoft **Visual Basic**. The choice of programming language generally depends on the language used for the overall project. This book uses the default C# selection unless otherwise noted.

2. Click OK in the New dialog box. The dialog box closes, and a new master page named *Untitled_1.master* appears in your workspace. If *Untitled_1.master* didn't open in Split view, click Split at the bottom of the workspace.

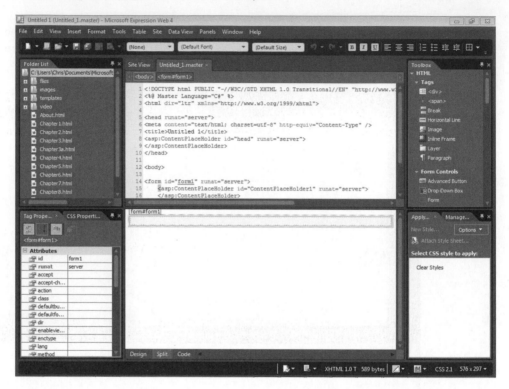

Take some time to examine the new master page. You can see in the Design pane that Expression Web has created a content placeholder named *ContentPlaceHolder1* within the body of the page. Notice in the Code pane that this placeholder is wrapped by a form tag. This is not a standard HTML form; it's used by the ASP.NET system. Scroll up to the head section of your master page in the Code pane, and you will see another content placeholder with an ID of *head*. This placeholder is there so designers can provide different content in the head sections of pages attached to the master page.

3. In the Folder List panel, expand the templates folder, and then double-click red.html to open it for editing. Click in the body of the page in the Design pane. On the Quick Tag Selector, point to the <body> tag, click the arrow, and then click Select Tag Contents.

4. In the Code pane, right-click the selected body tag contents. Select Copy from the context menu.

5. At the top of the workspace, click the Untitled_1.master tab to make that page the active document in the workspace. Click in the Design pane, and on the Quick Tag Selector, point to the <form#form1> tag. Click the arrow, and then click Select Tag Contents.

6. Right-click the selected body tag contents in the Code pane, and select Paste from the context menu. Expression Web pastes all the content from red.html into your new ASP.NET master page.

Notice in the Code pane that the *ContentPlaceHolder* control is gone. In the next few steps, you will replace it.

 Tip As mentioned earlier in this chapter, whenever you transfer an HTML file's body contents to a new file, you should check the <head> section of the original file for cascading style sheet links, JavaScript, and special metadata.

7. Click the red.html tab at the top of your workspace to make that page the active document. In the Code pane, scroll up to the head section of the page's source code.

8. In the head section of red.html, you will see a style sheet link and two JavaScript links. Highlight all three of those entries.

```
    Site View    Untitled_1.master*    red.html ×

  1 <!DOCTYPE html PUBLIC "-//W3C//DTD XHTML 1.0 Transitional//EN" "http://www.w3
  2 <html xmlns="http://www.w3.org/1999/xhtml">
  3
  4 <head>
  5 <meta content="text/html; charset=utf-8" http-equiv="Content-Type" />
  6         <title></title>
  7 <link rel="stylesheet" type="text/css" href="/templates/red/styles.css" media
  8 <script src="/templates/red/jquery-1.3.2.min.js" type="text/javascript"></scr
  9 <script src="/templates/red/design.js" type="text/javascript"></script>
 10 </head>
 11 <body>
 12 <div id="top">
 13 <div id="topover">
 14     <div id="www">www.yoursite.com</div>
 15     <div id="menu">
 16         <ul>
```

9. Right-click the highlighted lines of code in the Code pane, and select Copy from the context menu.

10. Click the Untitled_1.master tab at the top of your workspace to make that page the active document.

11. Scroll up to the head section of Untitled_1.master. Set your cursor between the *<asp: ContentPlaceHolder id="head" runat="server">* and *</asp:ContentPlaceHolder>*

ContentPlaceHolder control tags, and press Enter to insert an empty line. Set your cursor in this new empty line, right-click, and select Paste from the context menu. Expression Web pastes the style sheet and JavaScript links into the ContentPlaceHolder control.

> **Tip** Placing links or other content such as meta tags within a ContentPlaceHolder control enables the content to be changed on the content page to which they're attached. Conversely, if you want to make sure that certain content appears in the head section, place it *outside* the ContentPlaceHolder control, which will ensure that it will be persistent in all the pages to which the master page is attached.

```
Site View    Untitled_1.master* ×    red.html

 1 <!DOCTYPE html PUBLIC "-//W3C//DTD XHTML 1.0 Transitional//EN" "http://www.w3
 2 <%@ Master Language="C#" %>
 3 <html dir="ltr" xmlns="http://www.w3.org/1999/xhtml">
 4
 5 <head runat="server">
 6 <meta content="text/html; charset=utf-8" http-equiv="Content-Type" />
 7 <title>Untitled 1</title>
 8 <asp:ContentPlaceHolder id="head" runat="server">
 9 <link rel="stylesheet" type="text/css" href="/templates/red/styles.css" media
10 <script src="/templates/red/jquery-1.3.2.min.js" type="text/javascript"></scr
11 <script src="/templates/red/design.js" type="text/javascript"></script>
12 </asp:ContentPlaceHolder>
13 </head>
14
15 <body>
16
```

12. From the View menu, select Toolbars, and then choose Master Page. The Master Page toolbar opens.

13. In the Design pane, set your cursor in the PAGE NAME *<h1>* element. Then, on the Quick Tag Selector, click the <div#content> tab to select this tag and its contents.

14. Click the Manage Content Regions button on the Master Page toolbar. The Manage Content Regions dialog box opens. Type **MainContent** into the Region Name field, click Add, and then click Close.

You can see that the content *div* you selected has been wrapped with a
ContentPlaceHolder control.

> **Tip** If you can't see ContentPlaceHolder names in the Design view of your page, click the
> Template Region Labels button on the Master Page toolbar.

15. On the Common toolbar, click Save. The Save As dialog box opens. Type **red.master**
into the File Name field, and then click Save to save the new master page in the root
folder of the sample site.

16. On the Common toolbar, click the arrow on the New Document button, and then click
Create From Master Page. In the Select A Master Page dialog box, click the Browse but-
ton, double-click the red.master file located in the root of this site and then click OK.
Expression Web creates a new ASP.NET page named Untitled_1.aspx in your workspace.

Notice that the new page is a virtual duplicate of the master page it's based on.

17. On the Common toolbar, click Save. In the Save As dialog box, type **Chapter3b.aspx** in the File Name field, and then click Save to save the new file as Chapter3b.aspx in the root folder of the sample site.

18. In Design view, click the Content Tasks button on the right side of the MainContent region, and then click Create Custom Content. Highlight the PAGE NAME *<h1>* element in the content region and type **ASP.NET Content Page**.

Notice the difference between the Code pane of this page and the Code pane of Chapter3a.html that you made previously. The ASP.NET content and master page arrangement doesn't actually combine the two pages until it's processed by a server.

19. On the Common toolbar, click Save, and then click Preview. The Expression Development Server starts and passes your page to the browser.

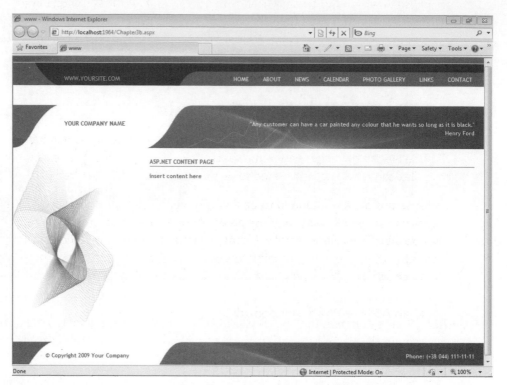

Examine your page in the browser. If you look at the source code, you will see that the Expression Development Server and ASP.NET combined the contents of your master page and content page and passed them to the browser. ASP.NET has built-in facilities such as navigation controls and AdRotator controls that you can use in this type of ASP.NET page.

20. Close the browser and return to Expression Web. On the Window menu, click Close All Pages.

Note Leave the SampleSite site open if you are proceeding directly to the next section.

You've just used the ASP.NET master page in the simplest of scenarios: a template page to assist in the layout and design of content pages that are attached to it. Even though this book isn't intended to be an ASP.NET manual, in Chapter 9, "Adding Functionality with ASP.NET and AJAX," you will learn more about this technology platform and some of the interesting ways that Expression Web 4 makes utilizing the power of ASP.NET easier for designers than ever.

Using ASP.NET Web User Controls

At its simplest, you can think of an ASP.NET Web user control as something analogous to an include file. At the higher end of the spectrum, an ASP.NET Web user control can consist of complex code that is programmed to perform actions within any Web page that includes it.

Because this book is intended to be an introduction to Expression Web 4, not a programming manual, you'll create and use an ASP.NET Web user control in the most elementary way possible. The user control will contain HTML content that you can include in ASP.NET pages by using a technique similar to the one you used for the design-time include earlier in this chapter.

Add an ASP.NET Web user control

 Note Use the SampleSite site you opened in the previous exercise. Open this book's sample site if it isn't already open.

1. On the Common toolbar, click the arrow on the New Document button, and then click Page. The New dialog box opens. Click the ASP.NET category, and then click Web User Control.

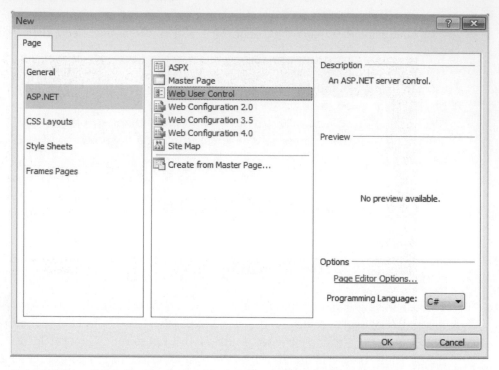

As in the New dialog box for a master page or an ASPX page, you will see a Programming Language field in the lower right corner. This book uses the default C# option, but you could choose to use Visual Basic instead, depending on your project requirements.

2. Click OK. Expression Web creates a new ASP.NET Web user control named Untitled_1.ascx in the workspace.

3. In the Folder List panel, double-click templates\ValidationLinks.html, which you created in the previous exercise.

4. On the Quick Tag Selector, click <p#w3cvalidity> to select the paragraph tag and all of its contents.

5. Right-click the selected contents in the Design pane of your page, and then, on the context menu, click Copy.

6. Click the Untitled_1.ascx tab at the top of your workspace to make that page the active document. Right-click the Design Pane, and in the context menu, click Paste.

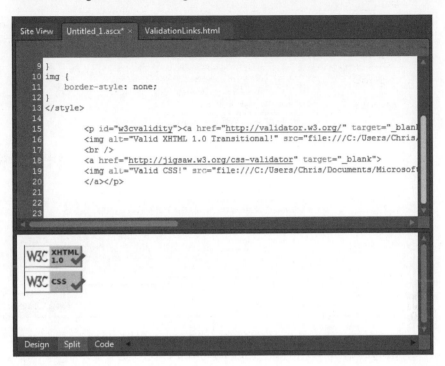

The content from your design-time include page is now pasted into your Web user control.

7. On the Common toolbar, click Save. In the Save As dialog box, type **ValidationLinks.ascx** in the File Name field, and then click Save to save the file in the root folder of your Web site.

8. In the Folder List pane, double-click the Chapter3b.aspx file that you created in the previous exercise to make it the active document in your workspace.

9. Drag ValidationLinks.ascx from the Folder List panel and drop it into the content area of Chapter3b.aspx.

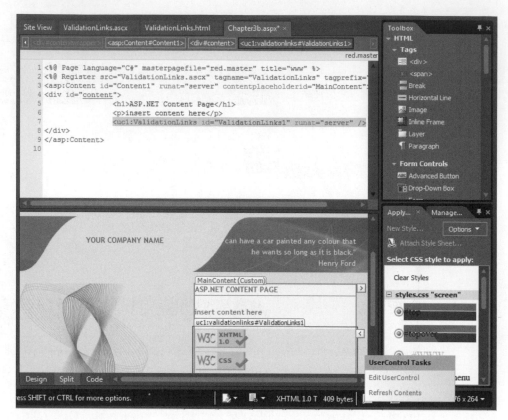

Notice that although there's a visual representation of the Web user control's content in the Design pane of Chapter3b.aspx, there is no such code in the Code pane. All you'll see there is the user control *<uc1:ValidationLinks id="ValidationLinks1" runat="server" />* in the body, and in the head section of the code you'll see an *@ Register* directive: *<%@ Register src="ValidationLinks.ascx" tagname="ValidationLinks" tagprefix="uc1" %>*.

10. On the Common toolbar, click Save, and then click Preview. The Expression Development Server starts and your page opens in a browser.

The result is similar to the functionality of the include page feature, except that the file contents were combined by the Expression Development Server rather than saved in a combined state by Expression Web.

11. Close your browser and return to Expression Web.

12. Click the Web user control in the Design pane to select it, and then click the Tasks button in the upper-right corner of the control.

As with the content control you added to the page, there are menu items for the most common tasks—in this case, Edit User Control, which opens the associated **ASCX** file in the workspace; and Refresh Contents, which refreshes the visual representation of the ASCX file's contents so you can see the results in the content page after you edit the ASCX file.

13. From the View menu, select Toolbars, and then click Master Page to close the Master Page toolbar. Then, on the Window menu, click Close All Pages.

Note Leave the SampleSite site open if you are proceeding directly to the next section.

In this exercise, you used the Web user control file to simply include some HTML content into an ASP.NET page, but be aware that, in Expression Web, you can also use ASCX files that contain programmatic scripting in Visual Basic or C#. ASCX files are a convenient way for developers to provide content to designers—or even a way to enable designers to create Web user controls for various site features and then include them on any number of pages. Unlike the design-time include page, the ASP.NET Web user control combines with other files on the server. If you had multiple pages with content from an include page and that include page's contents changed, you would have to publish all those changed pages to the server. With the Web user control, you'd *only* have to publish the control to the server, and every page that used it would automatically be served with this new content.

Using PHP Include Files

Like the ASP.NET Web user control, the PHP include file functionality uses the server to dynamically combine files before they're served to the browser. By using the PHP include file, you can gain the same advantages over a design-time include that you can with an ASP.NET Web user control.

Use PHP include files

> **Note** Use the SampleSite site you opened in the previous exercise. Open this book's sample site if it isn't already open.

In the following steps, you will create a new PHP page, attach a Dynamic Web Template to it, create a file to be included in the PHP page, and then use a PHP include to insert the contents into your page.

1. Click the arrow on the New Document button, and then click PHP. Expression Web creates a new PHP file named Untitled_1.php in your workspace.

2. On the Format menu, point to Dynamic Web Template, and then click Attach Dynamic Web Template. In the Attach Dynamic Web Template dialog box, navigate to the templates folder, click red.dwt, and then click Open. The DWT is attached to the new PHP file. Click Close in the File Update alert.

> **Note** Although PHP is a server-side scripting language, you can use Dynamic Web Templates with PHP files. In some cases, this option makes good sense, but in other cases you might choose a run-time template system or a content management system instead.

3. On the Common toolbar, click Save. In the Save As dialog box, type **Chapter3c.php** in the File Name field, and click the Change Title button. The Set Page Title dialog box opens. Type **My PHP Page** into the Page Title field, and then click OK. Click Save in the Save As dialog box, and save the page as **Chapter3c.php** in the root of the sample site.

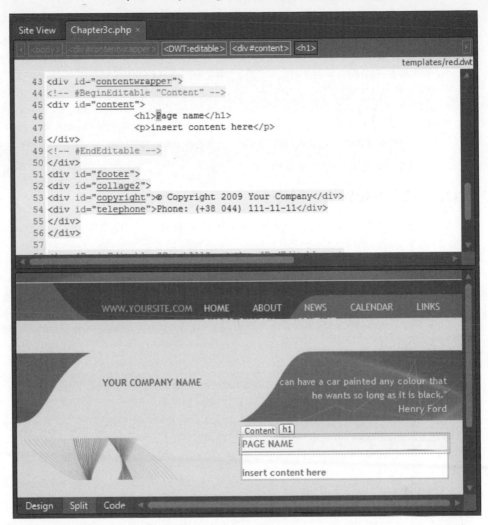

Next, you'll create a file to hold the content to be included via the PHP include.

4. Click the arrow on the New Document button, and then click PHP. A new PHP file named *Untitled_1.php* is created in your workspace.

5. On the Common toolbar, click Save. In the Save As dialog box, type **ValidationLinks.php** in the File Name field. Then click Save in the Save As dialog box and save the page as **ValidationLinks.php** in the root of the sample site.

> **Tip** Expression Web supports including HTML, INC, PHP, and TXT file types in PHP files. For both technical and tactical reasons, this book uses a PHP file and includes it in another PHP file.

6. In the Folder List panel, double-click the templates/ValidationLinks.html file that you created in the previous exercise to open it for editing.

7. On the Quick Tag Selector, click <p#w3cvalidity> to select the paragraph tag and all of its contents.

8. Right-click the selected contents in the Design pane, and then select Copy from the context menu.

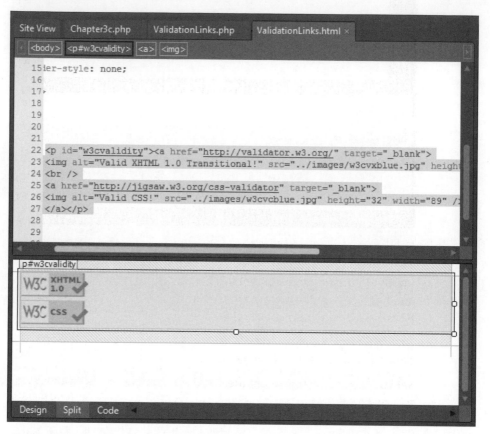

9. Click the ValidationLinks.php tab at the top of your workspace to make that page the active document. Set your cursor in the Code pane of the page, right-click, and on the context menu, click Select All. Then press Delete on your keyboard.

10. Right-click the Design pane, then select Paste from the shortcut menu.

11. Notice that Expression Web added <head> and <style> sections to your PHP file. Highlight those elements in the Code pane of your PHP file, and then press Delete on the keyboard.

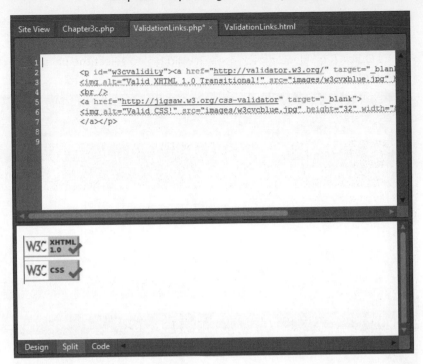

The reason you removed all the original content from this PHP file was because the file will be used to include the HTML content into other pages. If you left the <head> and <body> tags and other content in the page, you would wind up with multiple body and head tags on the page in which it gets included, thereby completely wrecking your HTML's validity and potentially the page's accessibility.

12. On the Common toolbar, click Save, and then click the Chapter3c.php tab to make that page the active file in your workspace.

13. Set your cursor in the content area, and then press Enter on your keyboard to break to a new line. On the Insert menu, point to PHP, and then click Include. The Select An Include File dialog box appears.

> **Tip** The Expression Web Insert PHP menu has four different kinds of PHP includes:
>
> - **Include** Includes the file each time it is referenced in the page.
>
> - **Include_once** Includes the file the first time it is referenced in the page.
>
> - **Require** Requires that the file be processed before the page is returned, and includes the file each time it is referenced in the page.
>
> - **Require_once** Requires that the file be processed before the page is returned, and includes the file the first time it is referenced in the page.
>
> For the purposes of this exercise, you will be using *Include*.

14. Double-click the ValidationLinks.php file that you created in the previous steps. The dialog box closes, and the content of your file is now displayed in the Design pane of the workspace. Click the Design pane, which will set focus there and refresh its rendering of what has occurred in the Code pane.

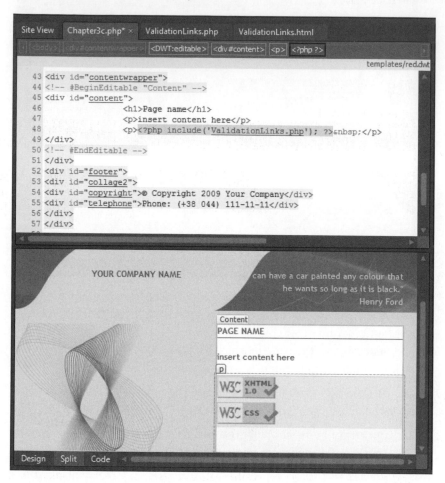

 Troubleshooting If you make a change in the Code pane or add something to the Design pane, and it doesn't appear, press F5 on your keyboard or select Refresh from the View menu.

Notice that—similar to the way the Web user control worked—there is no actual content in the Code pane other than the PHP include, *<?php include('ValidationLinks.php'); ?>*. In contrast, the Design pane renders the HTML content from ValidationLinks.php visually. That happens because this include is a server-side or run-time include, and uses the server to combine the files rather than saving the combination as a single file, which is what would occur with a design-time include.

> **Warning** To make sure that the Expression Development Server is able to process and serve PHP files to your browser, you must install PHP and set the Expression Web options to use it. For information on this, see Chapter 2, "Capitalizing on Expression Web 4 Functionality."

15. On the Common toolbar, click Save, and then click Preview. The Expression Development Server starts, and the Chapter3c.php file opens in a browser.

As with the previous include methods in this chapter—the design-time include page and the ASP.NET Web user control—the content of ValidationLinks.php is included within the HTML content of its parent page. This method of including and controlling content can go a long way in providing manageability and usability to designers and others who will work on the site.

> **Note** At this point, you can close the SampleSite site and any open browsers. If you are not continuing directly to the next chapter, exit Expression Web 4.

This chapter explored some key features in Expression Web 4. Regardless of whether an include or template method belongs to the design-time or run-time category, it can tremendously enhance the uniformity and manageability of your Web sites. By choosing and using a solid strategy to reuse and template elements of a Web site, you can influence the long-term efficiency of the site.

Expression Web 4 provides methods that are server independent, as well as methods appropriate for almost any server environment in which a Web site might be hosted. There is really no reason not to take advantage of at least one of these options, or maybe even a combination of design-time and run-time features, such as a Dynamic Web Template along with PHP includes.

Key Points

- Because Dynamic Web Templates don't have any specific server-side requirements, they are a good choice when you don't know the exact hosting environment for the production Web site.

- ASP.NET master pages reduce the overall file size of a Web site because their content is combined with their associated content page just before the server passes the file to the browser.

- You can use ASP.NET Web user controls in many scenarios, from a simple menu to be included into multiple pages, to a complex programmatic collection of code that provides functionality to a Web page.

- PHP include files are similar to ASP.NET Web user controls. They can be used in a number of scenarios, from including simple HTML code into multiple pages to advanced programmatic work.

- You can save time and effort by using a well-thought-out strategy, providing better uniformity across all the pages associated with a template or an include file.

- Run-time features such as master pages, Web user controls, and PHP includes require a server to combine files just before they're passed to the browser. Design-time features such as DWTs and include pages use Expression Web to combine the files when they're saved locally.

- Updating a site that uses run-time features requires publishing only the changed files that are included, but a site that uses design-time features requires that you publish all the pages associated with the DWT or design-time include.

Chapter 4
It's All About Content

After completing this chapter, you will be able to:

- Use tables properly
- Use lists to group information
- Use semantic markup
- Style the presentation of your content
- Add images to a Web page
- Edit images with Expression Design
- Use Photoshop files in a Web page
- Use Silverlight Video in a Web page
- Use Deep Zoom Composer projects in a Web page

Too often, when people think of "content," they think only of text. Whether that text consists of heavily marked-up HTML/XHTML code or just plain text, most people imagine the written word when they think of content. But today's modern Web—and most users—more than accept content such as video, images, and so forth; to a degree, it's expected.

In this chapter, you will learn how to present text content on your pages as well as how to present non-textual content of various kinds. For the purposes of this chapter, you can consider content as material that a visitor to your page can read, listen to, or view. That way, you won't fall into the potentially limiting mindset of thinking about content as simply readable text on a page. Instead, you will look at content in a more holistic light—anything that helps convey a message to a visitor. The chapter begins by discussing text, because that's still the backbone of information delivery on Web pages. You will see how to use Microsoft Expression Web and HTML to group, contain, and control your text content, and then you will discover how to present alternative forms of content on your pages.

Expression Web provides many ways to present content on your pages, both by itself and in conjunction with its Expression Studio stable mates—Expression Design and Expression Encoder. Together, these tools give you the capabilities to build rich Web pages that contain information users can consume in the most effective ways, in a broad range of scenarios.

 Important Before you can use the practice files in this chapter, you need to download and install them from the book's companion content Web site to their default location. For more information about downloading and installing the practice files, see the "Code Samples" section at the beginning of this book.

> **Troubleshooting** Graphics and operating system-related instructions in this book reflect the Windows 7 user interface. If your computer is running Windows XP or Windows Vista and you experience trouble following the instructions as written, please refer to the "Information for Readers Running Windows XP or Vista" section at the beginning of this book.

Using Tables Properly

Currently, professional Web developers consistently use cascading style sheets (CSS) for layout. For example, if you explore any of the templates that come with Expression Web 4, you won't find a single one that uses a table for layout purposes. In the not-so-distant past, designers used a table or a group of nested tables to lay out the design elements of a Web page. Although that method provided a fair amount of precision, layout was never the intended purpose of the *<table>* tag. As an unfortunate byproduct of "table heavy" design, the source code of the page is always much more complex, which makes it less than ideal for screen readers and search engines, not to mention additional download time for browsers. The big question seems to be whether it's still acceptable to use tables. The answer is a definite "Yes." Tables seem to have fallen out of favor for laying out pages; however, there are still a number of good reasons to use tables, the most obvious of which is to present data in clear, tabular form.

Display tabular data in a table

> **Note** Start Expression Web 4 before beginning this exercise. Open the SampleSite site by selecting Open Site from the Site menu, browsing to the companion media's default installation page, and double-clicking the SampleSite folder. With the sample site open in Expression Web, double-click the Chapter4.html page in the Folder List panel.

1. Set your cursor just after the *<h4>* element that contains the text, "Using Tables Properly," and press Enter on your keyboard to insert a new paragraph between the *<h4>* tag and the block quote beneath it.

2. From the View menu, select Visual Aids. Ensure that Block Selection and Visible Borders are both enabled.

   Visual Aids can help you see the various elements of a table in the Design pane.

3. In the Design pane, set the cursor in the new paragraph you created, and on the Table menu, click Insert Table.

4. In the Insert Table dialog box, configure the table to have two rows and three columns. Accept the default settings for all the other values in the dialog box.

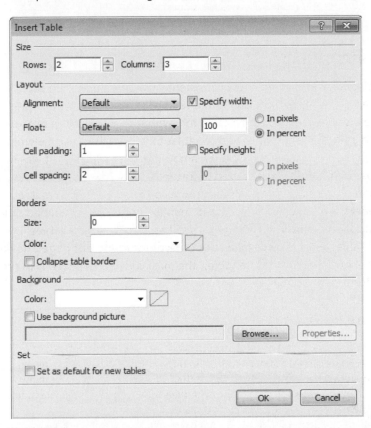

5. Click OK to insert the table. In the upper-left table cell, type **Name**. Press Tab to move into the next cell, and type **Email**. Tab to the next cell, and type **Phone**.

6. Press Tab again to move the cursor to the first cell in the next row. Type a name, an email address, and a phone number into the cells in the second row under the respective headings.

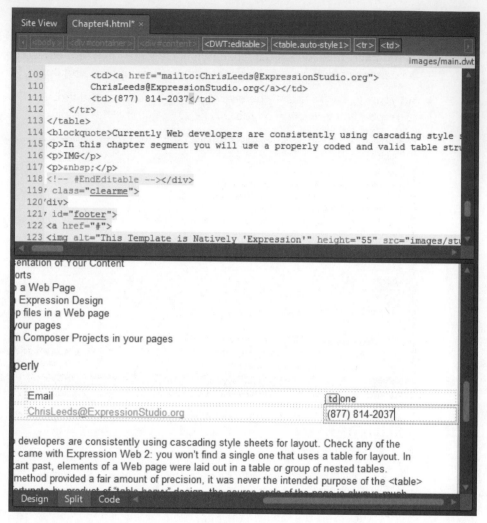

7. After you type a phone number in the last cell of the second row, press Tab to create a new, third row.

Note When you press Tab in the last cell of the last row in a table, Expression Web will insert a new row matching the row above it.

8. Type another name, email address, and phone number into the cells in the new third row.

    Next, you will change the code a little bit to make the table semantically more valuable. As it is now, there is no visual separation between the cells, even though the first row's cells are clearly headings for the contents of their respective columns.

9. Set your cursor in the cell where you typed "Name," click the drop-down arrow on the corresponding *<td>* entry on the Quick Tag Selector, and then click Edit Tag.

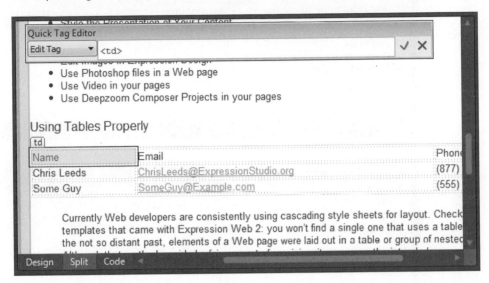

10. In the Quick Tag Editor, change *<td>* to *<th>*, and then click the green check mark to finish editing the tag.

    In HTML, the *<td>* tag is a table *body* cell, and *<th>* is a table *head* cell. Both are basically just cells but *<th>* explicitly denotes the head cell of a column. Think of it like this: Instead of creating undifferentiated cells with labels, you're giving alternative browsers such as screen readers and search engines a better chance of understanding the *function* of the heading cell contents and the contents of the cells below them in their columns.

11. Continue using the Quick Tag Editor to change *<td>* to *<th>* for the remaining two cells in the first row that contain "Email" and "Phone."

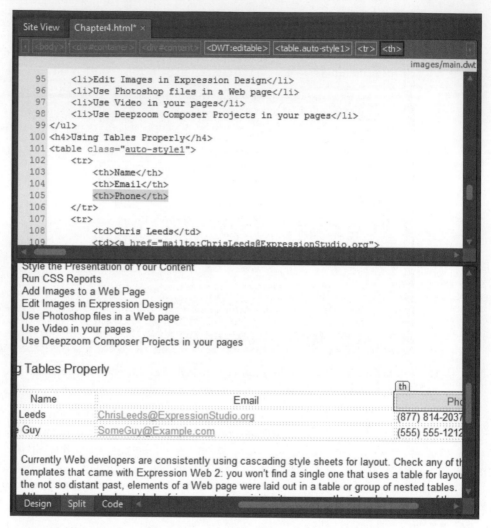

In the Design pane, notice that the *<th>* content alignment changes so that it's slightly different than when it was surrounded by the *<td>* tag. In addition to this obvious text centering, you will also be able to style these *<th>* cells using cascading style sheets easily, because they're a different HTML tag than a *<td>*. You will learn how to style basic HTML tags later in this chapter.

12. Click Save, and then click Preview on the Common toolbar to preview the page in a browser and make sure that the table structure appears as intended.

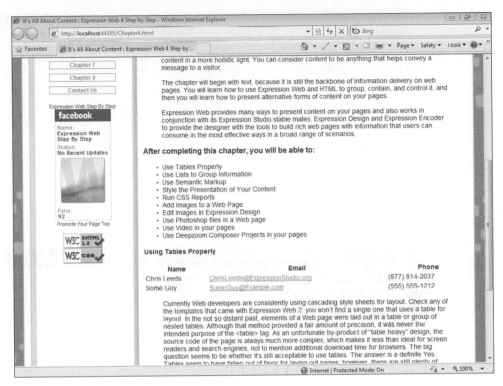

13. Close your browser and return to Expression Web.

    Note Leave the SampleSite site open if you are proceeding directly to the next section.

Using Lists to Group Information

Lists are among the essential tags for laying out information on a Web page. List tags include unordered (bulleted) lists (*<ul>*), ordered (numbered) lists (*<ol>*), and definition lists (*<dl>*), each of which adds semantic value to the information it contains. You can use lists when you need to display directions or procedures on a page, or even as the basis of a navigation structure. Lists also work well with advanced styling using cascading style sheets.

The following table provides a bit more information on the three basic types of lists.

List Type	Tag	Used For
Ordered list	<ol>	Numbered items such as procedures
Unordered list	<ul>	Bulleted items that relate to each other but without any specific order
Definition list	<dl>	Term and definition arrangement (similar to a typical dictionary)

Create an unordered list

> **Note** Use the Chapter4.html page of the SampleSite site you opened in the previous exercise. Open this book's sample site and Chapter4.html page, if they aren't already open.

Numbers (Ordered List)
Bullets (Unordered List)

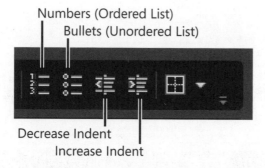

Decrease Indent
Increase Indent

1. In the Design pane, set your cursor immediately after the *<h5>* tag containing the text "Unordered," and press Enter to create a new paragraph.

2. Type **Benefits** as a title for the list that will follow. Press Enter to create another paragraph, and type **First Benefit**. On the Common toolbar, click the Bullets button.

   In Split view, the *<p>* tag that previously surrounded the words First Benefit is now a *<ul>* tag. The words for the individual list items are now wrapped in a *list item* (*<li>*) tag. In other words, the paragraph became an unordered list, and each line of text became a list item.

3. Press Enter again to create a new list item line, and type **Second Benefit**. Press Enter once more to advance to the next list line; but before you type anything, click the Increase Indent Position button.

> **Tip** The Tab key on your keyboard increases the indentation level, whereas Shift+Tab decreases it.

In the page code, you'll see that a *<ul>* tag appears within the preceding *<li>* tag; you now have a list within a list.

4. Type three items into this subordinate list, pressing Enter after entering each one, so that the inner list contains three items.

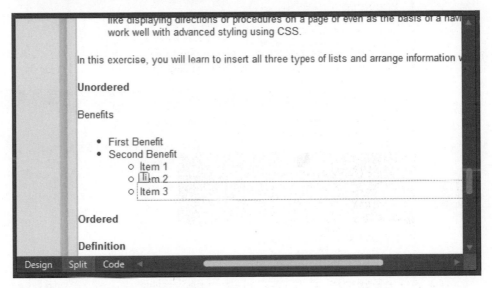

5. When you reach the final list item in this inner list, press Enter, and then click the Decrease Indent Position button (or press Shift+Tab).

6. In Split view, the code for the inner list and list element closes, so you're out of the inner list, and back in the original list you inserted.

7. Type two more entries: **Third Benefit** and **Fourth Benefit**, pressing Enter between them to set them each as list items. After typing "Fourth Benefit," press Enter twice to end the list and create a new paragraph.

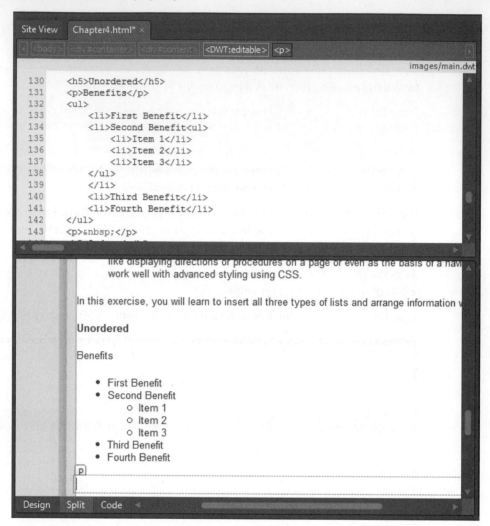

Notice the relationship between the list items as they appear in the Design pane and as they appear in the Code pane. Increasing or decreasing the indent actually is much more significant in the code than the toolbar button might lead you to believe, because increasing the indent actually creates a nested list.

8. Click Save, click Preview on the Common toolbar to preview the page in a browser and ensure that the list appears as it should, and then close your browser and return to Expression Web.

In the next list example, you will create a list of instructions, which lend themselves by nature to an ordered, step-by-step type of list.

Create an ordered list

1. In the Design pane, set your cursor immediately after the *<h5>* tag that contains the text "Ordered," press Enter on your keyboard to create a new paragraph, and then type **Instructions**, which serves as a heading for your next list.

2. Press Enter to create a new paragraph, type **First Step**, and then click the Numbering button.

   In Split view, the *<p>* tag that previously surrounded the words "First Step" becomes an *<ol>* tag, and the words themselves are now wrapped in a list item (*<li>*) tag. The paragraph is now an ordered list, and the text is a list item.

3. Press Enter to create a new list item line, and type **Second Step**. Press Enter again to create one more list item line; but before you type anything, click the Increase Indent Position button.

   As in the unordered list example, you'll see an *<ol>* tag appear within the preceding *<li>* tag; you've created a list within a list.

4. Type three items into the new subordinate list, pressing Enter after each entry.

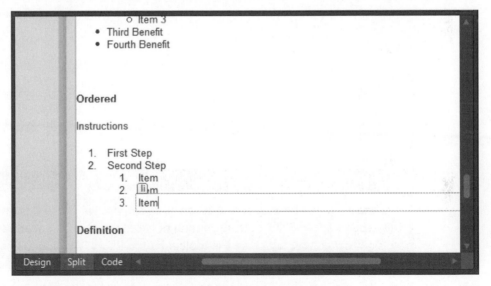

5. When you reach the final item for this inner list, press Enter on your keyboard, and then click the Decrease Indent Position button (or press Shift+Tab).

   In the Code pane, Expression Web closes the inner list and its final item, and returns to your original list.

```
                Site View    Chapter4.html* ×
           <body>  <div #container>  <div #content>  <DWT:editable>  <ol>  <li>
                                                                      images/main.dwt
    143         <p> </p>
    144         <h5>Ordered</h5>
    145         <p>Instructions</p>
    146         <ol>
    147             <li>First Step</li>
    148             <li>Second Step<ol>
    149                 <li>Item</li>
    150                 <li>Item</li>
    151                 <li>Item</li>
    152             </ol>
    153             </li>
    154             <li></li>
    155         </ol>
    156         <h5>Definition</h5>
```

6. Type two more entries: **Third Step** and **Fourth Step**, pressing Enter after each entry to create them as separate list items. After you type "Fourth Step," press Enter twice to end the list and create a new paragraph.

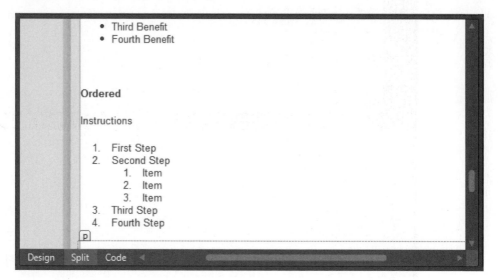

7. Click Save and then click Preview on the Common toolbar to preview the page in a browser. Verify that it appears as it should, then close your browser and return to Expression Web.

Definition lists aren't used as often as numbered and bulleted lists. In fact, you won't find a button on the toolbar for Definition Lists, but they are valuable for lists of terms and their definitions, similar to a dictionary or glossary.

Create a definition list

1. In the Design pane, set your cursor immediately after the *<h5>* tag that contains the text "Definition," and press Enter on your keyboard to create a new paragraph. Type the word **Definitions** as a heading for your next list.

2. Press Enter on your keyboard to create a new paragraph, and then type **First Term**. There is no button on the toolbar for Definition lists, so click the paragraph tag in the Quick Tag Selector that contains the text "First Term" to select the entire tag. On the Common toolbar, in the Style list, click the Defined Term *<dt>* drop-down arrow, and then click Defined Term.

Notice what has happened in the Code pane. The *<p>* tag has been wrapped by a *<dl>* tag, and the text within it, "First Term" was wrapped in a *<dt>* tag. Expression Web has created a definition list (the *<dl>*) and a term (the *<dt>*).

3. Press Enter to create a new line, which will be wrapped in a *<dd>* (definition) tag, and type **This is a definition to describe the term directly above it**.

4. Press Enter again. Expression Web sets up another *<dt>* tag for your next definition term. Type **Second Term**.

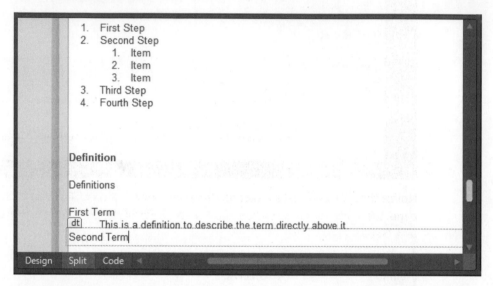

5. Press Enter again to create a new definition for Second Term and then type **This is a definition of "Second Term."**

It's common for a term to have multiple definitions. By pressing Enter on your keyboard, Expression Web will, by default, set up a new term rather than a secondary definition. In the next steps, you will create a secondary definition for "Second Term."

6. Press Enter on your keyboard to create a new line. Notice that Expression Web has set up a new *<dt>* (Term). Type **This is a secondary definition for "Second Term"** in this new line.

7. Click the drop-down arrow on the Quick Tag Selector for the *<dt>* that's surrounding the text. This text should be a secondary definition, so in the Style drop-down on the Common toolbar, click Definition *<dd>*.

```
Site View    Chapter4.html* ×

                                                                images/main.dwt
        152
        153        </li>
        154        <li>Third Step</li>
        155        <li>Fourth Step</li>
        156    </ol>
        157    <p> </p>
        158    <h5>Definition</h5>
        159    <p>Definitions</p>
        160    <dl>
        161        <dt>First Term</dt>
        162        <dd>This is a definition to describe the term directly above it.</dd>
        163        <dt>Second Term</dt>
        164        <dd>This is a definition of "Second Term".</dd>
        165        <dd>This is a secondary definition for &quot;Second Term&quot;.</dd>
        166    </dl>
```

Notice that you now have a second definition under "Second Term." In the Code pane, the *<dd>* tags are stacked above each other under the *<dt>* surrounding the text "Second Term."

8. Press Enter on your keyboard to create a new line. By default, this new line is a *<dt>* (definition term). Type **Third Term**.

9. Press Enter to create a definition for this third term and then type **This is a definition for "Third Term."**

10. Press Enter again. Expression Web inserts a new *<dt>* tag. To end the list, click the Block Selection label in the Design pane to select the new empty *<dt>* tag pair, and then press Delete on your keyboard to remove it and end the definition list.

> **Tip** Note that you end and close a definition list differently than the other list types described in this section.

Notice how the Code and Design panes display this definition list. The default layout is quite different from the other list types you've previously inserted. Besides having a comfortable and expected layout for a list of terms and their definitions, this list and its tags give semantic meaning to the words they surround. Search engines, screen readers, and other alternative browsers will all easily understand that it's a definition list, containing terms and their respective definitions.

11. Click Save, and then click Preview on the Common toolbar to preview the page in a browser and ensure that it appears as it should. Finally, close your browser and return to Expression Web.

> **Note** Leave the SampleSite site open if you are proceeding directly to the next section.

Using Semantic Markup

Rather than thinking of specific HTML tags as tools to make text "look" a certain way, think of tags as tools that describe the *purpose* of the text, and cascading style sheets as the tool to make the text within those appropriate tags appear the way you want it to.

For instance, lists, by nature, group similar elements together in a way that consecutive paragraphs don't. More specifically with lists, the definition list, ordered list, and unordered list mean different things based on their explicit intended use. An *<h1>* element gives text a more explicit meaning than the same words marked up with a large font size. Similarly, an *<em>* (emphasized) or a *<strong>* tag adds additional semantic meaning to a word, whereas a *<b>* (bold) tag simply changes the font but doesn't add any value to the word's perceived importance.

> **Use HTML and cascading style sheets that define the purpose and appearance of text**

> **Note** Use the Chapter4.html page of the SampleSite site you opened in the previous exercise. Open this book's sample site and Chapter4.html page, if they aren't already open.

1. If your workspace isn't already in Split view, click Split at the lower-left edge of the editing window. In the Design pane, scroll to the *h4* that contains the text, "Using Semantic Markup." Set your cursor at the end of the *h4* element and then press Enter on your keyboard to create a new paragraph.

2. Type the word **Strong**. Select the word in the Design pane, and then on the Common toolbar, click the Bold button.

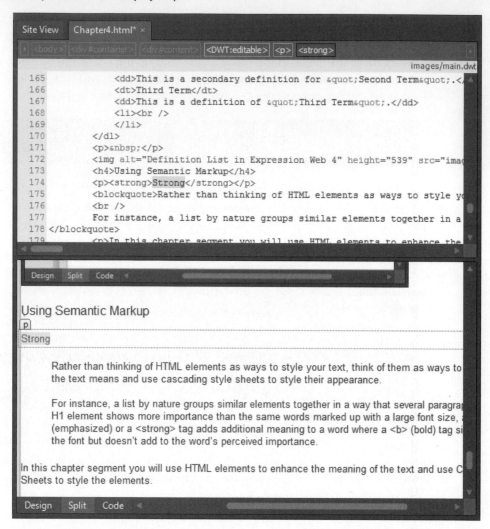

Notice that in the Design pane the word is now in a slightly bolder font, and that in the Code pane the word isn't inside of a *<b>* (*bold*) tag, as the toolbar button might lead you to believe, but instead it's inside of a *<strong>* tag. Expression Web will, by default, use tags that are current, modern, and semantically meaningful.

> **Tip** If you select a word that's already wrapped in a *<strong>* tag and click the Bold button again, the *<strong>* tag and its contents will be wrapped in a *<b>* (*bold*) tag. Semantically, this shouldn't hurt the meaning of the text wrapped in the *<strong>* tag and will provide additional bolding on the text. However, maintaining a distinction between the two is important, because you will learn how to control the level of bolding using cascading style sheets later in this chapter, based on the tag used.

3. Set your cursor just after the word "Strong," press Enter on your keyboard to create a new paragraph, and then type **Italic**.

4. Select the word "Italic" in the Design pane, and on the Quick Tag Selector, click the drop-down arrow on the *<strong>* tag that surrounds it, and click Remove Tag. Then press the Italic button on the Common toolbar.

Notice that in the Design pane the word "Italic" is now in an italic font style, but in the Code pane it isn't wrapped in the outdated *<i>* tag. Instead, it is wrapped in the *<em>* (emphasized) tag. Semantically the *<i>* tag means nothing. It's merely a font style, but the *<em>* tag literally means "emphasis."

5. Set your cursor at the end of the word "Italic" and press Enter on your keyboard to create a new paragraph. Click the Italic button on the Common toolbar to turn off the *<em>* tag insertion, and then type **This heading is more important than...**.

6. On the Quick Tag Selector at the top of the Code pane, click the *<p>* tag that is surrounding your newly entered text. Then on the Styles drop-down, click Heading 1 *<h1>*. Your paragraph tag changes to an *h1* tag.

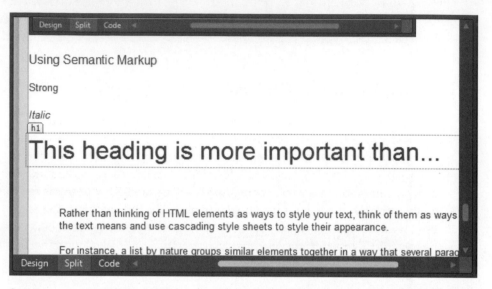

7. Set your cursor at the end of the newly entered h1 text; press Enter on your keyboard to create a new paragraph, and then type **This heading**. Select the *<p>* tag on the Quick Tag Selector that contains the newly entered text, and on the Styles drop-down, click Heading 3 *<h3>*. Your *<p>* tag changes to an *<h3>* tag.

8. Click Save, and then click Preview on the Common toolbar to preview your page in a browser and make sure that your content appears as it should. Close the browser and return to Expression Web.

The value of this shift from presentational markup (font tags, italic tags, bold tags, and so forth) to semantic markup is clear—the old way simply applied a visual appearance to the text, whereas the new way does something to lend a bit of description. It assists search engines and non-visual browsers to understand a level of meaning that font tag markup can't supply.

Note Leave the SampleSite site open if you are proceeding directly to the next section.

In this exercise, you have entered pieces of text and used HTML to mark them up based on meaning instead of appearance. Although this was a trivial example of the concept, you should be able to look at your content differently—marking up the text based on importance and actual meaning instead of simply designating different fonts for appearance or using HTML tags that don't serve to enhance the meaning of the text. Besides making your content more meaningful to users with alternative browsers such as screen readers, you can also enable search engines to better "understand" the importance of different segments of content based on the HTML tags that are used. In the next section, you will use cascading style sheets to change the style of these elements.

Styling the Presentation of Your Content

In the preceding exercises, you put several lists and a table on the page, as well as using various header tags and the strong and emphasis tags. They definitely serve the purposes for which they were intended. They contain the information they were designed to contain, and they keep it segregated from other information. Semantically, lists and tables are superior to using paragraph tags or one paragraph with line breaks between the relevant blocks, as are the strong and emphasis over bold and italic. The only problem one could have with the result is the default appearance rendered by these tags. Besides the possibility of not looking the way the designer would want them to, they will look different in various browsers. This is because every browser has its own default styles that it applies to HTML elements.

This is another case where cascading style sheets come to the rescue. You can maintain the semantic value of these tags for search engines and non-visual browsers, but style them so that they look the way you want them to look.

> ### Use cascading style sheets to style an HTML element

In this exercise, you will learn to style the presentation of your content by using a class and by styling the base HTML element.

 Note Use the Chapter4.html page of the SampleSite site you opened in the previous exercise. Open this book's sample site and Chapter4.html page, if they aren't already open.

1. In the Design pane, scroll to the table you created earlier in this chapter. Click anywhere inside of the table and then, on the Quick Tag Selector, click the table.auto-style1 button to select the entire table and all of its contents.

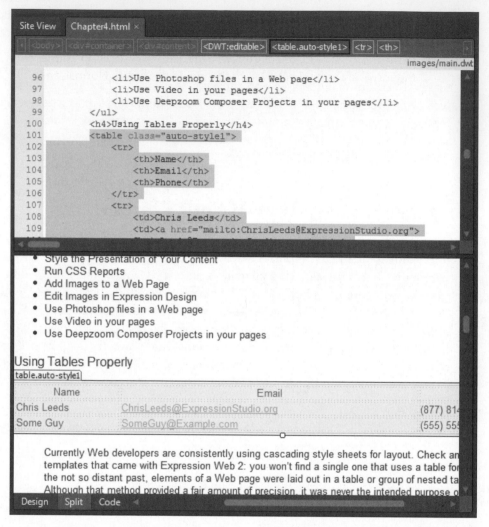

In the next steps, you are going to create cascading style sheet code to change the *<th>* cell appearance. Notice in the Code pane that Expression Web has already created and added a style (auto-style1) to the table. This is because of the specifications that existed in the Insert Table dialog box. Rather than marking up the table in the deprecated in-line fashion, a style was created to make it match the specifications in the dialog box.

2. In the Apply Styles pane, click New Style. In the New Style dialog box, name the style **.auto-style1 th**.

This will style any *<th>* tag that exists inside of any auto-style1 class, which this table already is classed as.

3. In the Define In field, select Current Page, set Font-Family to Courier New, Courier, Monospace. Set the Font-Weight to Bold, Font-Style to Normal, and Color to #FFFFFF.

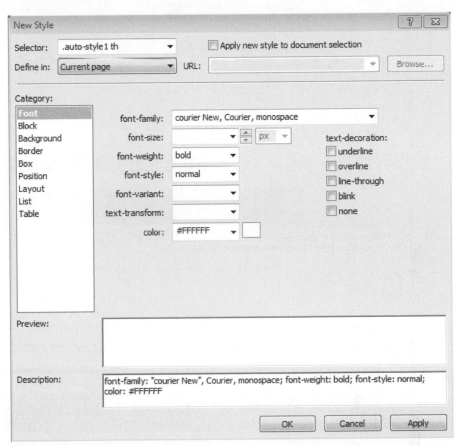

4. Beneath the Category label, click Background, and then set the Background-Color to #002D59, which is the color that has been defined for text in this site's style sheet. Click OK to close the dialog box.

The style that you're trying to create would be similar to a "reverse print" appearance where the font color is used for the background and the background color is used for the font.

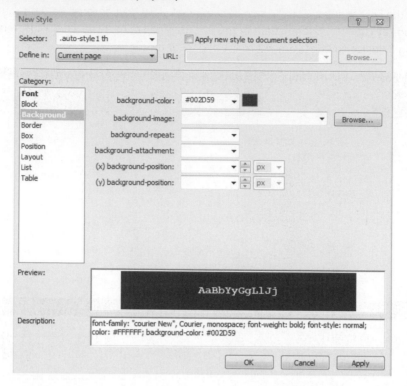

 Tip In the Style Builder dialog box, when you make a specification within a category, the category title is displayed in a bold font. This makes it easier to identify which categories have been styled.

You've modified the appearance of all of the *<th>* elements for any table that is classed as auto-style1.

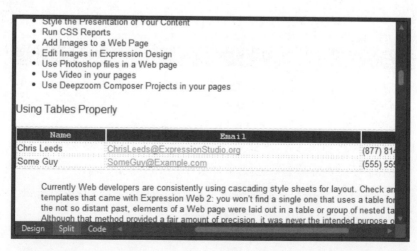

5. In the Design pane, scroll down to the benefits list you entered earlier in the chapter and set your cursor anywhere in the unordered list. Click the *<ul>* button on the Quick Tag Selector to select the entire list and all of its contents.

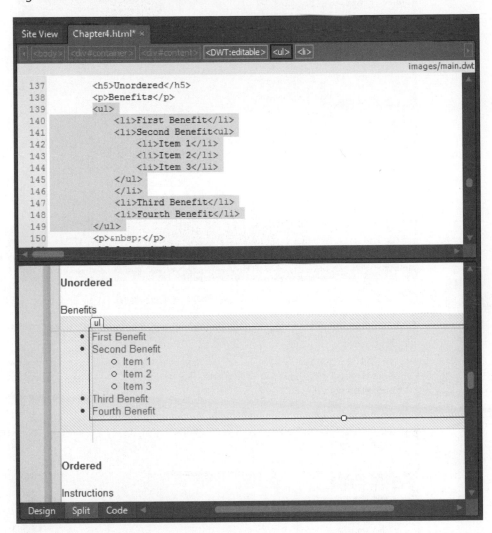

6. In the Apply Styles pane, click New Style. In the New Style dialog box, name the style **.benefitlist**, and then select the Apply New Style To Document Selection check box. In the Define In box, select Current Page.

7. In the List category, set List-Style-Type to Square. Then click Apply.

   The dialog box title changes from New Style to Modify Style.

8. The outer *<li>* elements now have a square bullet instead of the typical round bullet. The inner list items still have a round bullet.

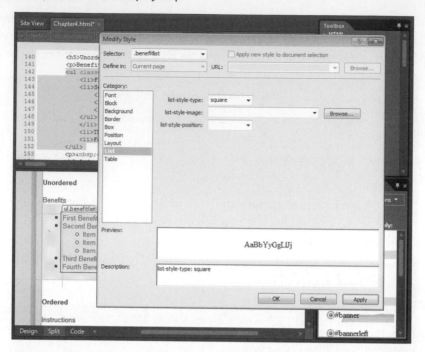

9. Change the Selector name from .benefitlist to **.benefitlist li**, and then click Apply.

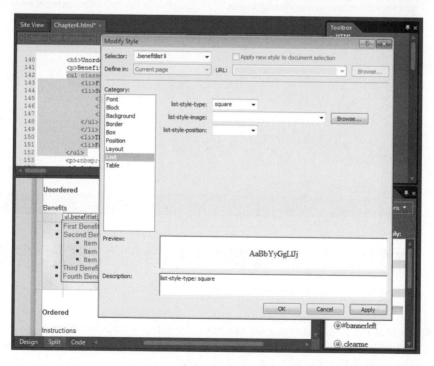

The inner list items now have a square bullet instead of a round bullet. This is because you classed the *<ul>* tag as .benefitlist but also added the *<li>* tag to that style specification in this step. This procedure creates an identical effect for both the inner and outer list items.

10. Click OK to close the Modify Style dialog box.

Modify ordered list style

In the next few steps, you will modify the style of the ordered list you created earlier in this chapter.

1. In the Design pane, set your cursor inside of the ordered list you created beneath "Instructions." On the Quick Tag Selector, click the *<ol>* button, and in the Apply Styles pane, click New Style.

2. In the New Style dialog box, name the style **.instructionlist**. Then select the Apply New Style To Document Selection check box.

3. In the Define In box, select Current Page.

4. Click the List category, and set the List-Style-Type to Upper-Roman. Then click OK to close the New Style dialog box.

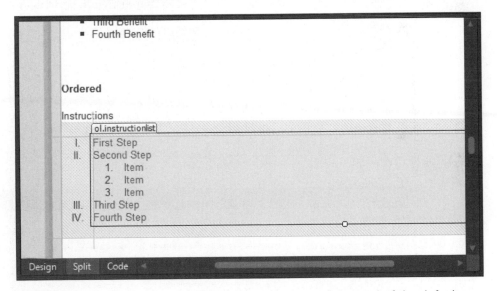

The outer list items now have uppercase Roman numerals instead of the default numbering.

5. So that the inner list items do not have the same formatting as the parent element, in the Apply Styles pane, right-click .instructionlist, and then click New Style Copy.

6. In the Selector field, type **.instructionlist li li**, and in the List category, change List-Style-Type to Lower-Alpha, and then click OK.

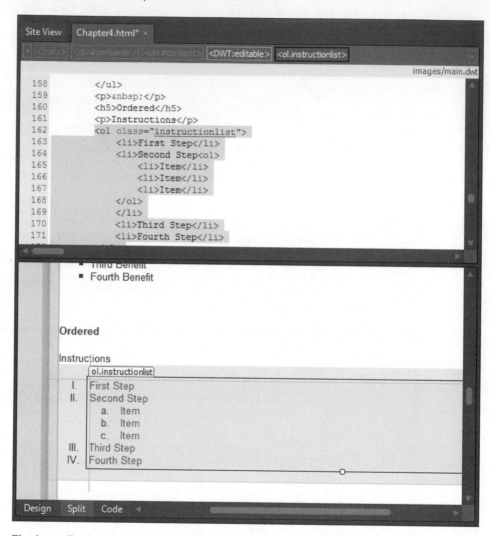

The inner list items now show lowercase alphabetic list items, and the outer list items are uppercase Roman numerals. The only code that has been added to the page is the containing <ol> tag that now has a class (class="instructionlist") applied to it.

Modify definition list appearance

In the next few steps, you will modify the default appearance of the definition list elements.

1. In the Apply Styles pane, click New Style, type **dt** for Selector, and make sure that the Define In field is set to Current Page. In the Font category, set Font-Family to Courier New, Courier, Monospace. Set Font-Weight to Bold, and Text-Transform to Uppercase.

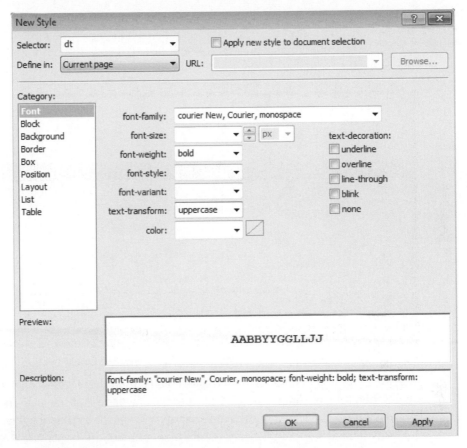

2. Click OK, and then in the Design pane, scroll down to the definition list you created earlier in this chapter. The definition list terms are now in all capital letters and are in Courier bold font.

> **Note** The method you used to style the definition terms is slightly different than the two previous lists. Previously, you created two classes (.benefitslist and .instructionlist), but in this instance, you styled the actual HTML tag *<dt>* (definition term). Unless otherwise specified, every definition term would take on the properties you just applied. There can be benefits and drawbacks to this method, but it's important to be familiar with the possibility of styling basic HTML tags.

3. In the Apply Styles pane, click New Style, add a Selector of **dd**, and make sure that the Define In field is set to Current Page. In the Font category, set Font-Family to Times New Roman, Times, Serif. Set the Font-Size to Small, Color to #808080, and then click OK.

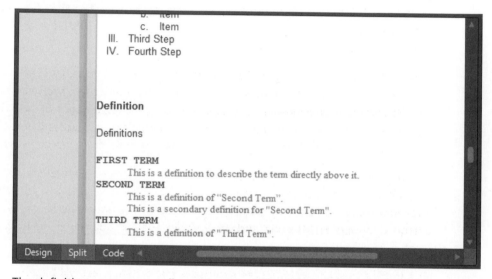

The definitions are now smaller and colored grey. These effects will apply to all definition list terms and definitions in this page. If you added these styles to an external style sheet, then the appearance would be present in any page that the style sheet is linked to. The code in the page hasn't changed at all. This style is applied to all definition list items by default without the need to class them or mark them separately.

This feature is a great advantage if you wanted to change the appearance of a styled HTML element. All you would need to do is change its entry on the style sheet, and every instance of that element in dozens, hundreds, or even thousands of pages would instantly change!

4. Click Save, click Preview on the Common toolbar to check your page in a browser to make sure that it looks the way you expect it to, and then return to Expression Web.

Cascading Style Sheets

When using cascading style sheets, several methods of altering the presentation of HTML elements are available, including the following:

- **CSS ID**   In the style sheet code, it will always begin with a number symbol (#). IDs are designed to be used only once in a page, and as such, are generally used for major page elements such as DIVs that make up major portions of a page.

- **CSS Class**   In the style sheet code, it will always begin with a period (.) and can be used multiple times in a page, if necessary.

You can also specify a style for a basic HTML element itself, such as an ordered list or an anchor tag. This can be particularly useful because you define the HTML element only once, and every time that element appears in a page, it's styled in accordance with the style sheet's specification.

What is the real value of all this? Let's consider the worst-case scenario that you didn't use the list elements or the style sheet and classes to create these segments of information. You would have extensive font tags describing the appearance of every line. You would have to resort to paragraph indents and perhaps block quotes where they didn't even belong, and the file size of your code would be many times greater than it is now.

The best-case scenario would be that you've contained your information in a semantically valid element that adds to the meaning of the text itself, and you've given it the appearance that you want by creating styles. You've prevented the necessity of using a large amount of HTML code, and you've given the text additional meaning beyond what can be seen.

As a tremendous added bonus, an externally linked style sheet will be downloaded by the browser just once, cached, and used on any page that's linked to it. Therefore, in addition to being cleaner and leaner, the code is also more efficient.

Though this small example isn't as telling as a large site would be, the fact remains that these techniques can save space on your server, save page load time for your site visitors, and add to content searchability as well as give meaning to visitors using alternative browsers such as screen readers.

Adding Images to a Web Page

Even with the most meaningful content in the best semantically valid HTML arrangement, there comes a time when text just isn't enough. Perhaps you need to use an image to reinforce a point made by the text, or perhaps you need to insert an image simply to break up the text and make it appear more approachable to visitors. Regardless of the reason, you do *need* to use images.

Expression Web provides very valuable and user-friendly tools that enable you to use images in a clean, professional way. A designer needs to keep in mind that images used on a Web site require a standardized file format, physical dimension, and file size. Expression Web contains tools to make virtually any image source file acceptable for Web display without even leaving the Expression Web interface.

When you complete this exercise, you will be able to insert images into your Web page in a number of different scenarios.

Insert images into a Web page

> **Note** Use the Chapter4.html page of the SampleSite site you opened in the previous exercise. Open this book's sample site and Chapter4.html page, if they aren't already open.

1. In the Design pane, scroll down to the *h4* that contains the text "Adding Images to a Webpage." Set your cursor at the end of that text, and press Enter on your keyboard to create a new paragraph.

2. From the Insert menu, point to Picture, and then click From File.

   While you're working on a Web site or Web page, the most common image insertion comes from outside of the Site folders. Often, these images aren't the right size or in the right format for displaying a picture on the Web. The following steps are intended to highlight several tools that Expression Web provides in order to make this task easier.

3. In the Picture dialog box, browse to this book's companion media installation folder (Documents\Microsoft Press\Expression Web 4 SBS), and then into the \Files folder.

4. Double-click the image ChickenDog.bmp. In the Accessibility Properties dialog box, type **Dog with Chicken** into the Alternate Text field, and then click OK.

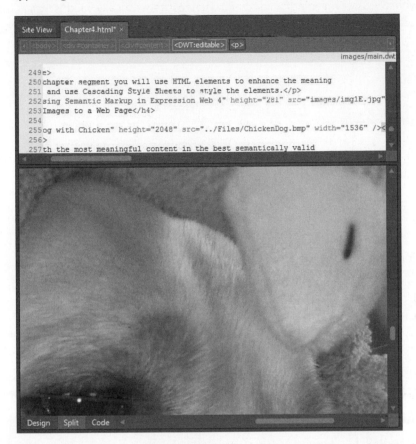

The image is inserted into the page at its original dimensions of 1536 pixels wide by 2048 pixels high and in its original file format (.bmp). This is far too big for our purposes here. In addition, a bitmap picture couldn't be more "wrong" for Web display. In the next steps, you will remedy several image issues using Expression Web.

5. Right-click the image you just inserted. From the context menu, select Picture Properties. In the Picture Properties dialog box, click the Appearance tab.

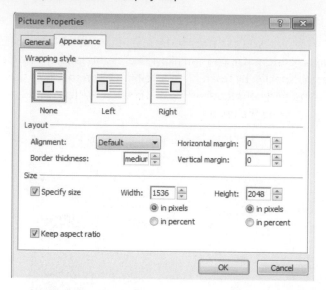

 Tip If you have a preferred graphics editor, you will see it in the Edit With group on the Context menu when you right-click an image.

6. At the bottom of the dialog box, under the Size group, make sure Keep Aspect Ratio and Specify Size are selected, type **350** in the Width field, and then click OK.

7. Click the image you just modified in the Design pane to set the focus to it. Notice the Resample icon that appears near the picture. Click that icon to show the available options.

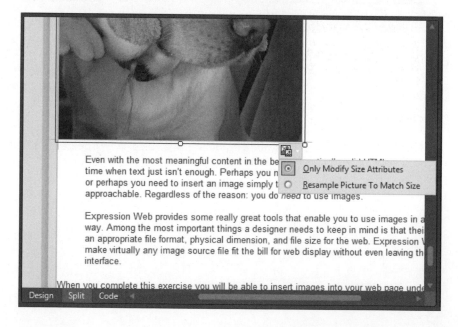

8. Select Resample Picture To Match Size.

   When you insert an image, you can specify the size in the HTML tag and leave the image at its original dimensions. Or, you can allow Expression Web to resample the image to match the size you specify. By resampling it to match the specified size, the file will become much smaller, and consequently it will deliver a much faster transfer from the server to the visitor viewing the image.

9. Click the Save button on the Common toolbar. The Save Embedded Files dialog box opens.

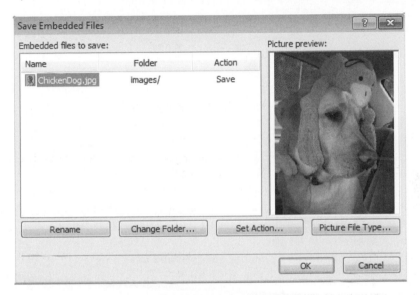

   This dialog box opens for two reasons in this case. First, it opens because you've inserted an image from outside of the site in which you're working, so Expression Web will import the file when you save the page. Second, the dialog box opens because you've specified that Expression Web should resample the image, so Expression Web needs to save that change as well.

10. Click Picture File Type. The Picture File Type dialog box opens.

    From here, you can change the file format in which Expressison Web saves the image, and you can also change quality settings or other properties.

11. Select JPEG for the file type, and change the Quality setting to **70**.

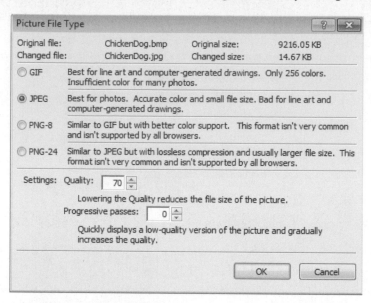

At the top of this dialog box, notice how drastically different the Original file size is compared to the Changed file size. The original was a Bitmap image that came into the site at over 9 MB, and you're saving it as a JPG file that's only about 15 KB. That's a huge reduction in file size, and the change will make a tremendous difference in how fast the page loads and its images are delivered to visitors.

12. Click OK in the Picture File Type dialog box, and then click OK on the Save Embedded Files dialog box.

You now have a new file saved as a resized and resampled image in an appropriate file format for the Web. Furthermore, you did it all from within Expression Web as opposed to preparing the image in a graphics application. In the next few steps, you will work on image placement within the page's content.

13. In the Design pane, click the image you inserted to give it the focus.

Look on the Quick Tag Selector. You can see that the image is inside a paragraph tag. That's unnecessary and will be a hindrance when you fine-tune the image's placement.

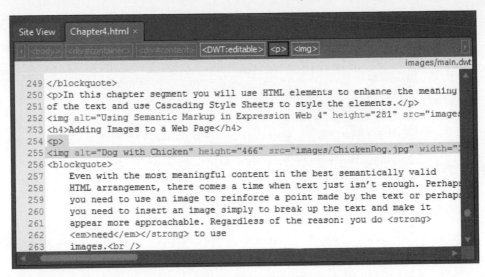

```
Site View    Chapter4.html ×

< <body>  <div#container>  <div#content>  <DWT:editable>  <p>  <img>  >
                                                             images/main.dwt

249  </blockquote>
250  <p>In this chapter segment you will use HTML elements to enhance the meaning
251  of the text and use Cascading Style Sheets to style the elements.</p>
252  <img alt="Using Semantic Markup in Expression Web 4" height="281" src="images
253  <h4>Adding Images to a Web Page</h4>
254  <p>
255  <img alt="Dog with Chicken" height="466" src="images/ChickenDog.jpg" width="
256  <blockquote>
257      Even with the most meaningful content in the best semantically valid
258      HTML arrangement, there comes a time when text just isn't enough. Perhaps
259      you need to use an image to reinforce a point made by the text or perhaps
260      you need to insert an image simply to break up the text and make it
261      appear more approachable. Regardless of the reason: you do <strong>
262      <em>need</em></strong> to use
263      images.<br />
```

14. On the Quick Tag Selector, click the drop-down arrow on the *<p>* tag that contains the image, and then click Remove Tag.

In the next few steps, you will place this image inside the block quote beneath it. Then you'll float it to the right, and add a little padding so that the text doesn't come into contact with it. Then you'll resize it appropriately for its new location.

15. Right-click the image you inserted, click Picture Properties, and then click the Appearance tab. In the Size field, change the height to **150** pixels. Make sure that Specify Size and Keep Aspect Ratio are both selected, and then click OK.

16. Click the resized image in the Design pane to show the Resize Options icon. Click Resize Picture To Match Size, and then click the Save button on the Common toolbar.

In the Save Embedded Files dialog box under the Action heading, the selected option is Overwrite.

17. Click Rename, and name this file **ChickenDog150.jpg**.

Notice that the Action changes from Overwrite to Save. By renaming the image, you won't overwrite the original image. Instead, you will save a copy of the image that's 150 pixels high under a different name.

18. Click OK on the Save Embedded Files dialog box.

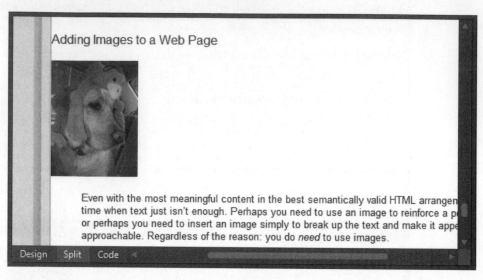

You now have a new copy of this image resized correctly for the block quote area.

19. Click and drag the image in the Design pane, releasing it just before the first letter in the block quote. The image is now "inside" the block quote.

20. Right-click the image and then click Picture Properties. Click the Appearance tab, and in the Wrapping style group, click Right. In the Layout group, set Border Thickness to **0**, Horizontal Margin to **5**, and Vertical Margin to **5**.

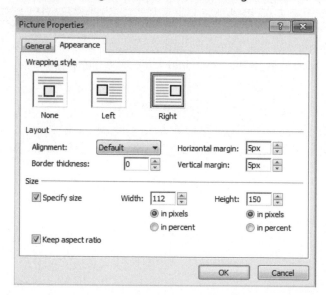

The Appearance tab of the Picture Properties dialog box provides the tools necessary to change image size, margin, float, and other common properties used in image layout.

21. Click OK in the Picture Properties dialog box.

22. Click the image that you just modified in the Design pane to give it focus.

> **Troubleshooting** Sometimes when you make a change to an image or other page element, the Design pane renders it somewhat differently than you might expect. Press F5 on your keyboard or click Refresh on the View menu to rectify the Design pane rendering.

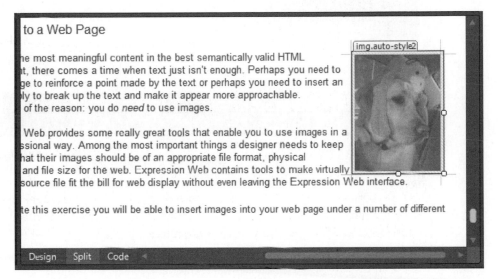

Notice that the image now has a style named *auto-style2* applied to it. Expression Web created that style and applied it to the image based on the selections you made on the Appearance tab of the Picture Properties dialog box.

23. In the Code pane, press and hold the Ctrl key and click the style that was added to the image tag. The Code pane jumps to the style block for auto-style2.

```
                                                              images/main.dwt
43  dd {
44      font-family: "times New Roman", Times, serif;
45      font-size: small;
46      color: #808080;
47  }
48  .auto-style2 {
49      float: right;
50      border-style: solid;
51      border-width: 0;
52      margin: 5px;
53  }
54  </style>
55  <!-- #EndEditable -->
56  <link href="images/main.css" rel="stylesheet" type="text/css" />
57  </head>
```

Notice the code that Expression Web created. It's fairly clear what it's supposed to do, which is to apply a border of 0, float the image to the right, and apply a margin of 5 pixels.

24. In the Design pane, scroll down to the image you've been working with, click it to select it and to set focus.

25. In the Apply Styles pane, right-click the entry for .auto-style2 and then click Modify Style.

26. In the Modify Style dialog box, click the Layout category, and change the float from right to **left**. Then click the Box category and change the margin to **10px**. Make sure the Same For All check box is selected, and then click OK.

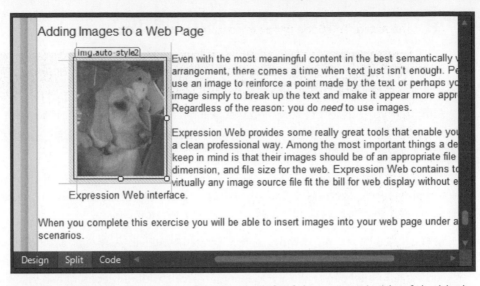

You can see that the image now floats to the left of the content inside of the block quote, and now it has twice the margin whitespace around it as before.

27. In the Code pane, press Ctrl and click the entry auto-style2 inside the image tag and take a look at the style block. You'll see that only the float and margin entries were changed. No change occurred in the image tag itself.

28. Click Save, and then click Preview. Check the page in a browser to make sure it looks the way you expect, and then return to Expression Web.

Hopefully, the preceding steps have given you insight into the tools that are available in Expression Web for image placement and conversion. The availability of these features makes it much easier for a designer to insert images from any location into a page and then exercise precise control over the physical dimensions and file size as well as the placement and appearance.

Note Leave the SampleSite site open if you are proceeding directly to the next section.

Editing Images with Expression Design

Since Expression Web now comes with Expression Design, you have near-seamless interoperability between your Web design, development interfaces, and a very capable graphics program.

Although some users of Expression Web will get their graphics and images from someone else and only be responsible for layout and deployment, the great majority of users will be responsible for creating and editing the images and graphics they use.

Expression Design is an excellent tool for creating an entire page/site graphics template. The template for this book's companion site was built in Expression Design. It's available as a native .design file that you can open directly in Expression Design.

In Chapter 6, "Creating a Web Site from Scratch," you will work with a template and create a custom template of your own, but in that case, the images would be considered "graphics." In this section, the images you are focusing on are considered "content," so you will begin with Expression Design by using it to perform basic image edits and then use the resulting image in Expression Web.

> ### Edit an image in Expression Design and use it in Expression Web

> **Note** Use the Chapter4.html page of the SampleSite site you opened in the previous exercise. Open this book's sample site and Chapter4.html page, if they aren't already open.

1. Click the Windows Start menu, click All Programs, select Microsoft Expression, and then click Microsoft Expression Design 4.

2. On the File menu in Expression Design, select Open. In the Open File dialog box, browse to this book's companion media installation folder (Documents\Microsoft Press\Expression Web SBS). Find the \Files folder, and then double-click the FishOutOfWater.jpg file.

The image opens in Expression Design. The layout of Expression Design should feel fairly familiar to you because it's similar to Expression Web. At the center of your display is the Artboard; to the left is the Toolbox, and on the right are the Properties, Layers, and Color Picker panes. At the bottom of the user interface is the action bar.

Expression Design is a full standalone graphics application. You should take some time to review the Help files (F1) and also take a look at the Microsoft Expression Design community tutorials, which you can find at *http://expression.microsoft.com/en-us/cc197142.aspx*.

> **Tip** Rather than typing in the link to the Expression Design tutorials, you can just click the link provided in the Chapter4.html file of this book's companion site.

One common image task is cropping, which is a process of removing a portion of an image and eliminating extraneous material around it. Because Expression Design is primarily a vector drawing tool, it doesn't have a crop tool like you'd find in most image editors. Instead, you will crop images with the slice tool. The next steps will show you how to crop the subject of this image (the fish) and eliminate the sand around it.

3. In the Toolbox, to the left of your Artboard, click the slice tool, and then move your cursor over the image.

   Notice that the cursor changed to a slice tool.

4. Click and drag to draw a square slice over the subject of the image.

   Don't worry if the slice isn't exactly square. It's easy to adjust. With the slice tool active, you can make multiple slices, and select and delete slices, but you can't adjust existing slices.

> **Tip** Whenever you select a slice, you can see the contents of that slice in the Properties panel. You can also control many aspects of the slice from the Properties panel, such as File Type, Layers, Color mode, size, and other parameters.

5. In the Toolbox, click the Selection button to switch to the selection tool and adjust the slice. Click and drag the anchor points on the slice to make the shape more appropriate to your intended outcome. Drag the slice until it has a more square shape.

> **Tip** Hold down the Shift key on your keyboard to maintain the slice aspect ratio while dragging.

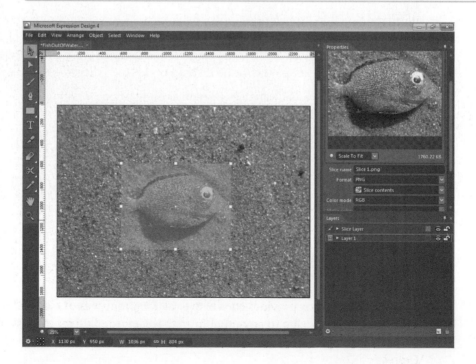

6. At the bottom of the user interface, you can see the dimensions of this slice in the action bar. Click the link icon between the Width and Height entry to unlock the aspect ratio of the slice. Enter equal numbers in each of the boxes, and then click the link icon to lock the ratio.

The action bar shows the dimensions and placement of any active selection. For instance, in this case the slice is selected, so the action bar shows you that. This slice's center point is 1130 pixels from the left side (X) and 950 pixels from the top of the base image. The slice itself is 1100 pixels by 1100 pixels.

> **Tip** Most graphics programs display these X and Y coordinates of objects relative to the upper-left corner. Click any of the points in the Registration Point button on the action bar for coordinates from that point on the object.

7. Make any final adjustments to the placement of the slice in the Artboard, and then right-click it. From the context menu, select Export.

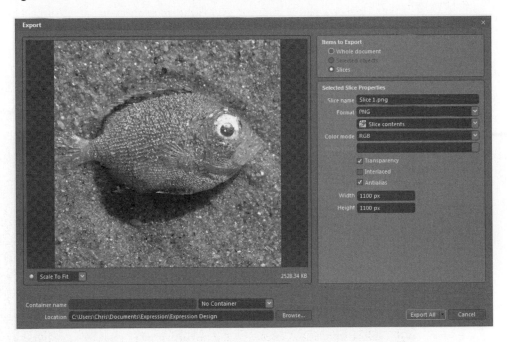

The Export dialog box provides control over all the properties of the slice. From here, you can adjust the image to an output form that's appropriate for the task at hand. By default, Expression Design saves and outputs its files to Documents\Expression \Expression Design.

8. In the Selected Slice Properties pane, change the slice name to **SquareFish.** Click the Format drop-down list and select JPEG.

When you export images from Expression Design, you can choose from 11 different formats:

- XAML
  - ❏ Silverlight 3 Canvas
  - ❏ WPF Drawing Brush
  - ❏ Silverlight 4 / WPF Canvas
- Raster
  - ❏ PNG
  - ❏ JPEG
  - ❏ GIF
  - ❏ TIFF
  - ❏ BMP
  - ❏ WDP (HD Photo)
- Adobe Formats
  - ❏ PSD
  - ❏ PDF

9. Change the Quality field to **Medium (60%)**, and then change the Width and Height to **150 px**.

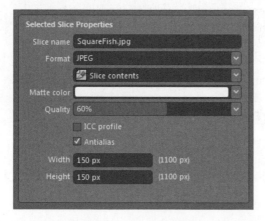

At the bottom of the Export dialog box are the Container Name and Location fields. Container Name, if enabled, will create an HTML file and images, or several XAML output containers that will let you work seamlessly in related applications, such as Expression Blend. By default, the dialog box will save your exports to Expression \Expression Design in the user's Documents folder.

10. Click Browse beside the Location field and then browse into this book's sample files location (Documents\Microsoft Press\Expression Web 4 SBS\SampleSite\images). Click OK in the Browse For Folder dialog box, and then click Export All.

   Expression Design exports the file with the parameters and to the location you specified.

11. Select File, click Save, and then save the open file as **FishOutOfWater.design**.

   You can see in the action bar that your original image is unchanged. Your slice is still a large square, and the size adjustment you made occurred only on the exported file.

12. Click the "sand" area of the picture outside your slice, and then look at the action bar.

   You'll see that the image size is still 2400×1800 pixels, despite the fact that you exported the subject of the image at only 150×150 pixels.

13. Return to Expression Web and scroll down the Design pane to the *<h4>* tag that contains the text, "Editing Images with Expression Design." Set your cursor at the end of that *<h4>* text and press Return on your keyboard to create a new paragraph.

14. In the Folder List panel, expand the Images folder to locate your newly saved file, SquareFish.jpg.

> **Tip** If you save a file to Expression Web from another application, and the file isn't visible, click Refresh on the View menu or press F5 on your keyboard. Recalculate Hyperlinks on the Tools menu is also handy because it causes Expression Web to reinventory all the files within the site.

15. Click and drag the file from the Images folder in the Folder List panel and drop it into the paragraph that you just created. In the Accessibility Properties dialog box, type **Expression Design Export Experiment**, and then click OK.

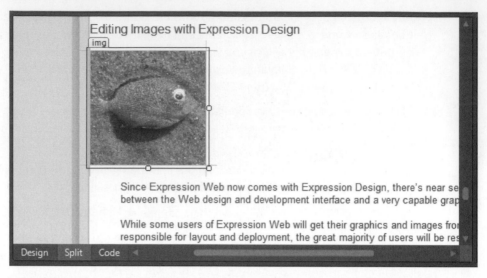

You can see in the Design pane that your image is now inserted into the page.

16. Click Save on the Common toolbar to save your changes to the Chapter4.html file.

Notice that the Save Embedded Files dialog box didn't open as it did in the previous exercises. This is because the image was already present in Expression Web from your export operation in Expression Design. In the next few steps, you will reopen the image in Expression Design, save some changes, and then update your page in Expression Web.

17. Double-click SquareFish.jpg in the Folder List panel to open it in Expression Design.

Troubleshooting See "Changing Application Options" in Chapter 2 if you haven't associated the image files with Expression Design.

18. Click Actual Size on the View menu. Hold the Shift key and drag one corner of the bounding box toward the center. Reduce the size of the square by about one third, and then click and drag it to the approximate center of the original image space.

19. Position the cursor over a corner anchor point, and when the selection icon turns to a Rotate icon, click and drag the image to change its rotation so that it's slightly skewed.

20. In the Properties pane, just below the Appearance group, you will find the Effects group. Click the Effects button on the lower right of this pane, point to Effects, and then click Outer Glow.

Every effect available from the Effects button has controllable properties. Each effect has a default setting, but by manipulating the settings, you can create literally limitless visual modifications for any object.

21. Click the Color Dropper tool and hold it over the fish subject until it picks up a bright orange area, and then click that area.

The idea is to make the image glow using one of the colors of the subject itself. The Color Dropper tool lets you sample colors from anywhere in the user interface, or even from windows open in other applications.

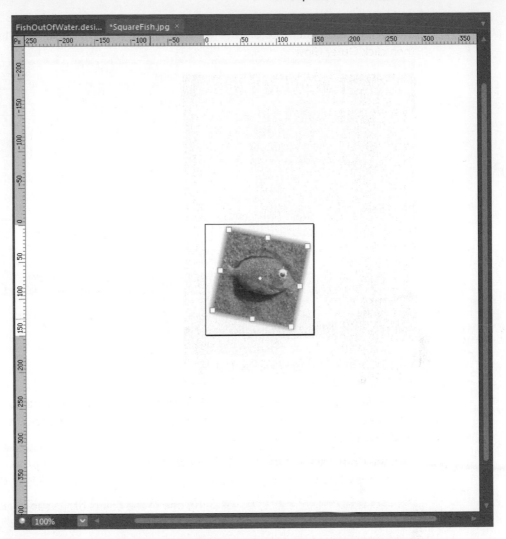

22. Click Export on the File menu. In the Export dialog box, click Browse beside the Location field, and select Documents\Microsoft Press\Expression Web 4 SBS\SampleSite\images. Click Replace in the Replace Files dialog box.

23. Return to Expression Web. If the image hasn't changed in your Design pane, click Refresh on the View menu or press F5 on your keyboard.

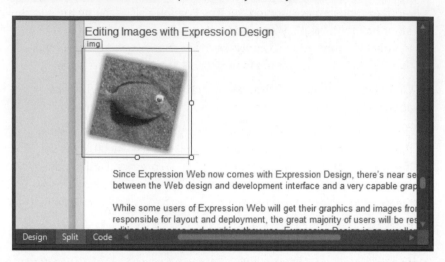

One of the benefits of working in an image editor application like Expression Design is that you have complete control over the exported images. For instance, in the previous exercise, you had to add padding to the image to keep the text from running into the image. This time, adding padding isn't necessary because you've added whitespace that will *appear* as padding during the image edit. This principal is even more important when you're laying out graphics for a Web page template, as you will do in Chapter 6.

24. In the Design pane, click and drag the image file into the block quote beneath it. Release it just before the first letter in the text. Right-click the fish image, and in the context menu, click Picture Properties. Click the Appearance tab, and then click Left in the Wrapping Style group. Finally, click OK to close the Picture Properties dialog box.

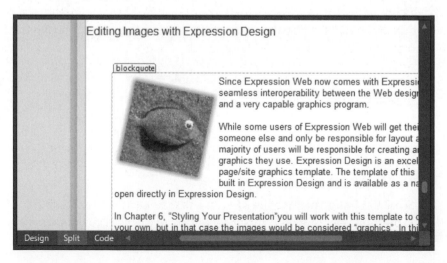

Notice that Expression Web created a new style because of the positioning change you made in the Picture Properties dialog box—*auto-style3*. If you're laying out a page that requires repeated positioning, such as floating half of the pictures to the left and the other half to the right, you need to create only two classes—one to float right and one to float left. Then you can apply those styles as needed to the images. This will reduce file size and limit complexity in your cascading style sheets code.

25. Click Save, and then click Preview. Check your page in a browser to make sure that it appears as expected and then return to Expression Web.

   Consider the outcome of this exercise. You now have an edited image in the SampleSite that you were able to use in your page that has a reasonable file size. The original image is still intact, and you have a third file in the Expression Design native format (.design), that you can edit and export as you wish. By using Expression Design, you've satisfied the need to create a Web-ready image, and benefited from the inherent original image protection that it enables.

Note Click Exit on the File menu to close Expression Design. Save the design document Square Fish.design if you want to keep it. Otherwise, click No on the Save alert. If you are continuing directly to the next exercise, leave Expression Web and Chapter4.html open. Otherwise, click Exit on the File menu to close Expression Web.

Using Photoshop Files in a Web Page

A very interesting feature of Expression Web is its ability to use Adobe Photoshop (.psd) files in Web pages. Expression Web enables you to import a Photoshop file, include or exclude any layers you want, and then Expression Web optimizes the resulting image for the Web. This feature comes in handy when you need to do a quick mock-up, and also when the person using Expression Web isn't same person doing the image preparation. One convenient feature of Expression Web's Photoshop file handling is that if the original source (.psd) file changes, you can update the image in an Expression Web page with a simple right-click.

Use a Photoshop file in a Web page

Note Use the Chapter4.html page of the SampleSite site you opened in the previous exercise. Open this book's sample site and Chapter4.html page, if they aren't already open.

1. Scroll the Design pane to the *<h4>* tag that contains the text "Using Photoshop Files in Expression Web." Set your cursor at the end of the *h4* text and press Enter on your keyboard to insert a new paragraph.

2. From the Insert menu, point to Picture, and then click From Adobe Photoshop (.psd) to open the Select Photoshop (.psd) file dialog box.

3. Browse to this book's companion media installation folder, and select PSImport.psd (Documents\Microsoft Press\Expression Web 4 SBS\Files\PSImport.psd). Then click Open to open the Import Adobe Photoshop File dialog box.

Tip Expression Web can import Photoshop files that have all the following properties:

- The color is 8 bits per channel (24 bits of color per pixel).
- The color mode is RGB Color, Grayscale, or Indexed Color.
- The resulting image size is 200 MB or less.
- The file is saved with the Photoshop Maximize Compatibility format option turned on.
- The file extension is .psd.

The file doesn't need to be created in Photoshop. In this example, the .psd file was created in Expression Design and exported as a .psd file.

4. In the Import Adobe Photoshop File dialog box, clear the Throw Me Away check box to exclude that layer and its text. Change the Encoding setting to JPEG, set the JPEG Quality setting to **75%**, and then click OK.

Tip In the Import Adobe Photoshop File dialog box, you can adjust the compression ratio of the resulting image and choose whether you want to save it as a .gif, .jpg, or .png. Below the individual layers is a Compatibility Layer, which is a single layer that combines all the PSD's individual layers into one image.

5. In the Save As dialog box, double-click the Sample Site's Images folder, and then click Save to save the file as PSImport-psd.jpg.

6. Type **Import Photoshop Experiment** in the Accessibility Properties dialog box and then click OK.

   The image is now inserted into the page, using the settings you chose in step 4.

7. Save your changes and preview the page in a browser to make sure that it appears as expected.

8. Return to Expression Web. Right-click the image you just inserted, and select Adobe Photoshop (.psd).

   When you click Update From Source, Expression Web will open the source PSD file in the Import Adobe Photoshop File dialog box. This is helpful if the image was changed in Photoshop or another PSD generating image editor and you want to update the resulting photo in your Web page.

9. Click Update From Source to open the Import Adobe Photoshop File dialog box. Clear all layers except the base image layer named Photo.

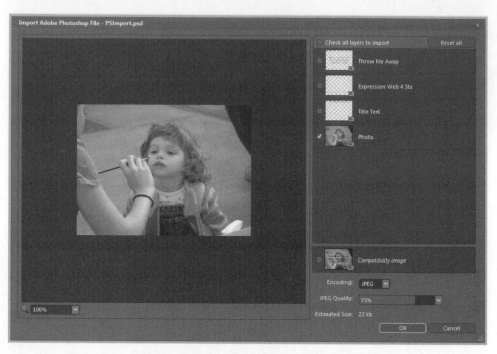

10. Click OK in the Import Adobe Photoshop File dialog box, click Save in the Save As dialog box, and then click Yes in the Confirm Save As alert to overwrite the previous version of the image in your site's Images folder.

> **Troubleshooting** If you don't have a photo editor assigned to .psd files, Edit Source will be unavailable.

> **Note** Leave the Chapter4.html file open if you are proceeding directly to the next section.

Consider the results of this exercise. Without leaving the Expression Web interface, you were able to use the Import Adobe Photoshop File feature to create a Web-ready, lightweight .jpg image and insert it directly into your page. You also retained the ability to quickly open the source file in your default .psd editor from within Expression Web and easily update the resulting Web-ready image in your page, while incorporating any changes made to the original Photoshop file.

> **Tip** If you elect to keep the original files within your Expression Web site, you may find it useful to right-click the files in the Folder List panel and then click Do Not Publish. Although you may find it convenient to keep original artwork and other files within your Web site, you'll most likely not want to waste hosting space or bandwidth by publishing the original files to the live Web site.

Using Silverlight Video in a Web Page

Every version of Expression Web now comes with Expression Encoder, which gives you the option of using Microsoft Silverlight Videos in your Web pages. Now you'll be able to insert high-quality streaming video directly into your pages. Expression Encoder resamples video files into a format appropriate for Web display. In addition, it creates a Silverlight video player that will play the movie in users' browsers. You can do all this with little more than a few mouse clicks.

Insert a Silverlight Video into a Webpage

> **Note** Use the Chapter4.html page of the SampleSite site you opened in the previous exercise. Open this book's sample site and Chapter4.html page, if they aren't already open.

1. Scroll through the Design pane until you find the *<h4>* tag that contains the text, "Using Silverlight Video in a Webpage." Set your cursor at the end of that text, and press Enter on your keyboard to create a new paragraph.

2. From the Insert menu, select Media, and then select Silverlight Video.

3. In the Select A Video dialog box, browse to this book's companion media installation folder (Documents\Microsoft Press\Expression Web 4 SBS\Files) and double-click CaseStudy.wmv.

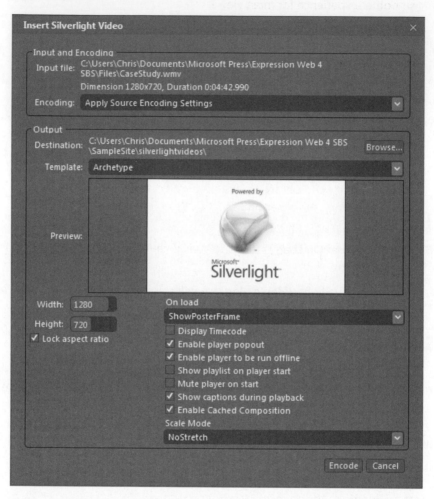

The Insert Silverlight Video dialog box opens. From this initial dialog box you can select one of 16 different Silverlight templates. Some of these templates are "gallery" styles that can contain multiple videos; some are designed strictly for audio files; still others are intended to show a single video.

> **Tip** Use the up and down arrows on your keyboard to cycle through the available templates and see previews of each. Double-click a template's preview to display it in Full Screen mode. Press Escape on your keyboard to return to the Expression Web interface.

4. Click the drop-down arrow beside the Encoding field, and select VC-1 256k DSL VBR. The VBR stands for Variable Bit Rate, which is an encoding format that results in a smoother experience for most viewers.

 Tip For information about these encoding formats, see the Online Help manual (press F1 in Expression Encoder).

5. Click the drop-down arrow beside the Template field and select Popup. Beneath the Width and Height fields, make sure the Lock Aspect Ratio option is selected, and change the width to **500**.

6. Beneath the On Load field, click the drop-down arrow, and then select ShowVideoPaused.

   The two option choices are ShowVideoPaused and ShowVideoPlaying, which are fairly self-explanatory; the other option, ShowPosterFrame will cause the video player to show the "Powered by Silverlight" image that you see in the preview.

7. Leave the other On Load settings at their defaults, and click Encode at the bottom of the dialog box.

   The Insert Silverlight Video dialog box will close and an Encoding dialog box will appear. The length of time it takes to complete the encoding process depends on the file size of the original video, the speed of your computer, and the output encoding you chose in the Insert Silverlight Video dialog box. When the encoding process finishes, a Silverlight object is placed in the page at your cursor.

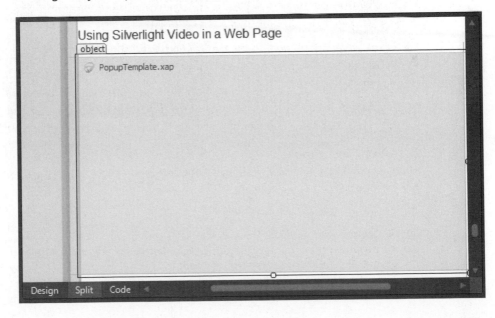

8. Click Save, and then click Preview on the Common toolbar. Check the page in a browser to view the appearance of your video as shown in the Silverlight Player.

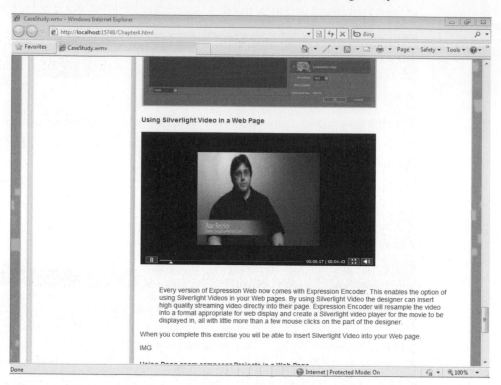

9. Try the controls on the Silverlight Player. Then close the browser and return to Expression Web.

10. Select the Silverlight Object in the Design pane, and then look at the highlighted code in the Code pane.

You can see in the Code pane and also on the Quick Tag Selector that a *<div>* with the ID *silverlightvideocontainer* has been inserted into the page. Inside that *<div>* is an *<object>* tag that has a number of parameters, such as source, background, minimum runtime version, and so forth. The last parameter in the list is very large. It contains the settings for the player. These settings reflect the choices you made in the Insert Silverlight Video dialog box in the previous steps. Even though this isn't a gallery type of Silverlight Video template, the settings contain a playlist, but it holds only one item.

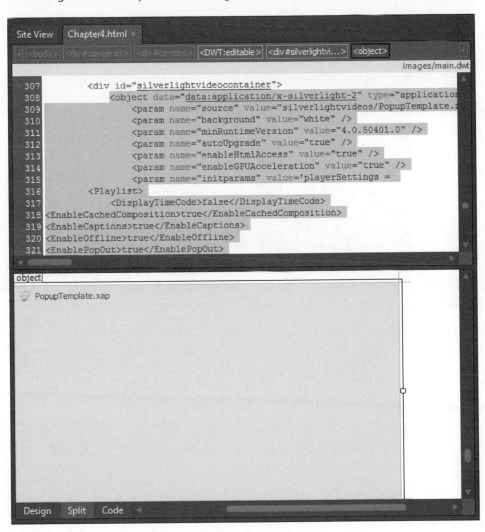

11. In the Folder List panel, expand the Javascript and Silverlightvideos folders. Expression Web created these two folders and their contents during the process of inserting the Silverlight Video into your page.

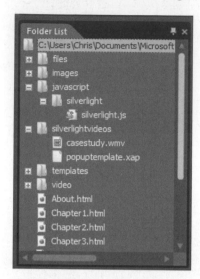

12. Click *<div#silverlightvideo>* on the Quick Tag Selector, and then press Delete on your keyboard to delete the Silverlight Player from the page.

Because the player you just inserted was designed for single video use, in the next few steps, you will see how to insert a Silverlight Player intended for multiple videos. Then you will learn how to modify its code so that your visitors will see a playlist from which they can choose videos. This is a useful technique for providing access to multiple videos within the constraints of a single interface.

13. From the Insert menu, choose Media, and then select Silverlight Video.

14. In the Select A Video dialog box, browse to this book's companion media installation folder (Documents\Microsoft Press\Expression Web 4 SBS\Files) and double-click BackPublish.wmv.

15. Click the drop-down arrow beside the Encoding field and select VC-1 256k DSL VBR. Again, this is a Variable Bit Rate encoding format that results in a smoother experience for most viewers.

16. Click the drop-down arrow beside the Template field, and select Silverlight Gallery. Beneath the Preview label, make sure Lock Aspect Ratio is selected, and then change the width to **500**.

17. Beneath the On Load field, click the drop-down arrow, and select ShowPosterFrame.

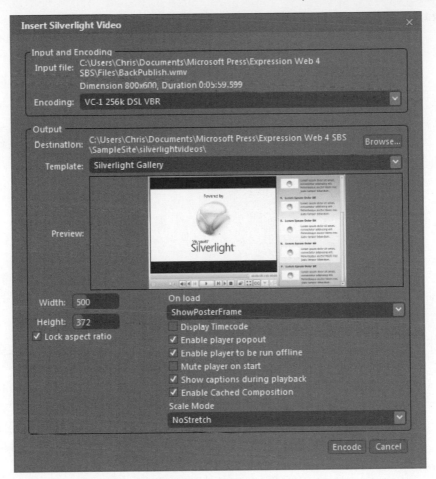

18. Leave the other On Load settings at their defaults, and click Encode at the bottom of the dialog box.

    This encoding process will be identical to the previous encode process—the video will be encoded and placed in the Silverlightvideos folder. Expression Web will also create a player in the page using the Silverlight Gallery template. You will see a silverlightgallery.xap file in the folder along with the video.

19. Click Yes when you see the warning message about overwriting the Silverlight.js file.

    Because you completed this process in the previous steps, Expression Web needs to overwrite or ignore the Silverlight.js file. This file contains JavaScript that enables the Silverlight Player.

20. Click the Silverlight Player in the Design pane to select it in the Code pane. Scroll downward through the Code pane until you find the first (and only) item in the PlaylistItem. Drag your cursor from the *<playlistItem>* tag to the *</PlaylistItem>* tag, selecting both of these tags and all the content between them. Press Ctrl+C on your keyboard to copy the selected text.

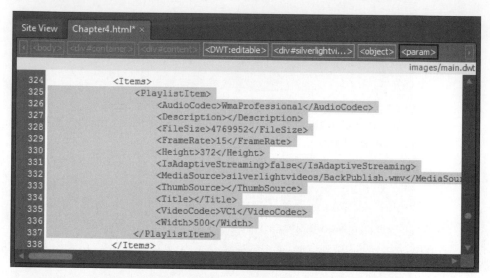

The Playlist contains "nodes" called *PlaylistItems*. Each *PlaylistItem* can contain several parameters that will affect the behavior of the Silverlight Player your visitors will see. For example, in the *<ThumbSource>* node, you can enter the path to a thumbnail picture that represents the *<MediaSource>* item (the video), and that thumbnail will be visible in the Silverlight Player's gallery pane.

21. Set your cursor just after the closing *</PlaylistItem>* tag and press Enter on your keyboard to insert a new line. Then press Ctrl+V on your keyboard to paste the content you copied into the page.

22. In your newly pasted *PlaylistItem* tag, change the *MediaSource* tag value from <Media Source>silverlightvideos/BackPublish.wmv</MediaSource> to **<MediaSource>silver lightvideos/casestudy.wmv</MediaSource>**

You're building a playlist that will be reflected in the gallery area of this Silverlight Player.

23. Change the empty *<Title></Title>* tag on the *PlaylistItem* for BackPublish.wmv to contain the text, **Back Publishing**. Change the second empty *PlaylistItem* for CaseStudy.wmv *<Title></Title>* tag so it contains the text, **Website Spark Case Study**.

It's not much of a "gallery" with only two items, so in the next few steps, you will import two more videos into the Web site and then repeat the preceding steps to add them to the playlist.

24. In the Folder List panel, click the Silverlightvideos folder. From the File menu, select Import, and then click File.

25. In the Import dialog box, click the File button, and browse to this book's installation file folder (Documents\Microsoft Press\Expression Web 4 SBS\Files). Hold down the Ctrl key and click EditWith.wmv and ImageTrick.wmv to select both files. Click Open, and then in the Import dialog box, click OK.

Expression Web imports those two videos into the site's Silverlightvideos folder.

26. Set your cursor in the Code pane just beneath the second *PlaylistItem* closing tag and press Ctrl+V twice to paste two more items into the code.

27. Change the last *PlaylistItem* entry so that the *<MediaSource>* tag contains **silver lightvideos/EditWith.wmv** and the Title tag contains the text **Edit any page with Expression Web**.

28. Scroll up to the next *PlaylistItem* entry, and change that entry's *<MediaSource>* tag contents to **silverlightvideos/ImageTrick.wmv** and its Title tag so it contains **Expression Web Image Trick**.

29. On the Common toolbar, click Save, and then click Preview.

Your video player now has a gallery pane on the right side, based on the items that you added in the previous steps.

30. View your newly customized Silverlight Video Player. Click the buttons on the control bar and try the links to the other videos you added when you edited the player's source code. Close the browser and return to Expression Web.

By combining Expression Encoder functionality with Expression Web, you can implement high-end video presentations into your pages with relative ease. Although this exercise focused primarily on Expression Web, using the Insert Silverlight Video functionality, you should explore Expression Encoder and review the online Help files (press F1 to view them), as well as the following resources:

- Microsoft Expression Encoder Product Overview (*http://www.microsoft.com /expression/products/Encoder_Overview.aspx*)

- Microsoft Expression Encoder Learning Center (*http://expression.microsoft.com /en-us/cc197144.aspx*)

- Microsoft Expression Encoder Forum (*http://social.expression.microsoft.com/forums /en-us/encoder/threads*)

- Official Team Blog for Expression Encoder (*http://blogs.msdn.com/expressionencoder/*)

Tip These links are in "clickable" form on the Chapter4.html file in this book's SampleSite.

Note Leave the Chapter4.html file open if you are proceeding directly to the next section.

Using Deep Zoom Composer Projects in a Web Page

Expression Web has the ability to insert a Deep Zoom Composer project into a Web page. Deep Zoom Composer is a free application from Microsoft that enables designers to build compelling projects that capitalize on Silverlight Deep Zoom technology.

Deep Zoom Composer images are very helpful in a situation where you want to show a collection of photos consisting of extremely high-resolution images, without taking up a lot of space on the page itself. Like a photo gallery—but much more—Deep Zoom Composer images are a truly unique feature for designers to consider.

Deep Zoom Composer is a standalone application. You should review the resources listed at the end of this section to learn the ins and outs of working with Deep Zoom Composer. You'll also find resource links in the Chapter4.html file of this book's SampleSite.

Insert Deep Zoom Composer images into your Web page

 Note Use the Chapter4.html page of the SampleSite you opened in the previous exercise. Open this book's sample site and Chapter4.html page, if they aren't already open.

1. Scroll through the Design pane until you find the *<h4>* tag that contains the text, "Using Deep Zoom Composer Projects in a Webpage." Set your cursor at the end of that text and press Enter on your keyboard to create a new paragraph.

2. From the Insert menu, select Media, and then click Deep Zoom. Browse to Documents\ Microsoft Press\Expression Web 4 SBS\Files\Composition-SeadragonAjax\ GeneratedImages, select the file dzc_output.xml, and then click Open.

3. Select Autodetect beneath the Insert Method label. Set the Width field to **500** and the Height field to **375**. Leave the Zoom Speed field at its default setting of 5.

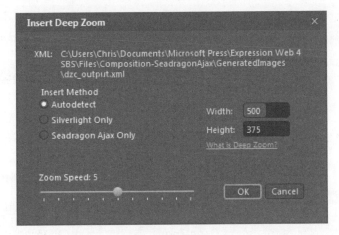

If your Deep Zoom Composer output is a Deep Zoom Composition (a single image), you can use Autodetect, which checks to see whether the browser has Silverlight installed. If so, Autodetect provides the Deep Zoom in Silverlight. If not, then it provides the Deep Zoom in Seadragon Ajax, a JavaScript version for non-Silverlight browsers. This is a necessary step because Deep Zoom Collections (multiple images) are compatible only with Silverlight, not with Seadragon Ajax.

 Tip Expression Web re-renders the Deep Zoom Composer project, which takes a long time. During the re-render process, the Expression Web interface is unavailable. In addition, the Cancel button in the Insert Deep Zoom dialog box is also unavailable. If you need to stop the process after it has begun, you must close Expression Web from the Windows Task Manager.

> **Important** If you want to skip this step and jump to the alternative method of including a Deep Zoom Composer image, click Cancel on the dialog box now. The Cancel button is not available after you click OK.

4. Click OK to begin the process of importing and inserting the Deep Zoom Composer image.

The length of time it takes Expression Web to re-encode the Deep Zoom Composer project depends on the number of images in the original project and the speed of the computer you're using. When the project finishes, you'll see the *<div>* tag with an ID of *deepzoomcontainer* in both the Design and Code panes of your workspace. You'll also find two new folders in the Folder List panel: /deepzooms, which contains the output files, and a /javascript/deepzooms folder, which contains the JavaScript necessary to make the project render in a visitor's browser.

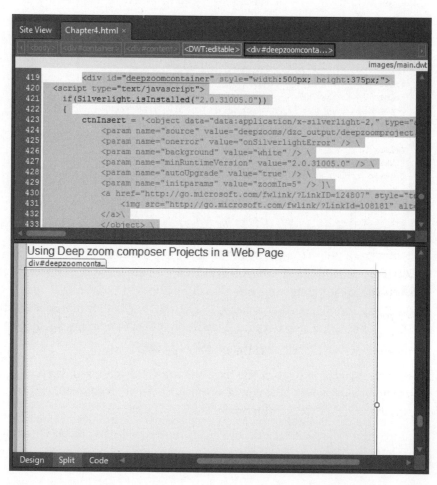

5. Click Save, and then click Preview on the Common toolbar to open the page in a browser. Review the browser version of the Deep Zoom Composer project, and then close your browser and return to Expression Web.

   Although this method does insert the Deep Zoom Composer project into the page, it doesn't maintain the original project's export settings. In the next few steps, you will learn how to insert a Deep Zoom project exactly as it was exported from Deep Zoom Composer.

6. Click the Deepzooms folder in the Folder List panel. From the File menu, select Import, and then click File. In the Import dialog box, click the Folder button. Browse to Documents\Microsoft Press\Expression Web 4 SBS\Files, select the Collection-DeepZoom folder, and then click Open.

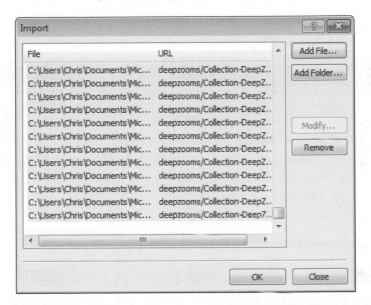

7. Click OK to import the folder you selected into the Deepzooms folder of the SampleSite.

8. Set your cursor in the Deep Zoom *<div>* tag you created in the previous steps, click the corresponding *<div#deepzoomcontainer>* button on the Quick Tag Selector to select the entire *div*, and then press Delete on your keyboard.

9. From the View menu, select Toolbars, and then click Standard. Set your cursor in the empty paragraph tag in Design view that you created earlier in this section, and then click the Include Page button on the Standard toolbar.

10. From the Include Page Properties dialog box, browse to the site's Deepzooms/ Collection-DeepZoom folder, double-click the default.html file, and then click OK.

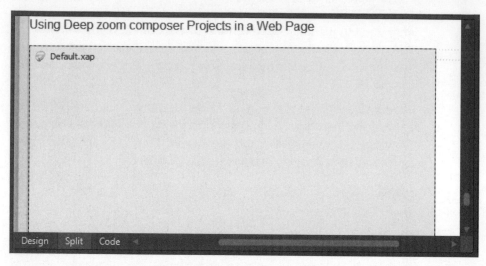

Expression Web inserts the Deep Zoom project into your page using the Include Page method. You can see that the object in the Design view has a Default.xap label. By using this method of importing the project and then using the Include Page to write it into your receiving page, you will insert the project with the exact output specifications it was given in Deep Zoom Composer, and the lag time is avoided while Expression Web re-renders the project.

11. From the View menu, select Toolbars, and then click Standard to close the Standard toolbar.

12. Click Save, and then click Preview on the Common toolbar to view the newly inserted Deep Zoom image in a browser.

Notice the difference in the quality of presentation between this method and the previous method. Not only does the Deep Zoom Composer project look better on the page, but the navigation controls are present, and the rendering is superior. Using the Include Page method to insert an imported Deep Zoom Composer project saves you time and produces a much better end-user experience on the page.

Troubleshooting You might see a JavaScript error on your page that will cause arrested slide show behavior. This error is a result of adding and removing the previous Deep Zoom image and adding the Silverlight Video, so it would not occur under normal circumstances. Feel free to delete the Deep Zoom JavaScript link from the head section of your page, because this implementation relies on Silverlight only and doesn't require JavaScript.

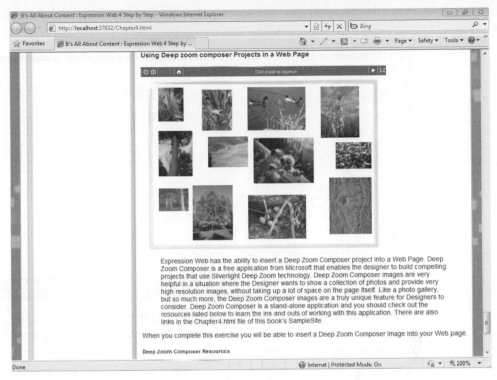

13. Close your browser and return to Expression Web.

Deep Zoom Composer images are an emerging technology on the Web. They're sure to draw attention and they can be useful tools as well. This section dealt with inserting the composition into the page. If you want to learn about how to use the Deep Zoom Composer application, the original project is available in the book's companion media installation folder in \Files\DeepZoomSample-Source\SampleProject. Open Deep Zoom Composer and from the File menu, click Open project. Browse to the sample folder location and double-click SampleProject.dzprj.

The following resources will help you learn how to use Deep Zoom Composer.

Deep Zoom Composer Resources

- Download Deep Zoom Composer (*http://www.microsoft.com/downloads/details.aspx?FamilyID=457B17B7-52BF-4BDA-87A3-FA8A4673F8BF*)

- MSDN Resources for Deep Zoom Composer (*http://msdn.microsoft.com/en-us/library/dd409068.aspx*)

- Microsoft Official Deep Zoom Composer Blog (*http://blogs.msdn.com/expression/archive/tags/Deep+Zoom+Composer/default.aspx*)

- Microsoft Deep Zoom Composer Forum (*http://social.expression.microsoft.com/ forums/en-US/deepzoomcomposer/threads*)

- Deep Zoom Composer Online Help Manual (*http://expression.microsoft.com/en-us/ library/cc295792.aspx*)

 Tip These links are available in "clickable" form in the Chapter4.html file in this book's SampleSite.

MIME Type

The previous sections dealt with rendering projects in a visitor's browser using Silverlight. Although they'll always preview for you in the Expression Development Server, they might not work when they're published to a production server unless that server has been set up for Silverlight.

For Silverlight to render properly in users' browsers, the following MIME types will need to be set on the server. A MIME type is code that identifies a specific type of content that is associated with a file extension. Some hosting services offer a control pane where you can set these MIME types yourself. In other cases, you can have the server administrator set them for you.

Ensure that all the MIME types below are included in your Web site:

- .dll application/x-msdownload

- .dmg application/octet-stream

- .flv video/x-flv

- .mp4 video/mp4

- .pdb Symbols file

- .psx Managed Jscript file

- .py IronPython file

- .xaml text/xml

- .xpi application/x-xpinstall

- .xap application/x-silverlight-app

Key Points

- In modern Web sites, content consists of more than just text.

- Using tables for Web page layout works well for certain content.

- By using XHTML and cascading style sheets, you can easily improve your site's appearance and its semantic meaning.

- HTML tags can help lend meaning to the content they contain.

- Cascading style sheets can help you make HTML render any way you want it to.

- Expression Web provides tools to make inserting images more efficient.

- Expression Design enables you to edit images in ways that Expression Web can't.

- Expression Web can insert Photoshop files into your pages as Web-ready images.

- You can add Silverlight Video to your pages in Expression Web using 16 different player templates.

- Expression Web provides several ways to display Deep Zoom Composer projects in your pages.

Chapter 5
Understanding Validity and Accessibility

After completing this chapter, you will be able to:

- Understand and change a DOCTYPE
- Verify and address W3C validity
- Verify and address accessibility
- Style text with cascading style sheets

Today's modern Web standards emphasize several key principles: validity, accessibility, cross-browser compatibility, and a clean separation of content and presentation. These principles pave the way for richer Web pages that are more easily indexed by search engines, more predictably rendered by browsers, more reliably rendered by alternative devices such as screen readers, and so on. You will be glad to know that Microsoft Expression Web 4 provides you with the tools you'll need to build Web sites that adhere to modern Web standards and best practices. In fact, Microsoft Expression Web actually makes development much easier than it once was.

For most of the key principles, you don't need to be an expert in behind-the-scenes code, because Expression Web 4 will either automatically ensure that your code follows these principals, or will provide you with a visual interface and tools to help you resolve any issues.

In this chapter, you will learn how to verify that HTML/XHTML is valid according to the World Wide Web Consortium (W3C) standards, and to address accessibility. You will also learn to use cascading style sheets (CSS) to style text and to choose and use the right Document Type Declaration (DOCTYPE). When you create new works in Expression Web 4, it reduces the need for these tasks, because the application is designed to ensure that your work complies with validity and accessibility standards. Where you will find the tools and features in Expression Web 4 most valuable is when you work with older sites, made when there were fewer common browsers in use and adherence to W3C standards and accessibility was much less emphasized. As an example, you will find fairly outmoded and deprecated HTML code in this chapter's accompanying page.

 Important Before you can use the practice files in this chapter, you need to download and install them from the book's companion content Web site to their default location. For more information about downloading and installing the practice files, see the "Code Samples" section at the beginning of this book.

Troubleshooting Graphics and operating system-related instructions in this book reflect the Windows 7 user interface. If your computer is running Windows XP or Windows Vista and you experience trouble following the instructions as written, please refer to the "Information for Readers Running Windows XP or Vista" section at the beginning of this book.

Understanding and Changing a DOCTYPE

A DOCTYPE is a declaration at the very beginning of an HTML/XHTML file that tells the browser what kind of document it's receiving. A valid DOCTYPE is the very first thing you need to make sure your page(s) will validate.

Expression Web 4 can work with any DOCTYPE. In fact, you'll find the following seven DOCTYPE declarations in the code snippets library.

Tip To display the code snippets library, set your cursor in the Code pane of a page and press Ctrl+Enter on your keyboard.

```
<!DOCTYPE HTML PUBLIC "-//W3C//DTD HTML 4.01 Frameset//EN"
"http://www.w3.org/TR/html4/frameset.dtd">

<!DOCTYPE HTML PUBLIC "-//W3C//DTD HTML 4.01//EN"
"http://www.w3.org/TR/html4/strict.dtd">

<!DOCTYPE HTML PUBLIC "-//W3C//DTD HTML 4.01 Transitional//EN"
"http://www.w3.org/TR/html4/loose.dtd">

<!DOCTYPE html PUBLIC "-//W3C//DTD XHTML 1.1//EN"
"http://www.w3.org/TR/xhtml11/DTD/xhtml11.dtd">

<!DOCTYPE html PUBLIC "-//W3C//DTD XHTML 1.0 Frameset//EN"
"http://www.w3.org/TR/xhtml1/DTD/xhtml1-frameset.dtd">

<!DOCTYPE html PUBLIC "-//W3C//DTD XHTML 1.0 Strict//EN"
"http://www.w3.org/TR/xhtml1/DTD/xhtml1-strict.dtd">

<!DOCTYPE html PUBLIC "-//W3C//DTD XHTML 1.0 Transitional//EN"
http://www.w3.org/TR/xhtml1/DTD/xhtml1-transitional.dtd">
```

For a complete list of DOCTYPES, see the W3C's list at *http://www.w3.org/QA/2002/04/valid-dtd-list.html*.

In addition to being the first step in making a valid page, there's an added benefit to specifying the correct DOCTYPE, which is a predictable browser rendering. To deliver consistent display in all browsers, the browser needs to be told what kind of file it's displaying.

Troubleshooting By default, Expression Web 4 inserts an XHTML 1.0 transitional DOCTYPE on every new HTML page it creates and ensures that the code is appropriate for that DOCTYPE. The only time you need to consider the DOCTYPE is when you're working on an existing site that was created by using another program. Similarly, it's used in a project where you want to use a different DOCTYPE than the standard one that Expression Web 4 provides.

Change a file DOCTYPE

In this exercise, you will change the DOCTYPE of a file and explore how Expression Web 4 uses DOCTYPES to verify code compliance.

Note Use the Chapter5.html file in the book's sample site located in the Documents\Microsoft Press\Expression Web 4 SBS folder. Launch Expression Web 4 before beginning this exercise, and open the SampleSite project by selecting Open Site from the Site menu, browsing to the companion media default installation page, and double-clicking the SampleSite folder. With the sample site opened in Expression Web, double-click Chapter5.html in the Folder List panel.

With the Chapter5.html file open, take a few minutes to examine the page. An area in this page serves as an example of deprecated HTML markup and contains an accessibility issue. You can easily identify it because it has a different background image than the rest of the page. This area will be the focus of the exercises in this chapter. Notice the HTML compatibility and code error warnings on the lower-right corner of your workspace.

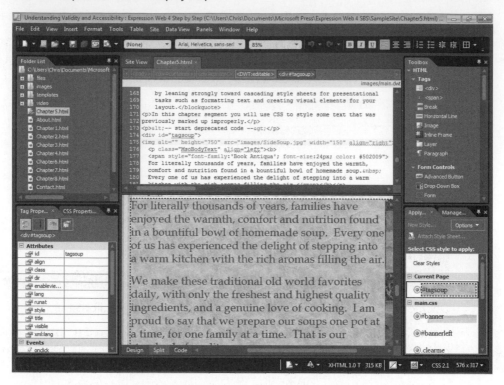

To learn how to work with the DOCTYPE, follow these steps:

1. If Chapter5.html didn't open in Split view, click Split on the lower left of the workspace to display the page in Split view.

   Before you move to the next step, notice the DOCTYPE listing on the lower right of the workspace. It's showing that the page is XHTML 1.0T.

2. Scroll to the top of the Code pane, and locate the following DOCTYPE information:

```
<!DOCTYPE html PUBLIC "-//W3C//DTD XHTML 1.0 Transitional//EN"
"http://www.w3.org/TR/xhtml1/DTD/xhtml1-transitional.dtd">
```

   Although you might consider altering the DOCTYPE to an earlier specification to elimi-nate the compatibility issues causing the warnings you see in the lower-right corner of your workspace, this exercise will highlight the futility of that approach.

3. In the Code pane, select the entire DOCTYPE, and then press Ctrl+Enter to open the code snippets list.

Notice that there are seven different DOCTYPEs that are available in the code snippets list.

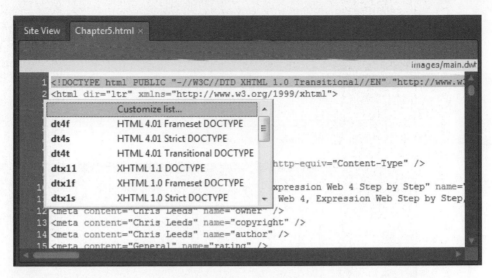

4. Double-click the HTML 4.01 Transitional DOCTYPE, and then click Save.

Notice all the red underlined code. Expression Web will apply red underlines whenever code in the page doesn't match acceptable code for the current DOCTYPE declaration. In this case, the page was originally created to comply with XHTML. Now, however, the page has a different DOCTYPE, and Expression Web 4 marks all the XHTML tags as incompatible with the changed DOCTYPE.

5. Because it should now be clear that modifying the DOCTYPE to bring the page to HTML compatibility isn't the way to go, you can change it back. To do that, follow the same sequence as before. First, select the newly added HTML 4.01 Transitional DOCTYPE declaration in the Code pane and then press Ctrl+Enter on your keyboard. The code snippet list appears. In the code snippet list, scroll down to and double-click the XHTML 1.0 Transitional DOCTYPE that was originally on the page and then click the Save button.

Notice that the code compatibility issues that appeared when you changed the DOCTYPE in step 4 have now disappeared.

This exercise showed how Expression Web uses the DOCTYPE to determine which tags are valid and which tags are not valid. Some of the most common DOCTYPE issues you will en-counter will occur in pages written without Expression Web, because Expression Web inserts a modern DOCTYPE by default, and ensures that any HTML code it writes is compliant with the DOCTYPE declaration. Besides pages with an incompatible DOCTYPE, you may also find pages with no DOCTYPE at all. The lack of a DOCTYPE will cause browser rendering issues and will prevent a page from being valid no matter what type of HTML/XHTML code you use.

Set a Default DOCTYPE

Besides manually modifying the DOCTYPE in the source of your document as you did in this exercise, you can use the Page Editor Options dialog box in Expression Web 4, which was detailed in Chapter 3, "Capitalizing on the Template Options in Expression Web 4."

To open the dialog box and access the settings, follow these steps:

1. From the Tools menu, choose Page Editor Options, and then click the Authoring tab in the dialog box.

2. To set the default DOCTYPE for all new files, set .htm or .html as the default file extension. Choose whether to use a Byte Order Mark with various file types, and an array of other options.

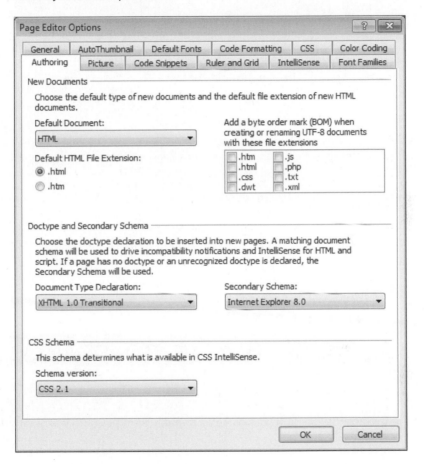

Tip The DOCTYPE of a file in Expression Web 4 dictates the IntelliSense, compatibility, validity, and accessibility testing rules. If you change a DOCTYPE, Expression Web 4 changes the way it treats the page code. Don't conclude, however, that using a looser or lower DOCTYPE is a cure for old sites that you're trying to clean up by using Expression Web 4. Generally, it's best to add a modern DOCTYPE and bring the code up to that standard.

Verifying and Addressing W3C Validity

One of the functions of the W3C is to maintain a set of standards that define valid code. You can visit the W3C Web site at *http://w3c.org*. Expression Web 4 is predisposed to meet those standards by writing valid HTML/XHTML code as required by the DOCTYPE declaration in the page, as you saw in the previous exercise. By ensuring that your page's code complies with validity standards, you will automatically make sure that it renders as consistently as possible in various browsers, and you'll also make it more understandable for search engines and alternative browsers.

Check page validity procedure

In this exercise, you will check the validity of the source code in the sample page, examine very old and invalid HTML code, and use Expression Web to fix it.

> **Note** Use the Chapter5.html page of the SampleSite site you opened in the previous exercise. Open this book's sample site and Chapter5.html page, if they aren't already open.

To check page validity, follow these steps:

1. Click Split at the lower left of your workspace if the page isn't already in Split view. Then, on the lower-right side of your workspace, click the drop-down arrow next to the Compatibility warning.

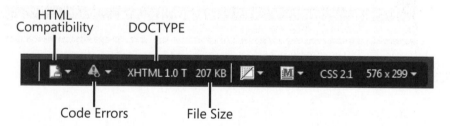

2. In the pop-up dialog box, click Run Compatibility Checker. The Compatibility Checker dialog box opens.

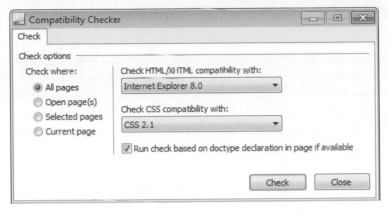

3. In the Compatibility Checker dialog box, select Open Page(s). Accept the other default values, and then click Check. The Compatibility panel opens at the bottom of your workspace. This panel shows all the issues that the Compatibility Checker uncovered.

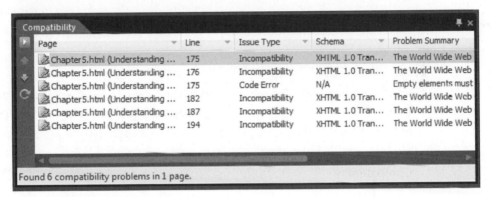

On the left side of the Compatibility panel, you will see a series of four buttons:

- Run Compatibility Checker

- Next Result

- Previous Result

- Refresh Changed Results

All the report panels in Expression Web have buttons with similar functions. You will learn more about other reports in subsequent chapters.

4. Click the Next Result button. Expression Web will focus on the very first incompatible segment of code in the Code panel of your workspace.

5. Point to the highlighted code, and you will see a tooltip that describes the particular issue that needs to be corrected. In most cases, the tooltip text will be identical to the Problem Summary displayed in the Compatibility pane.

6. Because the Compatibility Checker automatically selects the incompatible code, press the Delete key to remove the offending code from the page.

7. Click the Next Result button, and repeat the process to remove the *align* attribute from the next incompatible tag.

8. Click the Next Result button again to highlight the next issue. This time, the problem isn't an "outdated" tag, but an actual code error. Point to the highlighted code and examine the tooltip. The problem is that there's an image tag without a closing slash (/), and because the Compatibility Checker is checking the code for XHTML compatibility, tags without either a closing slash or a closing tag aren't allowed. Add a closing slash to the image tag just before the closing bracket. Thus, this existing code,

```
<img alt="" height="750" src="images/side.jpg" width="150" >
```

will look like this after you add the closing slash:

```
<img alt="" height="750" src="images/side.jpg" width="150" />
```

9. Continue to click the Next Result button and cycle through all the errors the Compatibility Checker has found. Each time your interface focuses on an incompatible tag or attribute, press the Delete key to remove it from the code.

10. When you've completed fixing the final issue in the list, click the Refresh Changed Results button.

    Congratulations! You've remedied all the incompatible code. You can see that there are no remaining issues in the Compatibility pane and that the Incompatibility Warning on the lower right of your workspace now shows a green checkmark. The check mark indicates that the page is fully compatible with the DOCTYPE declaration at the beginning of the page's source code.

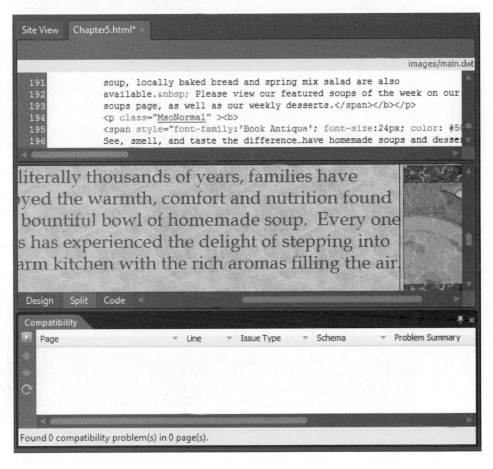

11. Click the Save button and then close the Compatibility pane by clicking the small "x" icon at the upper-right side of the panel. Your interface returns to Split view.

You might notice that the page is visibly different than it was when you began repairing the compatibility issues. This is because without the *align* attribute or some other method to make the image float to the right of the text, it will float left and displace the text or any other content that was located on its right side.

12. Right-click the image that was previously floated to the right, and from the context menu, select Picture Properties. The Picture Properties dialog box opens. Click the Appearance tab.

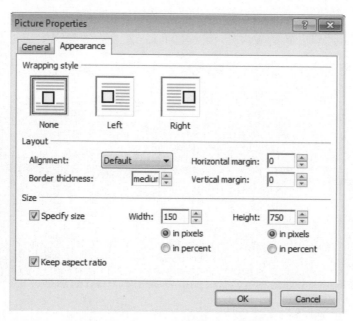

13. Under the Wrapping Style category, click Right, and then click OK. The page returns to its previous appearance.

The image now floats to the right of the text because Expression Web added the *class="auto-style1"* to the image tag, and then defined that class in the <head> section of the page as *.auto-style1 {float: right;}*.

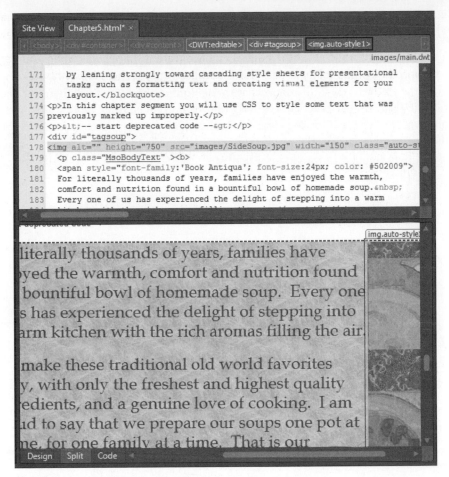

14. Click Save on the Common toolbar to save your changes.

 Note Leave the SampleSite site open if you are proceeding directly to the next section.

In this exercise, you used Expression Web's Compatibility tools to rectify several existing issues in a page's HTML code. Although this was a trivial example designed to let you become familiar with the Compatibility tools and the work you can do with them, consider the much more powerful scenario of using the All Pages selection on the Compatibility Checker to find and address every code incompatibility in an entire Web site.

 Tip To see this validation process in effective use, visit the W3C validation engine at *validator.w3.org*, and test a page from any popular Web site. You may be shocked by how badly some popular sites fail validation.

Verifying and Addressing Accessibility

Accessibility relates to the way a page is structured, and how it will render in devices that are used by people who have vision problems or who need other special browser considerations.

Good HTML/XHTML practices such as using valid code, meaningful *alt* tags, avoiding reliance on JavaScript or Flash for key elements such as navigation, and selecting font colors and sizes that will not present problems to differently abled individuals. Using meaningful descriptive text within object tags for videos, Flash, Microsoft Silverlight, and so forth, will also help to prevent most accessibility problems.

Use the Accessibility Checker

In this exercise, you will set up an accessibility issue and then use the Accessibility Checker in Expression Web to identify the issue and correct it.

Tip A side benefit of building accessible pages is the fact that when you create and structure pages so that they're accessible to alternative devices, they automatically become easier for search engines to derive meaning from.

Note Use the Chapter5.html page of the SampleSite site you opened in the previous exercise. Open this book's sample site and the Chapter5.html page, if they aren't already open.

To verify and address accessibility, follow these steps:

1. From the Tools menu, select Accessibility Reports to open the Accessibility Checker.

   In the Accessibility Checker dialog box, you will see three groups of options: Check Where, Check For, and Show. Check Where is self-explanatory, as is Show. The Check For category contains three options:

   - **WCAG Priority 1**   Web Content Accessibility Guidelines released in May, 1999 (*http://www.w3.org/TR/WCAG10/*)

   - **WCAG Priority 2**   Web Content Accessibility Guidelines released in December, 2008 (*http://www.w3.org/TR/WCAG20/*)

   - **Access Board Section 508**   Section 508 of the U.S. Rehabilitation Act, which outlines the U.S. Government accessibility standards for a wide range of information sources and technologies (*http://www.access-board.gov/sec508/standards.htm*)

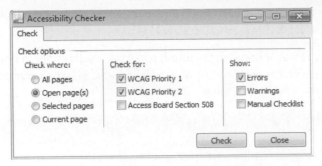

2. Using the default Accessibility Checker settings, click Check. The Accessibility panel opens below the Design pane and shows errors that exist in the open page. In this page, you won't find any accessibility issues. Close the Accessibility panel. Because there aren't any accessibility issues in this page, you will need to create one for example purposes.

3. In the Design pane, click the image on the right side of the *div id="tagsoup"* code to select it. Expression Web also selects the code for the image in the Code pane. In the Code pane, remove the *alt* attribute (*alt=""*) from the *image* tag. WCAG requires that every image must have an *alt* attribute even if the attribute is empty (such as *alt=""*).

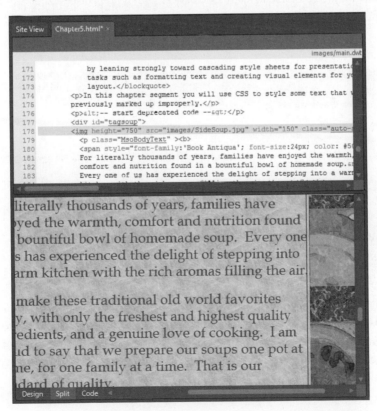

4. On the Common toolbar, click Save. From the Tools menu, select Accessibility Reports to open the Accessibility Checker. In the Check Where category, click Open Page, and in the Check For category, make sure WCAG Priority 1 and WCAG Priority 2 are selected, and then click Check.

Errors are now visible in the Accessibility panel.

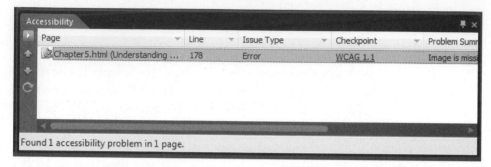

Rather than simply replacing the previously removed *alt* attribute, it's better to put something meaningful there.

5. Set the cursor in the *image* tag that you modified in step 3, and type **alt="Homemade soups from our family to yours"**.

6. In the Accessibility panel, click Refresh. The error disappears.

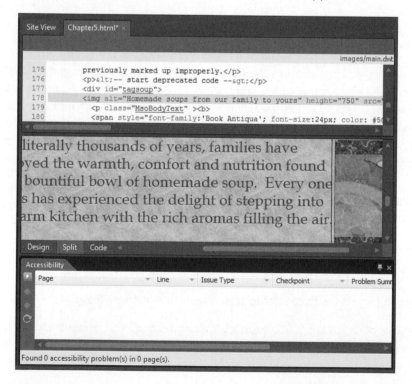

7. Click the Close icon on the Accessibility panel to close it, and then click Save on the Common toolbar.

Although this was a trivial error and remedy, the Accessibility Checker is a powerful tool, especially when you consider that the designer can check every page in an entire Web site at once, and then use the Accessibility panel to cycle through all of the issues while they remedy them.

Note Leave the SampleSite site open if you are proceeding directly to the next section.

Tip You can find another excellent accessibility checker at *http://contentquality.com*. This is the HiSoftware Cynthia Says Portal, an education and outreach project of HiSoftware, ICDRI, and the Internet Society Disability and Special Needs Chapter. At the time of this writing, the site provided a link to a document entitled "The Accessibility Handbook," which serves well as an enhanced learning aid for this topic.

Styling Text with Cascading Style Sheets

Separation of content from presentation is a cornerstone of modern Web standards and practices. Expression Web 4 helps you with this separation by leaning strongly toward cascading style sheets for presentational tasks, such as formatting text and creating visual elements for your layout.

In this exercise, you will examine the deprecated HTML markup that you used when addressing the compatibility issues earlier in this chapter. By doing so, you'll gain an understanding of what the deprecated markup was supposed to do. Then you can improve it by stripping the markup from the HTML code and restyling it with cascading style sheets. These improvements will reduce the overall amount of HTML code and make the code easier to manage and modify in the future.

Use cascading style sheets to style text

Note Use the Chapter5.html page of the SampleSite site you opened in the previous exercise. Open this book's sample site and Chapter5.html page, if they aren't already open.

To begin styling text with cascading style sheets, follow these steps:

1. If your page isn't in Split view, click Split at the bottom of the workspace to display the page in Split view. In the Design pane, click within the *div* containing the soup text, and

then on the Quick Tag Selector, click the *<div#tagsoup>* button. Set your cursor just before *<div id="tagsoup">* in the Code pane and press Ctrl+/ to insert an HTML comment.

```
175        previously marked up improperly.</p>
176        <p>&lt;-- start deprecated code --&gt;</p>
177        <!-- --><div id="tagsoup">
178        <img alt="Homemade soups from our family to yours" height="750" src="
179          <p class="MsoBodyText" ><b>
180          <span style="font-family:'Book Antiqua'; font-size:24px; color: #5(
181          For literally thousands of years, families have enjoyed the warmth,
182          comfort and nutrition found in a bountiful bowl of homemade soup.&r
183          Every one of us has experienced the delight of stepping into a war
184          kitchen with the rich aromas filling the air.</span></b></p>
185          <p class="MsoBodyText" ><b><span style="font-family:'Book Antiqua',
186          We make these traditional old world favorites daily, with only the
187          and highest quality ingredients, and a genuine love of cooking.&nbs
```

2. In the Code pane, scroll down a few lines until you see this segment of HTML code: *<span style="font-family:'Book Antiqua'; font-size:24px; color: #502009">*. That selection of markup gets repeated continually in this *div* and it serves as the main text styling. Copy that code and paste it inside of the HTML comment you created in step 1.

This method of making a note works well so that you don't forget which markup was controlling the appearance of the text after you remove that markup in the next few steps. Notice also that the code contains bold tags *<b>*, which are also deprecated.

```
175        previously marked up improperly.</p>
176        <p>&lt;-- start deprecated code --&gt;</p>
177        <!-- <span style="font-family:'Book Antiqua'; font-size:24px; color: #502
178        <img alt="Homemade soups from our family to yours" height="750" src="imag
179          <p class="MsoBodyText" ><b>
180          <span style="font-family:'Book Antiqua'; font-size:24px; color: #502009
181          For literally thousands of years, families have enjoyed the warmth,
182          comfort and nutrition found in a bountiful bowl of homemade soup. 
183          Every one of us has experienced the delight of stepping into a
184          kitchen with the rich aromas filling the air.</span></b></p>
185          <p class="MsoBodyText" ><b><span style="font-family:'Book Antiqua'; fon
186          We make these traditional old world favorites daily, with only the fres
187          and highest quality ingredients, and a genuine love of cooking.  I
```

3. Return to the Design pane and click inside of the *div* that you just added the HTML comment to above. On the Quick Tag Selector at the top of the Code pane, click the button *<div#tagsoup>*, and then click the drop-down arrow that appears. From the pop-up menu, choose Select Tag Contents.

4. Right-click the Design pane, and in the context menu, click Cut. From the Edit menu, click Paste Text. In the Paste Text dialog box, select Normal Paragraphs Without Line Breaks, and then click OK.

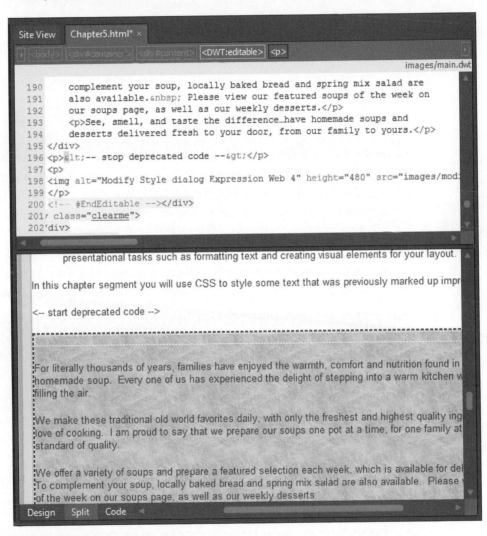

In addition to the <p> tags, every piece of markup in this segment has been removed, including the image, which you'll replace in the next few steps.

Examine both the Code and Design panes. You can see that all the formatting has been removed. The text looks like other text on the page outside the <div> you've been working on. It's now time to apply cascading style sheets markup and restore the text's original appearance, but this time, in a clean and manageable way.

5. In the Apply Styles panel at the lower right of the workspace, click New Style. The New Style dialog box opens.

6. Make sure the Define In field shows Current Page, and in the Selector field, type **#tagsoup p**. You're targeting the *p* tags that fall within the *#tagsoup div* in which you have been working. In the Font-Family field, type **Book Antiqua, Palatino, Palatino Linotype, Serif**.

   This multi-font specification warrants deeper explanation. Although the original font specification was Book Antiqua, you can't be sure that all visitors will have that font installed on their computer systems. If they don't, their browsers will substitute another font—a substitution over which you have no control. To regain a measure of control, you can specify multiple fonts. Palatino Linotype is for Windows systems that lack Book Antiqua, Palatino is for Mac systems, and Serif will at least result in a serif font when a visitor's system has none of the previously listed fonts installed.

> **Note** In cascading style sheets, you are required to enter double quotes around font names that contain a space (such as Book Antiqua and Palatino Linotype), but to make working in cascading style sheets a little easier, Expression Web 4 wraps multi-word font names in quotes for you automatically.

7. In the Font-Size field, type **150**, and in the drop-down list beside it, click the percent sign (%).

   Although the original code specified a font size of 24 pixels, it is much better to specify the font size as a percentage of normal size, because that gives users with alternative browsers or with custom browser settings the ability to see fonts as they prefer, but the designer still retains some styling control.

8. In the Font-Weight field, click the drop-down, and then click Bold. Lastly, in the Color field, type **#502009**, which was the color specified in the original font markup.

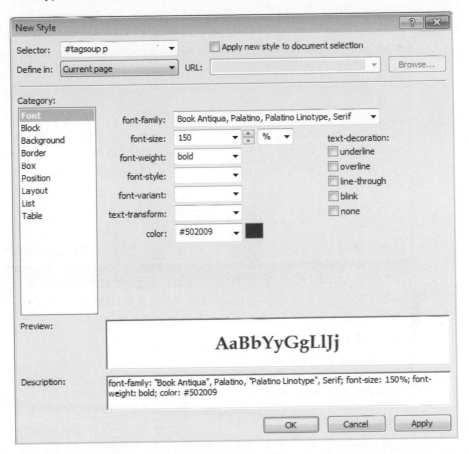

Tip You can probably see why you were instructed to make the HTML comment containing the original font specification. Putting a note in the code of a page before you clear formatting from page elements is a big advantage. Also, because you can copy and paste from your original source code comment, it's a better method than using pencil and paper.

9. Click OK to save your changes and return to Split view in Expression Web. Take a moment or two to look at the Design pane view of the *#tagsoup div*. You will see text that looks very similar to its original appearance. However, if you look in the Code pane representation of this *div*, you will notice that absolutely no markup was added.

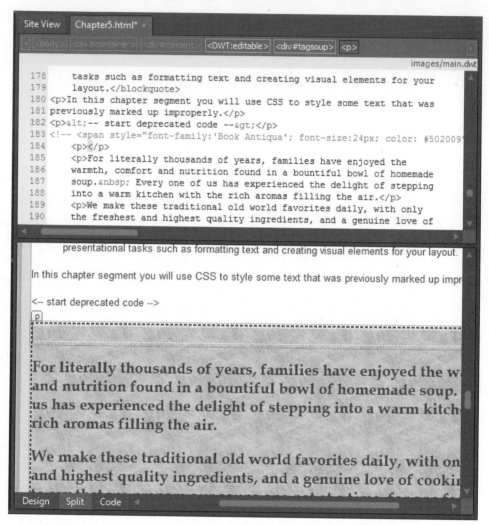

10. To see where all your new formatting specifications occurred, scroll to the top of the file in the Code pane and look for the *style* entries just below the *<title>* element. The first one (*#tagsoup*) was there before you started, but the second entry (*#tagsoup p*) is the direct result of what you just did in the New Style dialog box.

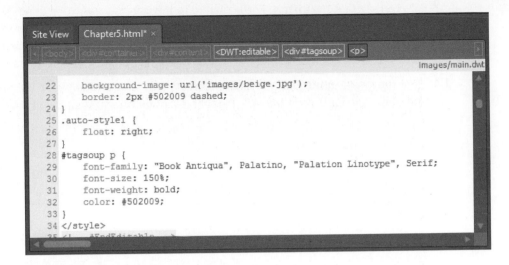

```
Site View    Chapter5.html* ×

<body>  <div=container>  <div=content>  <DWT:editable>  <div #tagsoup>  <p>

                                                              Images/main.dwt
22     background-image: url('images/beige.jpg');
23     border: 2px #502009 dashed;
24 }
25 .auto-style1 {
26     float: right;
27 }
28 #tagsoup p {
29     font-family: "Book Antiqua", Palatino, "Palation Linotype", Serif;
30     font-size: 150%;
31     font-weight: bold;
32     color: #502009;
33 }
34 </style>
35
```

Tip If you noticed the empty *<p>* tag at the top of the *div*, that's there because of the image that was inside of the *div* originally. When an image is in your clipboard, and you paste it as text in paragraphs, Expression Web places an empty paragraph tag where the image was.

11. Set your cursor inside the empty paragraph tag at the top of the text, and then expand the images folder in the Folder List panel. Drag SideSoup.jpg from the Folder List panel to the paragraph where your cursor was set. In the Accessibility Properties dialog box, type **Homemade soups from our family to yours** into the alternate text field, and then click OK.

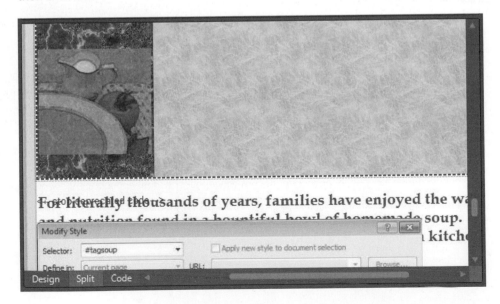

You can see that the image is now aligned to the left as it was when you first removed the *align* attribute earlier in the chapter. Instead of just reapplying the *auto-style1* class that Expression Web generated to get it to float to the left, you will use the cascading style sheets inheritance to make it float to the right.

12. Click the image in the Design pane to select it, and then on the Quick Tag Selector, click the drop-down arrow on the *<p>* tag that it's inside of, and then click Remove Tag.

You're removing the paragraph tag for two reasons. First, it's unnecessary, and secondly, you've already specified the *#tagsoup p* style.

13. In the Apply Styles pane, click New Style, and then type **#tagsoup img** in the Selector field. Click Layout in the Category field, click the drop-down arrow beside Float, and then select Right.

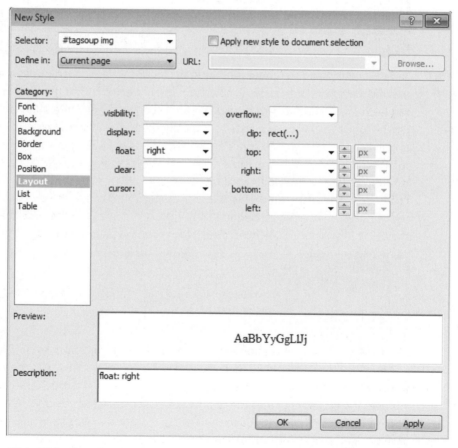

14. Click OK in the New Style dialog box to save your changes, and then click Save on the Common toolbar.

r literally thousands of years, families have enjoyed the
armth, comfort and nutrition found in a bountiful bowl
homemade soup. Every one of us has experienced the
elight of stepping into a warm kitchen with the rich
omas filling the air.

e make these traditional old world favorites daily, with
ly the freshest and highest quality ingredients, and a
nuine love of cooking. I am proud to say that we
epare our soups one pot at a time, for one family at a
me. That is our standard of quality.

e offer a variety of soups and prepare a featured

Design   Split   Code

Take a look in the Code pane rendering of this *div*. What started out as a heavily
marked-up segment of code, is now completely free of all but the most basic HTML
tags—the *<p>* and the *<img>* tags. You've used cascading style sheets to style them,
not by specifically adding a style to the element as Expression Web did for you in the
previous exercise, but by leveraging the inheritance property of cascading style sheets.
Just because these *<p>* and *<img>* tags exist inside of the *<div id="tagsoup">*, they will
take on the style and appearance that you specified using the New Style dialog box.
Look at the file deprecatedHTML.txt in the Files folder to see the exact code that was
inside of this *div* when you began this chapter. Compare it to the code that's inside of
the *div* now, and you'll see how "clean" the code has become through the use of cascading style sheets.

Note You can close the SampleSite site and any open browsers. If you are not continuing
directly to the next chapter, exit Expression Web 4.

In this exercise, you used Expression Web to strip the formatting from some deprecated
HTML. Then you used the Style Builder to create a new style that restored the text's original
appearance. Using styles not only requires less code and results in much cleaner HTML, but
also improves the probability that the text rendering occurred as you intended on systems
without the preferred Book Antiqua font installed. In addition, you have made it easier for
users with unusual screen settings to see and read your text.

Although the 24-pixel font originally specified would be fairly easy for anyone to read, the percentage method you've applied works with text specified in unusually small sizes as well.

You've only just scratched the surface of what you can accomplish with cascading style sheets and Expression Web 4, but hopefully you are beginning to see several powerful and flexible benefits you can enjoy by becoming proficient with this markup methodology.

Key Points

- Using the correct DOCTYPE is necessary for building valid, accessible pages.
- Expression Web 4 helps you maintain W3C validity standards.
- Expression Web 4 helps you check and address accessibility issues.
- Using cascading style sheets helps you style text with fewer markups, simplifies maintenance, and enhances accessibility for people using adaptive browsers.

Chapter 6
Creating a Web Site from Scratch

After completing this chapter, you will be able to:

- Work with a graphics template
- Create an HTML layout
- Style major HTML elements
- Design the site architecture and navigation
- Style for alternative media

In the previous chapters, you have seen some of the basic skills necessary to work efficiently in Microsoft Expression Web, but so far, you've worked only with existing graphics and templates.

In this chapter, you will build on the skills you already know by discovering ways to create graphics for your own custom design, and how to use those graphics to create a Web site template from scratch. These skills will be important whether you decide to create your own graphics or work with an existing Web site template that you customize.

Important Before you can use the practice files in this chapter, you need to download and install them from the book's companion content Web site to their default location. For more information about downloading and installing the practice files, see the "Code Samples" section at the beginning of this book.

Troubleshooting Graphics and operating system-related instructions in this book reflect the Windows 7 user interface. If your computer is running Windows XP or Windows Vista, and you experience trouble following the instructions as written, please refer to the "Information for Readers Running Windows XP or Vista" section at the beginning of this book.

Working with a Graphics Template

A designer can do only so much with colors and basic HTML/CSS layout techniques. At some point, graphics are required. Whether those graphics are used as backgrounds for various page areas, as buttons, icons, other elements, or a combination of these, designers must either create the graphics, or at the very least, be able to work with existing graphics to fine-tune them for use in their Web site layout.

Most Web site designs start with a sketch and an idea of what the end result will be. In this chapter, you will make a very simple Web site layout, and then create the graphics to go with it. The reason that you're going to work with the graphics first is simple: How can you create a layout if you don't know what it's going to look like?

Create and export a simple graphics template

> **Note** Use the Chapter6.html page in the sample site. This site is located in the Documents\ Microsoft Press\Expression Web 4 SBS\ folder. Open the SampleSite site by clicking Open on the Site menu, and then display the Chapter6.html page.

1. From the Site menu, click New. Select One Page Site, and in the location field, replace the automatically generated folder name by typing **Chapter6**. Save the site in the Documents\Microsoft Press\Expression Web 4 SBS\Chapter6 folder.

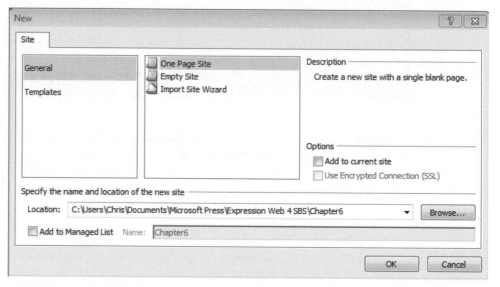

2. Click OK to begin the process of creating the new site.

   This book's Sample Site closes and Expression Web opens your newly created one-page site.

3. Double-click the default.html file to open it in the workspace. If your Editing window isn't already in Split view, click Split at the bottom of the workspace.

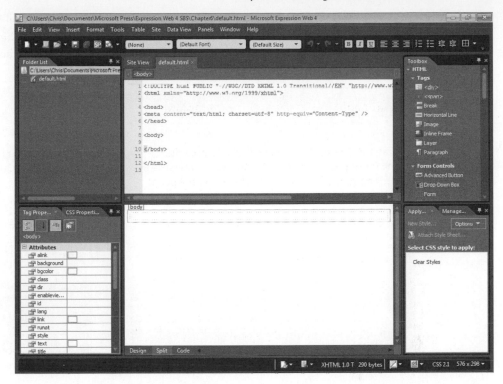

Notice that this is a truly minimal site. The Folder List panel contains just one file, and even the file open in the editing window has bare-minimum content. During the course of this chapter, all this will change radically.

4. From the Windows Start menu, click All Programs, select Microsoft Expression, and then click Microsoft Expression Design 4.

> **Tip** If you don't want to draw your own template, you can open the finished file with Expression Design (Documents\Microsoft Press\Expression Web 4 SBS\Files\CH6-template .design), and then skip forward to step 38.

5. From the File menu, select New. In the New Document dialog box, type **Chapter6** in the Name field; **900 px** in the Width field and **600 px** in the Height field. Type **96 px/inch** in the Resolution field and then click OK.

6. From the View menu, select Show, and then enable Grid, Guides, and Edges.

By showing the visual aids, you will have a better point of reference as you create your layout.

7. In the Toolbox, click the Rectangle tool, and then click and drag a rectangle onto the Artboard.

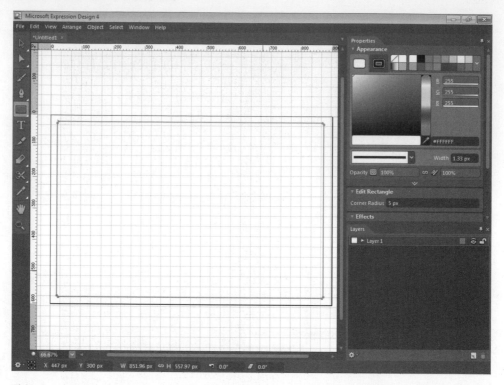

This simple rectangle will serve as the basic "container" for the Web page template. In the next few steps, you will add some visual enhancements to it.

8. Click the Selection tool at the top of the Toolbox, and then click the Artboard outside of the rectangle to hide its marquee so you can see the rectangle's appearance more clearly.

This rectangle is a vector shape and you can manipulate all its properties in Expression Design.

Using the Properties panel, you can adjust most of the shape's appearance properties The size of the shape at this point is not important. Just work on the shape as if it were the outside edge of the content area in a page and adjust it for balance and general appearance.

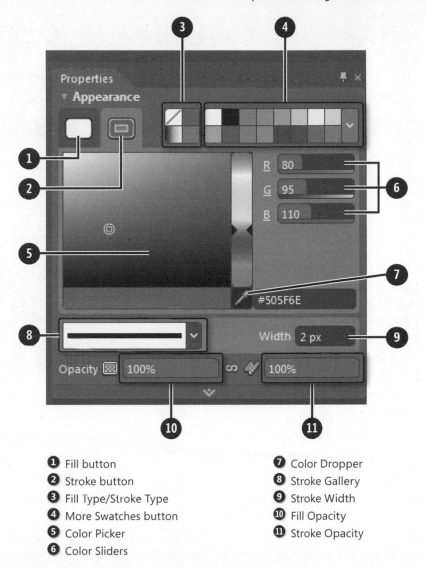

- ❶ Fill button
- ❷ Stroke button
- ❸ Fill Type/Stroke Type
- ❹ More Swatches button
- ❺ Color Picker
- ❻ Color Sliders
- ❼ Color Dropper
- ❽ Stroke Gallery
- ❾ Stroke Width
- ❿ Fill Opacity
- ⓫ Stroke Opacity

 Tip Every shape has a "fill" and a "stroke." The tabs at the top of the appearance category of the Properties panel enable you to control the appearance of each, independently from the other.

9. Click the edge of the rectangle to select it, click the Fill button on the Appearance tab, and then click the white swatch. Click the Stroke button, click the drop-down arrow on the More Swatches button, and then click the #505F6E swatch in the Beach Swatches category.

10. Click the drop-down arrow beside the Stroke Gallery, click Basic Stroke, and then type **2px** in the Width field.

11. In the Effects Panel below the Appearance Panel, click the Add Effects button, point to Effects, and then click Outer Glow. Type **3** in the size field, **0.5** in the Opacity field, and use the Stroke color (#505F6E) for the Glow Color.

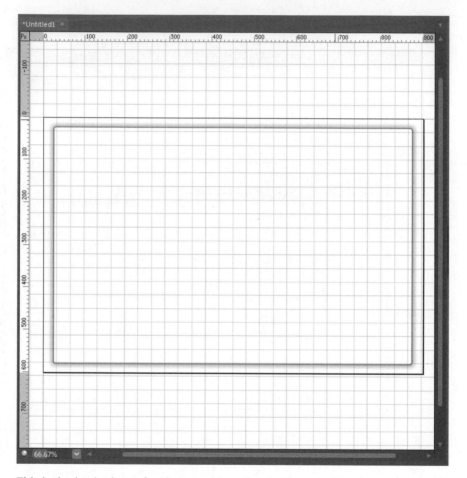

This is the basic shape for the page's content background. In the next few steps, you will create some of the common page areas.

12. Using the action bar at the bottom of your workspace, set the Width to **850 px** and the X position to **450 px**, which centers the rectangle in the middle of the 900-pixel-wide document.

    Because this design will stretch to accommodate any height necessary to contain the Web page content, there is no reason to adjust the height of the shape.

13. Click the Paintbrush tool in the Toolbox, and then drag a horizontal line across the top of your shape to serve as the header area of the template.

14. Click the Stroke button, click the Stroke Gallery drop-down arrow, and then in the General group, click Thin Multi-layer. Set the width to **60px** in the Width field.

15. Click the More Swatches drop-down arrow. Click the #3C78C3 swatch in the Beach Swatches group, and then click the Selection tool in the Toolbox. Drag the anchor points on the selection to adjust the width and height of the brush stroke as necessary. Click the Artboard outside the objects so that you can see the results without the marquee guides.

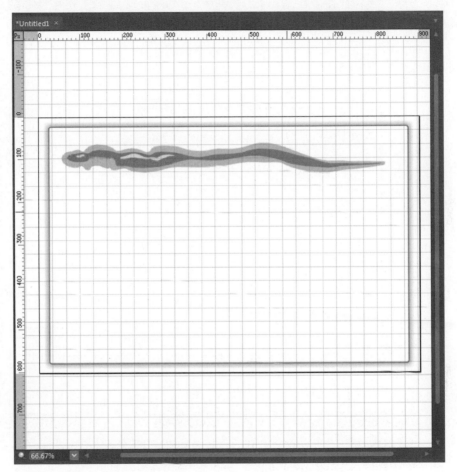

16. Click the Paintbrush tool again. This time, drag a line at the bottom of the rectangle shape where the footer would be.

> **Tip** Drag in the opposite direction than you did for the header to get a more balanced appearance. The Paintbrush tool is designed to behave like a paintbrush, leaving a heavier mark at the beginning of a stroke and a lighter mark at the end.

17. Click the More Swatches drop-down arrow, and then click the #EBDCC3 color in the Beach Swatches category to give this stroke a sandy color. Click the Stroke Gallery drop-down arrow and then click the Fuzzy Thick Wet Brush in the Watercolor category.

18. Click the Selection tool in the Toolbox, and adjust the width and height of the stroke as necessary. As needed, click the Artboard outside of the objects so that you can get a clear view of your work so far.

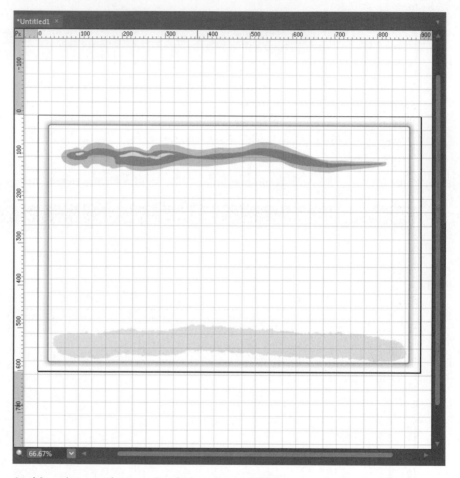

At this point, you have a simple header and footer area; in the next few steps, you will add some additional strokes to help define other page areas.

19. Click the Pen tool, and draw a vertical line starting at approximately the 200 pixel mark from the left side of the Artboard. Click the Stroke Gallery drop-down arrow, and then click Fuzzy Brush in the Ink category.

20. Click the Stroke button at the top of the Appearance panel; click the drop-down arrow beside the More Color Swatches button, and then click #EBDCC3 in the Beach Swatches group.

21. Click the Selection tool in the Toolbox and adjust the height of this line so that it's just touching the stroke at the top and bottom, but not overlapping them.

22. Click and hold the triangle in the lower-right corner of the Rectangle button, and then click the Ellipse button in the pop-up that appears. Drag a circular shape in the upper left of the header.

> **Tip** When you're drawing a line and want it to be straight, hold the Shift key down as you draw. This technique works similarly with the Ellipse tool (to keep a shape circular) and with the Rectangle tool (to keep a shape square).

23. Click the Fill button in the Appearance panel, and then click #EBDCC3 in the Beach Swatches group. Click the Stroke button, and then click #F5C38C to give the shape a different outline. Click the Stroke Gallery drop-down arrow, and then click Geometric Flowers With Stars in the Design Elements category. Drag the Width slider beside the Stroke Gallery to adjust the size of the stroke.

24. Click the Selection tool again and adjust the shape to fit the overall drawing.

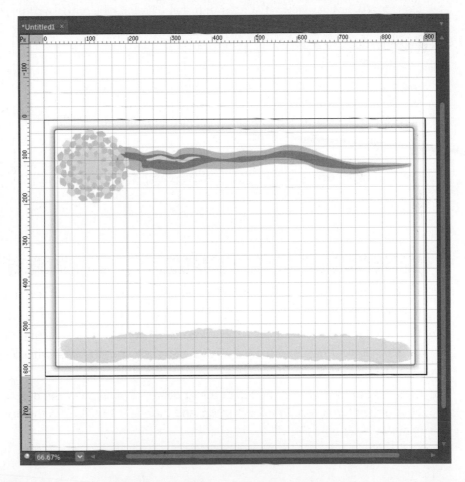

Now that you've drawn these page areas, the next steps are to create some color sample squares and slice the image, so that you can use it in your Web page.

25. Click the Text tool, and set your cursor on the left side of the blue brushstroke at the top of your document. Type **Summer Beach Template**.

Notice that the text follows the center line of the brushstroke. If the text doesn't follow the brushstroke, then you've set the text cursor near—but not on—the centerline of the brushstroke.

26. Press Ctrl+A on your keyboard to select all the text you entered, then in the Text group of the Properties panel, select **Lucida Calligraphy, 36 pt**. Click the More Swatches drop-down arrow, and then click #967878 in the Beach Swatches category.

27. Click the Stroke button, and then click the black swatch to put an outline around the text, which will give it better separation from the background.

28. Click and hold the triangle in the lower right of the Ellipse button, and then click the Rectangle tool in the pop-up. Drag six small rectangles onto the document just above the footer brush stroke.

Don't worry about uniformity or size and shape here. Think of these squares as simple containers to hold the color samples that you will use in Expression Web to color your text, headers, links, and so on.

29. Click the Selection tool, and organize the squares so that they're out of the way of the other page elements. Click the first square on the Artboard. Then, in the Beach Swatches category, click a color that you would like to use in your HTML template. Repeat this process to assign a different color from the Beach Swatches category to each of the six shapes.

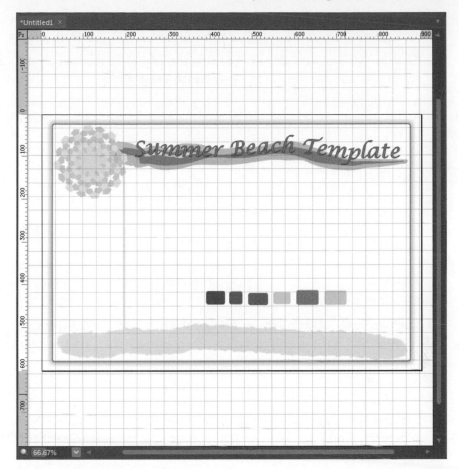

The colors that designers choose are up to them, based on individual preferences and the end goals of their design, but for this exercise, use these colors: **#1E4173**, **#55555A**, **#505F6E**, **#F5C38C**, **#967878**, and **#EBC3C3** (from left to right). These choices give you three cool colors and three warm colors to work with. By putting these colored squares on the Artboard, you can easily select the colors for your HTML and CSS as you build your page template in Expression Web.

30. Click the Slice tool in the Toolbox, and drag a slice from the upper-left corner of your document to the right side. Create a slice around the header graphics. The slice will be **900px** wide and the height will be such that it will contain the circular shape and the horizontal brushstroke.

 Tip You can switch from the Slice tool to the Selection tool to adjust the size and shape of a slice, just as you can a shape.

31. Click and drag a slice at the bottom of the document to contain the footer graphics. This slice will be similar to the header slice but with a little less height.

32. Next, drag a slice across the width of your document just below the header slice. This slice should be **900px** wide, and about **20px** high. Finally, draw a slice around the color squares you added to the document.

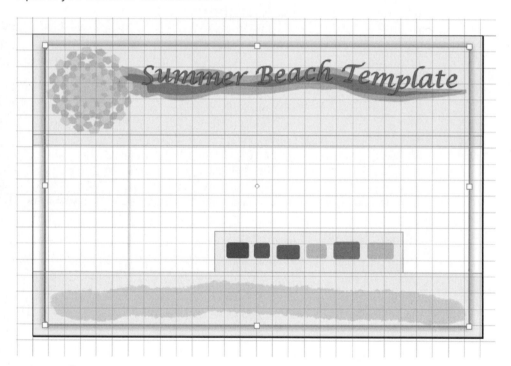

Now that the slices are drawn, you will use the Properties panel to name them and specify their export file format.

33. Click the Selection tool, and then click the top slice on the document. In the Properties panel, click **JPEG** beside the Format field, and type **header** into the Slice Name field.

34. Click the next slice below the header slice. Click **JPEG** beside the Format field, and type **container** into the Slice Name field.

35. Click the slice that contains the colored squares, select **JPEG** beside the Format field, and type **colors** into the Slice Name field.

36. Click the bottom slice, select **JPEG** beside the Format field, and type **footer** into the Slice Name field.

37. Click File, click Save, and then in the Save As dialog box, navigate to the One Page Site you made at the beginning of this section (Documents\Microsoft Press\Expression Web 4 SBS\Chapter6), type **template.design** into the File Name field, and then click Save.

38. Click File, click Export, and then in the Export dialog box, select Slices in the Items To Export field. Click the drop-down arrow beside the Container Name field, and select **HTML & Images**. Click the Browse button beside the Location field, and browse to Documents\Microsoft Press\Expression Web 4 SBS\Chapter6 in the Export Location dialog box. Then click Save.

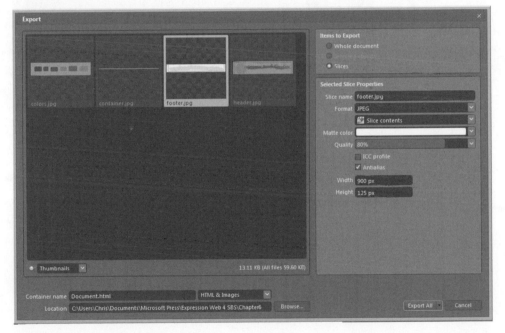

39. Click Export All in the Export dialog box. Expression Design *rasterizes* all the slices and exports a document (Document.html) and the images into the One Page Site you created at the beginning of this exercise.

40. Close Expression Design, return to Expression Web, select Recalculate Hyperlinks from the Tools menu, and then double-click Document.html in the Folder List panel to open it in the editing window.

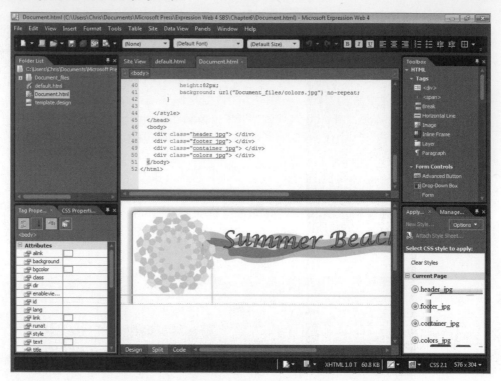

Take a few minutes to examine the Design and Code panes of the Document.html file. You can see that Expression Design has created a page with a *div* for each of the slices that you created, and created CSS code to utilize the sliced images as the backgrounds of these areas.

41. Switch to the default.html file and expand the Document_files folder in the Folder List panel. Click colors.jpg, and then press the Shift key while clicking header.jpg to select all the files in that folder. Drag the files from the folder onto the Design pane of the default.html file. Click OK on each of the Accessibility Properties prompts, because you're just dropping the files onto the page for reference and not for an actual production use. Click Save on the Common toolbar to save the page.

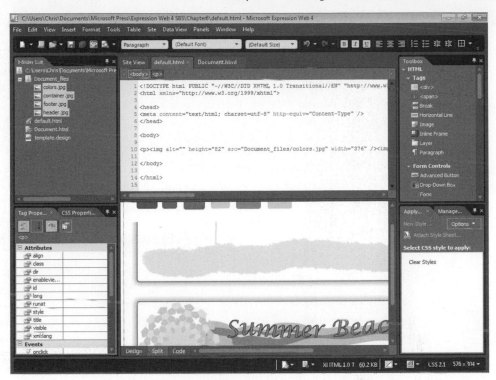

By following these steps, you've just created a graphics package that you can use as build-ing blocks for a Web page template. Although the work in Expression Design was purpose-fully simple, the level of detail that a designer can control is virtually unlimited. Consider gradients, multiple layers, live effects, and so on. For modern Web sites, the graphics tool is in many ways more pivotal to being able to create or modify a Web page template than the HTML editor.

If you liked using Expression Design, you might consider the book *Microsoft Expression Design Step by Step* as a learning resource. You'll also find more good tutorials and sample files for Expression Design on the Microsoft Web site.

 Tip There are links to more Expression Design materials in the Sample Site's Chapter6.html file.

 Note Click Exit on the File menu to close Expression Design. If you are continuing directly to the next exercise, leave Expression Web and the Chapter6.html file open. Otherwise, click Exit on the File menu to close Expression Web.

Creating an HTML Layout

Now that you have the basic graphics layout created, sliced, and exported, you can go about the tasks required to implement these graphics in an HTML layout. Because of the steps in the previous chapter, such as naming the slices with meaningful names and slicing the graphics in specific sizes, the following steps will be much easier and require much less trial and error, and fewer revisions.

In this exercise, you will create your initial layout in an HTML page even though it will eventually be moved to a Dynamic Web Template (DWT). This is because you can easily preview an HTML page in a browser, but it's not so easy with a DWT. The cascading style sheet (CSS) you create will also be written in the HTML layout page itself, instead of an external style sheet. Eventually you will move the CSS from the HTML file to its own style sheet, but for speed and ease of use, it's just more efficient to work with a single file as you refine the HTML layout.

Create an HTML layout

> **Note** Using the Chapter6 site that you created in the previous exercise, open the default.html file if it isn't still open from the previous exercise.

1. Click and drag the *<div>* tag from the Toolbox on the upper-right side of the user interface to the Code pane just below the *<body>* tag of the default.html file.

```
Site View    default.html* ×    Document.html

1  <!DOCTYPE html PUBLIC "-//W3C//DTD XHTML 1.0 Transitional//EN" "http://www.w3
2  <html xmlns="http://www.w3.org/1999/xhtml">
3
4  <head>
5  <meta content="text/html; charset=utf-8" http-equiv="Content-Type" />
6  </head>
7
8  <body>
9  <div></div>
10 <p><img alt="" height="82" src="Document_files/colors.jpg" width="376" /><img
11
12 </body>
13
14 </html>
15
```

The *<div>* tag is the backbone of CSS/HTML layout. Its meaning is "division" and it's a block element that works as a container. With CSS, you can apply virtually limitless appearance modifications to it. This template you're using will contain 5 divs when you're done.

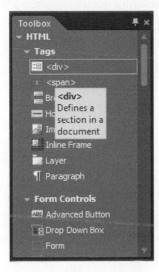

2. In the Design pane, click the Block Selection label to select this entire *div*, and then click New Style in the Apply Styles panel.

3. In the Selector field, enter **#container**. Select the Apply New Style To Document Selection check box, and set the Define In field to Current Page.

4. Click the Background category on the left side of the New Style dialog box. Click the Browse button beside the Background-Image field. Browse to and select container.jpg in the site's Document_files folder. Set the Background-Repeat field to **repeat-y**.

 Tip X is always horizontal and Y is always vertical.

5. Click the Box category and set the padding to **0px** and leave its Same For All check box selected. Clear the Same For All check box beside the Margin field and set the following values: Top: **0px**, Right: **auto**, Bottom: **0px**, Left: **auto**.

    The margin-right and margin-left selections enable you to float the container in the middle of the screen. This is one of the most common questions with CSS layout and it's remarkably simple to do.

6. Click the Position category, and then set the width to **900px**, and the height to **100%**.

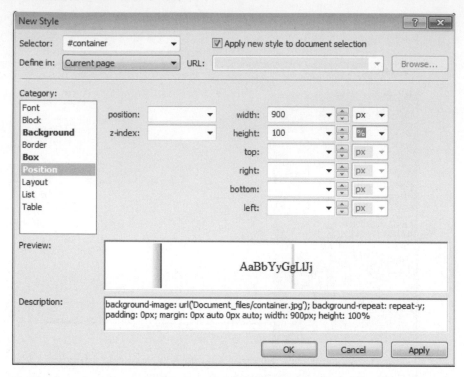

Notice that you can see all the styles in the Description field of the New Style dialog box.

7. Click OK in the New Style dialog box to set your changes.

Although it might not look like much at this point, you've just set up the basic container for this entire template.

8. Drag another *<div>* from the Toolbox panel into the *div* that you just styled.

Before you begin styling this *div*, you will need to know the height and width of the underlying image. Click the header image in the Design pane of your workspace. Look at the Code pane. You can see that it's 900 pixels wide and 200 pixels high.

9. Select the *div* that you just added to the page by clicking its Block Selector tag in the Design pane, and then click New Style in the Apply Styles pane.

10. Enter **#header** in the Selector field, select the Apply New Style To Document Selection check box, and make sure that the Define In field is set to Current Page.

11. Click the Background category, click the Browse button beside the background-image field, and then browse to and select header.jpg in the site's Document_files folder. Set the Background-Repeat field to **no-repeat**.

12. Click the Box category and set padding and margin to **0px**. Leave both the padding and margin Same For All check boxes selected.

13. Click the Position category, and type **900px** in the Width field and **200px** in the Height field.

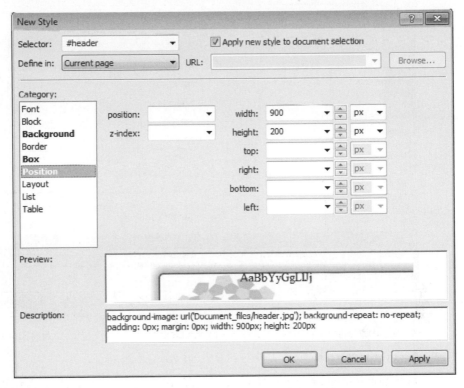

14. Click OK in the New Style dialog box to set your changes.

15. In the Design pane, set your cursor in the Header *div* you just styled, and then type **Header**.

This is recommended for two reasons: some browsers won't display *div* tags that have no content, and it provides good visual reference in the Design pane.

16. Drag another *<div>* from the Toolbox panel into the Code pane just after the closing *</div>* tag that you just typed the word "Header" into. Type **Menu** into this *div*.

> **Important** It's imperative that you're careful in these steps. You want the *divs* that you're inserting to be "nested" inside the Container *div*, but not inside each other.

17. Drag another *<div>* from the Toolbox panel into the Code pane after the closing *</div>* tag that you typed the word "Menu" into. Type the word **Content** inside it.

18. Drag another *<div>* from the Toolbox panel into the Code pane after the closing *</div>* tag that you typed "Content" into, and then type **Footer** into this *div*. Click Save on the Common toolbar.

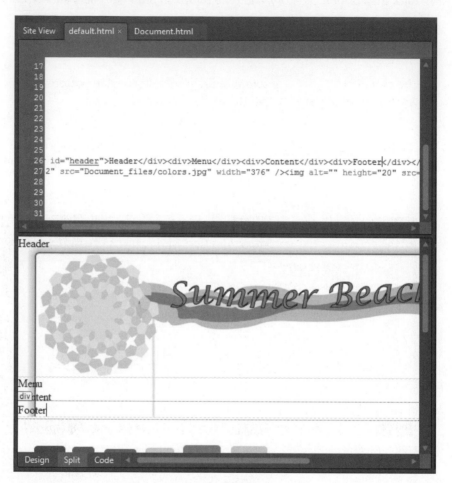

19. Right-click the Code pane, and from the Context menu, select Reformat HTML.

This step will organize the Code pane for you and make working on this template easier.

20. Click the Block Selection tab in the Design pane for the Footer *div*, and then click New Style in the Apply Styles panel.

21. Enter **#footer** in the Selector field, select the Apply New Style To Document Selection check box, make sure the Define In field is set to Current Page, and then click the Background category.

22. Click the Browse button beside the Background-Image field, and then browse to and select footer.jpg in the site's Document_files folder. Set the Background-Repeat field to **no-repeat**.

23. Click the Box category, set padding and margin to **0px**, and then leave both padding and margin Same For All check boxes checked.

24. Click the Position category, and type **900px** in the Width field and **125px** in the Height field.

25. Click the Layout category, and set the Clear field to **both**, and then click OK to set your changes and close the New Style dialog box.

The *clear: both* style will ensure that the footer stays at the bottom of the design and won't be overlapped by either the content or menu divisions.

> **Tip** The reason you were instructed to drag the images into the page is to serve as a reference while you're building these styles. Click the image in the Design pane and then look at the height and width attributes in the Code pane.

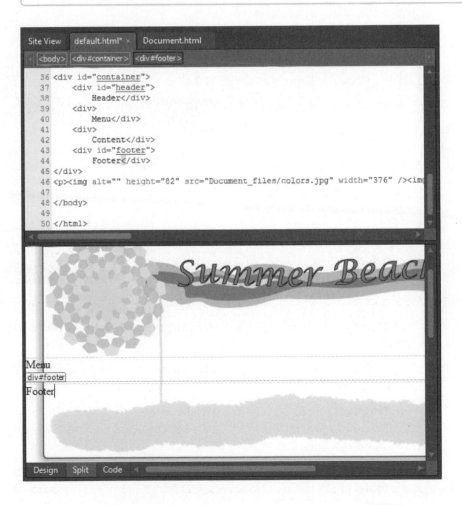

At this point, your HTML template is starting to take shape. Notice how the Menu and Content divisions are stacked horizontally. This is because the default appearance of a *div* is a *block element* 100% wide. In the next few steps, you will adjust these *divs* so that they line up beside each other vertically.

26. Click the Block Selection tag in the Design pane for the Menu *div*, and then click New Style in the Apply Styles panel.

27. Enter **#menu** in the Selector field, select the Apply New Style To Document Selection check box, and make sure Current Page is set in the Define In field.

28. Click the Position category, and type **200px** in the Width field.

29. Click the Layout category, set the Float field to **left,** and then click OK to set the style and close the dialog box.

30. Click the Block Selection tag in the Design pane for the Content *div*, and then click New Style in the Apply Styles panel.

31. Enter **#content** in the Selector field, select the Apply New Style To Document Selection check box, and make sure Current Page is set in the Define In field.

32. Click the Position category, and type **700px** in the Width field.

33. Click the Layout category, and set the Float field to **right**.

> **Tip** If you designed the graphics template in Expression Design yourself, it's very likely that your image dimensions will be different. That's why you were instructed to insert the images into the page so you could have quick reference to their sizes by clicking them in the Design pane and looking at their sizes in the Code pane. Just substitute your image measurements where appropriate.

34. Click the colors.jpg image in the Design pane, and press Ctrl+X on your keyboard to cut it. Then set your cursor in the Content *div* and press Ctrl+V to paste it into the *div*.

35. Press the Ctrl key while clicking each of the three images below the Footer *div* tag, and press Delete on your keyboard to delete all of them. Then click the Block Selector tab for the *<p>* tag that contained them.

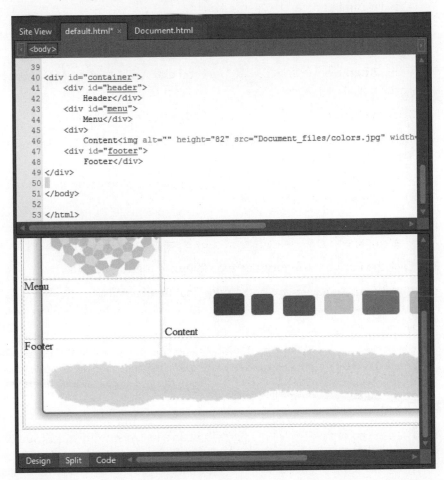

36. Click Save and then click Preview on the Common toolbar to check your work in a browser.

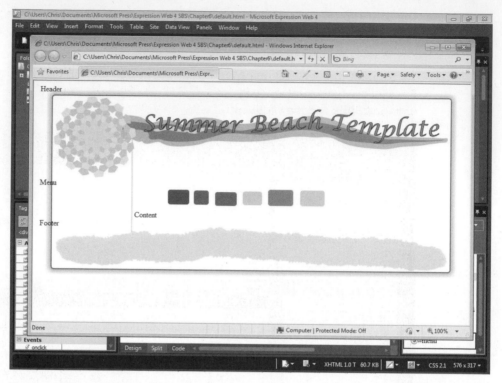

The browser rendering of this template is starting to look close to how it should. There are some details to take care of such as making sure that content inside the *divs* you created will be in the appropriate place, but the point that it's at right now is well past the halfway mark as far as layout is concerned.

37. Close the browser window and return to Expression Web.

The next steps are going to revolve around the CSS Box Model. You can think of a *div* as a box. If you're experienced in layout using tables, you can think of the *div* as a cell. What this template needs is some basic padding so that the content in each cell falls in the approximate location that it should. That will help transition into the next section where you will fine-tune the placement of content.

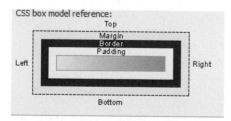

38. Click the CSS Properties tab on the lower left of the user interface to display the CSS Properties panel. Because the Folder List panel isn't going to do anything for you at this point, click the thumbtack icon on its upper-right corner to autohide it.

The CSS Properties panel is ideal for making quick modifications to existing styles, and you'll be using it to take care of the padding requirements for the layout *divs* that you've been working with.

39. Set your cursor in the Design pane, Header *div*. Scroll the CSS Properties down to the Box section. Type **25px** in the Padding field. In the Position group, change the height entry to **150px** and the width entry to **850px**.

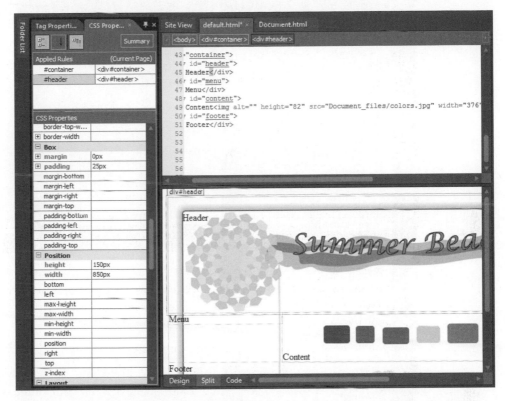

Because you've added 25px of padding to each side of the box model for the header, you have to reduce the width and height specifications to compensate for it.

> **Tip** Notice that many of the categories in the CSS Properties panel have expandable en-tries, such as the padding entry you just worked on. If you make your entries in the fields that are exposed when the item is expanded, you will be creating shorthand CSS code. The entries below the expandable item will create longhand CSS code.

40. Set your cursor in the Menu *div* and scroll the CSS Properties panel down to the Box category again. In this *div*, we don't want padding at the top and the bottom, so click the plus (+) sign next to the padding entry, and enter these values: **0px** in Padding-Top, **25px** in Padding-Right, **0px** in Padding-Bottom, and **25px** in Padding-Left.

This will result in *shorthand CSS* code, which you will look at and compare to similar entries for another *div* in *longhand CSS*.

41. Change the width entry in the Position category to **150px** in order to compensate for the padding you added.

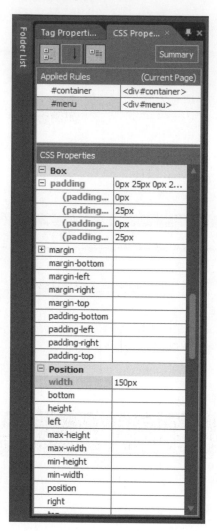

42. Set your cursor in the Content *div* and then scroll the CSS Properties panel down to the Box category. If the padding entry is expanded, click the minus (-) sign to close it and set the padding entries below it to: Padding-Bottom: **0px**, Padding-Left: **10px**, Padding-Right: **35px**, and Padding-Top: **0px**. Change the width entry under the Position category to **655px** to factor for the padding you just added.

43. Set your cursor in the Footer *div* and then scroll the CSS Properties panel down to the Box category. Enter **25px** in the Padding field and then click the plus (+) sign beside it. Notice how the 25px was added to all four padding fields.

44. In the Position category, change the height to **75px** and the width to **850px**, and then in the Block category set the Text-Align field to **center**.

45. Click Save and then click Preview on the Common toolbar to check the results in a browser.

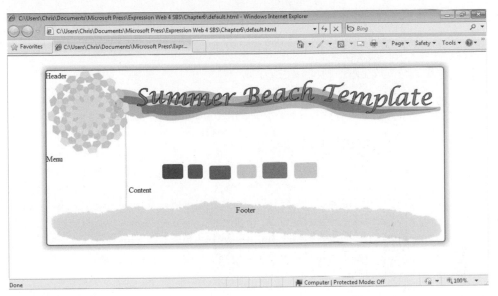

Just by adding some padding specifications to these page divisions, you now have text in the approximate place that it belongs. To further tune the placement, you will style the HTML tags that surround the content itself in the next section.

46. Close the browser and return to Expression Web. Scroll the Code pane to the top so that you can see the style block.

```
33 #menu {
34     padding: 0px 25px 0px 25px;
35     width: 150px;
36     float: left;
37 }
38 #content {
39     width: 655px;
40     padding-bottom: 0px;
41     padding-left: 10px;
42     padding-right: 35px;
43     padding-top: 0px;
44     float: right;
45 }
46 body {
47     font-family: arial, Helvetica, sans-serif;
48     color: #565559;
```

Notice that the #*menu* ID has its padding set in shorthand, and the #*content* ID has its padding set in longhand. This is a direct result of which fields you entered these specifications in using the CSS Properties panel. There isn't all that much difference in the end results when you choose longhand or shorthand CSS, but many users find it easier to read and modify longhand CSS.

> **Note** If you are continuing directly to the next section, leave the Chapter6 site open; otherwise, you can close it.

Although this section took you through the tasks of laying out your graphics in an HTML template, it shouldn't be considered the end of what you need to learn about CSS/HTML layout. You will continue to learn about this topic through trial and error and research that you will conduct as you employ new methods to achieve the results you want. Consider that HTML 5 and CSS 3 are getting closer to release and general usage. As with everything in the Web design and development field, these techniques and standards are in a constant state of flux. The skills you learn by following examples in this book should give you enough familiarity with the concepts so that you can transition into higher-level techniques. There are a lot more books available on CSS than there are on Expression Web, so that should give you an indication of the breadth of knowledge out there on this topic.

Styling Major HTML Elements

In the previous segment, you used cascading style sheets code to style the divisions of an HTML template. Those exercises achieved the goal of getting the page layout arranged, but it also set up the ability to easily style the content that appears within the divisions.

In this section, you will work on styling HTML tags in specific page divisions using cascading style sheets to refine the entire template and the appearance of content that will be included in it.

Using cascading style sheets in this way provides benefits, particularly with a growing site. For instance, all an author has to do is enter text in basic HTML tags, such as heading tags, paragraph tags, and lists. Because the designer set up the cascading style sheets for the template in a well thought out way, the content anyone enters will take on the appearance that the designer intended.

Create CSS styles for HTML markup

> **Note** Using the Chapter6 site that you created in the previous exercise, open the default.html file if it isn't still open.

1. Click the Folder List tab on the upper left of the workspace that you set to autohide, and then click the thumbtack icon to lock it into place. Click the root folder in the Folder List, click File, click Import, and then select File.

2. In the Add File To Import List dialog box, browse to the Documents\Microsoft Press\ Expression Web 4 SBS\Files folder, double-click LazyDogText.txt, and then click OK in the Import dialog box. The file is imported into the root of your site.

3. Double-click LazyDogText.txt in the Folder List panel to open it in the workspace.

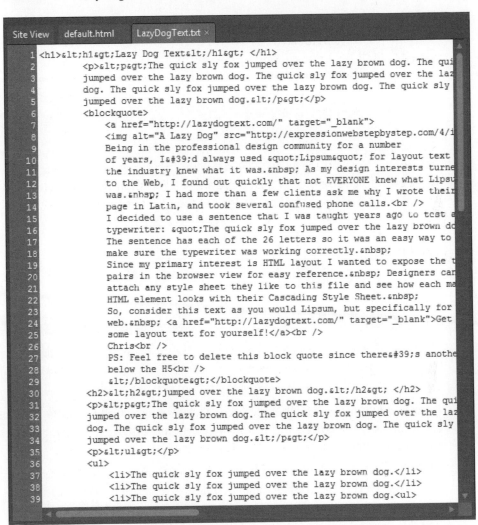

Because you've opened a text file, with a .txt extension, Expression Web will open it in Code view. This text file has been designed to expose each of the 26 letters in the alphabet as well as a collection of the HTML tags most often used in Web page content. This file is helpful when designing CSS styles for content areas of a Web page.

4. Set your cursor in the text file and press Ctrl+A on your keyboard to select all the text. Then press Ctrl+C to copy all the code, and close the file.

5. Double-click the word "Content" in the Design pane, inside the content division of the default.html page, and then in the Code pane, right-click the highlighted word and select Paste from the context menu.

6. Scroll the Design pane to the bottom and click the colors.jpg image to select it. Press Ctrl+X on your keyboard to cut it and then scroll back to the top of the Design pane.

7. Set your cursor in the Design pane just after the *<h1>* text, press Enter on your keyboard to create a new paragraph, and then press Ctrl+V to paste the image into the paragraph.

By moving the colors.jpg image to the top of the page, it'll be easier to sample the colors for use in the CSS work that you're about to do. One of the first things you will accomplish is to get the text colored to match the graphics.

8. In the Apply Styles panel, click New Style, and type **body** into the Selector field. Leave the Apply New Style To Document Selection check box unselected, but make sure the Define In field is set to Current Page.

What you're about to do is style the basic *<body>* tag using cascading style sheets. This is a very global selector, in that any text that isn't specifically styled will take on the properties you're about to set.

9. In the Font category, click the drop-down arrow beside Font-Family and then select Arial, Helvetica, Sans-Serif. Click the drop-down arrow beside the Color field, and then click More Colors. In the More Colors dialog box, click the Select button, then hold the color dropper over the grey color square in the Design pane of your page, click it to set the color (*Hex={56,55,59}*), and then click OK.

10. Click the Background category and then click the drop-down arrow beside the Background-Color field. Click the white swatch (*#FFFFFF*).

Although it might not seem like it's important to set the background to white, it actually is. If an element isn't styled, then it's up to the browser to decide how to present it. In this case, it could be very unattractive because the shadow and background of the graphics are white; the illusion would be ruined if the browser substituted a grey background.

11. Click the Box category. Leave the Same For All check boxes selected and enter **0px** in both Margin and Padding fields, and then click OK to set your changes and close the dialog box.

12. Click Save and then click Preview on the Common toolbar to check the page in a browser.

If you look closely at the browser view, you'll notice that there's less room between the header area of the page and the top of the browser viewport. Because there wasn't any specific margin and padding set for the body tag, the browser simply applied a default padding and margin setting. That's why specifically styling an HTML tag's properties gives you a high level of control. When a page has cross-browser differences, it's usually because of an unstyled HTML element that each browser chose to display your page with a different appearance.

Also notice that all the text now appears in the grey color that you specified. Even though you didn't specifically set the text color for the content division, the parent container of everything on the page is the body tag. So, unless you specify a different font color for one of your divisions, it will appear in grey. By leveraging this inheritance property in CSS, the designer can achieve the maximum visual change with the minimum CSS code.

13. Close the browser and return to Expression Web.

The next styling alteration you will make is to change the color of all the heading tags. You can do this easily by setting up a global style for all the heading tags and then, if needed, specifically styling the headings within certain page divisions.

14. In the Apply Style panel, click New Style. In the New Style dialog box, enter **h1, h2, h3, h4, h5** into the Selector field. Make sure the Apply New Style To Document Selection check box is not selected, and that the Define In field is set to Current Page.

15. Click the drop-down arrow beside the Color field and then click More Colors. Click the Select button, click the color dropper on the mauve color (*Hex={96,78,78}*) in the colors.jpg image in Design view, and then click OK in the More Colors dialog box.

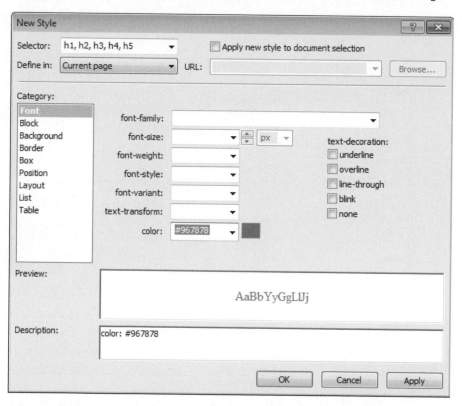

This is a very simple style change. As you can see in the Description field, the only thing that has been added is a color specification. With this slight modification, every heading in the page will now have this color applied to it.

16. Click OK to set your change and close the dialog box.

17. Scroll through the content division in the Design pane of your page. Notice that everything in there is styled except for the links. In the next few steps, you will style those.

18. In the Apply Styles panel, click New Style, and in the Selector field, type **#content a:link, a:visited, a:active**. Make sure that the Apply New Style To Document Selection" check box is not selected, and that the Define In field is set to Current Page.

    In CSS, links are known as Anchor Pseudo-classes. There are four states to a link: default (*a:link*), visited (*a:visited*), active (*a:active*), and hover (*a:hover*). By setting Selector as you did, you've set up all the links which appear in the *#content division* of the page to take on the properties you're about to set. You can also set the style of all links using the *[a]* tag (without the state), which you will see later in this chapter.

19. Click the drop-down arrow beside the Color field and then click More Colors. Click the Select button, click the first blue square in the Design pane view of colors.jpg (Hex={1D,41,73}), and then select the Underline check box, under the text-decoration field.

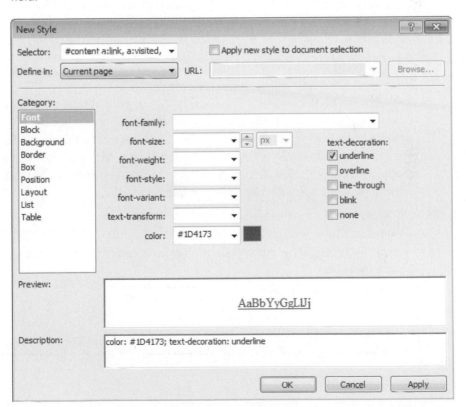

20. Click OK to set your changes and close the dialog box.

Take a look at the Design pane of your page. You'll see that both links in this pane are now styled with the color you selected in the previous step. In the next step, you will use CSS to style what the link looks like when it's hovered.

21. In the Apply Styles panel, click New Style, and type **#content a:hover** into the Selector field. Make sure the Apply New Style To Document Selection check box is not selected, and that the Define In field is set to Current Page.

22. Click the drop-down arrow beside the Color field and then click More Colors. Click the Select button and then click the color dropper over the grey-blue (Hex={4F,5F,6E}) square in the Design pane view of colors.jpg. Click OK in the More Colors dialog box.

23. Select the None check box beneath the Text-Decoration field and then click OK to set your changes and close the dialog box.

24. Click Save and then click Preview on the Common toolbar to check your page in a browser.

Take a few minutes to examine the page and most importantly, the newly styled links in the content area. Make sure that the hover property is working as expected. Styling links is an easy way to provide some interactive feedback to the user. In a content area of a page, you should keep in mind that you don't want to style the link to such an extent that the user doesn't realize that it's a "clickable" link. This isn't a problem in menu areas where the user will assume that your highly styled links are navigation elements.

25. Close the browser window and return to Expression Web.

In the next steps, you will deal with the header division in the page. The end goal of this work will be to create an *h1* that will be below the site title image, and as a bonus, you will learn a technique to include invisible text. The reason for this is simple: the site title is part of the graphics; therefore, it can't be read by screen readers or search engines. We could never achieve this text appearance with plain text so we've used a graphic. To counter this situation, we will use text that will be invisible to a visitor, yet present for search engines and screen readers.

26. Set your cursor in the header division and select the text "Header". Double-click the *<span>* tag in the Toolbox panel on the right side of the editing window. The word "Header" is replaced by *<span></span>*. Set your cursor in this span and type **Summer Beach Template**.

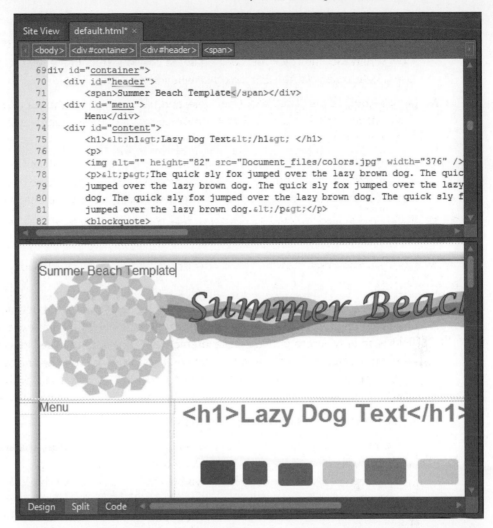

A *<span>* is very similar to a *<div>* with the main difference that a division is a block element by default, and a span is an inline block by default. What that means is you can have a number of spans next to each other horizontally without any modification of the default styles like you have to do with a *<div>*.

27. Click the *<span>* tag on the Quick Tag Selector to select the entire tag and all its contents. Then click New Style on the Apply Styles panel.

28. Type **#sitetitle** into the Selector field, select the Apply New Style To Document Selection check box, and make sure the Define In field is set to Current Page.

29. Click the Block category and enter **-850px** in the Text-Indent field.

This causes the text to be negatively indented by 850px.

30. Click the Position category and enter **850px** in the Width field and **50px** in the Height field.

31. Click the Layout category, set the Overflow field to **hidden**, and then set the Display field to **block**.

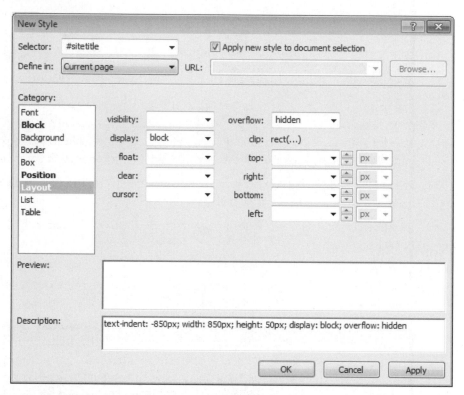

32. Click OK to set your changes and close the dialog box.

Notice in the Design pane of your page that you clearly have a span, but the text isn't visible. This result could also be accomplished by using the display property of "none" or "hidden," but these techniques can be misinterpreted by search engines and your site could be penalized in search results for it.

33. Set your cursor in the Code pane just after the closing *</span>* tag and type **Page Title Goes Here**.

34. Select this text in the Design pane, click the drop-down arrow on the Styles box of the Common toolbar, and then click Heading 1 *<h1>*.

The first *<h1>* in your page is a key to good search engine results. Having an *<h1>*, page title, and URL all matching the meaning of the page content is virtually unbeatable for search engine positioning. Fortunately, CSS can enable you to make this most important heading look like whatever you need it to in order to fit your overall design.

35. Select New Style in the Apply Styles panel. Enter *#header h1* in the Selector field and make sure that the Define In field is set to Current Page.

36. Click the Box category and enter **0px** in the top padding field. Leave the padding Same For All check box selected.

37. Clear the Same For All check box for the margin field and enter **75px** in the Top field, **0px** in the Right field, **0px** in the Bottom field, and **185px** in the Left field. Click OK to set your changes and close the dialog box.

Those simple margin changes have moved the <*h1*> that appears in the Header division to an appropriate position.

38. In the Design pane, double-click the text "Footer" in the footer division of the page to select it and then type **Top**.

In the next few steps, you will create a bookmark link to the top of the page, add some text to the footer, and then fine tune the presentation.

39. Select the word "Top" and then right-click it. In the context menu, choose Hyperlink. In the Insert Hyperlink dialog box, type **#header** into the Address field, and then click OK.

This is a nice little bonus of using CSS IDs on various page elements. You don't need to set up bookmarks and their respective hyperlinks as you would have in the past. Any link to an ID element will behave as a bookmark. So, when you click this link in a browser, the page will automatically reposition to the top.

40. Set your cursor just after the link you inserted and press Shift+Enter on your keyboard to create a line break. Type **Copyright 2010 Summer Beach Template** and then press Shift+Enter on your keyboard again to break to a new line. Type **Terms of Use | Privacy | Contact**.

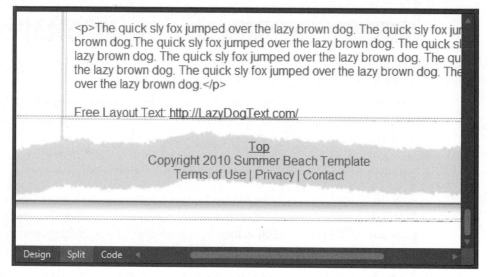

The footer content is beginning to take shape, but it needs a little work to style it appropriately to match the rest of the template.

41. In the Apply Styles panel, point to *#footer*, click the drop-down arrow on it, and then click Modify Style.

42. In the Modify Styles dialog box, enter **12px** in the Font-Size field, **600** in the Font-Weight field, and **#FFFFFF** (white) in the Color field. Click OK to set your changes and close the dialog box.

43. Click New Style on the Apply Styles panel and type **#footer a** into the Selector field. Make sure that the Apply New Style To Document Selection check box is clear and that the Define In field is set to Current Page.

44. Set the color field to #FFFFFF (white) and then click OK to set the change and close the dialog box.

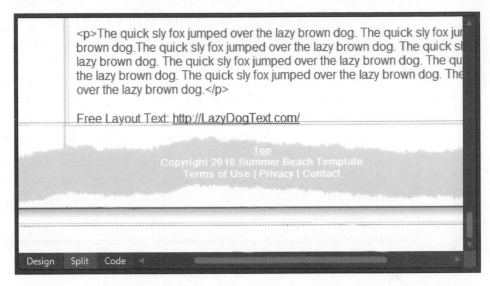

That minor change to the anchor pseudo classes has now matched the current, and any future hyperlinks in the footer, to the rest of the footer text.

45. Scroll the Design pane so that the colors.jpg image is visible, because you'll need to sample the grey color out of it. Click New Style on the Apply Styles panel, and then type **#footer a:hover** into the Selector field. Make sure the Apply New Style To Document Selection check box is not selected, and that the Define In field is set to Current Page.

46 Click the drop-down arrow beside the Color field and then click More Colors. In the More Colors dialog box, click the Select button, and then click the color dropper on the grey color swatch (Hex={56,55,59}) in the colors.jpg image in the Design pane, and then click OK. Click OK in the New Style dialog box to set your changes and close the dialog box.

47. Right-click the Code pane of the page and then in the context menu, choose Reformat HTML. Click Save and then click Preview on the Common toolbar to check your page in a browser. Scroll the page to the bottom and check your footer division and make sure that it appears as expected. Check the hover state of the link you styled and make sure that it does refocus the page to the header division.

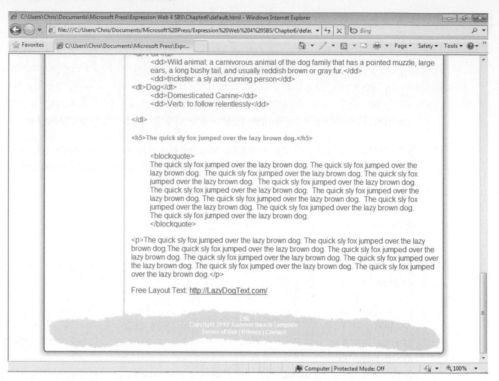

Review the visual presentation of your page. Think about what else you might want to do as a designer, such as setting up CSS styles for the *<blockquote>* or other HTML tags, perhaps adding some style to the HTML list elements, and so on. The choices are endless, and you should feel free to experiment as much as you like.

Although you didn't work on the Menu page division, that's only because the site architecture and navigation haven't been established yet. You will complete those tasks in the next section.

This exercise has been fairly significant, whether it's apparent to you or not. You've styled an HTML template based on a custom graphics composition in a very logical and efficient way, and all the while maintained the appearance you wanted without sacrificing semantic value or HTML validity. You were also able to do this significant work with user-friendly New Style and Modify Style dialog boxes as opposed to manually writing CSS code.

Note If you're not continuing directly to the next exercise, you can close the default.html file and then exit Expression Web.

Designing the Site Architecture and Navigation

The folder structure, page organization, and navigation of a site go hand in hand. Besides keeping the site "clean" and logically organized, the designer has an opportunity to improve usability by designing the basic folder structure of the site. By naming the folders intuitively and pertinently to the information their pages contain, they can actually attain higher search engine results and make it easier for people to share links to specific pages or sections of the site.

In this section, you will arrange the structure of the site, create a Dynamic Web Template to ease the creation, deployment, and maintenance, and then add navigation to tie it all together.

Design the folder structure and navigation for a site

> **Note** Using the Chapter6 site that you created earlier, open the default.html file if it isn't still open from the previous exercise.

1. Double-click the word "Menu" inside the menu page division and type **Home**. Click the bullets button on the Common toolbar to change this text to a list item in an unordered list.

An unordered list is ideal for a navigation menu. What is a navigation menu at its most basic other than a list of links? By creating this list, you'll be able to get an understanding of the coming folder structure, plus when the structure is complete, these list items can be converted to links and styled heavily with CSS.

2. Press Enter on your keyboard after each term, and then type the next term so that you create a list containing **Products**, **Services**, **About Us**, and **Contact Us**. Press the Enter key twice more after the last list item to close the list.

3. Click Save on the Common toolbar to save your changes to the page.

Besides being the beginning of your site navigation, this list also gives you some direction as to how you will need to design the folder structure of the site.

4. Click the root folder in the Folder List panel, click the drop-down arrow beside the New Document button, and then click Folder. Type **Products** as the folder name.

5. Repeat the folder creation steps to create four more folders in the root of your site named **Services**, **About**, **Contact**, and **Legal**.

You added the folder "Legal" to the site so that you'd have a place to keep the Terms of Use and Privacy page that you'll link to on the footer.

6. Right-click the Document_files folder in the Folder List panel and then choose Rename from the context menu. Rename the folder to **Images**.

   When you rename a folder in Expression Web, all the references to files within it are automatically updated. Although it's not a necessity to rename this folder, it's always a good practice to keep folders and files named in a way that will mean something to you and anyone who might need to work on the site in the future. As the number of files and folders in a site becomes greater, the value of this practice becomes more and more important.

7. In the Folder List pane, press Ctrl while clicking default.html, Document.html, LazyDogText.txt, and template.design to select them all, and then drag them into the Images folder.

   By dragging all the files from the root of the site into the Images folder, you've cleaned up the root folder and you will make the process of building a site within this folder structure much easier. By keeping a clean and orderly folder structure, you will greatly reduce the difficulty of maintaining and modifying a site over the long-term.

> **Tip** Although the folders and files in this demonstration are limited, you won't often find this to be the case in a production site. Click the Site View tab at the top of the editing window to put the site into Folders View, which will make your file and folder tasks much easier.

8. Click the drop-down arrow on the New Document button on the Common toolbar and then click CSS. A new cascading style sheet named Untitled_1.css is created.

9. Click the Save button on the Common toolbar, and in the Save As dialog box, double-click the site's Images folder, and then type **Main.css** in the File Name field.

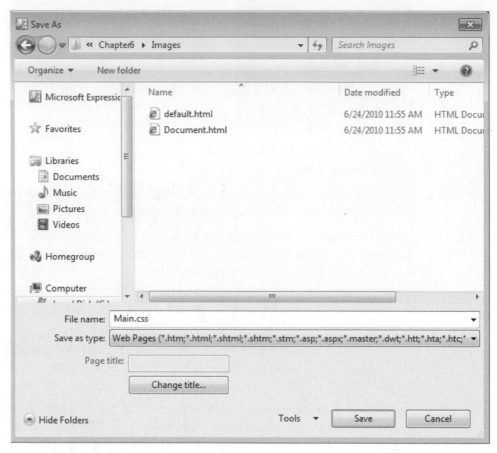

10. Click Save to save the style sheet in the Images folder and close the dialog box.

> **Tip** Saving a style sheet in your site's Images folder makes it much easier to use images in the CSS file. There isn't any folder path that needs to be considered, and keeping the style sheet in the same folder as the images is a good technique to make using images in your CSS easier.

Up to this point, you've been using Expression Web to write the CSS code into the HTML file you've been creating your layout on. This has been the easiest and most efficient way so far, but in the next steps, you will transfer that code to an external style sheet to make the rest of your work easier.

11. Switch to the default.html file that you've been working on. Click Format, select CSS Styles, and then click Attach Style Sheet. In the Attach Style Sheet dialog box, click the browse button. Browse into the site's Images folder, double-click Main.css, and then click OK.

12. To the right of the Apply Styles tab in the Apply Styles panel that you've been using, you will see the Manage Styles tab. Click the Manage Styles tab to activate that panel. Click the thumbnail icon on the Toolbox panel to autohide it, because it's not necessary at this time and it'll give you more space for the Manage Styles panel.

You will use this tab to easily drag the styles from the default.html file into the newly created and linked external CSS file.

13. Click the first style entry beneath the Current Page heading in the Manage Styles panel and then press Shift while clicking the last entry to select all the entries at once.

For this screen shot image, the *#container* is *#footer a:link, a:visited, a:active*.

14. Drag the selected style entries onto the Main.css heading below them and release them there.

All the styles you created are moved from the original location within the page to the external style sheet.

15. From the File menu, select Save All.

16. Click the drop-down arrow on the New Document button and then click Page. In the New dialog box, in the General category, click Dynamic Web Template.

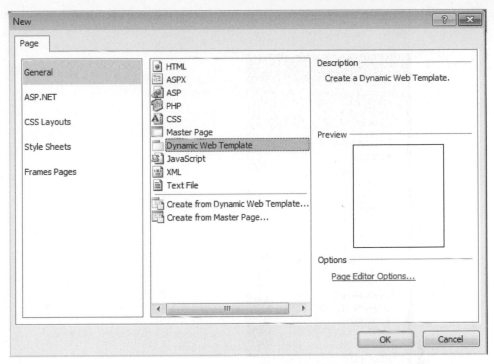

17. Click OK. A new Dynamic Web Template named Untitled_1.dwt is created. Click the Save button on the Common toolbar, and in the Save As dialog box, navigate to the site's Images folder, type **Main.dwt** in the File Name field, and then click Save.

18. Click the default.html tab at the top of the editing window and set your cursor in the Design pane of the page. Click the drop-down arrow on the *<body>* tag button on the Quick Tag Selector, and then click Select Tag Contents. Right-click the selected code in the Code pane, and in the context menu, choose Copy.

19. Click the Main.dwt tab at the top of the editing window to make that page the active document. Set your cursor in the Design pane of the page, click the drop-down arrow on the *<body>* button on the Quick Tag Selector, and then click Select Tag Contents. Right-click the selected code in the Code pane, and in the context menu, choose Paste.

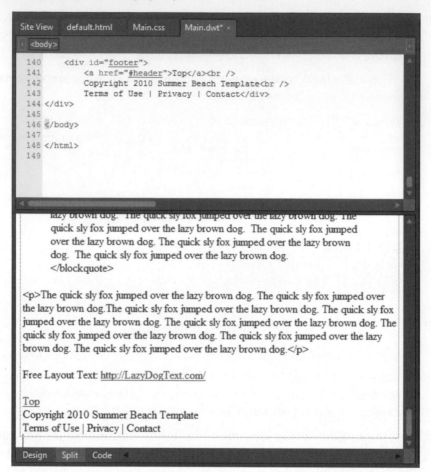

All the divisions you worked on in the default.html page have now been transferred in one easy move to your new DWT. It won't look like the template you have worked on though, because the style sheet isn't attached yet. You'll take care of that in the next step.

20. Click Format, select CSS Styles, and then click Attach Style Sheet. Click Browse in the Attach Style Sheet dialog box, browse into the site's Images folder, double-click Main.css, and then click OK in the Attach Style Sheet dialog box.

As soon as the Main.css style sheet is attached, your Dynamic Web Template will look identical to the HTML file you've been working with.

21. Click Save on the Common toolbar. Click View, select Toolbars, and then click Dynamic Web Template. The DWT toolbar appears at the top of your workspace.

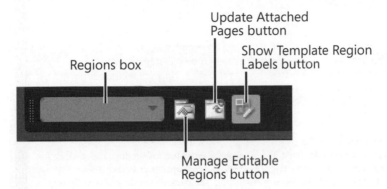

Update Attached
Pages button

Show Template Region
Labels button

Regions box

Manage Editable
Regions button

The Dynamic Web Template toolbar is fairly small, but it makes working with setting up editable regions easier because every major operation is represented by a button, as opposed to selections several levels into the Format menu. In the next few steps, you will set up two Editable Regions in the Dynamic Web Template.

22. Set your cursor in the Design pane of the first *h1* that reads Page Title Goes Here. On the Quick Tag Selector, click the drop-down arrow on the *<h1>* tag, and then click Select Tag Contents.

23. Click the Manage Editable Regions button on the Dynamic Web Template toolbar. In the Editable Regions dialog box, type **PageBanner** in the Region Name field, click Add, and then click Close.

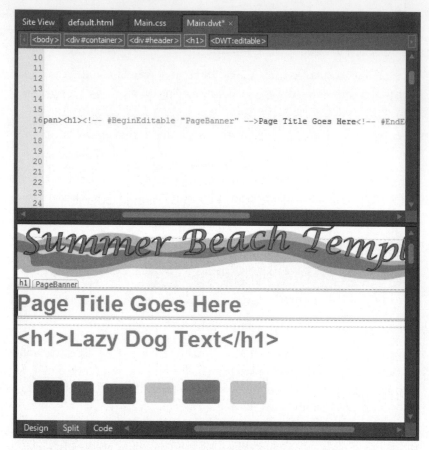

Notice what has occurred in the page. Instead of putting the *<h1>* tag and its contents inside the Editable Region, you have the *<h1>* tags outside of the Editable Region, and the region is inside the tag pair. This will prevent a user from using a tag other than the *<h1>* in this semantically critical page area.

24. Set your cursor in the content area of the page. Click the drop-down arrow on the *<div#content>* button on the Quick Tag Selector, and then click Select Tag Contents.

25. Click the Manage Editable Regions button on the Dynamic Web Template toolbar. In the Manage Editable Regions dialog box, type **Content** in the Region Name field, click Add, and then click Close.

Similarly to how you added the Editable Region inside the *<h1>* tag in the previous step, this editable region is inside the content *div* tag. By setting up the Editable Region this way, it will prevent a user from inadvertently deleting or changing the content division's tag in any way. Although you may be the only designer to ever work on a site you build, using practices such as this will go a long way in keeping the site uniform and durable in any editing situation.

26. Right-click the Code pane, and from the context menu, choose Select All. Right-click the Code pane again and choose Reformat HTML from the context menu. Click Save on the Common toolbar.

> **Tip** You are about to begin adding pages to the site based on this DWT. If you want to add custom Meta tags to the <head> section's Editable Region, you will achieve easier and more consistent results if you do so now, as opposed to after the pages are created based on the Dynamic Web Template.

27. From the File menu, point to New, and then click Create From Dynamic Web Template. In the Attach Dynamic Web Template dialog box, double-click Main.dwt in the site's Images folder, and then click Close on the file update alert.

A new file based on the Dynamic Web Template, named Untitled_1.html is created in your workspace.

28. Click the Save button on the Common toolbar. In the Save As dialog box, navigate up one level to the root of your site. Make sure that the File Name field reads default. html and then click the Change Title button. In the Set Page Title dialog box, change Summer Beach Template to Home: Summer Beach Template, and then click OK.

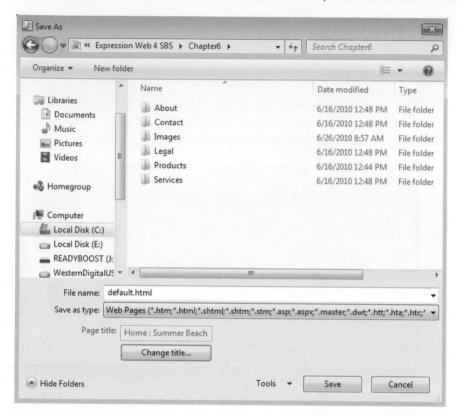

Obviously, if you were building a production site, Summer Beach Template would be the name of the site or text relative to the particular site you were building.

29. Click Save in the Save As dialog box to save your new site's new home page as default.html in the root folder.

30. Right-click default.html in the Folder List panel and then, in the Context menu, choose Copy.

31. You now have a copy of your default.html page on your Clipboard. Next, you will make it the default file for each of the folders in the root of your site.

32. Right-click the About folder in the Folder List panel and then, from the context menu, select Paste. Repeat this process for each of the remaining folders: Contact, Legal, Products, and Services. The Images folder already has a default file in it, so you can skip that one.

> **Tip** Click a folder in the Folder List panel and then press Ctrl+V on your keyboard to quickly paste a file into it. It's much faster than using the context menu.

You now have a default file in each of your site's folders and you're just a few steps away from having a working navigable site.

33. Using the page tabs above the Quick Tag Selector, close all the open pages except for the Main.dwt file.

> **Tip** You've closed all the open pages except for the DWT because you're about to set up the navigation for the site. These updates automatically occur in closed pages, but open pages would need to be saved manually.

34. In the Menu division of your page, double-click the list item text "Home" to select it. Right-click the selected text, and choose Hyperlink from the context menu. In the Insert Hyperlink dialog box, click the default.html file in the site's root. The Address field will be populated with "..*default.html*." Backspace through the page name, erasing characters until the Address field contains only the two periods and the backslash (**..**).

For the navigation in this site, you won't use any page names or extensions. Instead, you will use folder path navigation. It results in cleaner addresses in visitor's address bars, and if you decide to change the default document, you can easily switch that in a folder without having to change the navigation at all. For instance, if you decide to use a dynamic page such as a PHP or ASP.NET page, you can easily put a default. php or default.aspx file in a folder, delete or rename the default.html file, and there-fore upgrade the page without changing the site navigation. Search engine placement and visitor's bookmarks stand a much better chance of remaining correct using this method.

35. Click OK on the Insert Hyperlink dialog box to set the link.

36. Double-click Products to select the list item text. Right-click the selected text and then select Hyperlink in the context menu. Click the site's Products folder to select it. The Address field will be populated with ".\Products," rather than .".\Products\default.html."

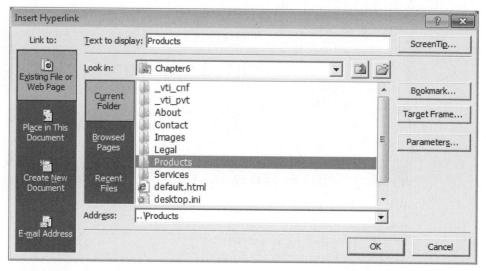

37. Continue hyperlinking the remaining list items (Services, About Us, and Contact Us) to their respective folders.

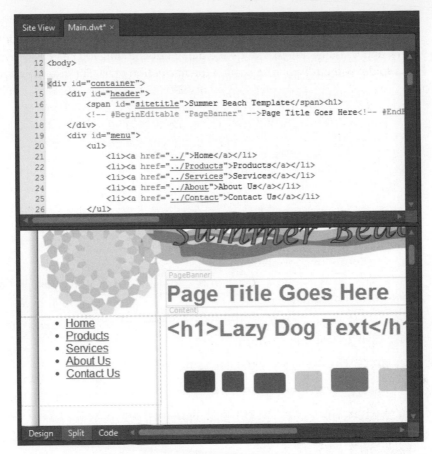

Although the navigation at this point clearly needs some adjustment for its visual appearance, take a look in the Code pane representation. It's clean and simple, and what is a navigation bar really other than a list of links? This navigation will be easy to understand for search engines, screen readers, and conventional visitors alike.

38. Click New Style in the Manage Styles panel. In the New Style dialog box, type **#menu ul** into the Selector field. Set the Define In field to **Existing Style Sheet**, click the Browse button beside the URL field, and in the Select Style Sheet dialog box, double-click the Main.css file in the site's Images folder.

39. Click the Box category and set both the Padding and Margin fields to **0px**, leaving the Same For All check box selected.

40. Click the List category and set the List-Style-Type field to **none**. Click OK to set the style and close the dialog box.

You've set these specifications to remove the "bullets" from the list items in your menu and remove any inherent padding and margin that the list could be given by browsers.

41. Click New Style on the Manage Styles panel. In the New Style dialog box, type **#menu li a** into the Selector field. Make sure that the "Define In" field is set to **Existing Style Sheet** and the URL field shows **Main.css**.

42. Set the Font-Weight field to **bolder**, click the drop-down beside the Color field, and then click More Colors. In the More Colors dialog box, click the Select button, and then click the pink color square in the Design view of the colors.jpg image. Beneath the Text-Decoration field, select the check box beside none, to remove the link's inherent underline.

43. Click the Block category and set the Text-Align field to **center**.

44. Click the Background category and set the Background-Color field to **#FFFFFF** (white).

45. Click the Border category. Leaving the Same For All check boxes selected, set the Border-Style to **solid**, the Border-Width to **2px,** and the Border-Color to **#EBC3C2** (the same as the font color).

46. Click the Box category. Leaving the Same For All check boxes selected, enter **2px** for the padding and **10px** for the margin.

47. Click the Position category and enter **140px** in the Width field.

48. Click the Layout category and set the Display field to **block**.

You're setting the Display field to block because it will make the links act more like buttons where the user doesn't need to click the text, but can click anywhere on the list item.

49. Click OK to close the dialog box and set your style changes.

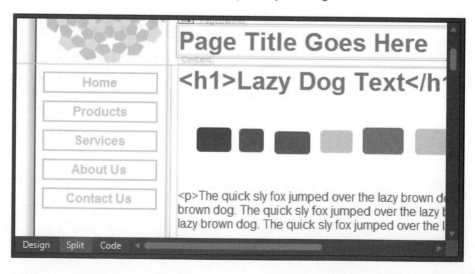

Your links look a lot more like buttons now. There's just the matter of assigning a different color to them for their hover state so that the user will get a little visual feedback when they mouse-over them.

50. Click New Style on the Manage Styles panel and type **#menu li a:hover** into the Selector field. Make sure the Define In field is set to **Existing Style Sheet** and the URL field shows **Main.css**.

51. Click the drop-down arrow beside the Color field in the Font category and then click More Colors. Click the Select button in the More Colors dialog box, and then click the mauve color square in the Design view rendering of colors.jpg.

52. Click the Border category and, leaving the Same For All check boxes selected, enter **solid** in the Border-Style field, **2px** in the Border-Width field, and **#967878** (the same color as the font) in the Border-Color field. Click OK to set the styles and close the dialog box.

53. Scroll the Design pane down to the footer of the page and select the words "Terms of Use." Right-click the selected words and then, from the context menu, choose Hyperlink. Click the Legal folder and then click OK.

54. Select the word Privacy and right-click the selection. Select Hyperlink from the context menu, click the Legal folder, and then click OK.

55. Select the word "Contact" and right-click. From the context menu, click Hyperlink, click the Contact folder, and then click OK.

56. Click Save on the Common toolbar. In the Save Embedded Files dialog box, click OK to let the Main.css file overwrite and save. Click Yes on the file update alert to allow Expression Web to update all the files attached to the Dynamic Web Template you're working on, and then click Close on the confirmation alert.

57. Choose Site Settings from the Site menu, and then click the Preview tab in the Site Settings dialog box. Select the For All Web Pages option beneath the Use Microsoft Expression Development Server label, and then click OK to set your change and close the dialog box.

   Because this site is using folder paths for the navigation, you will need the Expression Development Server to preview the pages. If the Development Server wasn't used, the default behavior would be for your folder-based links to open in Windows Explorer and show you the folder contents. It takes a server to know what the default document of a folder is.

58. Click default.html in the Folder List panel and then click the Preview button on the Common toolbar to open the page in a browser.

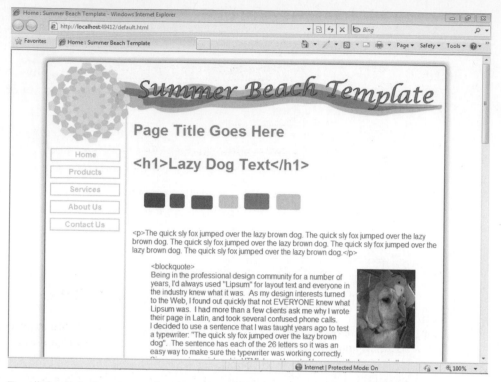

59. Try all the links in your navigation structure, both in the menu division and footer division of the pages, to make sure they behave as expected, then close the open browser and return to Expression Web.

    As you were clicking around in the browser, you probably noticed that all the pages were virtually identical. Although this section isn't about writing content for pages, we will wrap it up by making each of the pages unique by adding their page title and the page banner *<h1>* element.

60. Double-click default.html in the Folder List panel to open it for editing. Change the text "Page Title Goes Here" to **Our Home Page**.

    By having the page title, which you added when you first created the page, the first *<h1>* element on the page, and the URL in the address bar all relate to each other, the search engine placement of the page will be much greater than if these steps weren't taken.

61. Expand the About folder in the Folder List panel and then double-click its default.html file. Change the "Page Title Goes Here" text to **About Us**.

62. Right-click the Design pane of the page, and from the context menu, choose Page Properties. On the General tab, change the title from Home: Summer Beach Template to **About Us: Summer Beach Template**.

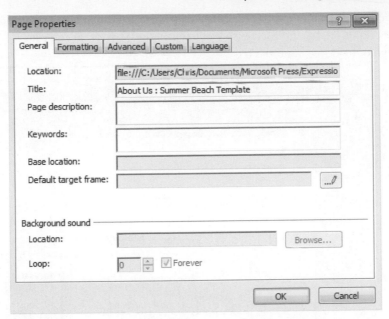

The Page Properties dialog box also provides a convenient place to enter a page description and keywords. If you fill in these fields, you will see these meta tags written into the *<head>* section of your page. Currently, keywords aren't relied on by search engines, but a page description tag will appear in search engine results pages.

63. Type **This is the About Us page of the Summer Beach Template site**, into the Page description field, and then click OK to set your changes and close the dialog box.

64. Expand the Contact folder in the Folder List panel and then double-click the default.html file to open it for editing. Change the "Page Title Goes Here" text to **Contact Us**. Right-click the Design pane and from the context menu, select Page Properties. Enter a page title of **Contact Us: Summer Beach Template**, insert a Page description in the appropriate field, and then click OK.

65. Continue changing the default *<h1>* text, Title, and Page descriptions in each of the remaining pages: Legal/default.html, Products/default.html, and Services/default.html.

> **Tip** If you open a page and it doesn't match the other pages, it is most likely a rendering issue in Expression Web. Press F5 on your keyboard or select Refresh from the View menu before trying to remedy such an issue by other means.

66. Click File, and then click Save All to save all the page changes you've made while entering heading text, titles, and descriptions.

67. From the Panels menu, click Reset Workspace Layout, to return all your panels to their original state, and then click View, select Toolbars, and then click Dynamic Web Template to close that toolbar.

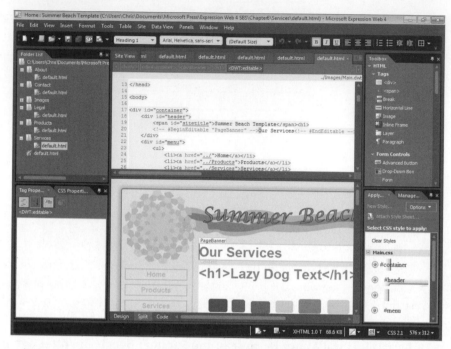

Although there would still be the significant outstanding work of creating and tuning content for the pages of this site, what you have at this point is a multiple page, custom designed, and fully navigational site. The techniques that you've learned and employed in this section can serve as the basis of how you lay out the folder architecture and navigation of sites you build in the future. By using the Dynamic Web Template and cascading style sheets, this site will be easy to expand, manage, and maintain.

Note If you're not continuing directly to the next exercise, you can close all the open pages (select Close All Pages from the Window menu) and then exit Expression Web.

Styling for Alternative Media

One of the really great things about cascading style sheets is the separation of content and presentation. More than just a "buzz phrase," this section will show you exactly what that means in a tangible way. You will create a style sheet specifically for print and attach it to your master page using the media attribute in the style sheet link. This is interesting because you don't have to change a single line of HTML on your Dynamic Web Template or any of the pages that it's attached to. You also don't need to make additional pages specifically for printing, nor do you need to do any kind of server-side programming. All you will have to do is link the print style sheet to the DWT.

By employing this method, you will be able to make your Web pages print completely differently than they appear on screen. Although it's a simple technique, it's an underused feature. Many sites that could benefit from a clean print layout don't even make an attempt. So if you employ this technique for your own and/or your client's sites, you will be providing the visitors with a benefit that most sites simply overlook.

Create a cascading style sheet for the print version of your pages

> **Note** Using the Chapter6 site that you created earlier, open the Main.dwt file in the Images folder if it isn't still open from the previous exercise.

1. In the Folder List panel, expand the Images folder and then right-click Main.css. Choose Copy from the context menu, then right-click again, and select Paste from the context menu. A copy of this file named "Main_copy(1).css" is pasted into the Images folder.

2. Right-click the newly created copy and choose Rename from the context menu. Rename the file to **Print.css**, and then double-click the file to open it in the editing window.

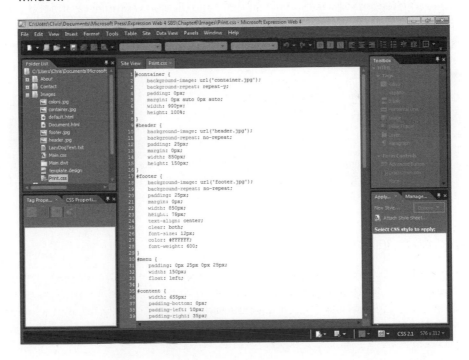

The next few steps will give you an opportunity to edit a style sheet directly. Until this point, you've relied on the Style dialog box in Expression Web. Although you could use the Style dialog box here, it will be much more efficient to just directly edit this style sheet. You'll be removing much more than you'll be adding so it's not going to take very long.

3. Starting with the *#container* ID, remove all specifications except for *height: 100%,* and change the width from 900px to **100%**.

4. Remove all specifications from the *#header* ID and enter **width: 100%.**

> **Tip** Notice that as you begin typing in a style block, options begin to pop up over your workspace. This is Intellisense for CSS. As you learn how to manually write CSS, this tool will become very helpful.

5. Edit the *#footer* ID to remove all specifications except:

```
width: 100%;
text-align: center;
clear: both;
font-size: smaller;
color: #000000;
```

6. Remove all specifications from the *#menu* ID and give it the style **display:none;.**

The reason for *display:none;* on the menu division is simple: what good is a navigation menu when a Web page is printed?

7. Change the *#content* ID to:

```
width: 100%;
text-align: left;
```

8. Change the body selector to:

```
font-family: "Times New Roman," Times, serif;
font-size: medium;
color: #000000;
```

In print, the serif fonts are more readable than the sans-serif fonts commonly used on screen.

9. Change the h1, h2, h3, h4, h5 selector to **color: #000000;**.

10 Change the #content a:link, a:visited, a:active selector to **#content a** and give it the following styles:

```
color: #000000;
text-decoration: none;
```

Because readers won't be able to click the link, there's really no reason to underline it.

11. Completely remove the *#content a:hover* selector and its specifications, because there's no hover event in printed pages.

12. Edit the *#sitetitle* selector so it has the following styles:

```
width: 100%;
display: block;
font-size: large;
```

This is an interesting point. The original styling of this division contained the site title but not shown on screen because there was a stylized title in the graphics of the site. Because the user won't be printing the background images, we can just style this title to print.

13. Remove the selectors *#header h1* and *#footer a:hover* along with their specifications. They won't be needed so you can just remove them from the style sheet.

14. Edit *#footer a* so it contains only **display: none;**.

There's no need to give footer links to visitors that have printed the page, so that line of CSS will cause them to not even print.

15. Remove the *#menu ul*, *#menu li a*, and *#menu li a:hover* selectors and styles from the style sheet.

16. Although you've already specified that the #menu division is *display:none*, and as such, none of its content should display, there's nothing wrong with keeping a clean, tight style sheet.

17. Right-click the style sheet and select Reformat CSS from the context menu. Then click the Save button on the Common toolbar.

```
Site View    Print.css ×

 1  #container {
 2      width: 100%;
 3      height: 100%;
 4  }
 5  #header {
 6      width: 100%;
 7  }
 8  #footer {
 9      width: 100%;
10      text-align: center;
11      clear: both;
12      font-size: smaller;
13      color: #000000;
14  }
15  #menu {
16      display: none;
17  }
18  #content {
19      width: 100%;
20      text-align: left;
21  }
22  body {
23      font-family: "Times New Roman", Times, serif;
24      font-size: medium;
25      color: #000000;
26  }
27  h1, h2, h3, h4, h5 {
28      color: #000000;
29  }
30  #content a {
31      color: #000000;
32      text-decoration: none;
33  }
34  #sitetitle {
35      width: 100%;
36      display: block;
37      font-size: large;
38  }
39  #footer a {
```

You now have a style sheet that specifically hides the page areas that provide no benefit to print, and refined the styles for the page areas that you are keeping to be more print friendly.

18. In the Folder List panel, double-click the Main.dwt file in the site's Images folder to open it in the editing window, and then scroll the Code pane to the *<head>* section of the page.

19. Set your cursor inside this line...

```
<link href="Main.css" rel="stylesheet" type="text/css" media="screen" />
```

...just after *type="text/css"* and then type **media="screen"**.

20. Notice that Intellisense pops up as you begin to type this line; when it shows the item you want, just press Enter on your keyboard to enter it automatically.

21. Set your cursor below the line you just edited, and type:
<link href="Print.css" rel="stylesheet" type="text/css" media="print" />

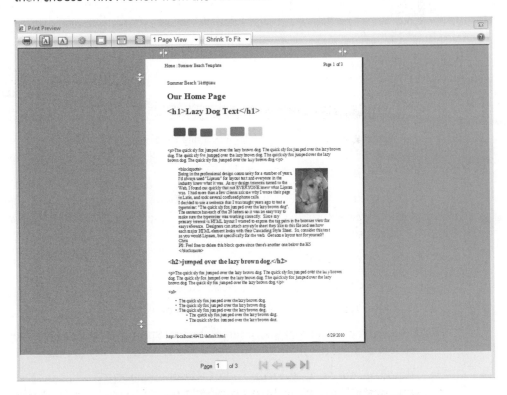

```
    Site View    Print.css    Main.dwt* ×

1  <!DOCTYPE html PUBLIC "-//W3C//DTD XHTML 1.0 Transitional//EN" "http://www.w3
2  <html dir="ltr" xmlns="http://www.w3.org/1999/xhtml">
3
4  <head>
5  <meta content="text/html; charset=utf-8" http-equiv="Content-Type" />
6  <!-- #BeginEditable "doctitle" -->
7  <title>Untitled 1</title>
8  <!-- #EndEditable -->
9  <link href="Main.css" rel="stylesheet" type="text/css" media="screen" />
10 <link href="Print.css" rel="stylesheet" type="text/css" media="print" />
11 </head>
12
13 <body>
14
```

22. Click Save on the Common toolbar, click Yes on the file update prompt, and then click Close on the update confirmation.

23. Click default.html in the root folder in the Folder List panel, and then click the Preview button on the Common toolbar to open the page in a browser.

24. In Internet Explorer, press the Alt key on your keyboard to show the Menu bar, and then choose Print Preview from the File menu.

Print preview is a real help when you're spending time to get the print version of a page to an exact specification. Besides just saving ink and paper, it's much faster than actually printing the pages.

25. With the Print Preview open, press Escape on your keyboard to return to Internet Explorer, and then close the browser and return to Expression Web.

What you've just done and seen is a good example of some of the benefits that a CSS-based design affords the designer because of the separation of content and presentation. By simply adding a style sheet for print, the designer is able to provide a completely different appearance to the page than would be present on the screen. It's a powerful technique that requires very little effort and shouldn't be overlooked. Although you used the media types Screen and Print, there are 10 different media types you can use:

- all
- aural
- braille
- embossed
- handheld
- print
- projection
- screen
- tty
- tv

 Note Close any open pages, and then select Exit from the File menu to close Expression Web.

Key Points

- As the basis of every site, the graphics are key to creating an attractive and usable template.

- Expression Web provides tools to help you lay out your graphics into an HTML template.

- By providing thoughtful site architecture, the designer can improve search engine results, while at the same time providing better accessibility to visitors.

- Using CSS, the designer can provide different appearances for pages on the screen, in print, and a number of other media types.

Chapter 7
Adding Client-Side Functionality

After completing this chapter, you will be able to:

- Understand server-side versus client-side scripting
- Use layers and behaviors
- Use Data View in an HTML page
- Create and use HTML forms

Virtually all the functionality you've seen and used in Microsoft Expression Web to this point has been intrinsic to Expression Web as an application. The goal of this chapter is to show you how you can use features within Expression Web to add functionality to an HTML page.

To provide a page with more than static information, you must use some mechanism to provide the active content. This functionality can come by virtue of code you send to the visitor's browser, known as *client-side scripting* and performed almost exclusively by JavaScript, or you can enable this functionality using code on the Web server where the site is hosted, which is commonly known as *server-side scripting*.

Expression Web provides methods to work with client-side and server-side scripting through its tools and the Expression Development Server.

 Important Before you can use the practice files in this chapter, you need to install them from the download site to their default location. For more information about practice files, see the "Code Samples" section at the beginning of this book.

 Troubleshooting Graphics and operating system–related instructions in this book reflect the Windows 7 user interface. If your computer is running Windows XP or Windows Vista, and you experience trouble following the instructions as written, please refer to the "Information for Readers Running Windows XP or Vista" section at the beginning of this book.

Understanding Server-Side vs. Client-Side Scripting

Before you forge ahead in this chapter, it's important to understand the difference between server-side and client-side scripting. Without a foundation in the benefits of each and the differences between them, you won't be able to make an appropriate choice.

Server-side scripting is programming code that is processed or executed on the server, and then the server passes the resulting content back to the browser. It doesn't matter what kind of browser is visiting your page, nor does it usually matter if that browser has disabled JavaScript. The server passes a completed page back to the browser. The only downside is that the server needs to process the script before it passes it to the browser, which results in a full page reload and a slight delay in delivery to the browser. Whether you use ASP.NET, PHP, or even SHTML, the server must complete the scripting operations before the content is passed back to the visitor.

In contrast, client-side scripting occurs completely in the visitor's browser. The page extension isn't an issue with this. JavaScript will run on any page type: ASP.NET, PHP, HTML, and so on. Client-side scripting requires no special server capabilities or processing. The main issue is that client-side scripting relies on the visitor's browser to execute the script properly, and you don't have the luxury of knowing that the script will be executed as expected. On the other hand, delivering content through client-side scripting is much faster, because it doesn't have to go through a full round-trip from server to client and back.

Using Layers and Behaviors

Expression Web 4 provides a visual interface for performing complicated Dynamic HTML (DHTML) tasks. You accomplish these tasks by using the Expression Web 4 Layers and Behaviors task panels. In this exercise, you will examine these capabilities, and insert a DHTML-driven "viewer" into one of your pages. This viewer shows information to a visitor in several ways, without requiring navigation to different pages.

Use Interactive Buttons and the Layers and Behaviors panels to create a multimedia display area

Note Start Expression Web 4 before beginning this exercise. Open the SampleSite site by selecting Open Site from the Site menu, browsing to the companion media's default installation page, and double-clicking the SampleSite folder. With the sample site opened in Expression Web, double-click the Chapter7.html page in the Folder List panel. Turn on Visual Aids, Block Selection, and Empty Containers if they're not already on.

1. In the Design pane, set your cursor at the end of the <h4> containing the text "Using Layers and Behaviors." Press Enter on your keyboard to insert a new paragraph between that heading and the block quote below it.

2. Click the new paragraph's Block Tag Selector in the Design pane of the page to select the entire paragraph. On the Insert menu, point to HTML, and then click <div>.

Expression Blend inserts a new *<div>* element in the page, replacing the paragraph tag.

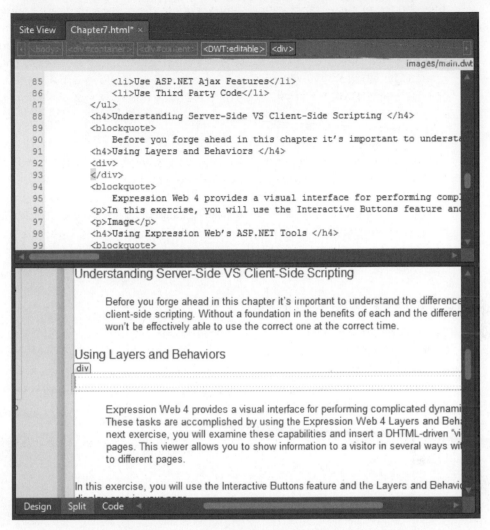

3. Click *<div>* on the Quick Tag Selector for the *<div>* element that you just placed in the page. In the Apply Styles panel, click New Style.

The New Style dialog box opens.

4. In the New Style dialog box, change the Selector field to #controls, select the Apply New Style To Document Selection check box, click Existing Style Sheet in the Define In list, and then double-click images/main.css (the document's current style sheet) in the Select Style Sheet dialog box.

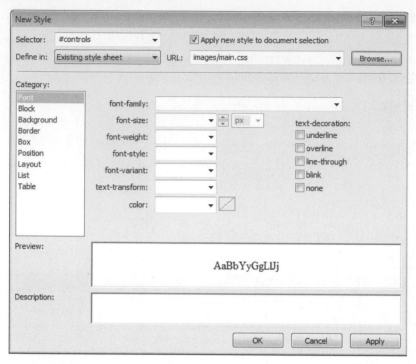

5. In the Category list, click Background. Enter a value of **#5aac65** into the Background Color field.

6. Click the Position category and, type **300px** in the Width field, and then type **270px** in the Height field. Click OK to apply your changes and close the New Style dialog box.

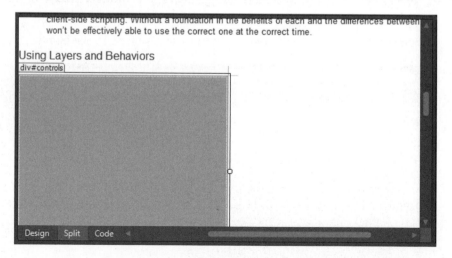

7. In the Design pane, click inside this newly styled *<div>* element. From the Insert menu, select Interactive Button to open the Interactive Buttons dialog box.

8. In the Buttons list of the Interactive Buttons dialog box, click Soft Tab 1. In the Text box, type **Text**, and leave the Link field empty.

9. Click OK to insert the button into the page.

10. Repeat steps 8 and 9 twice more, using **Flash** and **Windows Media** for the button text and leaving the Link box empty.

You should have created a row of three buttons, with no space between them.

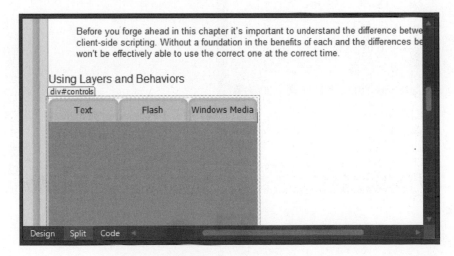

11. From the Insert menu, select HTML, and then click *<div>*.

A new *<div>* element is inserted into the page inside of the #controls division.

12. In the Design pane, set your cursor inside this *<div>* element, and then, on the Quick Tag Selector, click its corresponding button to select the entire tag.

13. In the Manage Styles panel, click New Style to open the New Style dialog box.

14. In the Selector box of the New Style dialog box, type **#presentation**, and select the Apply New Style To Document Selection check box. In the Define In list, click Existing Style Sheet, and then click main.css in the URL list.

15. In the Category list, click Box, and then enter **30px** in the Top field, below Padding.

16. In the Category list, click Position, and then enter **240px** in the Width field and **180px** in the Height field. Click OK to save your changes and close the New Style dialog box.

17. Set your cursor inside the new *<div>* element, and then on the Format menu, click Layers.

The Layers panel opens in the panel group with the Apply and Manage Styles panels.

Insert Layer
Draw Layer

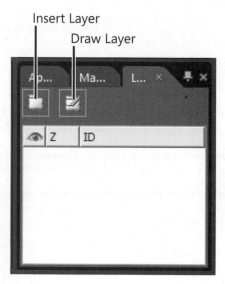

18. Click the Insert Layer button. Expression Web 4 inserts a layer below your row of buttons.

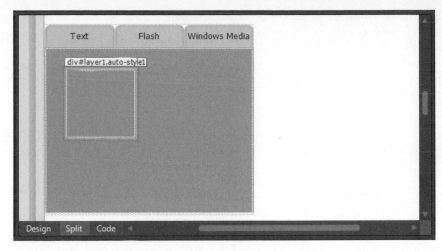

19. In the Layers panel, right-click *layer1*, and then click Modify ID. Change the ID to **player**.

20. Right-click *player*, and then click Borders And Shading. On the Shading tab, change the Background Color to white, and then click OK.

21. Right-click *player* again, and then click Positioning. Type **240px** in the Width box, type **180px** in the Height box, and then click OK.

22. Click inside this newly styled *<div>* element, and type **Please select a viewing option by clicking one of the buttons above**.

23. Click Save on the Common toolbar, and then click OK in the Save Embedded Files dialog box.

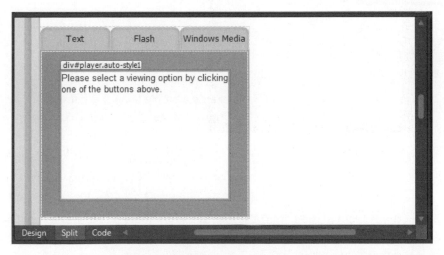

24. In the Folder List, expand the /files folder and open the text-code.txt file. Select the code, right-click, and in the context menu, click Copy. Close the file and switch to Chapter7.html.

25. In the Design pane, click the Text interactive button, and then on the Format menu, click Behaviors to display the Behaviors panel in the same panel group where the Layers panel appeared.

26. In the Behaviors panel, click the Insert button, point to Set Text, and then click Set Text Of Layer.

> **Troubleshooting** Sometimes, depending on how the styling is applied to a division, the CSS code may be placed in the <head> section of the page. For a div to be accessible by the Behaviors panel, it must have an inline style of position: absolute. If you find that the Set Text Of Layer option is unavailable, add: style="position:absolute" in code view to the division with the ID of "player."

27. In the Set Text Of Layer dialog box that opens, paste the code from the Clipboard into the New HTML box.

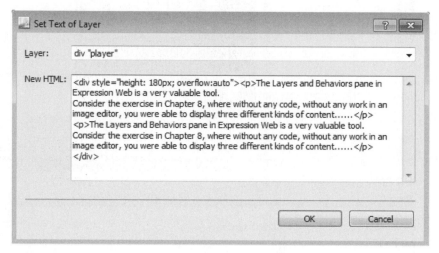

28. Click OK to set your changes.

29. In the Folder List, open the Flash-example.txt file from the /files folder. Select the code, and then right-click. In the Context menu, click Copy. Close the file and switch to Chapter7.html.

30. In the Design pane, click the Flash interactive button. In the Behaviors task panel, click Insert, point to Set Text, and then click Set Text Of Layer. Paste the code from the Clipboard into the New HTML box, and then click OK to set your changes.

31. In the Folder List, open the WindowsMedia-example.txt file inside the /files folder. Select the code, and then right-click. In the Context menu, click Copy. Close the file, and switch to Chapter7.html.

32. In the Design pane, click the Windows Media interactive button. In the Behaviors task pane, click Insert, point to Set Text, and then click Set Text Of Layer. Paste the code from the Clipboard into the New HTML box, and then click OK to set your changes.

33. Click Save and then click Preview on the Common toolbar to preview your page in a browser.

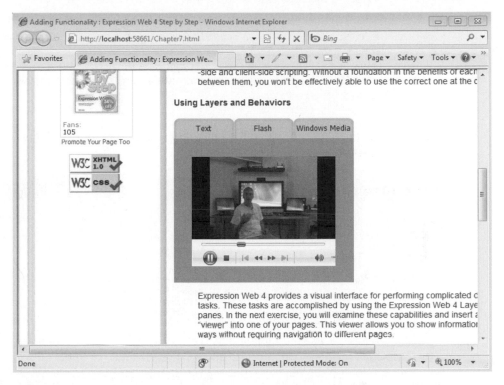

Explore your creation in the browser by clicking the buttons to check each delivery method.

Note Leave the SampleSite open if you are proceeding directly to the next section.

Although the video and audio files were provided for this exercise, consider the outcome: using only the user interface in Expression Web 4, you were able to set up a three-button rollover bar and exploit the capability to deliver content to a visitor in three different ways. Consider also that by using the Set Text Of Layer function, no extra files will be downloaded unless the site visitor clicks one of the buttons. This way, the visitor can receive your page quickly, and can then click for "heavy" content such as video or audio. It's a much better user experience than if the running media content were placed on the surface of the page.

Using Data View in an HTML Page

Based on just the fact that Data View has a menu of its own in Expression Web 4, one can assume that it's fairly important. That would be an accurate assumption. Not only can the Data View work on ASP.NET pages, but there's even functionality to include a Data View in an HTM/HTML page. Including the Data View in an HTM/HTML page is another good example of client-side scripting. Expression Web uses JavaScript, XML, and XSLT to make this feature work.

In this exercise, you will insert a Data View into the Chapter7.html page and then modify its code to yield results that aren't available through the Expression Web Graphical Interface.

> **Note** Use the Chapter7.html page of the SampleSite site you opened in the previous exercise. Open this book's sample site and Chapter7.html page, if they aren't already open.

Insert a Data View into an HTM/HTML page

1. Set your cursor in the Design pane of Chapter7.html, at the end of the heading "Using Data View in an HTML Page," and then press Enter on your keyboard to insert a new paragraph between the heading and the block quote beneath it.

2. From the Data View menu, click Insert Data View. The Data Source Library panel becomes visible in the same panel area as the Toolbox.

3. In the Local XML Files group, click Add An XML File. In the Data Source Properties dialog box, click Browse and then select feed.xml from this book's sample /files folder. Click OK in the alert dialog box to allow Expression Web to import the file into your site, and then OK in the Import dialog box that follows.

Expression Web imports the feed.xml file into the root of the Web and makes it available in the Data Source Library panel. This XML file is just a local copy of my activities feed available at *http://social.expression.microsoft.com/profile/chris%20leeds,%20 mvp/?type=forum*.

 Tip There is a clickable link in the SampleSite's Chapter7.html page.

4. Hold your cursor over the new feed.xml entry in the Data Source Library panel, click the drop-down arrow that appears, and then click Show Data.

The Data Source Details panel appears in the same panel group as the Data Source Library panel. This panel is where you'll select and insert the nodes of the XML file into your page.

5. Press the Ctrl key while clicking the nodes—*title*, *link*, and *description* in the channel group. With all three nodes selected, click the Insert Selected Fields As drop-down arrow, and then select Single Item View.

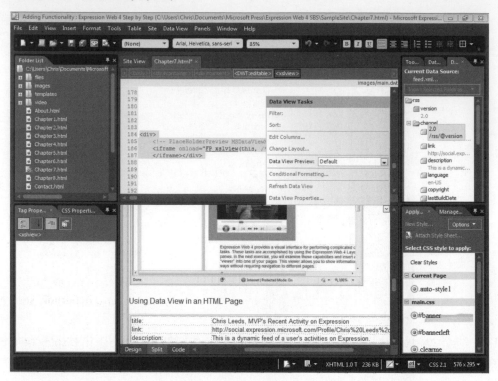

Expression Web Inserts a Data View in the Code pane of your page, and upon saving the page you inserted the Data View in, creates files named feed.xsl and xslview.js, which provide the formatting and functionality to make the Data View work. In the next few steps, you will format the heading that has been inserted into the page, and set up the table for more data.

> **Troubleshooting** Sometimes the Data View Tasks pop-up loses focus and is therefore hidden. You will see its pop-up button on the upper-right corner of the Design pane. Click the Data View in the Design pane to re-focus on it and then click the button to open the Data View Tasks pop-up.

6. In the Design pane of the page, select the table cell to the right of the word "link." With the entire cell selected, click the Insert Selected Fields As drop-down, select Formatted, click Hyperlink, and then click Yes in the Confirmation dialog box.

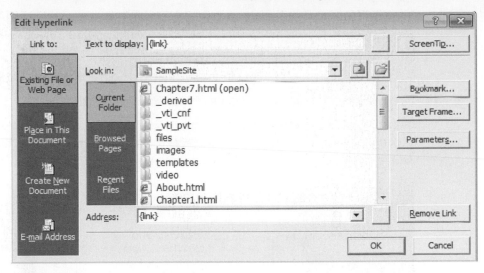

The Edit Hyperlink dialog box appears. In this dialog box, you can format the link. You have all the controls that you would normally have over a hyperlink, such as the Target Frame, Parameters, and so on.

7. Type **Expression Studio Community Profile** in the Text To Display field at the top of the Edit Hyperlink dialog box, and then click OK to set your change and close the dialog box.

   Notice that the content of the table cell is now formatted as a link using the text you specified.

8. Set your cursor in the Design pane at the end of the text in the cell to the right of the title description, and then press the Tab key on your keyboard to insert a new row.

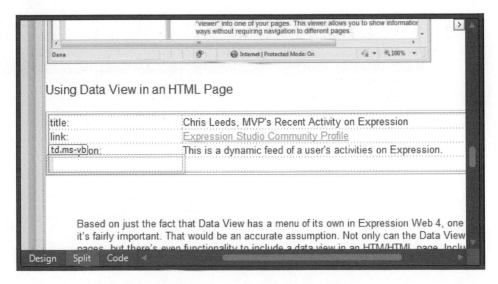

This new table row will contain an entire list of links and activity descriptions. In the next few steps, you will prepare this area for the intended Data View.

9. Drag from the first cell of your new row to the next cell to select them both. Right-click the selected cells, select Modify from the Context menu, and then click Merge Cells.

10. Set your cursor in your newly merged cell.

11. In the Data Source Details panel, scroll down to the item group and press Ctrl while clicking the *title*, *description*, and *pubDate* fields. With all three cells selected, click the drop-down arrow on the Insert Selected Fields As button, and then click Sub View.

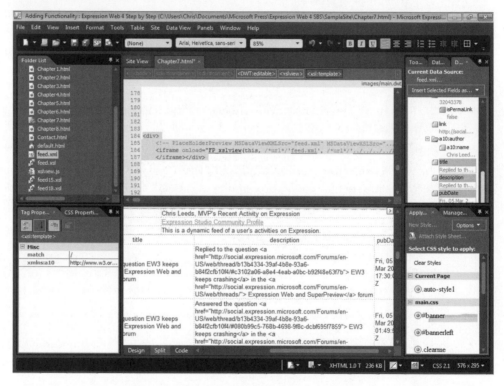

Expression Web sets the appropriate columns and data into the page. Although this layout needs additional work, in the next few steps you will save and preview the page to help you decide how to format this Data View.

12. Click Save on the Common toolbar, click OK in the Save Embedded Files dialog box, and then click Preview.

Note The Save Embedded Files dialog box appears because Expression Web has added files to the root of the site.

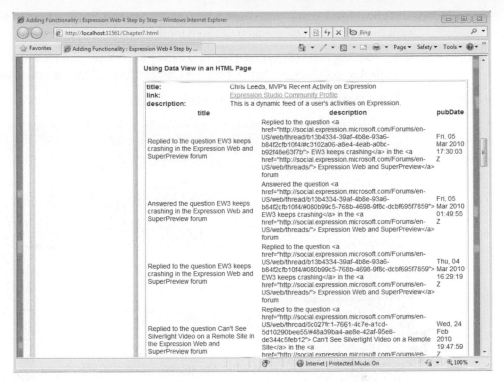

Take a few minutes to examine the Data View in the browser. With little more than a few selections, you have inserted a complex Data View based on content in an XML file, which runs using client-side scripting. In the next few steps, you will apply more customizations to the Data View.

13. Close the browser and return to Expression Web.

> **Note** Leave the SampleSite and Chapter7.html open if you are proceeding directly to the next section.

The browser preview revealed several areas that need improvement. Because the title and description contain the same information, you will remove the title column and then move the pubDate field to the left of the description.

Customize the Data View source code

> **Note** Use the Chapter7.html page of the SampleSite site you opened in the previous exercise. Open this book's sample site and Chapter7.html page, if they aren't already open.

1. Set your cursor in the Design pane, title column heading, of the data sub view. Click the Data Tasks button in the upper right of the Design pane, and then click Edit Columns.

2. In the Edit Columns dialog box, click Title in the Displayed Columns panel, and then click the Remove button.

3. Click the *pubDate* entry in the Displayed Columns panel and then click Move Up.

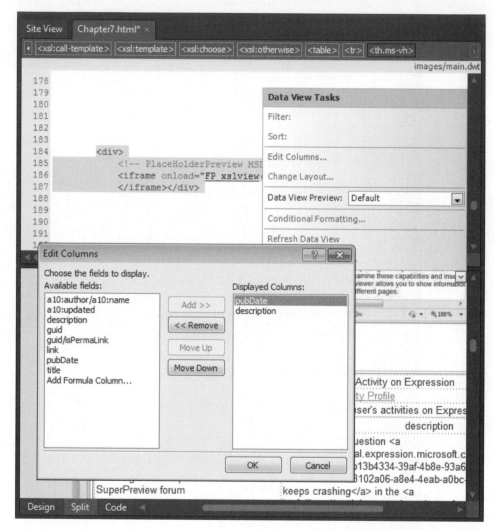

The Edit Columns dialog box contains entries for all the available fields in the feed.xml file, or any file to which it is attached. This enables the designer to set up custom Data Views of any XML file.

4. Click OK in the Edit Columns dialog box to set your changes and return to the Design pane.

The description column has now been removed from the page, but the Data View is rendering the HTML in the description field improperly. This is because the Data View component is predisposed to protect the browser from any malicious activity. In the next step, you will edit the code in feed.xsl, so that the Data View displays the resulting markup and not the HTML tags.

5. In the Folder List panel, double-click the feed.xsl file to open it for editing in Expression Web.

```
Site View    Chapter7.html*    feed.xsl ×

 1 <xsl:stylesheet xmlns:a10="http://www.w3.org/2005/Atom" version="1.0" exclude
 2     <xsl:param name="dvt_adhocmode"></xsl:param>
 3     <xsl:param name="dvt_adhocfiltermode">xsl</xsl:param>
 4     <xsl:param name="dvt_fieldsort"></xsl:param>
 5     <xsl:param name="dvt_sortfield"></xsl:param>
 6     <xsl:param name="dvt_groupfield"></xsl:param>
 7     <xsl:param name="dvt_groupdisplay"></xsl:param>
 8     <xsl:param name="dvt_sortdir">ascending</xsl:param>
 9     <xsl:param name="dvt_groupdir">ascending</xsl:param>
10     <xsl:param name="dvt_grouptype"></xsl:param>
11     <xsl:param name="dvt_sorttype">text</xsl:param>
12
13
14
15
16     <xsl:param name="dvt_groupsorttype">text</xsl:param>
17     <xsl:param name="dvt_filterfield"></xsl:param>
18     <xsl:param name="dvt_filterval"></xsl:param>
19     <xsl:param name="dvt_filtertype"></xsl:param>
20     <xsl:param name="dvt_firstrow">1</xsl:param>
21     <xsl:param name="dvt_nextpagedata"></xsl:param>
22     <xsl:param name="dvt_apos">'</xsl:param>
23     <xsl:param name="filterParam"></xsl:param>
24     <xsl:template match="/">
25         <xsl:call-template name="dvt_1"/>
26     </xsl:template>
27     <xsl:template name="dvt_1">
28         <xsl:variable name="StyleName">RepForm3</xsl:variable>
29         <xsl:variable name="Rows" select="/rss/channel"/>
30         <xsl:variable name="RowCount" select="count($Rows)"/>
31         <xsl:variable name="IsEmpty" select="$RowCount = 0"/>
32         <xsl:choose>
33             <xsl:when test="$IsEmpty">
34                 <xsl:call-template name="dvt_1.empty"/>
35             </xsl:when>
36             <xsl:otherwise>
37                 <table border="1" width="100%">
38                     <xsl:call-template name="dvt_1.body">
39                         <xsl:with-param name="Rows" select="$Rows"/>
```

An XSL file contains XSLT (Extensible Stylesheet Language Transformations) code, which is an XML-based language used to transform XML documents (in this case feed.xml) into other XML documents (in this case rendered to your browser through Chapter7.html).

> **Troubleshooting** If you've generated several Data Views while working on this section, you may have noticed that the XSL file gets incremented automatically by Expression Web. To verify the XML and XSL files that your Data View is referring to, just check the Code pane and you will see the file references in the *PlaceHolderPreview* tag that Expression Web uses: `<!-- PlaceHolderPreview MSDataViewXMLSrc="feed.xml" MSDataViewXSLSrc="feed.xsl" -->`

6. From the Edit menu, click Find, and then in the Find And Replace dialog box, enter `<xsl:value-of select="description" />` into the Find What field. Set Find Where to current page, and then click Find All.

7. In the Find panel that opens below your Code pane, double-click the second entry to set the focus in the Code pane to the place where you will make your edit.

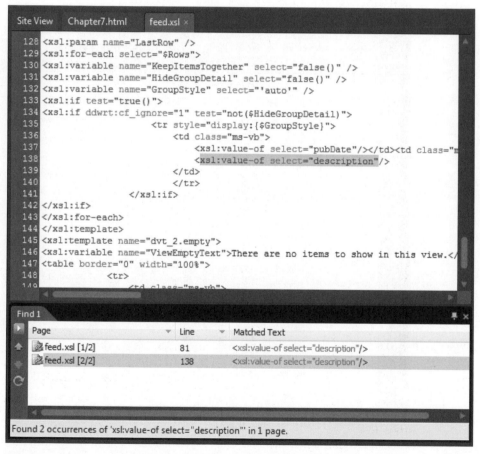

8. Set your cursor in the Code pane just before the closing bracket in the tag (`/>`) and start typing **disable-output-escaping="yes"**. Intellisense will pop up as you begin to type; just press the Enter key on your keyword when the code you want is highlighted

in the Intellisense pop-up. Make sure the value of your new addition is "yes," which results in a tag that looks like this:

```
<xsl:value-of select="description" disable-output-escaping="yes"/>
```

 Tip When XML data contains HTML tags, they're considered plain data by default, and are not parsed as HTML. In the *xsl:value-of* element, use the XSL Disable-Output-Escaping property, and then set it to Yes in order to render HTML results in the browser.

9. Click Save on the Common toolbar to save your change to the XSL document. Close the Find panel, and then close the feed.xls file to return to Chapter7.html.

10. Click Preview on the Common toolbar to view the Chapter7.html file in a browser. Look at the Data View segment.

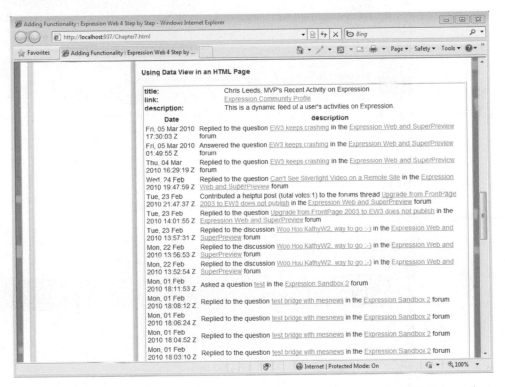

You can see the result of your edits to the XSL document, because the HTML tags that were previously rendering in the browser have now been parsed into HTML results (the clickable hyperlinks).

11. Close the browser and return to Expression Web.

In the next few steps, you will refine the appearance of the Data View slightly.

12. In the Data Views you've worked with in this exercise, there are five fields—*title*, *link*, *description*, *date*, and *description*. Retype them so they become: **Title**, **Link**, **Description**, **Date**, and **Description**. After you retype each label, use the Bold button on the Common toolbar to apply bold formatting, which will make them render differently than their content labels.

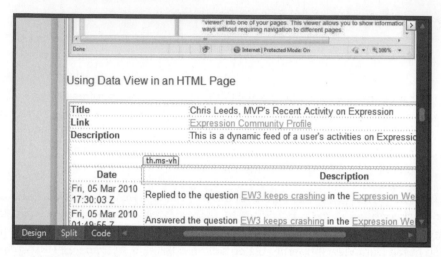

13. Click Save, and then click Preview on the Common toolbar to view your changes in a browser.

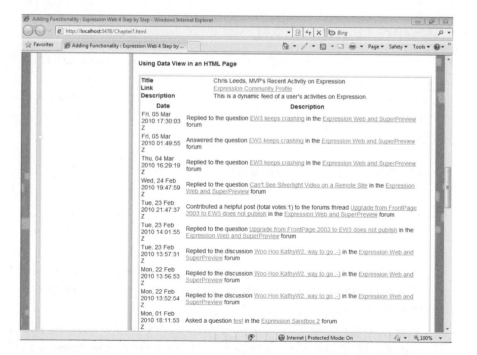

As you look at the browser preview of your page, consider what's occurred: Expression Web has exposed an XML file and enabled you to create a Data View on an HTML page as well as modify its presentation. Additionally, since the page you've inserted the Data View on is styled by cascading style sheets, the links and other aspects of the Data View automatically match those of the page.

14. Close the browser and return to Expression Web.

> **Note** Leave the SampleSite open if you are proceeding directly to the next section.

In a production environment, the ability to write the contents of an XML file into a page dynamically can save time and aid in the overall efficiency of maintaining a Web site. The capability isn't limited to RSS feeds; Microsoft Excel and other applications can create similar XML documents that you can use. For information that changes frequently, the Data View can be a good choice for a presentation mechanism.

Expression Web provides a number of different Data View templates that you can apply. Take some time to return to Chapter7.html to apply and experiment with the available Data View Styles. From the Data View Tasks pop-up menu, select Change Layout to show the Layout Tab of the Data View Properties dialog box. You will find a number of HTML View Styles and their respective descriptions.

Creating and Using HTML Forms

HTML forms provide a way for you to collect user input and provide varied levels of user interaction. Forms can be used for anything from the most complex database application to the simplest of email-producing contact forms. Expression Web provides several tools to assist in the creation of forms. All the tools are available in the Toolbox panel within the Form Control group.

> **Create and configure a simple contact form to send user input to a results page**

> **Note** Use the Chapter7.html page of the SampleSite site you opened in the previous exercise. Open this book's sample site and Chapter7.html page, if they aren't already open.

1. In the Design pane, set your cursor immediately after the text in the heading that reads "Creating and Using HTML Forms," and then press Enter on your keyboard to insert a new paragraph.

2. Type **Contact Form**, and then press Enter again to create a new paragraph. Select the text you just typed, click the Style drop-down arrow on the Common toolbar, and then click Heading 5 *<h5>*.

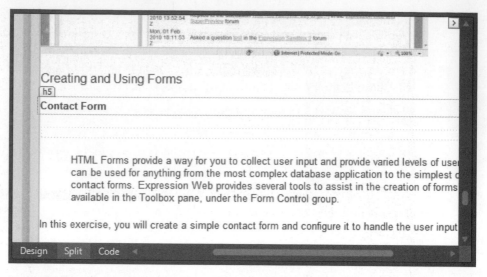

3. In the Design pane, set your cursor in the paragraph below the new *<h5>* element. If the Toolbox panel isn't visible, click Toolbox on the Panels menu. In the Toolbox panel itself, expand Form Controls.

These form controls can be added to your page either by dragging them from the Toolbox to where you want them or by setting the cursor in the design surface of the page where you want them and double-clicking their entry in the toolbox.

4. In the Design pane, click the *<p>* element below the heading you entered. Click its Block Selection tag to select the entire element, and then in the Toolbox panel, double-click Form.

An empty form is inserted into your page in place of the paragraph.

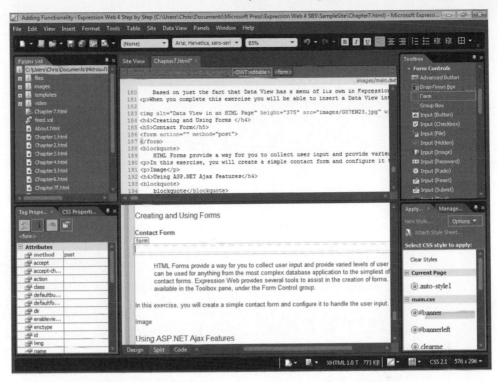

5. Type **Name** and then press Shift+Enter to insert a line break. In the Toolbox panel, double-click Input (Text) to insert a text field.

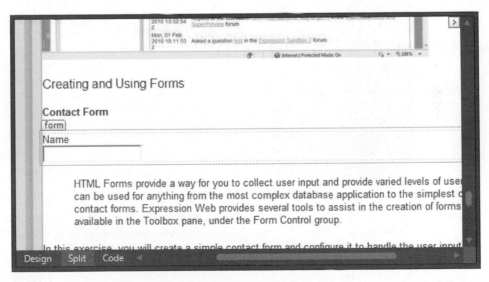

6. Right-click the text field and then click Form Field Properties to open the Text Box Properties dialog box. Type **name** in the Name field, and then enter **1** in the Tab Order field.

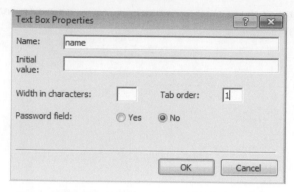

7. Click OK to apply the changes and close the dialog box.

8. Set your cursor just after the newly inserted text field, and then press Shift+Enter to insert a line break.

9. Type **E-mail** and then press Shift+Enter to insert a line break. In the Toolbox panel, double-click Input (Text) to insert another text field.

10. Right-click the new text field, and then click Form Field Properties. Type **email** in the Name field, type **2** in the Tab order field, and then click OK to apply the changes and close the dialog box. Set your cursor just after the text field, and then press Shift+Enter to insert a line break.

11. Type **Phone**, and then press Shift+Enter to insert a line break. In the Toolbox panel, double-click Input (Text) to insert another text field.

12. Right-click the new text field, and then click Form Field Properties. Type **phone** in the Name field, type **3** in the Tab order field, and then click OK to apply the changes and close the dialog box. Set your cursor just after the text field, and then press Shift+Enter to insert a line break.

13. Type **Your Message**, and then press Shift+Enter to insert a new line break. In the Toolbox panel, double-click Text Area to insert a text area field into your form.

14. Right-click the text area field and then click Form Field Properties to open the TextArea Box Properties dialog box. Type **message** in the Name field, type **40** in the Width In characters field, type **4** in the Tab order field, type **10** in the Number Of Lines field, and then click OK to apply the changes and close the dialog box.

15. Set your cursor just after the text area field, and then press Shift+Enter to insert a line break. In the Toolbox panel, double-click Input (Reset), and then double-click Input (Submit).

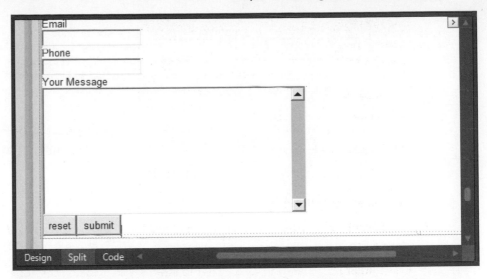

After setting the form field names and tab order, you can configure what happens when a site visitor uses the form by filling in the requested information and clicking the Submit button.

16. In the Design pane, right-click anywhere inside the form, and then click Form Properties to open the Form Properties dialog box.

The Send To Other option should be selected.

> **Tip** There are options on the Form Properties dialog box for features that require Microsoft Office FrontPage server extensions. These options also require email transport to be enabled in some cases, and require FrontPage publishing. FTP publishing will cause them to fail. These FrontPage options are present only so that an Expression Web user can edit pages that were originally created in FrontPage and that use FrontPage extensions.

17. Type Contact in the Form Name field, and then click Options. In the Action field of the Options For Custom Form Handler dialog box, type **files/confirmation.aspx**.

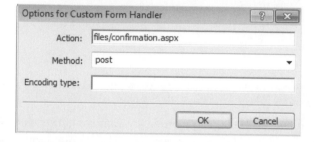

> **Tip** In the Options For Custom Form Handler dialog box, you can change the method to post or get. *Post* may involve anything, such as storing or updating data, or sending email. *Get* is basically used just for retrieving data, and it passes the form data in a URL string. Each can be helpful depending on the purpose of the form itself.

18. Click OK to save your changes in the Options for Custom Form Handler dialog box, and then click OK in the Form Properties dialog box.

19. Click Save and then Preview on the Common toolbar to view the Chapter7.html file and your new form in a browser.

20. In the browser, fill out the form, and then click Submit.

> **Troubleshooting** If the confirmation.aspx file doesn't show any user input, check the browser's address bar and make sure that it shows a beginning URL of http://localhost. That indicates that the Expression Development Server is passing the page to the browser. For an .aspx page like the confirmation file to run, it must be served by a browser. Set your Site Settings (Preview tab) to Use Microsoft Expression Development Server, for all Web pages.

> **Tip** The confirmation page is intended solely to illustrate how to create and direct an HTML form in Expression Web 4. It is assumed that the site developer will have a script or form handler in order to process the HTML form. See the links beneath the Resources heading on the Chapter7.html file. You'll find a "Readers Only" bonus on the confirmation.aspx page, too.

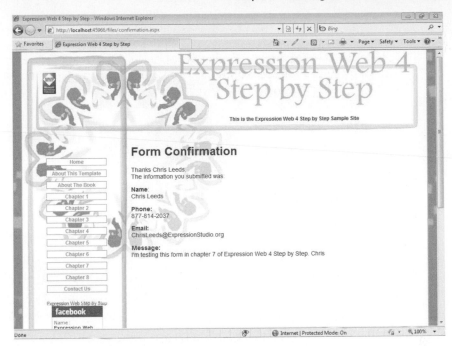

The confirmation page shows the form input.

 Note At this point, you can close the SampleSite site and any open browsers. If you are not continuing directly to the next chapter, exit Expression Web 4.

From the most basic contact form to the most complex database application, the way users will interact and provide input is almost always through a form. The HTML form has been around since virtually the beginning of the World Wide Web, and it's as important today as it was then to learn how to create forms and use them.

Key Points

- Scripting functionality can take place on the server or in the browser.

- Expression Web's Layers and Behaviors enable you to create client-side functionality.

- Expression Web enables you to insert a Data View on an HTML page.

- HTML Forms are one of the oldest and most common ways users interact with a Web page.

Chapter 8

Adding Functionality with jQuery and PHP

After completing this chapter, you will be able to:

- Use jQuery in Expression Web
- Use the Expression Web PHP tools

Microsoft Expression Web 4 provides support not only for Microsoft technologies, but also for other popular Web development tools. This chapter shows you how to take advantage of the jQuery JavaScript library and the PHP Web development language using Expression Web 4.

 Important Before you can use the practice files in this chapter, you need to download and install them from the book's companion content Web site to their default location. For more information about downloading and installing the practice files, see the "Code Samples" section at the beginning of this book.

 Troubleshooting Graphics and operating system-related instructions in this book reflect the Windows 7 user interface. If your computer is running Windows XP or Windows Vista and you experience trouble following the instructions as written, please refer to the "Information for Readers Running Windows XP or Vista" section at the beginning of this book.

Using jQuery in Expression Web

jQuery is a lightweight JavaScript library that makes authoring JavaScript faster and easier than ever. It's currently very popular among designers and developers alike, because it's easy to use, flexible, and has a plug-in ecosystem that lets you add additional functionality.

With jQuery, you can write simplified JavaScript that's compatible with multiple browsers, letting you create functionality more easily than ever before.

Because jQuery is a framework library it's possible for developers to create "plug-ins" for the framework, which add specialized functionality that extends jQuery for specific needs. Many plug-ins have already been written; you can find a list of them at *http://plugins.jquery.com/*. After installing a plug-in, you can use its features on your pages with little to no coding.

In this exercise, you will write some jQuery-compatible JavaScript and use a jQuery plug-in.

Link a page to a jQuery library, write a simple function, and use a jQuery plug-in

 Note Start Expression Web 4 before beginning this exercise. Open the SampleSite site by selecting Open Site from the Site menu, browsing to the companion media's default installation page, and double-clicking the SampleSite folder. With the sample site opened in Expression Web, double-click the Chapter8.html page in the Folder List panel.

1. Scroll the Code pane of Chapter8.html to the *<head>* section and set your cursor just before the closing *<!-- #EndEditable -->* in the "doctitle" editable region and then press Enter on your keyboard to break to a new line.

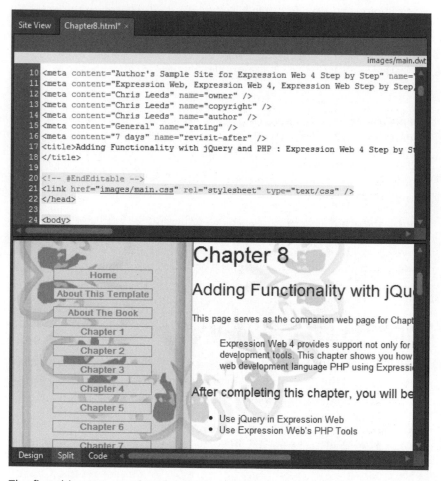

The first thing you need to do when using jQuery is link to the library itself; that's what you will do in the next few steps.

2. With your cursor on a new line in the editable region within the page's *<head>* section, begin to type **<script**... and the Expression Web Intellisense will appear. Each time the Intellisense pop-up displays the code fragment you want, press Enter on your keyboard. When complete, you will have a line that looks like this:

```
<script type="text/javascript" language="javascript" src="files/jquery-1.4.2.min.
js"></script>
```

In this example, you are linking to the jQuery file that resides physically in the Sample-Site's folder structure—specifically, the site's /files folder. Using a local copy of the jQuery library as in this example is just one option for linking to the library; many designers link to the jQuery library via an external URL. Both Google and Microsoft host this library, and anyone can link to it freely. The following example script tags would link a page to the Google or Microsoft hosted jQuery library:

```
<script language="javascript" type="text/javascript" src=
 "http://ajax.googleapis.com/ajax/libs/jquery/1.4.2/jquery.min.js">
</script>
```

```
<script language="javascript" type="text/javascript" src=
 "http://ajax.Microsoft.com/ajax/jQuery/jquery-1.3.2.min.js">
</script>
```

 Note In this example, you are linking to the jQuery library locally so that you don't need an active Internet connection to complete the examples.

 Tip If you're going to use the jQuery library in many or all of your pages, you can add the link to a template file so it will be available automatically on all the pages based on that Dynamic Web Template (DWT) or ASP.NET master page.

3. The next step in this jQuery example is to write actual script into the page. Press Enter on your keyboard to create a new line beneath the script tag that you inserted. Enter the following code:

```
<script type="text/javascript">
$(document).ready(function() {
  $("a[href^='http:']:not([href*='" +
  window.location.host +   "'])").each(function() {
    $(this).attr("target", "_blank");
  })
});
</script>
```

```
Site View    Chapter8.html* ×

                                                          images/main.dwt
14 <meta content="Chris Leeds" name="author" />
15 <meta content="General" name="rating" />
16 <meta content="7 days" name="revisit-after" />
17 <title>Adding Functionality with jQuery and PHP : Expression Web 4 Step by St
18 </title>
19 <script type="text/javascript" language="javascript" src="files/jquery-1.4.2
20 <script type="text/javascript">
21 $(document).ready(function() {
22    $("a[href^='http:']:not([href*='" +
23    window.location.host +  "'])").each(function() {
24       $(this).attr("target", "_blank");
25    })
26 });
27 </script>
28 <!-- #EndEditable -->
```

If you don't want to type that entire block of code, you can continue this exercise by copying and pasting from within the comment tags in the file /files/external_blank.js, or simply link to the file in the same way that you did the jQuery library:

```
<script language="javascript" type="text/javascript"
  src=" files/external_blank.js"></script>
```

4. Click Save, and then click Preview on the Common toolbar to open your page in a browser. Scroll down to the jQuery Resources list.

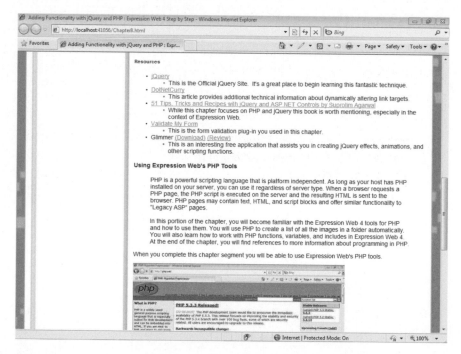

5. Click a few of the hyperlinks in the list. Notice that they open in a new window. Return to the browser view of Chapter8.html and click one of the page links on the upper-left navigation area of the page. Notice that the internal links now open within the *current* browser window. The JavaScript you added works with the jQuery library to read all the hyperlinks in the page, and if they contain an HREF attribute that begins with "http," gives them a *_blank* target attribute. The result: All the external links open in a new window, and all the internal links open conventionally.

> **Tip** Using jQuery or another method to alter HTML elements is particularly useful in an instance where the actual content you want to alter doesn't exist in your source code or isn't under your control. In the previous chapter, the Data View isn't compiled in Expression Web. The content may change constantly. The Data View is designed to consistently render content the same way even with a potentially changing XML file, so altering the links dynamically is virtually required. Try steps 1 through 3 on Chapter7.html and take note of how you were able to change the behavior of the hyperlinks in the Data View when you test it in the browser.

6. Close the browser window and return to Expression Web. Click one of the jQuery Resource links in the Design pane and notice the Code pane. There is no `target="_blank"` attribute in any of the links in the list, which is how you would normally make hyperlinks open in a new window.

In the next exercise, you will link to a jQuery plug-in, which is a pre-written set of functions designed and tested to work with the jQuery Library. You'll use this particular plug-in to validate the input fields of the form you created in Chapter 7, "Adding Client-Side Functionality."

Link to a jQuery plug-in and use it to validate user input

1. Set your cursor in the *<head>* section of the page where you've been working and press Enter on your keyboard to insert a new line after your most recent script block.

2. Using the Expression Web Intellisense pop-up as you did previously, enter the following script tag, which links to the jQuery plug-in:

```
<script type="text/javascript" src=" files/validateMyForm/jquery.
validateMyForm.1.1.js"></script>
```

To use this plug-in, you must link to it just as you linked to the jQuery library. This plug-in is called Validate My Form. You can find a link to it beneath the Resources heading in the Chapter8.html file.

3. In the Code pane, press Enter on your keyboard to start a new line beneath your link to the form validation plug-in and then enter the following script tag and style sheet link:

```
<script type="text/javascript">
<!--
    $(document).ready(function(){
        $("#form1").validateMyForm();
    });
-->
</script>
<link href="files/validateMyForm/css/plugin.css"
    rel="stylesheet" type="text/css" />
```

4. Scroll the Design pane of your page to the Resources heading in the jQuery segment. Set your cursor in the Design pane at the end of the heading text and press Enter on your keyboard to create a new paragraph.

5. In the Folder List panel, expand the site's /files folder and then double-click Chapter7 Form.txt to open it in your workspace. Set your cursor in the code of that file and press Ctrl+A to select all of the text, and then Ctrl+C to copy it all to your Clipboard. Close Chapter7Form.txt and return to Chapter8.html.

6. Set your cursor inside of the new paragraph tag in the Design pane and then click the *<p>* tab on the Quick Tag Selector to select the entire tag. Right-click the highlighted code in the Code pane, and in the Context menu, click Paste. Then click Save on the Common toolbar.

The HTML form from Chapter 7 is now pasted into the page where your paragraph tag was, and the page is saved.

7. Set your cursor inside the Form tag in the Code pane and add the ID attribute **id="form1"** to the tag.

By adding the ID to the form tag, you have given the plug-in the ability to manipulate the form and apply the validation functionality. This plug-in not only identifies the form by its ID, but enables validation simply by applying a class to the form field in question.

8. Click the Name form field in the Design pane to select it, and then in the Code pane, add **class="required"** to the tag.

9. Click the Email form field in the Design pane and then add **class="required email"** to the tag in the Code pane.

10. Click the Phone form field in the Design pane and add **class="required numeric"** to the tag in the Code pane.

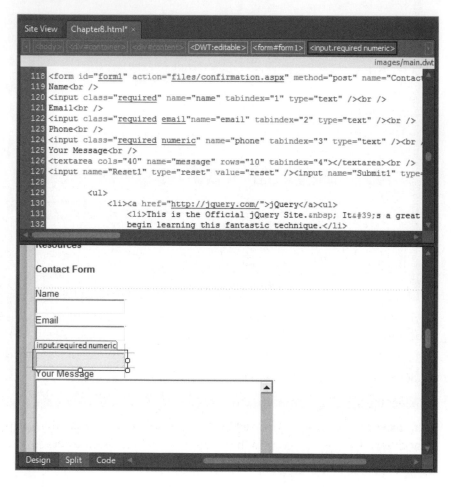

Tip If you find that you routinely use certain selectors, you can add them to your style sheet and then apply them to individual elements using the Apply Styles panel or by exposing the classes in Intellisense while you're entering them into the tags manually.

11. Click Save and then click Preview on the Common toolbar to view your page in a browser. In the browser view, scroll down to your form and enter some input values to test the validation. Click the Submit button and watch the form validation in action.

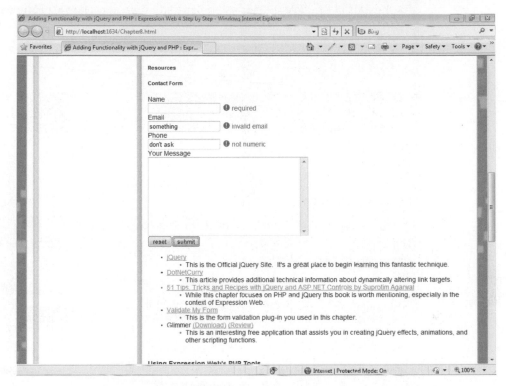

In the image above, I entered nothing into the Name field, entered an invalid email address into the *Email* field, and typed some text into the Phone field. In each case, this input failed to pass the validation function that the jQuery plug-in provides.

12. Close the browser window and return to Expression Web.

13. Select the Phone input field in the Design pane.

In many cases, designers will need to modify and experiment with the jQuery, JavaScript, or other attributes they add to their page. Expression Web provides tools that make this task quick, easy, and accurate. The Tag Properties panel is ideal for this operation.

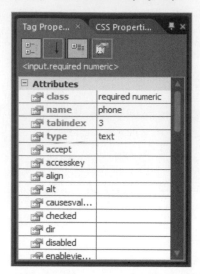

14. With the form field still selected, notice the Tag Properties panel on the lower left of your workspace. Using the Tag Properties panel, remove the class *(required numeric)* from the form field's Tag Properties.

15. In the Design pane, select the message text box of your form and, using the Tag Properties panel, enter **required** in the Class field.

    The idea is to require users to enter something in the message field, but not the phone field.

> **Tip** Use the Set Properties On Top button at the top of the Tag Properties panel to make working with tags much easier. Any attribute that exists for the tag will be at the top of the list.

16. Click Save, and then click Preview on the Common toolbar to check your page in a browser again. This time, test the validation by leaving the phone field blank. Submit the form. You should see a screen similar to the following one.

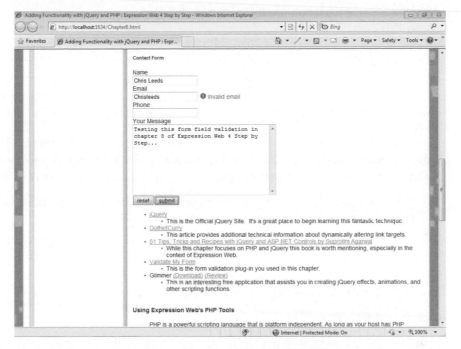

17. Close the browser window and return to Expression Web.

Although some HTML editors produce JavaScript code, such as the JavaScript that Expression Web created for the Interactive Buttons you used in the media player segment, the HTML editor is best suited for editing the code produced by JavaScript tools such as jQuery and its myriad of plug-ins. By using an open and pre-coded approach such as jQuery, you can make the latest and greatest scripting solutions available in your pages, without having to be a programmer. Using code libraries such as jQuery within Expression Web gives you virtually unlimited client-side scripting capabilities.

> **Tip** Check below the Resources heading in Chapter8.html for links pertinent to this section.

> **Note** Leave the SampleSite open if you are proceeding directly to the next section.

Using the Expression Web PHP Tools

PHP is a powerful, platform-independent server-side scripting language. As long as your server has PHP installed, you can use it regardless of the server type (such as Linux or Windows). When a browser requests a PHP page, the server executes the PHP script and sends the resulting HTML and other content to the browser. PHP pages may serve text, HTML, and script blocks, and function similarly to "Legacy ASP" pages. In other words, PHP pages can mix PHP code with HTML markup and other content.

Microsoft Expression Web 4 provides several tools to make working with PHP easier, and also provides assistance in creating and previewing PHP files. Programming in PHP is a very broad topic, and is well outside the scope of this book. This section serves purely as an introduction to the PHP tools in Expression Web.

In this portion of the chapter, you will become familiar with the Expression Web 4 tools for PHP and how to use them. You will use PHP to create a list of all the images in a folder automatically. You will also learn how to work with PHP functions, variables, and includes in Expression Web 4. At the end of the chapter, you will find references to more information about programming in PHP.

The PHP coverage in this book is not intended to be an example of best practices, or current PHP coding standards. It is here to expose the reader to the PHP tools available in Expression Web, particularly the Insert menu items, IntelliSense, and the Expression Development Server.

> **Important** Before you can complete the rest of the chapter, you must install PHP for the Expression Development Server. See Chapter 2, "Capitalizing on Expression Web 4 Functionality." You will also find some PHP information in Chapter 3, "Capitalizing on the Template Options in Expression Web 4" as it relates to using PHP in template scenarios.

Using PHP in Expression Web

1. From the File menu, select New, and then select PHP. Expression Web creates a new PHP file named Untitled_1.php in your workspace.

2. From the Format menu, select Dynamic Web Template, and then select Attach Dynamic Web Template.

3. In the Attach Dynamic Web Template dialog box, browse to the site's Images folder and double-click main.dwt. Click Close on the Update Confirmation alert.

The method of adding a Dynamic Web Template to a PHP file was originally shown in Chapter 3, so it may seem familiar to you.

4. In the Design pane, set your cursor inside the Content editable region. On the *<DWT:editable>* tab on the Quick Tag Selector, click the drop-down arrow, click Select Tag Contents, and then press Delete on your keyboard.

5. Type **Automatic Image Gallery** and then select the text. On the Styles drop-down menu, click **Heading 1 <h1>**, and then press Enter on your keyboard to create a new paragraph below your heading.

6. Click Save on the Common toolbar. In the Save As dialog box, make sure the root folder of the site is selected, and type **Chapter8.php** into the File Name field.

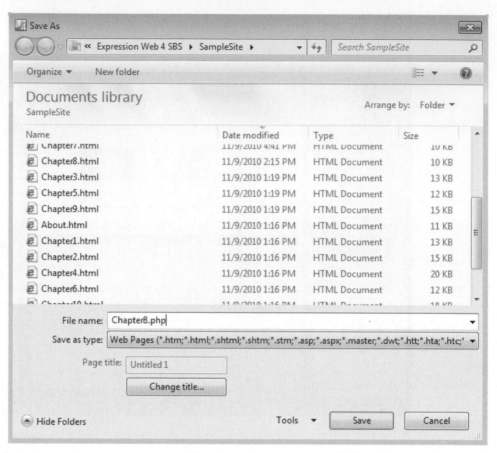

7. Click Save in the Save As dialog box.

Now that the PHP file is attached to the site's Dynamic Web Template and saved, you need to add it to the site navigation by editing the Dynamic Web Template.

8. From the Format menu, select Dynamic Web Template, and then select Open Attached Dynamic Web Template.

The file main.dwt opens for editing in your workspace.

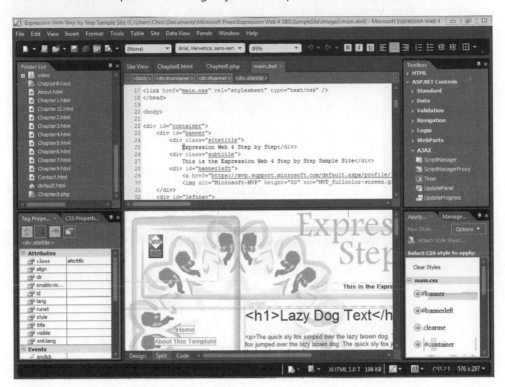

9. Set your cursor at the end of the text in the list item containing the link to the Chapter 8 file, and then press Enter on your keyboard to insert a new list item.

10. Type **Chapter 8 (PHP)** in the list item, and then triple-click the text to select it. Right-click the selected list item text, and from the context menu, select Hyperlink.

11. In the Insert Hyperlink dialog box, click Chapter8.php and then click OK to close the dialog box and insert the link.

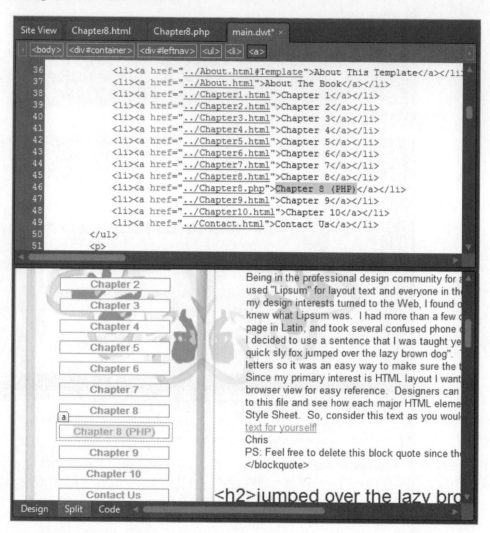

12. Click Save All on the Common toolbar, click Yes on the File Update alert to save your navigation change to the DWT and all the pages it's attached to, and then click Close on the Confirmation alert.

13. Close the Dynamic Web Template and return to Chapter8.php.

Notice how the navigation change you made in the DWT is now present on the new PHP file. The usefulness of a template for maintaining and managing a Web site can't be overstated.

14. In the Design pane, set your cursor in the empty paragraph below the heading that you previously entered, and from the Insert menu, point to PHP and then click Code Block.

15. Set your cursor between the PHP tags in the Code pane, and press Enter twice on your keyboard to create an empty line. Then move your cursor to the new empty line between the PHP tags.

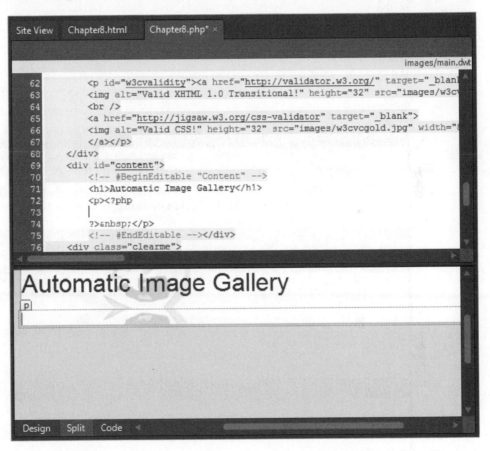

In the next few steps, you will use PHP to create an unordered list of all the files in a particular folder.

16. Enter the following code:

```
$dir = new DirectoryIterator('images/gallery1');
while($dir->valid()) {
   if(!$dir->isDot()) {
      print "<li><img src='images/gallery1/";
      print $dir->current()."'/></li>";
   }
   $dir->next();
}
```

> **Tip** You don't have to type those lines if you don't want to. You can copy and paste them from the file DirectoryIterator1.txt in the site's /files folder.

The code retrieves all the files in the images/gallery1/ folder, and creates a set of HTML list items (*<li></li>*), to display those images, skipping the two "dot" directory items (the directory itself and its parent) that appear in all child directory listings. The code creates the list items and image tags, but you need to add the unordered list (*<ul>*) tag that surrounds the items to make the list render properly.

17. On the Quick Tag Selector, click the drop-down arrow on the *<p>* tag that's surrounding your PHP code, and then click Edit Tag. On the Quick Tag Editor, change the *<p>* tag to a *<ul>* tag and then click the Checkmark button.

```
Site View    Chapter8.html    Chapter8.php* ×

<body> <div #container> <div #content> <DWT:editable> <ul>
                                                   images/main.dwt
69    <div id="content">
70       <!-- #BeginEditable "Content" -->
71       <h1>Automatic Image Gallery</h1>
72       <ul>
73          <?php
74       $dir = new DirectoryIterator('images/gallery1');
75  while($dir->valid()) {
76    if(!$dir->isDot()) {
77      print "<li><img src='images/gallery1/";
78      print $dir->current()."'/></li>";
79    }
80    $dir->next();
81  }
82       ?> </ul>
83       <!-- #EndEditable --></div>
```

18. Click Save and then click Preview on the Common toolbar to run the PHP code and preview your page in a browser.

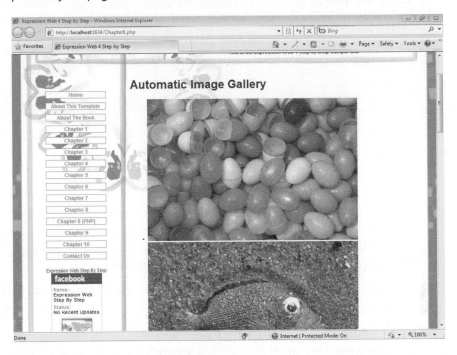

Troubleshooting For the Expression Development Server to process PHP code, you must install PHP and set the path in either the Expression Web Application or Site Settings. See Chapter 2 for more details.

Take a few minutes to examine the page in a browser. Consider what you've been able to do with just a few lines of PHP. You have created a script that gets the file name of every file in a specific folder, and then displays them as a list of images. If you were to add additional image files to the /images/Gallery1/ folder, those images would also be included in the list; in other words, the list updates itself automatically.

19. Close the browser window and return to Chapter8.php in Expression Web.

Although the PHP worked, there are a couple of things that are sub-optimal. First, if you scroll through the list, you will see a broken image icon. This is because the PHP script looks for all the files in the Image folder, and one of those files is a hidden metadata folder that Expression Web uses to manage the site. PHP tries to display that directory in an image tag, which of course doesn't work. Secondly, the bulleted list is hardly a "gallery." In the next few steps you will remedy both those issues.

Improve the image list

1. Find your PHP code block from the previous steps in the Code pane. Change the code so that it looks like the following:

```
$dir = new DirectoryIterator('images/gallery1');
$FileType=".jpg";
while($dir->valid()) {
    if(!$dir->isDot()) {
        if(strpos($dir->current(),$FileType)) {
            print "<li><img src='images/gallery1/";
            print $dir->current()."'/></li>";
        }
    }
    $dir->next();
}
```

   What you've done is added a variable to contain the file extension ".jpg" (the first bold line in the preceding code) and an *if* statement that makes sure the file name contains ".jpg" (the second bold line). The *if* test skips any file name that doesn't include the text ".jpg"—in other words, non-image files.

2. Click Save and then click Preview on the Common toolbar to check your modifications in a browser.

   Notice that the previous broken image list item is gone. The list now includes only files with .jpg extensions, which is ideal for this particular gallery.

3. Close the browser and return to Expression Web.

   In the next few steps, you will use more of the Expression Web PHP tools to make the code you've been working with more useful and reusable as well.

4. In the Code pane, locate the PHP code you have been working on. Select all of it (including the opening PHP delimiter "*<?php*" and the closing delimiter "*?>*").

5. With the entire PHP block selected in the Code pane, right-click the highlighted code, and select Cut from the context menu.

   In the next few steps, you will move this PHP code from Chapter8.php to its own file, and then bring it back into play via a PHP include.

6. From the File menu, select New, and then select PHP. Expression Web creates a new PHP file in your workspace.

7. Set your cursor in the Code pane of this new page, and press Ctrl+A on your keyboard to select all of the contents, and then press Delete on your keyboard.

   Because you are creating a PHP file that will be included into a different page, you don't want any head, body, or other tags to be present in it.

8. With the new PHP file completely empty, press Ctrl+V on your keyboard to paste in the PHP block that you cut from Chapter8.php.

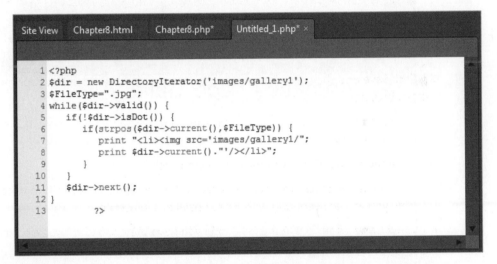

```php
1  <?php
2  $dir = new DirectoryIterator('images/gallery1');
3  $FileType=".jpg";
4  while($dir->valid()) {
5      if(!$dir->isDot()) {
6          if(strpos($dir->current(),$FileType)) {
7              print "<li><img src='images/gallery1/";
8              print $dir->current()."'/></li>";
9          }
10     }
11     $dir->next();
12 }
13         ?>
```

9. Click Save on the Common toolbar, and in the Save As dialog box, name this file **AutoGal.php**. Save it in the root of the sample site.

10. Click the Chapter8.php tab at the top of your workspace to continue editing that file.

11. In the Code pane, set your cursor between the *<ul>* tags where you cut the PHP code block from the page. From the Insert menu, select PHP, and then click Include. In the Select File To Include dialog box, double-click the AutoGal.php file you saved in step 9.

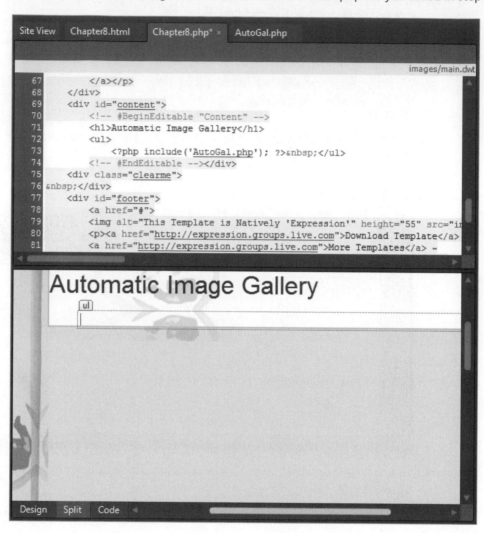

The content from AutoGal.php will now be included in Chapter8.php via a server-side include. This is helpful, because you can use an include file on any page you want, and if you need to modify the file, you only need to make the modifications in one location.

12. Click the AutoGal.php tab at the top of your workspace to continue editing that file.

Remember what this code does: it looks in a specific folder, retrieves all the files in that folder, and then filters the list for just the .jpg files, creating an *<img>* tag for each .jpg file, and surrounding each item with *<li></li>* tags. So, you could insert it into any file you like but it would always do the same thing. That's not very flexible. In the next few steps, you will modify this file so it's much more flexible in a designer's workflow.

13. The code returns the images as list items. Remember, you had to add the unordered list *<ul>* tag to surround the list before. To make things a little more sensible, you can add the unordered list tags to this include file. Enter a *<ul>* at the very beginning of the file, and a closing *</ul>* at the very end of the file.

14. Set your cursor after the opening PHP delimiter *<?php*, and then press Enter to create a new line.

Because you will replace some of the hard-coded variables in this block with variables you will be able to set in the page it'll be included on, it's important to make some notes here so that you and or anyone else will be able to easily see what's going on.

15. On the new line just below your opening PHP tag, type the following comment (comments begin with two forward slashes in PHP).

```
// Don't forget to add the following variables before you include this file:
//$TargetFolder $FileType $GalleryClass
```

```
1  <ul><?php
2  // Don't forget to add the following variables before you include this file:
3  //$TargetFolder $FileType $GalleryClass
4  $dir = new DirectoryIterator('images/gallery1');
5  $FileType=".jpg";
6  while($dir->valid()) {
7      if(!$dir->isDot()) {
8          if(strpos($dir->current(),$FileType)) {
9              print "<li><img src='images/gallery1/";
10             print $dir->current()."'/></li>";
11         }
12     }
13     $dir->next();
14 }
15         ?></ul>
```

By using the PHP comments feature (*//*), you can leave a message in the code file. The PHP engine ignores comment lines when it processes the page, so the comments will never appear in a browser, even if users view the HTML source of the page.

16. Change the *<ul>* tag at the top of this file to:

```
<ul class="<?php echo $GalleryClass ?>">
```

The *echo* command causes PHP to insert the contents of the following variable (in this case *$GalleryClass*). Because you can set this variable from outside the include file, that means you can define the unordered list class that's in the host file. This will make it easier to apply any gallery style you like.

17. Change the next line from:

```
$dir = new DirectoryIterator('images/gallery1');
```

to:

```
$dir = new DirectoryIterator($TargetFolder);
```

You're using a variable to set the script's path to an appropriate folder. This way, you'll be able to point the script at any folder you like from the page that contains the calls to the include file.

18. Change the following line from:

```
print "<li><img src='images/gallery1/";
```

to:

```
print "<li><img src='$TargetFolder";
```

Because you created a variable for the folder path, you want to replace the hard-coded path with the variable name.

19. Finally, remove the following line:

```
$FileType=".jpg";
```

You will define which file type to filter for in the Chapter8.php file, so it doesn't belong in the include file now.

```
Site View   Chapter8.html   Chapter8.php*   AutoGal.php* ×

 1  <ul class="<?php echo $GalleryClass ?>"><?php
 2  // Don't forget to add the following variables before you include this file:
 3  //$TargetFolder $FileType $GalleryClass
 4  $dir = new DirectoryIterator($TargetFolder);
 5  while($dir->valid()) {
 6      if(!$dir->isDot()) {
 7          if(strpos($dir->current(),$FileType)) {
 8              print "<li><img src='$TargetFolder";
 9              print $dir->current()."'/></li>";
10          }
11      }
12      $dir->next();
13  }
14          ?></ul>
```

20. Click the Chapter8.php tab at the top of your workspace to switch back to that file. Scroll the Code pane of Chapter8.php to the *<head>* section and enter the following code using the Expression Web IntelliSense pop-up:

```
<script type="text/javascript" src=
  "/files/jquery-ulslide/js/jquery.js"></script>

<script type="text/javascript" src=
  "/files/jquery-ulslide/js/jquery.mousewheel.js"></script>

<script type="text/javascript" src=
  "/files/jquery-ulslide/js/jquery.ulslide.js"></script>

<script type="text/javascript">
  $(function() {
    $('.slide1').ulslide({
      width: 443,
      height: 'auto',
      bnext: '#e1_next',
      bprev: '#e1_prev',
      axis: 'y',
          mousewheel: true,
          autoslide: 3000});

      $('.slide2').ulslide({
        width: 443,
        height: 300,
        duration: 1000,
        affect: 'fade',
        bnext: '#e2_next',
        bprev: '#e2_prev',
        direction: 'f',
        duration: 350,
        autoslide: 3000});
    });
</script>
```

> **Tip** You can copy and paste this content from DirectoryIterator1.txt in the site's /files folder.

The three *<script>* tags at the beginning of this code are includes for a jQuery library file and a plug-in called ULSlide. The actual JavaScript below that defines the appearance and behavior of the gallery. You can use other plug-ins that build a gallery based on an unordered list, or you can modify the PHP to create the chosen output that the plug-in requires.

Tip If you are going to use jQuery or some other script in all or many pages, you can include a link to it in your Dynamic Web Template. That way, you would only have to call the plug-in on specific pages because the main library file would automatically be included on all pages.

21. Scroll down through the Code pane until you reach the area in the Content region where you have the PHP Include.

    The final work here requires defining a few variables and removing the *<ul>* remnants from the earlier version.

22. Remove both the opening *<ul>* tag before the PHP include and the closing *</ul>* tag after it.

 Note You moved those tags to AutoGal.php, so leaving them in place in the Chapter8.php file would create duplicate HTML tags, which would cause rendering and validity problems.

23. Enter the following code just above the PHP include file:

```php
<?php
$TargetFolder="images/gallery1/";
$FileType=".jpg";
$GalleryClass="slide1";
?>
```

```
Site View   Chapter8.html   Chapter8.php* ×   AutoGal.php*

                                                    images/main.dwt
 98          <img alt="Valid CSS!" height="32" src="images/w3cvcgold.jpg" width="8
 99          </a></p>
100      </div>
101      <div id="content">
102          <!-- #BeginEditable "Content" -->
103              <h1>Automatic Image Gallery</h1>
104  <?php
105  $TargetFolder="images/gallery1/";
106  $FileType=".jpg";
107  $GalleryClass="slide1";
108  ?>
109  <?php include('AutoGal.php'); ?>
110          <!-- #EndEditable --></div>
111      <div class="clearme">
112   </div>
```

24. Click the Save All button, and then click the Preview button on the Common toolbar to test the gallery in a browser.

By using a small amount of PHP code and an easy-to-use jQuery plug-in, you have created a system that you can use over and over on any page or any number of pages you like. You've made it easy to turn a folder full of images into a self-maintaining image gallery of sorts.

25. Close the browser window and return to Expression Web.

Most of the work you just completed on the AutoGal.php include file was intended to make it more flexible. To explore that flexibility, you will now change the variables in Chapter8.php and cause the script to get a different kind of file, from a different folder, and apply a different gallery treatment to them.

Explore the power of generic include files

1. Return to the Chapter8.php file. Locate the variables you added to your page just above the PHP include statement and change them from this:

```php
<?php
$TargetFolder="images/gallery1/";
$FileType=".jpg";
$GalleryClass="slide1";
?>
```

to this:

```php
<?php
    $TargetFolder="images/gallery2/";
    $FileType=".png";
    $GalleryClass="slide2";
?>
```

These new variables tell the script to look into a different folder (images/gallery2/), for a different type of picture file (.png), and then (by changing the $GalleryClass class name), apply a different style to the result.

2. Click Save and then click Preview on the Common toolbar to check your changes in a browser.

As you can see, by changing the variables that pertained to the folder you wanted to use, the file type that you wanted to find, and the jQuery effect you wanted to apply, you were able to include a totally different gallery into Chapter8.php. Using PHP variables and an include file makes it easy and flexible to drop a gallery on any page you like.

3. Close the browser and return to Expression Web.

Note At this point, you can close the SampleSite site and any open browsers. If you are not continuing directly to the next chapter, exit Expression Web 4.

Tip Check below the Resources heading in Chapter8.html for links pertinent to this section.

PHP isn't necessarily a "programmers only" tool. Like ASP.NET or any other server-side scripting, with a little knowledge and some creative use, designers can save a great deal of time, and do some truly interesting things automatically.

By using server-side code appropriately, you can create almost anything a site requires. Knowing how technologies work together helps a great deal. As you've seen in this section, combining PHP with a little jQuery can create interesting and useful results.

Key Points

- Using jQuery in Expression Web can help you enhance your pages with client-side functionality.
- Using the Expression Web PHP Tools can help you add server-side functionality to your pages.
- jQuery plug-ins add tremendous functionality.
- Designers can use jQuery and PHP code together to create interesting and reusable functionality.

Chapter 9
Adding Functionality with ASP.NET and AJAX

After completing this chapter, you will be able to:

- Use ASP.NET tools in Expression Web
- Convert a DWT to a master page
- Use site navigation controls
- Use the AdRotator control
- Link to data sources and use data controls
- Use ASP.NET Ajax features

Microsoft ASP.NET is a server-side scripting technology. At a high level, ASP.NET works in much the same way as the PHP code you worked with in the previous chapter. One big difference is that ASP.NET separates code from markup more cleanly than is typical with PHP. In fact, ASP.NET typically stores markup in one file and code in a separate, related file. When a browser requests a page, the ASP.NET engine loads both pages, letting the code interact with the markup to create a response that the server returns to the browser.

What can you do with ASP.NET? Literally, anything that can be done with Web programming!

Together, Microsoft Expression Web and ASP.NET make a great combination. Expression Web has solid support for ASP.NET files. Using that support, you can, for example, insert advanced controls into your pages without writing any programming code.

One feature that facilitates using ASP.NET within Expression Web is the ASP.NET group in the Toolbox panel, which contains many ASP.NET controls commonly used in Web pages.

Important Before you can use the practice files in this chapter, you need to download and install them from the book's companion content Web site to their default location. For more information about downloading and installing the practice files, see the "Code Samples" section at the beginning of this book.

Troubleshooting Graphics and operating system-related instructions in this book reflect the Windows 7 user interface. If your computer is running Windows XP or Windows Vista and you experience trouble following the instructions as written, please refer to the "Information for Readers Running Windows XP or Vista" section at the beginning of this book.

Using ASP.NET Tools in Expression Web

Before starting to use the various tools that Expression Web provides for ASP.NET, it's worth exploring them briefly.

The ASP.NET Segment of the Toolbox

The ASP.NET segment of the Toolbox panel is divided into the following seven groups, each of which contains controls that you can use in your pages:

- **Standard**   Standard ASP.NET controls such as radio buttons, image controls, content placeholders, and other standard controls that are common on Web pages.

- **Data**   Controls that allow you to easily connect to data sources and insert data that the controls gather from those data sources into a Web page.

- **Validation**   Controls that support validation of data entered into ASP.NET forms.

- **Navigation**   Controls designed to help create navigation systems without having to write any programming code.

- **Login**   Controls that support implementing a user interface for membership systems in an ASP.NET site.

- **WebParts**   Controls for creating customizable Web sites in which end users can modify the content, appearance, and behavior of Web pages directly from a browser.

- **AJAX**   Controls for creating rich client behavior with little or no client script, such as asynchronous partial-page updating (dynamically refreshing selected parts of the page without reloading the entire page). Asynchronous partial-page updates avoid the visible "blink" that happens when a browser reloads an entire page.

> **Tip** When you're adding ASP.NET controls to your page, it will be much easier if you can see a visual representation of them. To make that happen, select Visual Aids from the View menu, and then enable Block Selection, Visible Borders, Empty Containers, ASP.NET Non-visual Controls, and Template Region Labels.

Another great feature in Expression Web is the Expression Development Server. This development server provides value because you can build a site in any folder-based location, and Expression Web will preview that page through the built-in server. Having a built-in server is far more convenient and straightforward than having to set up a server on your local computer and previewing your pages by browsing them through that server. It definitely beats having to publish your pages to an external Web server just to preview them.

In addition to the Toolbox panel and the Expression Development Server, Expression Web provides the Tag Properties panel, which you can use to modify ASP.NET control properties in much the same way that you modify cascading style sheets or HTML elements.

From a designer's perspective, some of the most interesting controls that Expression Web provides are master pages, site navigation controls, data access components, AJAX controls, and DataView controls.

> **Note** Expression Web helps you work with ASP.NET controls and features, but if you're interested in full-scale ASP.NET programming, you're going to need more than this book and a copy of Expression Web. You'll need Microsoft Visual Web Developer, Microsoft Visual Studio, or another code editor, and you'll need to learn a full set of programming skills. You can use books to learn ASP.NET programming, or you can use online resources such as MSDN or any of the many sites dedicated to teaching people ASP.NET. You will find a list of resources in the Chapter9.html file of this book's Sample Site.

This chapter focuses on the ASP.NET capabilities available from within Expression Web, and how the design-related features can assist you in creating ASP.NET Web pages that make use of those features.

Converting a DWT to a Master Page

Although you created an ASP.NET master page/content page arrangement in Chapter 3, "Capitalizing on the Template Options in Expression Web 4," the ability to quickly convert a Dynamic Web Template (DWT) to an ASP.NET master page is useful, because there are many more templates available based on the DWT file than the master file, so a quick conversion is often quite handy, plus the skill set is identical to making use of the most commonly available HTML templates.

Earlier in this book, you saw how easy it was to keep all the pages in a site uniform by using the master page/content page arrangement, or the more commonly available Dynamic Web Template format. It's surprisingly easy to move content from one to the other.

Convert a Dynamic Web Template into an ASP.NET master page

> **Note** Start Expression Web 4 before beginning this exercise. Open the SampleSite site by selecting Open Site from the Site menu, browsing to the companion media's default installation page, and double-clicking the SampleSite folder. With the sample site opened in Expression Web, double-click the Chapter9.html page in the Folder List panel.

1. With the Chapter9.html page open in Split view, you can see, as indicated just above the Code pane, that this page is attached to /images/Main.dwt. On the Format menu, point to DWT and then click Open Attached Dynamic Web Template.

2. With the DWT open, select New from the File menu, and then select Page. In the New Page dialog box, click the ASP.NET category on the left. The display will list all the ASP.NET-related files you can create.

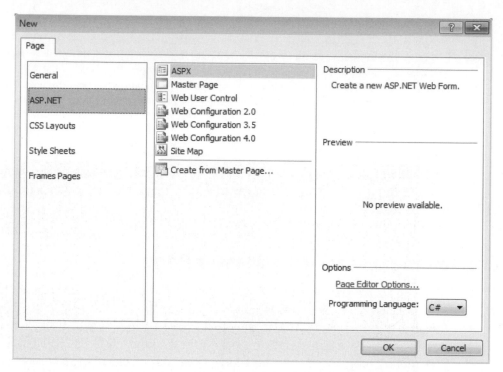

 Tip Refer to Chapter 3 for additional detailed information regarding master pages and other template techniques.

3. In the center pane of the New Page dialog box, select Master Page. In the right pane, make sure that the programming language is set to C#, and then click OK.

   Expression Web creates a new ASP.NET master page in your workspace.

4. From the Format menu, select CSS Styles, and then click Attach Style Sheet. In the Attach Style Sheet dialog box, browse to and double-click the file /images/main.css.

   Due to the way this book's site template is built, linking to the style sheet will give you default design parameters that will work in master pages, HTML pages, DWT files, or even PHP files. The flexibility that style sheets deliver is well worth the effort of learning the skill, and using them appropriately in your designs.

5. Click Save on the Common toolbar, and in the Save As dialog box, save the master page as **default.master** in the site's root folder.

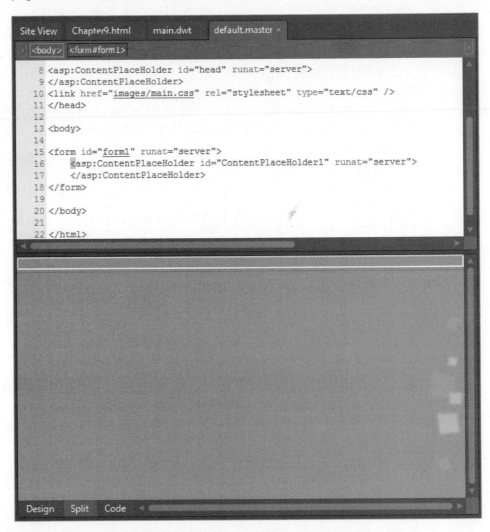

In the next few steps, you will transfer the design from the DWT to the master page.

6. Click the main.dwt tab at the top of your workspace to switch to that file. Set your cursor in the content area in the Design pane. On the Quick Tag Selector, click the drop-down arrow on the *<body>* tag, and then click Select Tag Contents. Right-click the selected code in the Code pane, and then click Copy.

7. Click the default.master tab at the top of your workspace to continue editing the master page. Set your cursor in the Design pane. On the Quick Tag Selector, click the drop-down arrow on the *<form>* tag, and then click Select Tag Contents. Right-click the selected code in the Code pane, and then click Paste.

The ASP.NET master page is an ASP.NET forms page. Even though there's no HTML form, ASP.NET needs a form inside of the body tag; that's why you're leaving this one in place.

8. Click Save on the Common toolbar. You may see a content region confirmation alert. Click Yes to paste the DWT's body tag contents into your master page.

An ASP.NET master page needs a content placeholder inside of the body. You may see this warning because Expression Web is trying to protect you from creating a non-functional master page. You will be converting the Dynamic Web Template editable regions into ASP.NET content placeholder in the next few steps.

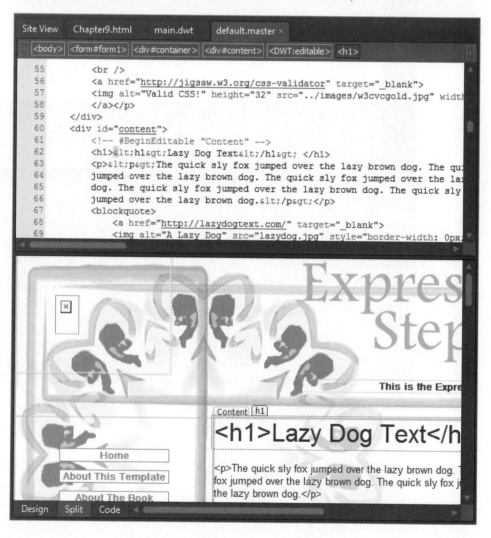

Tip You may notice the broken image icons in the Design pane of the master page. This is because of a path issue. Ignore it for now. You will replace the images with ASP.NET image controls later in this section.

9. Scroll the master page's Code pane to the top so that the *<head>* section is visible.

```
Site View    Chapter9.html    main.dwt    default.master ×

<body>  <form#form1>  <div#container>  <div#content>  <DWT:editable>  <h1>

 1 <!DOCTYPE html PUBLIC "-//W3C//DTD XHTML 1.0 Transitional//EN" "http://www.w3
 2 <%@ Master Language="C#" %>
 3 <html dir="ltr" xmlns="http://www.w3.org/1999/xhtml">
 4
 5 <head runat="server">
 6 <meta content="text/html; charset=utf-8" http-equiv="Content-Type" />
 7 <title>Untitled 1</title>
 8 <asp:ContentPlaceHolder id="head" runat="server">
 9 </asp:ContentPlaceHolder>
10 <link href="images/main.css" rel="stylesheet" type="text/css" />
11 </head>
12
13 <body>
14
15 <form id="form1" runat="server">
```

The master page has a *ContentPlaceHolder* control in the head of the page that looks like this:

```
<asp:ContentPlaceHolder id="head" runat="server">
</asp:ContentPlaceHolder>
```

This placeholder is there to contain content that will show up in all the pages based on the master page, but you can also change the contents on a page-by-page basis. This is a particularly useful area for content such as Meta tags, JavaScript, and CSS links that you want to apply on a page-by-page basis.

This site's Dynamic Web Template has a considerable amount of code in the head section's editable region. A DWT's editable regions and a master page's content placeholder provide similar results using different technology.

10. Click the main.dwt tab at the top of your editing window to switch to that file and scroll the Code pane to the *<head>* section.

```
Site View    Chapter9.html    main.dwt ×    default.master

 2 <html dir="ltr" xmlns="http://www.w3.org/1999/xhtml">
 3
 4 <head>
 5 <!-- #BeginEditable "doctitle" -->
 6 <meta content="text/html; charset=utf-8" http-equiv="Content-Type" />
 7 <meta content="english" name="language" />
 8 <meta content="Author's Sample Site for Expression Web 4 Step by Step" name=
 9 <meta content="Expression Web, Expression Web 4, Expression Web Step by Step,
10 <meta content="Chris Leeds" name="owner" />
11 <meta content="Chris Leeds" name="copyright" />
12 <meta content="Chris Leeds" name="author" />
13 <meta content="General" name="rating" />
14 <meta content="7 days" name="revisit-after" />
15 <title>Expression Web Step by Step Sample Site</title>
16 <!-- #EndEditable -->
17 <link href="main.css" rel="stylesheet" type="text/css" />
```

11. Highlight all the Meta tags in the DWT's "doctitle" editable region, but don't highlight the *<title>* tag, because that gets handled a little differently in a master page.

12. Right-click the highlighted code, and in the context menu, click Copy. Click the default.master tab at the top of your workspace to switch back to that file.

13. Set your cursor in the Code pane just after the opening *ContentPlaceHolder* tag (*<asp:ContentPlaceHolder id="head" runat="server">*) in the *<head>* section, and press Enter on your keyboard to break to a new line. Press Ctrl+V on your keyboard to paste the Meta tags from the DWT into the master page.

```
Site View    Chapter9.html    main.dwt    default.master* ×

 5 <head runat="server">
 6 <meta content="text/html; charset=utf-8" http-equiv="Content-Type" />
 7 <title>Untitled 1</title>
 8 <asp:ContentPlaceHolder id="head" runat="server">
 9 <meta content="text/html; charset=utf-8" http-equiv="Content-Type" />
10 <meta content="english" name="language" />
11 <meta content="Author's Sample Site for Expression Web 4 Step by Step" name=
12 <meta content="Expression Web, Expression Web 4, Expression Web Step by Step,
13 <meta content="Chris Leeds" name="owner" />
14 <meta content="Chris Leeds" name="copyright" />
15 <meta content="Chris Leeds" name="author" />
16 <meta content="General" name="rating" />
17 <meta content="7 days" name="revisit-after" />
18 </asp:ContentPlaceHolder>
19 <link href="images/main.css" rel="stylesheet" type="text/css" />
```

Just as the editable region and *ContentPlaceHolder* in the *<head>* sections of the two templates correspond, you will create new placeholders in the DWT's body to match the body of the master page.

14. Set your cursor in the Design pane of the master page. On the Quick Tag Selector, locate the tab *<DWT:editable>*, click its drop-down arrow, and then click Select Tag Contents. Right-click the selected code in the Code pane, and then select Cut from the context menu.

The editable region is now completely empty in both the Code and Design panes.

 Tip The cut-and-paste technique you're about to learn is very helpful to keep content while modifying or eliminating its parent element (in this case the editable region).

15. Click the *<DWT:editable>* tab on the Quick Tag Selector to select the entire tag, and then in the Toolbox panel, expand the ASP.NET controls, and in the Standard group, double-click *ContentPlaceHolder*.

An ASP.NET *ContentPlaceHolder* replaces the editable region.

16. Set your cursor in the Code pane, between the start and end tags for the new *ContentPlaceHolder*, and press Ctrl+V on your keyboard to paste the content you cut from the DWT's editable region.

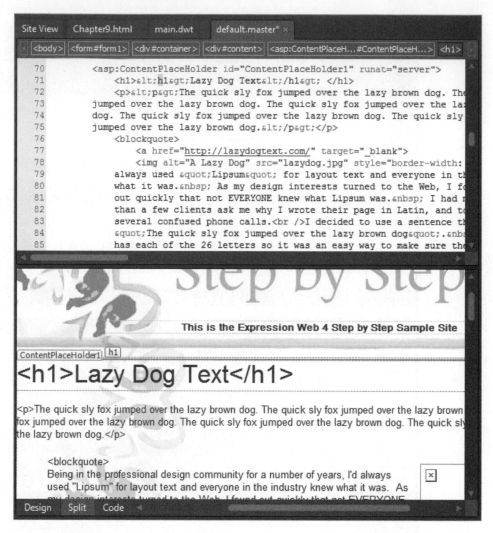

Using the Quick Tag Selector along with creative cut and paste, Toolbox selections, or keyboard shortcuts is a skill that's easy to learn and yields a great return in speed and accuracy.

17. Click Save on the Common toolbar.

Not only does a Dynamic Web Template have editable regions, it also keeps track of paths to images, hyperlinks, and so on. This happens at the desktop level before you save attached pages. ASP.NET master pages can do that too—and much more—but you need to take certain techniques into account. One such technique that you will learn in the next few steps involves inserting an ASP.NET image control into a master page, which is different than the procedure to place an image in a DWT, where you can rely on Expression Web to maintain the file path to that image.

18. In the upper-left corner of the page, you will see a broken image where the blue Microsoft MVP logo was. Click it in the Design pane to select it.

When you make a selection in the Design pane like this, the convergence of Design pane, Code pane, and Quick Tag Selector give you immediate orientation in the HTML code. For example, you can see in the Code pane and on the Quick Tag Selector that this image is inside of a hyperlink, and that the hyperlink is inside of a division (*#bannerleft*).

19. Right-click the selected code in the Code pane, and then select Cut from the context menu. Press Ctrl+/ on your keyboard to insert an HTML comment, and then press Ctrl+V to paste the image inside the HTML comment tag.

Cutting the image tag from the code and then inserting it back into the page inside an HTML comment provides two benefits. First, it lets you refer back to the previous code. Second, it hides the content in the Design pane.

20. Set your cursor in the Code pane, just before the HTML comment you inserted. In the Toolbox panel, double-click Image in the ASP.NET Controls Standard group.

Expression Web inserts an ASP.NET image control into your page. In the next few steps, you will use the Tag Properties panel to edit the control.

21. Select your newly inserted *image* control in the Design pane, and then, in the Tag Properties panel, set your cursor in the ImageUrl field of the Appearance group.

By using the Tag Properties panel, you can refer back to the original image that you hid with the HTML comment, and apply size, alt text, and file path information to the ASP.NET tag.

22. Click the ellipsis button beside the ImageUrl field label. In the Select Image dialog box, browse to and double-click the file MVP_fullcolor-screen.gif in the site's /images folder. Enter **MVP Logo** in the AlternateText field. In the Layout group of the Tag Properties panel, enter **31px** in the Width field, and **50px** in the Height field.

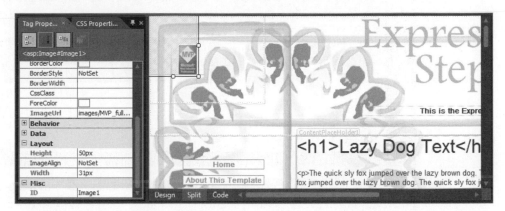

 Tip The Tag Properties panel can be very lengthy. Collapsing or expanding categories and using the Show Set Properties button at the top of the panel judiciously helps tame these property lists.

23. Scroll the Design pane of your page to the bottom, and click the image on the left side of the footer to select it.

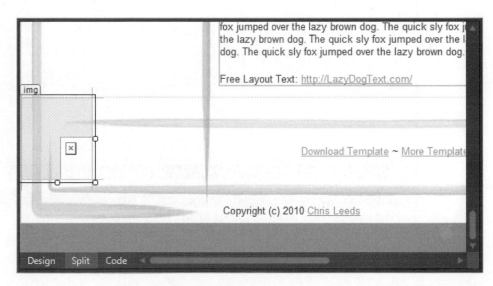

Look at the Quick Tag Selector. You can see that this image is also inside of a hyperlink tag, as well as a division *(#footer)*.

24. Right-click the selected code in the Code pane, and select Cut from the Context menu. Press Ctrl+/ on your keyboard to insert another HTML comment, and then press Ctrl+V to paste the image into the comment.

25. Set your cursor in the Code pane, just before the HTML comment you inserted. In the Toolbox panel, double-click Image in the ASP.NET Controls Standard group. Select the new image control in the Design pane.

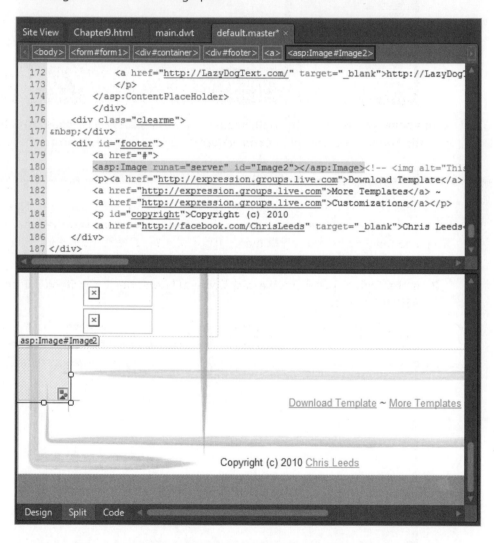

26. Enter **images\studiobox.jpg** in the ImageUrl field, **This Template is Natively Expression** in the AlternateText field, **55px** in the Height field, and **42px** in the Width field.

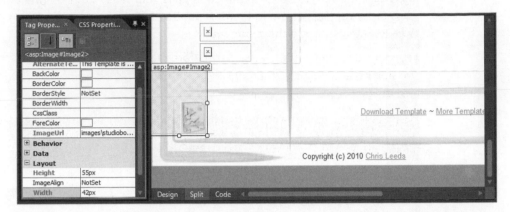

At this point, you've converted both images in the template's HTML code to ASP.NET image controls. You will add one more *ContentPlaceHolder* to make the template more flexible.

Make the template more flexible

1. Select one of the master page's navigation links on the left side of the page in the Design pane. On the Quick Tag Selector, click the drop-down arrow on the *<div#leftnav>* tab, and then click Select Tag Contents. Right-click the selected contents in the Code pane, and then select Cut from the Context menu.

2. In the Toolbox panel, double-click ContentPlaceHolder in the Standard group of the ASP.NET controls.

3. In the Code pane, set your cursor between the start and end tags for the new *ContentPlaceHolder* and then press Ctrl+V on your keyboard to paste the contents of the navigation division back into the page, and then click Save on the Common toolbar.

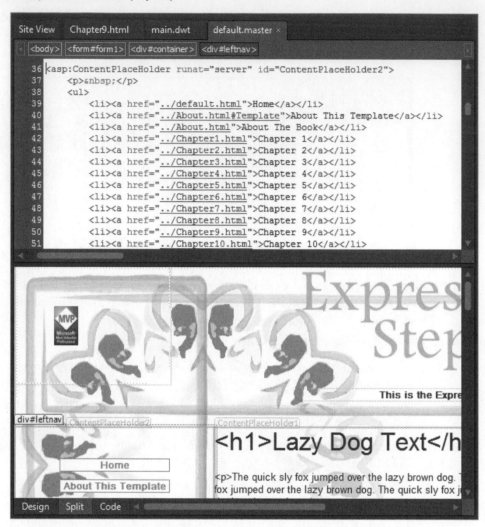

By adding this navigation division's contents to a *ContentPlaceHolder* now, you can save time and effort later if you need to add custom content in pages already created from the master page.

4. Click Save on the Common toolbar. Then, from the File menu, select New, and choose Create From Master Page.

5. In the Select A Master Page dialog box, click Browse. Double-click default.master in the site's root folder, and then click OK in the dialog box.

   Expression Web creates a new file named Untitled_1.aspx in your workspace.

6. Click Save on the Common toolbar. In the Save As dialog box, name this new page **Chapter9.aspx,** and then click Save to save it in the site's root folder.

7. Click Preview on the Common toolbar to preview this page through the Expression Development Server.

   The page should look identical to new pages created with the site's Dynamic Web Template.

8. Close the browser and return to expression Web.

   You may have noticed in the browser preview that there was no entry in the navigation menu for this new page. In the next few steps, you will add this page to the menu and see how a server-side run-time template such as the master page works differently than a save-time template such as a DWT.

9. Click the default.master tab at the top of your workspace to switch to that file. Set your cursor in the Design pane at the end of the text in the list item that reads "Chapter 9," and press Enter on your keyboard to insert a new list item below it. Type **Chapter 9 (ASPX)**.

10. Select the text you just entered, right-click the selected text, and select Hyperlink from the context menu. In the Insert Hyperlink dialog box, click chapter9.aspx, and then click OK. Click Save on the Common toolbar to save your change to the master page's navigation list.

Tip One of the most common tasks is setting a hyperlink. You'll find that using the Ctrl+K keyboard shortcut can be a time saver.

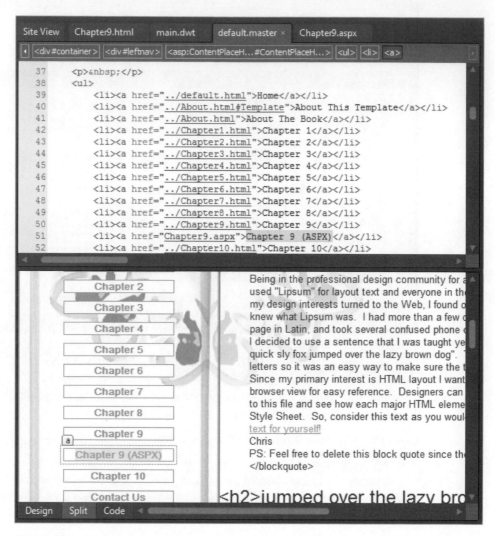

Notice that the only page you saved a change to was default.master. You made no edits and saved no changes to Chapter9.aspx.

11. Click the Chapter9.aspx tab at the top of your workspace to switch to that file, and then click Preview on the Common toolbar.

As you can see in the browser preview, the Chapter 9 (ASPX) link now appears in the Chapter9.aspx file. Also note the broken image on the right side of the content area of the page. Had you not converted the images in the banner and footer to ASP.NET image controls, they would appear as broken images as well. The image in the main content *ContentPlaceHolder* control in the master page would be another good place to replace an HTML image tag with an ASP.NET image control.

12. Close the browser and return to Expression Web. From the Window menu, click Close All Pages.

> **Note** Leave the SampleSite open if you are proceeding directly to the next section.

In this section, you converted a DWT to an ASP.NET master page, replaced image tags with ASP.NET image controls, used the Tag Properties panel to modify the image controls, and created a new page based on the master page. The new master page and Chapter9.aspx files will serve as practice files for the remaining segments of this chapter.

Using Site Navigation Controls

The ASP.NET controls segment of the Toolbox panel contains a group named Navigation, which contains three types of site navigation controls—*Menu*, *SiteMapPath*, and *TreeView*. All these controls draw their navigational information from an XML file named Web.sitemap, which is saved in the root of your site.

- *Menu* is a Dynamic HTML type of menu control that you might already be familiar with. When you point to a link that has child pages below it, a secondary menu appears.

- *TreeView* is a control that organizes items hierarchically—similar to what you see when browsing a site such as msdn.microsoft.com. It is appropriate for organizing very large sites that have many levels of hierarchical information.

- *SiteMapPath* provides what you might know as "breadcrumb navigation." It indicates the page the browser is currently showing and pages in the navigation structure that come before and after it.

In this exercise, you will replace the original navigation in the master page that you created in the previous exercise with an ASP.NET navigation control.

Add an ASP.NET navigation control

> **Note** Use the Chapter9.aspx file that you created in the previous exercise. Open the SampleSite site if it isn't already open, and then open the Chapter9.aspx file.

> **Troubleshooting** To follow the steps in this exercise, you will need to have completed the preceding exercise. Specifically, you need to have created the files default.master and Chapter9.aspx.

1. Click the link to the master page (default.master) above the Code pane of Chapter9.aspx to open the master page in your workspace.

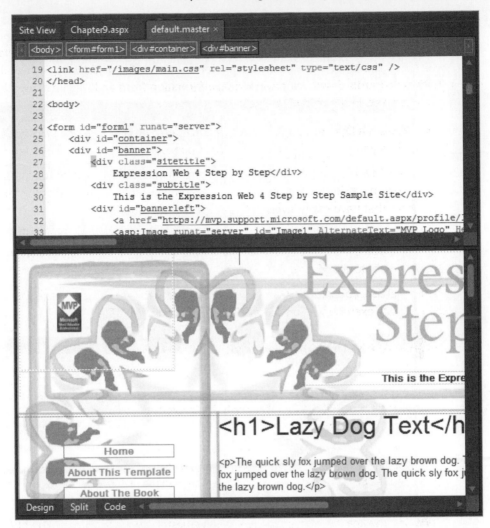

As a designer using Expression Web with a master page/content page arrangement, you're in an interesting situation. You can either put your new ASP.NET navigation control in the content page (Chapter9.aspx) or in the master page (default.master). For the purposes of this section, you will work on it in the content page because after you're done, you can transfer the work to the default.master file, and then reset the content file back to the master page's contents. You'll have a more "secure" workflow with this technique.

2. Click the Chapter9.aspx tab at the top of your workspace to switch back to that file. In the Design pane, click the navigation area (*ContentPlaceHolder2*) to select it.

3. Click the Content Tasks button on its upper-right corner, and then click Create Custom Content.

Notice what has just happened in the Code and Design panes. When you created the custom content, Expression Web placed an ASP.NET content control into Chapter9.aspx and filled the control with the contents that were inside the *ContentPlaceHolder* in the default.master file, thereby making that content editable on this individual page.

> **Tip** *ContentPlaceHolder* controls will show either (Custom) or (Master) depending on where the visible content is coming from.

4. In the Design pane, click Home in the navigation area at the top of the page. Click the *<ul>* tab on the Quick Tag Selector to select the entire tag and its contents, and then press Delete on your keyboard to eliminate it.

   In the next few steps, you will replace this list of navigation links with an ASP.NET menu control.

5. In the Toolbox panel, expand the ASP.NET controls group, and then expand navigation. Double-click Menu to insert an ASP.NET menu control into the page.

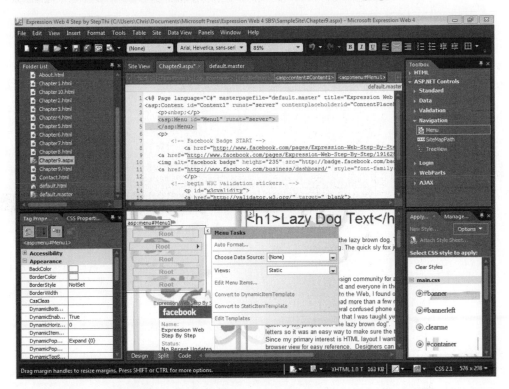

An ASP.NET menu control is now visible in both the Design and Code panes, as well as available in the Tag Properties panel, and so on.

 Tip Notice how the visual presentation of the default ASP.NET menu control looks fairly similar to the original menu that you removed from the page. This is a side benefit of a site design that makes use of cascading style sheets.

To use the menu control, you need a file named Web.sitemap in the root folder of the SampleSite.

6. From the File menu, select New, and then choose Page. Click the ASP.NET category on the left side, and then double-click Site Map.

The file that defines the navigation structure for the menu control is an XML file. XML is inherently hierarchical, so the nodes in the XML structure work naturally to define subpages and hierarchical structure for the menu control.

7. Double-click the file Sitemap.txt in the site's /files folder and copy its entire contents to your Clipboard. Close Sitemap.txt and return to Web.sitemap. Set your cursor in the page and press Ctrl+A to select all the content, and then press Ctrl+V to paste the contents of the text file into the site map.

> **Tip** When you copy and paste XML or work on an XML file, right-click the code and then click Reformat XML and/or Verify Well Formed XML in the context menu.

8. Click Save on the Common toolbar. Save the file as Web.sitemap in the root folder of the site, and then click the Chapter9.aspx tab at the top of your workspace to switch to that file.

9. Click the Menu Tasks button on the upper right of the menu control. In the Menu Tasks pop-up window, in the Choose Data Source box, click New Data Source. In the Data Source Configuration Wizard, click Site Map.

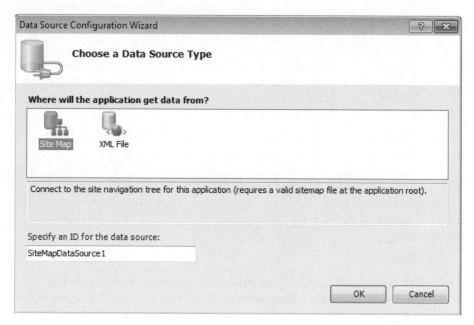

10. Click OK in the Data Source Configuration Wizard to apply your changes and close the wizard.

11. Click the menu control in the Design pane of your workspace to select it. In the Tag Properties panel, scroll down to the Behavior group, and type a **2** in the StaticDisplayLevels field. Then scroll down to the Layout group, and make sure the Orientation field is set to **Vertical**.

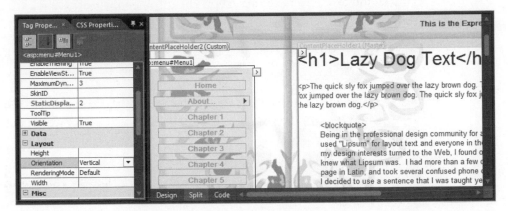

> **Tip** When you're working with a lengthy Tag Properties panel list, make use of the options at the top of the panel. You can choose to sort by group, alphabetically, place all the properties with set values on top, and so on. Usually you can apply several view modifications to find exactly what you're looking for much more quickly than scrolling through the item list.

12. Click Save and then click Preview on the Common toolbar to start the ASP.NET Development Server and preview your page in a browser.

    Although the navigation is not identical to the original menu bar, the file looks fairly close for a first draft.

    Take note of the functionality of the site navigation control. The page displayed in the browser has two links on the navigation bar, each of which has a small arrow icon. When you point to it, a fly-out menu appears.

    You can modify all the visual aspects of this site navigation control easily by using the Tag Properties panel. This menu can be formatted to fit better with the rest of the site template.

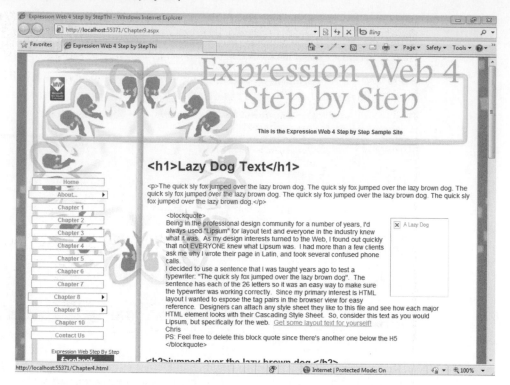

Tip You can insert the other site navigation controls into a page and modify them using the same workflow that you've applied to the menu control. Take some time to experiment with them after you complete this exercise.

13. Close the browser and return to Expression Web.

Because the menu control is working and requires only minor adjustments for its appearance, you will move it from the Chapter9.aspx file into the master page, and then reset the Chapter9.aspx file to the master page's content.

14. In the Design pane of Chapter9.aspx, right-click the ASP.NET menu control, and select Cut from the Context menu.

15. Click the default.master tab at the top of your workspace, and then set your cursor in the navigation list on the left of the page.

16. Click the *<ul>* tab on the Quick Tag Selector, and then press Ctrl+V to paste the *menu* control into the master page, where the unordered list of navigation links was previously located.

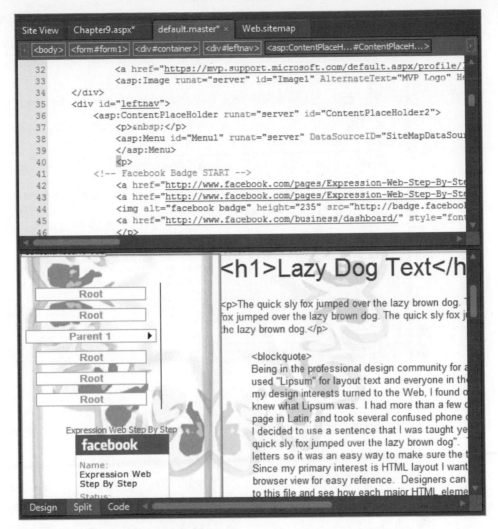

Notice that because the *SiteMapDataSource* isn't present on the master page, the *menu* control shows a default list of links.

17. Click the Menu Tasks button on the upper right of the menu control, and in the Menu Tasks pop-up window, in the Choose Data Source box, click New Data Source. In the Data Source Configuration Wizard, click Site Map, click OK, and then click Save on the Common toolbar.

18. Click the Chapter9.aspx tab at the top of your workspace, and then click the Content Tasks button on the upper right of the *ContentPlaceHolder* you were working with. In the Content Tasks pop-up window, click Default to Master's Content, and then click Yes on the Confirmation alert.

The next steps will show you how to create a new page and add it to the site map file.

19. From the File menu, select New, and then choose Create From Master Page. In the Select A Master Page dialog box, click Browse, double-click default.master, and then click OK.

Expression Web creates a new page named Untitled_1.aspx in your workspace.

20. From the File menu, click Save All. In the Save As dialog box, name the page **Chapter9b.aspx**, and then click Save.

Now you've created a new page, and you're ready to add it to the site navigation.

21. Click the Web.sitemap tab at the top of your workspace to open it for editing. Locate the following code for the original chapter9.aspx file's entry.

```
<siteMapNode url="Chapter9.aspx" title="Chapter 9 (ASP.NET)"
  description="Chapter 9 (ASP.NET)" />
```

22. Just below that node, add the following code to the site map file:

```
<siteMapNode url="Chapter9b.aspx" title="Chapter 9B (ASP.NET)"
  description="Chapter 9B (ASP.NET)" />
```

These XML SiteMap nodes work much like nested HTML tags. A node can be a single entry, or it can contain sub-nodes of its own.

23. Click Save to save your change to the site map file. Switch back to Chapter9b.aspx and then click Preview on the Common toolbar. In the browser, point to the Chapter 9 entry on the menu control.

Your new page is now represented in the site navigation control.

24. Close the browser and return to Expression Web. From the Window menu, click Close All Pages.

Note Leave the SampleSite open if you are proceeding directly to the next section.

In this exercise, using nothing but an easily updated XML site map file, a few clicks of the mouse, and a couple of adjustments in the Tag Properties panel, you've generated an easily styled and very usable menu.

Creating this type of menu would typically have required substantial hand-coded JavaScript or the use of a third-party application to build the menu.

As you use these ASP.NET site navigation controls, you should experiment with modifying the properties by using the AutoFormat option on the Common Tasks pop-up. There are literally limitless combinations of color, action, placement, and orientation that you can achieve by editing the properties of the entire menu, or by modifying specific levels through the Tag Properties panel.

> **Note** You can add, remove, and modify pages in the site map within a single XML file. You don't need to edit any other pages, yet your changes are displayed on every page that's attached to the master page that contains the control. These site navigation controls can open a whole new world to you in your site design workflow.

Using the AdRotator Control

Now that you have had a chance to explore master pages and site navigation controls, you will learn about another control from the Standard group of the Toolbox panel—the AdRotator control. This control uses the information in an XML file to display advertising banners in an ASP.NET page.

For this exercise, you will add the banner to the master page, ensuring that the banner will display in all the pages that are based on it. Like the *menu* control, you will put the AdRotator inside a *ContentPlaceHolder* control in the master page so that users can change it on a page-by-page basis, if necessary.

Insert an ASP.NET AdRotator control and modify its XML information file

> **Note** Use the Chapter9.html page of the SampleSite site you opened in the previous exercise. Open this book's sample site and Chapter9.html page, if they aren't already open.

1. Double-click the default.master file in the Folder List panel to open it in your workspace. In the Design pane, click one of the W3C validation images on the left side of the page, click the *<p#w3cvalidity>* tab's drop-down arrow on the Quick Tag Selector, and then click Select Tag Contents.

2. In the Toolbox panel, expand the ASP.NET controls, expand the Standard group, and then double-click *AdRotator* to insert that control where the paragraph tag's contents were.

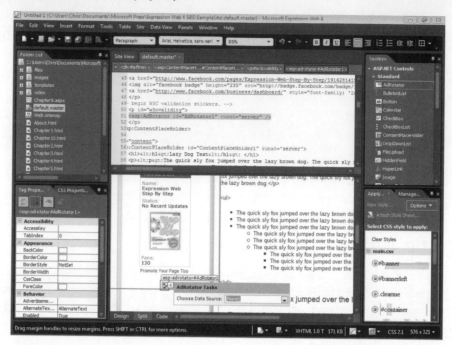

3. Click the AdRotator's Tasks button. In the AdRotator Tasks pop-up, click New Data Source in the Choose Data Source box. In the Data Source Configuration Wizard, click XML File, and then click OK. In the Configure Data Source dialog box, click Browse (next to the Data File field), click banners.xml inside of the site's /files folder, and then click Open.

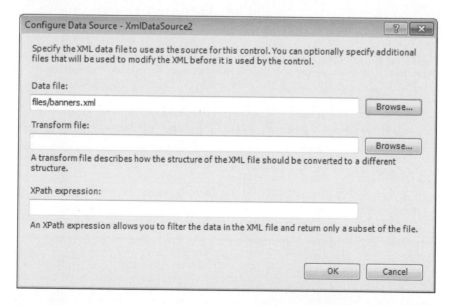

4. In the Configure Data Source dialog box, click OK. On the toolbar, click Save to save the change you made to the master page. Click Chapter9.aspx in the Folder List panel, and then click Preview on the Common toolbar.

5. Scroll down to the AdRotator's rendering in the browser. Refresh the browser several times and notice that the banner image changes each time the page loads.

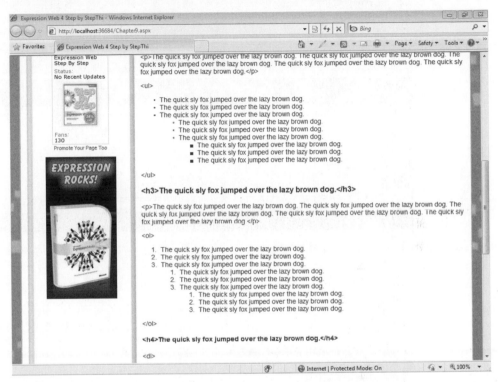

6. Close the browser and return to Expression Web. In the Folder List panel, double-click the Banners.xml file inside of the site's /files folder to open it.

You will add another node to the file to display another banner image.

7. Insert the following code just before the closing </Advertisements> tag.

> **Tip** You don't actually have to type the code. Just copy the last node in the file from the start <Ad> tag to the end </Ad> tag (Expression Web), paste it above the closing </Advertisements> tag, and then replace the instances of "Web" with "Studio." If your edits cause the XML nodes to become out of alignment, just right-click the page and in the context menu, click Reformat XML.

```
<Ad>
    <ImageUrl>~/images/studio-banner.jpg</ImageUrl>
    <NavigateUrl>http://www.microsoft.com/expression/products/overview.
aspx?key=studio</NavigateUrl>
    <AlternateText>Visit Microsoft's Expression Studio Site</AlternateText>
    <Height>300</Height>
    <Width>150</Width>
    <Keywords>
    </Keywords>
    <Impressions>
    </Impressions>
</Ad>
```

```
Site View    default.master    banners.xml* ×

31          <Keywords>
32          </Keywords>
33          <Impressions>
34          </Impressions>
35      </Ad>
36      <Ad>
37          <ImageUrl>~/images/web-banner.jpg</ImageUrl>
38          <NavigateUrl>http://www.microsoft.com/expression/products/overview.as
39          <AlternateText>Visit Microsoft's Expression Web Site</AlternateText>
40          <Height>300</Height>
41          <Width>150</Width>
42          <Keywords>
43          </Keywords>
44          <Impressions>
45          </Impressions>
46      </Ad>
47      <Ad>
48          <ImageUrl>~/images/studio-banner.jpg</ImageUrl>
49          <NavigateUrl>http://www.microsoft.com/expression/products/overview.as
50          <AlternateText>Visit Microsoft's Expression Studio Site</AlternateTex
51          <Height>300</Height>
52          <Width>150</Width>
53          <Keywords>
54          </Keywords>
55          <Impressions>
56          </Impressions>
57      </Ad>
58  </Advertisements>
```

8. Click Save on the Common toolbar. In the Folder List panel, click the Chapter9.aspx file, and then click Preview on the Common toolbar.

9. Refresh the browser several times to make sure that you eventually see the Expression Studio image.

10. Close the browser window and return to Expression Web. From the Window menu, click Close All Pages.

Note Leave the SampleSite open if you are proceeding directly to the next section.

In this exercise, you inserted a dynamic banner rotator into your master page that gets its content data from an XML file. You added a new banner to the XML file by editing its contents directly. Rather impressively, you were able to do all this without writing one single line of programming code!

Tip Just because it's called an AdRotator control doesn't mean that it's useful only for displaying rotating ads. For example, you could use this control to draw users' attention to graphical links to pages within your own site.

Linking to Data Sources and Using Data Controls

The ability to draw information from a database and display it on a Web page has previously been a fairly complicated task. Not so with Expression Web ASP.NET tools.

Since ASP.NET uses providers and has the ability to deal with data natively, you don't need to write any programming code to display data from a database on your ASP.NET Web pages.

ASP.NET can work with Microsoft Access databases, Microsoft SQL Server databases, XML files, Microsoft Excel files, and even Oracle, IBM DB2, and MySQL databases.

Display Access database information using GridView and ListView controls

Note Use the Chapter9.html page of the SampleSite site you opened in the previous exercise. Open this book's sample site and Chapter9.html page, if they aren't already open.

1. In the Folder List panel, double-click the Chapter9.aspx file to open it for editing. In the Design pane, click *ContentPlaceHolder1*, and then click the Content Tasks button on its upper-right corner. In the Content Tasks pop-up, click Create Custom Content.

2. With all the text from the master page still selected, type **Contact Our People**. Highlight the text in the Design pane and click Heading 1 *<h1>* in the Styles drop-down list on the Common toolbar. Set your cursor at the end of the heading and press Enter to create a new paragraph.

3. In the ASP.NET controls group in the Toolbox panel, expand the Data section, and then double-click GridView to insert an ASP.NET GridView control.

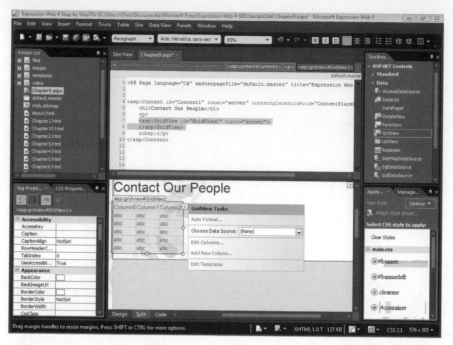

4. Click the GridView Tasks button on the upper right of the GridView control. In the GridView Tasks pop-up window, in the Choose Data Source box, click New Data Source. In the Data Source Configuration Wizard, click Access Database.

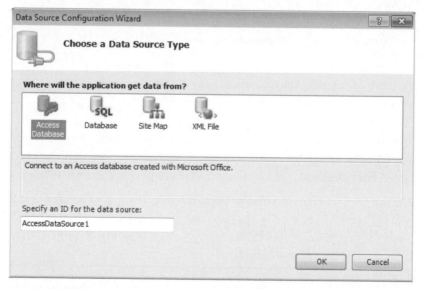

5. Click OK in the wizard. In the Configure Data Source dialog box, click Browse, click the ContactList.mdb file in the site's /files folder, and then click Open.

6. Click Next.

This part of the wizard helps you select the data you want to display.

7. In the Name field, make sure the drop-down list is set to **employees**. Under Columns, se-lect the FirstName, LastName, E-mail Address, Business Phone, and Job Title check boxes.

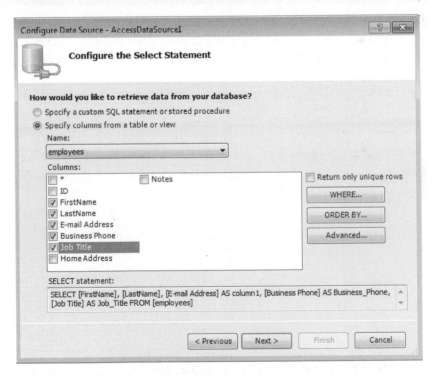

8. Click Next. On the Test Query page, click Test Query to ensure that you are connecting to the database.

If the query test passes, you will see a table of the data that you selected in step 7.

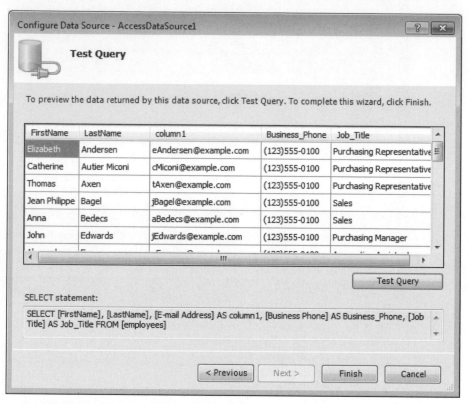

9. Click Finish to close the Configure Data Source Wizard.

10. On the Common toolbar, click Save, and then click the Preview button to view the page and its GridView control in a browser.

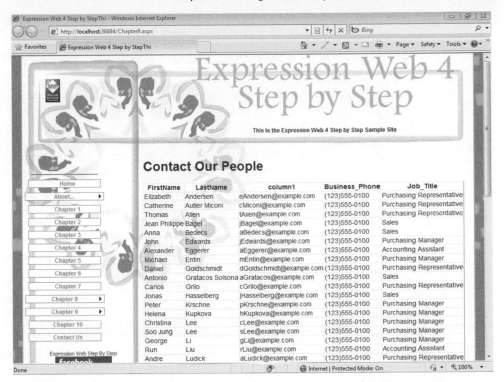

11. Close the browser window, return to the Chapter9.aspx file in Expression Web, and examine the *GridView* that you inserted into the page.

    Notice that there are now more options on the GridView Tasks pop-up window.

12. Click the GridView Tasks button on the *GridView* control's upper-right corner, and then click Edit Columns in the GridView Tasks pop-up to open the Fields dialog box.

13. In the Selected Fields list, click Business_Phone, and then under BoundField properties, in the HeaderText field, replace Business_Phone with **Phone**. Repeat the process to replace Job_Title with **Title**, FirstName with **First Name**, LastName with **Last Name**, and column1 with **E-mail**.

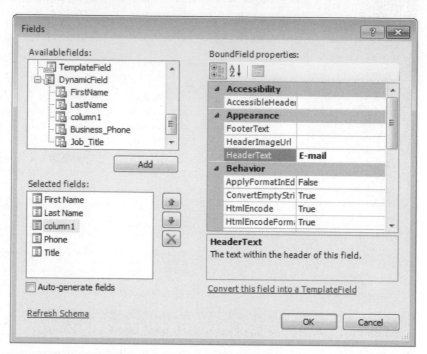

14. Click OK in the Fields dialog box. In the GridView Tasks pop-up window, select the Enable Paging and the Enable Sorting check boxes.

Paging sets up the grid view so that the user doesn't have to look at the entire list at once, and has numerical links at the bottom for the user to view segments of the data. Sorting turns the column titles into hyperlinks that will sort the data by alphanumeric means based on the column title that the user clicked.

15. With the *GridView* control still selected, in the Tag Properties panel Layout group, type **700px** in the Width field.

16. Click Save and then click Preview on the Common toolbar to preview your work.

The column headers are now hyperlinks that sort the rows below them, in addition to having better column heading text. If you scroll to the bottom of the page, you'll see that numerical paging (getting data page by page rather than all at once) is also set up for the employee list.

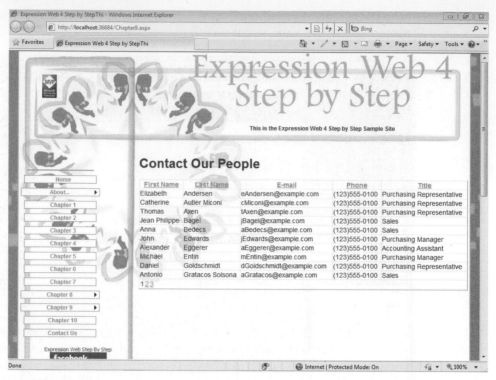

17. Close your browser and return to Expression Web. Double-click Chapter9b.aspx in the Folder List panel to open it for editing.

18. In the Design pane, click *ContentPlaceHolder1*. Click the Common Tasks button on its upper-right corner, and then click Create Custom Content.

19. With all the text from the master page still selected, type **Our Staff**. Highlight the text in the Design pane and click Heading 1 *<h1>* in the Styles drop-down list on the Common toolbar. Set your cursor at the end of the heading and press Enter to create a new paragraph.

20. In the Data group of the ASP.NET controls in the Toolbox panel, double-click ListView to insert an ASP.NET ListView control.

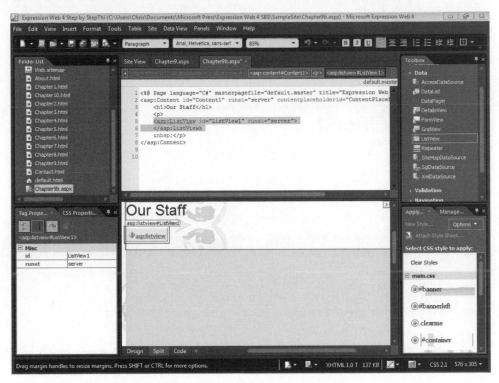

21. Click the red warning (*asp:listview*) link in the Design pane.

The Confirm alert opens.

The *ListView* control requires the Microsoft .NET Framework 3.5, which needs a web.config file in your site.

22. Click Yes on the Confirm alert and then click Save on the Common toolbar.

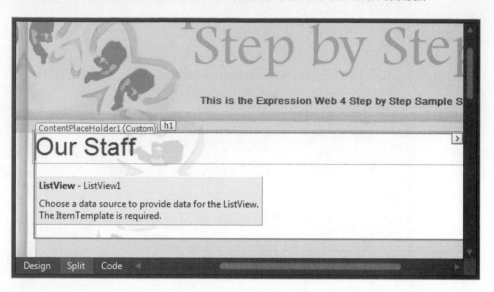

> **Troubleshooting** If you don't have a visual representation of the ListView control at this point, press F5 on your keyboard to refresh the page in the workspace.

23. Click the ListView Tasks button. In the ListView Tasks pop-up, click the Choose Data Source drop-down list and then click New Data Source.

The Data Source Configuration Wizard opens.

24. Click Access Database, and then click OK to open the Choose A Database dialog box. Browse to the ContactList.mdb database in the SampleSite's /files folder and double-click it.

25. In the Choose A Database dialog box, click Next to open the Configure The Select Statement dialog box. Select the FirstName, LastName, Job Title, and Notes check boxes.

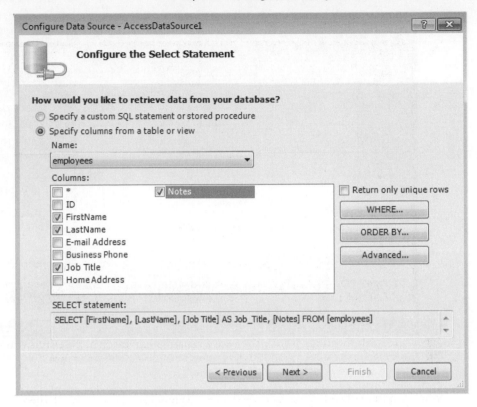

26. Click Next, and then click Finish.

> **Tip** The Test Query step isn't mandatory. Because Expression Web was able to read from the same database in the previous steps, we've skipped the step here.

27. In the ListView Tasks pop-up window, click Configure ListView.

28. Under the Select A Layout label, click Bulleted List. Select the Enable Paging check box and ensure that Next/Previous Pager is in the field below it.

29. Click OK to close the Configure ListView dialog box. Click Save and then click Preview on the Common toolbar to test your new *ListView*.

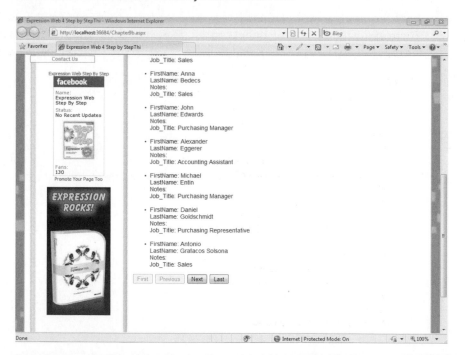

Examine your bulleted list. Notice the paging buttons at the bottom of the list.

30. Close the browser window and return to Expression Web. Click the ListView Tasks button on the *ListView* control, and in the ListView Tasks pop-up, change Current View to ItemTemplate.

The next two steps involve editing the source code of the *ListView* control to eliminate text that was included in the control, and to change the layout slightly.

31. Click the *ListView* control in the Design pane to focus on its code in the Code pane. There are two nodes in the templates that need a little customization. Edit the *<AlternatingItemTemplate>* node. At this point, it should contain the following code:

```
<AlternatingItemTemplate>
      <li style="">FirstName:
      <asp:Label id="FirstNameLabel" runat="server"
        Text='<%# Eval("FirstName") %>' />
      <br />
      LastName:
      <asp:Label id="LastNameLabel" runat="server"
        Text='<%# Eval("LastName") %>' />
      <br />
      Job_Title:
      <asp:Label id="Job_TitleLabel" runat="server"
        Text='<%# Eval("Job_Title") %>' />
      <br />
      Notes:
      <asp:Label id="NotesLabel" runat="server"
        Text='<%# Eval("Notes") %>' />
      <br />
      </li>
    </AlternatingItemTemplate>
```

Modify the code so it looks like this:

```
<AlternatingItemTemplate>
  <li style="">
  <asp:Label id="FirstNameLabel" runat="server"
    Text='<%# Eval("FirstName") %>' />
  <asp:Label id="LastNameLabel" runat="server"
    Text='<%# Eval("LastName") %>' />
  <br />
  <asp:Label id="Job_TitleLabel" runat="server"
    Text='<%# Eval("Job_Title") %>' />
  <br />
  <asp:Label id="NotesLabel" runat="server"
    Text='<%# Eval("Notes") %>' />
  </li>
</AlternatingItemTemplate>
```

In the preceding edit, you removed the default text: *FirstName:*, *LastName:*, *Job_Title:*, and *Notes*. They're unnecessary and the item template will be better without them.

32. In the Code pane, scroll to the *<ItemTemplate>* node, and modify it as you did the *<AlternatingItemTemplate>* node in step 31.

Changing this:

```
<ItemTemplate>
  <li style="">FirstName:
    <asp:Label id="FirstNameLabel" runat="server"
      Text='<%# Eval("FirstName") %>' />
    <br />
    LastName:
    <asp:Label id="LastNameLabel" runat="server"
      Text='<%# Eval("LastName") %>' />
    <br />
    Job_Title:
```

```
      <asp:Label id="Job_TitleLabel" runat="server"
        Text='<%# Eval("Job_Title") %>' />
      <br />
      Notes:
      <asp:Label id="NotesLabel" runat="server" Text='<%# Eval("Notes") %>' />
      <br />
    </li>
  </ItemTemplate>
```

into this:

```
<ItemTemplate>
  <li style="">
    <asp:Label id="FirstNameLabel" runat="server" Text='<%# Eval("FirstName") %>' />
    <asp:Label id="LastNameLabel" runat="server" Text='<%# Eval("LastName") %>' />
    <br />
    <asp:Label id="Job_TitleLabel" runat="server" Text='<%# Eval("Job_Title") %>' />
    <br />
    <asp:Label id="NotesLabel" runat="server" Text='<%# Eval("Notes") %>' />
  </li>
</ItemTemplate>
```

Similar to the previous edit, you've removed the default label content from the code. Click Save and then click Preview on the Common toolbar to check your modifications in a browser.

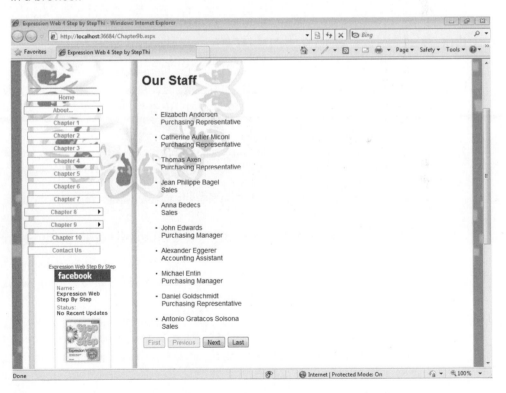

Because the contents of the database are sent to the page as an unordered list, by using an easily editable template such as the one you just modified, a *ListView* control can be a real time saver and efficiency booster for Web designers and developers.

33. Close your browser window and return to Expression Web. Select Close All Pages from the Window menu.

> **Note** Leave the SampleSite open if you are proceeding directly to the next section.

In the past, creating a connection to a database, selecting the data you needed, transferring it into a page, and formatting it was a fairly technical and difficult task. With ASP.NET and Expression Web, you can do all that and more, without writing a single line of programming code. Consider also that when ASP.NET renders this data to the page, it's just (X)HTML code, so you can use CSS to style it with limitless different appearances.

These data source controls and data views become even more impressive as you dig deeper into their capabilities. If you've ever had to write code by hand, you will undoubtedly appreciate the added, advanced features that are available, such as enabling sorting or even enabling users to edit the data in a browser.

Using ASP.NET Ajax Features

Using the ASP.NET AJAX controls, you can create client-side functionality such as partial-page updating. Partial-page updating and rendering eliminates the need for the browser to reload an entire page, and instead update only those individual regions of the page that have changed.

In many ways, AJAX is similar to jQuery. AJAX's particular specialty is exchanging data with a server and then updating parts of a Web page, without reloading the whole page.

AJAX is used in millions of sites including Google Maps, Gmail, YouTube, and Facebook.

Use ASP.NET AJAX to cycle AdRotator items without refreshing the page

> **Note** Use the Chapter9.html page of the SampleSite site you opened in the previous exercise. Open this book's sample site and Chapter9.html page, if they aren't already open.

1. In the Folder List panel, double-click default.master to open it in your workspace. Locate the *AdRotator* control that you added in the previous section. On the Quick Tag Selector, click the *<p#w3cvalidity>* tab to select the paragraph that surrounds the *AdRotator*.

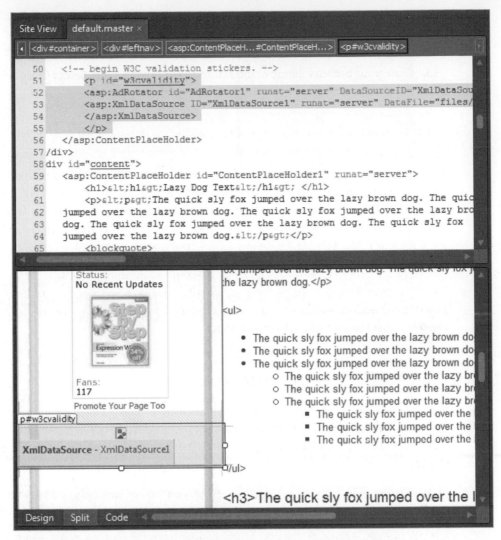

In the next few steps, you will use AJAX tools from the Toolbox panel to create an area of the page that updates the AdRotator without reloading the page.

2. In the Code pane, set your cursor inside the *<p>* tag that contains the *AdRotator*. In the Toolbox, expand the Ajax group, and then double-click the *ScriptManager* control.

Expression Web places a ScriptManager inside the paragraph.

3. Double-click the Timer control in the AJAX group. Click Save on the Common toolbar, and then select the *Timer* control in the Design pane. With the Timer control still selected in your workspace, change the Interval field to **1000** in the Tag Properties panel.

The timer interval is in milliseconds. You need to assign a specific time interval to the *Timer*, or it will default to 60000 (one minute). Notice that in the source code, Expression Web adds *Interval="1000"* to the *Timer* definition.

4. Double-click UpdatePanel in the AJAX group. With the UpdatePanel still selected, in the Tag Properties panel, click the button beside (Collection) in the Triggers field to open the UpdatePanelTrigger Collection Editor.

   The trigger is necessary because it works with the timer to cause an action to occur at automatic intervals.

5. Click Add. Under the *AsyncPostBack* properties, set the Control ID field to **Timer1** and the EventName field to **Tick**.

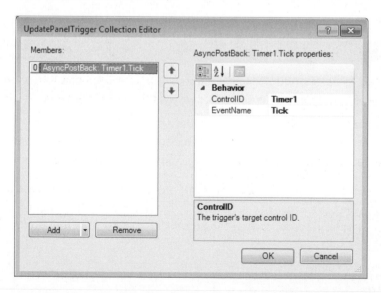

6. Click OK to apply your changes and close the UpdatePanelTrigger Collection Editor.

7. In the Design pane, click the *AdRotator* to select it, and then press Ctrl+X to cut it from the page.

8. In the Design pane, set your cursor inside the *UpdatePanel*. Press Ctrl+V to paste the *AdRotator* inside the *UpdatePanel*, and then click Save on the Common toolbar.

9. Click Chapter9.aspx in the Folder List panel, and then click Preview on the Common toolbar to open the file in a browser and test the *UpdatePanel*.

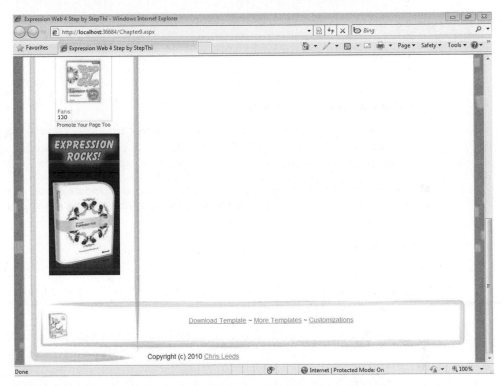

Unlike the last time when you used the *AdRotator*, the AJAX features cause the segment of the page that contains the *AdRotator* to refresh at a set interval—without reloading the whole page.

 Troubleshooting For your ASP.NET AJAX controls to display correctly, your Web server must support the .NET Framework 3.5 or a later version.

10. Close the browser window and return to Expression Web. On the Window menu, click Close All Pages.

 Note If you are not continuing directly to the next chapter, exit Expression Web.

In this section, with just three clicks in the Toolbox, and two simple tag edits in the Tag Properties panel, you were able to create an area in your page that updated itself at a set interval—and you did it all without any handwritten code.

 Note At this point, you can close the SampleSite site and any open browsers. If you are not continuing directly to the next chapter, exit Expression Web 4.

Key Points

- The Expression Web ASP.NET tools enable complex functionality with minimal coding.

- The Toolbox panel contains a group of commonly used ASP.NET controls.

- You can quickly convert a DWT to a master page.

- Site Navigation controls enable you to create server-side navigation for your pages.

- The AdRotator Control uses an XML file to load a different ad each time a page loads.

- ASP.NET data controls enable designers to easily work with Data Sources.

- ASP.NET AJAX tools make it easy for a designer to create partial page updates.

Chapter 10
Managing and Publishing Your Work

After completing this chapter, you will be able to:

- Understand hosting requirements and publishing protocols

- Find and register a domain name

- Use Microsoft Office Live Small Business

- Understand the publishing protocols available in Expression Web

- Understand and evaluate security requirements

- Publish with FTP, HTTP, or File System

- Create a subsite

- Import and export Web packages

- Use SEO reports

After you've taken all the time and trouble to create a Web site and have gotten everything set up the way you want, you are probably going to want people to be able to access it. Whether your site is intended for only a select group of users (an intranet site), or for the general public (an Internet site), you will need to place the files and folders from your development site onto a more generally available server.

From a Microsoft Expression Web standpoint, moving your site's local files and folders to a server is a process called *publishing*. Although publishing might, on its surface, seem like a simple copy operation, there's actually a lot more going on during the publishing process; Expression Web not only copies files, it keeps tabs on what's been published, where it's been published to, and when each file was last published. In addition, with Expression Web, you can publish not only from your local site to a server, but also from a server back down to your local computer, or even from one server to another server without copying the files to your local computer at all. Given these capabilities, the complexity and usefulness of the publishing functions become quite apparent.

 Important Before you can use the practice files in this chapter, you need to download and install them from the book's companion content Web site to their default location. For more information about downloading and installing the practice files, see the "Code Samples" section at the beginning of this book.

Troubleshooting Graphics and operating system-related instructions in this book reflect the Windows 7 user interface. If your computer is running Windows XP or Windows Vista and you experience trouble following the instructions as written, please refer to the "Information for Readers Running Windows XP or Vista" section at the beginning of this book.

Considering Hosting Requirements

You can host your domain and site on many different server types. For the purposes of this discussion, you can divide servers into two main categories: those that run a Windows operating system, and those that do not.

The decision about which server type to use depends solely on what kind of files and functionality you either currently have in your site or plan to include in the future. Use these guidelines:

- If your site has or will have Microsoft dynamic pages such as ASP.NET, or ASP files, or if the site requires a Microsoft Access or Microsoft SQL Server database, you should choose a Windows server with the appropriate Microsoft .NET Framework version and the appropriate database capabilities.

- If your site has or will have non-Windows dynamic pages such as PHP or a MySQL server, then you can use either a non-Windows server or a Windows server configured properly to allow PHP and MySQL to run.

- If your site has only static pages (.htm/.html) and you don't intend to add server-side functionality, it really doesn't matter which server type you choose.

When choosing a server to host your site, it's important to make a good initial decision. It can be a tremendous hassle to move a site after it's been deployed to a server. The decision is complicated by the fact that there are literally tens of thousands of hosting companies you can choose from. A little due diligence is definitely required on this topic. A good place to start, by using the experience of others, is at *www.webhostingtalk.com*.

Some of the things you'll need, and should be provided to you after signing up for hosting space, include:

- A user name and password for publishing. Whether you opt for HTTP, FTP, FTPS, SFTP, or WebDAV, your host will provide you with a unique user name and password.

- The URL or folder you are supposed to publish into. Some hosts designate a specific folder in your Web space into which you must publish.

- The DNS settings your host requires you to use. To enable visitors to arrive at your site on your hosting space, you will need to use the appropriate DNS settings. These settings are changed within the account where you registered your domain name. At least two DNS entries are required. For example, *NS1.EXAMPLE.COM* and *NS2.EXAMPLE.COM*. When you change these settings at your registrar, it can take up to 72 hours for the settings to propagate throughout the Internet.

After you set up your hosting space, you'll be ready to move on to publishing your files and folders to the Internet. Resist the urge to find the cheapest host, or to make a quick decision. This is one of those points where taking some additional time in the beginning can save you much more time and trouble in the future.

Reseller Accounts

If you're a professional Web designer, or if you intend to get into the business, you should look into what's commonly known as a *reseller account*. Such an account will allow you to host your own site and all your customers' sites. You'll be able to access all the sites through a common control panel, and your clients will be able to access their own domain settings through their own unique domain control panel.

One provider of reseller accounts with a concentration in Microsoft Expression Studio products is *www.ExpressionStudioHosting.com*. Because a reseller account hosts not only your site but also the customer sites for which you're responsible, due diligence in the beginning carries even more weight. Reselling hosting to your customers can be easy and profitable if you have the right host, but it can be a recipe for disaster if you choose the wrong host. You can check *www.webhostingtalk.com* for reseller accounts also.

Finding and Registering a Domain Name

In addition to acquiring hosting space for your site, you'll also need a domain name. A domain name is the base of the alphanumeric address called a Uniform Resource Locator (URL), and it's the address visitors use to find your site. For example, the URL for Microsoft is *http://microsoft.com*; their domain name is *microsoft.com*.

When you register your domain name, you will want to choose something directly related to your name, your company's name, or a word or phrase that the potential readers associate with the products or services your company provides. It's important to give a great deal of thought to the domain name you choose, because the name will have a direct impact on search engine relevance for all the pages within your site. In addition, it's the name people will use to access your site. Whether you're giving them that name in print advertising, by phone, or in person, the name needs to be descriptive, easy to remember, and easy to spell.

> **Tip** Even if you need only one site, you may need more than one domain. For example, you might want to register your company name with several extensions, such as *example.com*, *example.net*, and *example.org*. Another tactic is to register common misspellings of your "main" domain. That way, if visitors happen to type the domain name improperly, you can still get them to the correct site.

Part of the choice you make when registering a domain name is selecting the extension. Common domain extensions are *.com* (intended for company and commercial sites), *.net* (intended for network sites), *.org* (intended for organizations), and *.edu* (intended for educational institutions). The Internet started with only a few domain extensions, but these have been extended over the years; there are a great number of domain extensions available today, but you should initially use the one that was designed for your site's purpose and profile.

For domain names to function as intended, each name must be unique. Therefore, domain names are centrally registered and managed by the Internet Corporation for Assigned Names and Numbers (ICANN). However, you can submit a domain name for registration through secondary companies, called *registrars*.

Because there are a tremendous number of registrars where you can set up and register your domain name, you should do some research on this topic as well. ICANN's site, at *www. internic.com*, maintains a list of accredited registrars along with invaluable information on the topic. Choosing a registrar is another situation where learning from other people's experience pays off exponentially. Expect to pay from $8 to $30 per year for a registered domain.

Another way to find great domain names that have just become recently available is to use a service like *www.justdropped.com*. This particular service enables its users to find recently expired domain names, and they can search and filter the results.

> **Tip** People who are in business as Web site designers or developers might want to look into reselling domain name registrations as well as reselling hosting. Domain name registration is less lucrative than reselling hosting space, but the added level of convenience of having all your customers' domains registered through a common domain control panel might be worth it for you. Two of the most popular options are *www.wildwestdomains.com* and *www.enom.com*, although they each have different methodologies. To resell hosting and domains with a concentration on Expression Studio products, see *www.ExpressionStudioHosting .com*. A large number of domain name reselling options are available, so this, as with all major decisions, also requires some research.

Using Microsoft Office Live Small Business

The Microsoft Office Live Small Business site offers one possible solution by which you can register a domain name and set up hosting in one step. You'll find various feature levels available at *http://smallbusiness.officelive.com*. The site offers free domain registration and a free basic Web site, but also provides you with the opportunity to add paid services such as extra storage space, a set of e-commerce features, and email newsletter functionality. Office Live Small Business might be just what you're looking for, so you should spend some time checking it out.

> **Tip** In my research for this book, I found the Office Live servers to be the absolute fastest servers I'd ever published to. I also found it convenient that the user name and password were the same as the Windows Live ID that I used when I signed up.

Understanding the Publishing Protocols Available in Expression Web

From within Expression Web, you can choose to publish in six different ways:

- FTP
  - ❏ Requires FTP to be set up on the server. Check with your host for FTP parameters for your site.
  - ❏ FTP is the most common and widely available form of publishing.

- SFTP
  - ❏ Secure Shell (SSH) File Transfer Protocol
  - ❏ FTP over SSH is fairly rare on shared hosting. You will most likely find this option available only on dedicated servers.

- FTPS
  - ❏ FTP over Secure Sockets Layer (SSL)
  - ❏ Not a "default" setup with most hosts. If you're interested in, or required to use the enhanced security afforded by this method, you should contact your host and see what they have available. In most cases, you will use FTPS as opposed to SFTP, because it's much more common to install an *SSL certificate* for a site than to provide Secure Shell access.

- HTTP (Microsoft Office FrontPage Server Extensions)

  - Requires *FrontPage Server Extensions* on the server. Check with your host to see if they are available.

  - Provides for encrypted transfer of user name and passwords by using the HTTP protocol to publish.

  - If you have any FrontPage legacy components in your site, you should have the host enable FrontPage Server Extensions and publish via this method. For instance, if you have a form in your site that uses FrontPage Server Extensions, just publishing it via FTP instead of HTTP will cause the form to stop working.

- WebDAV

  - Requires *Distributed Authoring and Versioning (DAV)* to be set up on the server. Check with your host to see if this is an option for your site.

  - Is currently fairly rare but provides a feature set that is otherwise not available, such as file locking, properties, and namespace management.

  - For more information about WebDAV, visit *www.webdav.org* and see "WEBDAV: IETF Standard for Collaborative Authoring on the Web" by E. James Whitehead, Jr. and Meredith Wiggins available at *www.ExpressionWebStepByStep.com/Files /WebDavIntro.pdf*.

- File System

  - Publishes a disk-based site from one folder structure to another.

  - This method is generally used to "copy" a site from one location on your computer to another for administrative purposes.

  - Has no requirements, but also results in minimal capabilities at the publish location.

Considering Security Requirements

Although publishing via HTTP using FrontPage Server Extensions will protect the user name and password, it only protects your site from being logged into by a malicious user due to an exposed user name and password.

If you have sensitive files such as an encryption key or a database of sensitive user information such as credit card numbers, you need to do more than protect just the logon credentials. You need to encrypt the files as they're passed from your local computer to the server.

Encryption has been a staple of e-commerce sites since the very beginning of commerce on the Internet. Generally an SSL certificate is added to the server. The browser and server encrypt all the data that is transferred during a secure session (https). Although browser and server security is essential in e-commerce transactions, the same level of security should be considered while publishing sensitive files from the local computer to the server or from the server to the local computer.

If you're using HTTP publishing via FrontPage Server Extensions or WebDav, you can publish securely using HTTPS and therefore use the site's SSL certificate to encrypt the files you publish.

In the absence of HTTPS, you can choose to publish from Expression Web 4 using FTPS or SFTP, both of which securely encrypt your files as they're transferred.

Ask your host what they have available to securely publish your files.

Publishing with FTP

Publishing with FTP is a valuable capability, because virtually every server and every hosting space has FTP publishing available. It's definitely the most common method of transferring files to a server. Even if you prefer to use HTTP publishing over FrontPage Server Extensions, as many people do, a time will come when you need to use FTP. For example, you may have a new customer with an existing Web site and you need to copy the customer's current online assets down to your local computer. If his current hosting provider does not support FrontPage Server Extensions, you won't have a choice; you'll have to use FTP to transfer the content. Knowing when and how to use FTP is a valuable skill, and it's one you will undoubtedly need.

In the next exercise, you will publish a site to a server via FTP, and become familiar with the publishing settings available in Expression Web for FTP publishing.

Publish a site using FTP

> **Note** Use the SampleSite located in the Documents\Microsoft Press\Expression Web 4 SBS folder. Start Expression Web, and have your FTP user name and password available before beginning this exercise. Open the SampleSite by selecting Open Site from the Site menu and then double-click Chapter10.html in the Folder List panel.

1. From the Site menu, choose Site Settings.

   The Site Settings dialog box opens, displaying the Publishing tab and any saved Publishing Destinations.

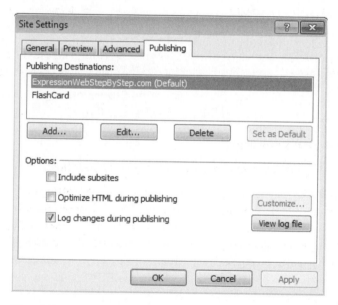

The ability to keep multiple publishing destinations for each site is a real boost to efficiency. For instance, a user can keep their remotely hosted site, a local backup location, and a development location for testing new changes to the site. In addition to using different locations for different purposes, the more locations that files exist in, the more secure they are from loss.

Important In the exercises in this chapter, you will see references in the graphics to *ExpressionWebStepbyStep.com*. This domain was set up specifically for the publishing operations demonstrated in this book, and used as a support site for its readers. You should have your own site publishing parameters.

2. Click Add. In the Connection Settings dialog box, type **SampleSite** in the Name field and select FTP from the Connection Type drop-down list.

3. The next segment of the dialog box that you need to configure is the Location group. Type the FTP address into the Location field.

4. If your host requires you to use a specific folder for your public files, type the name of that folder in the Directory field. Finally, add the text **SampleSite** to the Directory field.

 Important If you have a required folder from your host, the path you enter in the Directory field might look like Public_HTML/SampleSite. If there's no public folder required, the Directory field will contain just the text SampleSite. The reason for adding SampleSite is to protect the rest of your Web site and so that the root of your Web site doesn't end up with all the practice files from this book's SampleSite in it, leaving you with a mess to clean up. If there's no folder named SampleSite on your server (and there shouldn't be) Expression Web will create that folder for you during the publishing operation.

5. The next group you need to fill in is the Credentials field. Enter your user name and password in their respective fields.

   The user name and password will be provided to you by your host.

6. The final group in the Connection Settings dialog box is the Settings group. It contains choices for Maximum Simultaneous Connections, which is a number that Expression Web limits multiple simultaneous uploads to, and a check box for Use Passive FTP. In most cases, you should leave these selections at their default of 4 simultaneous connections and Passive FTP enabled.

Tip You can use passive FTP or normal FTP from Expression Web. Some network configurations work only with passive FTP mode turned on, whereas others work only with it turned off; however, most network configurations support both modes. The passive FTP mode is considered more secure. You can also choose how many simultaneous connections Expression Web uses during transfer. Although you can choose from 1 to 10, the ideal number seems to be the default selection of 4, but feel free to adjust this as you experiment and progress in your publishing skills.

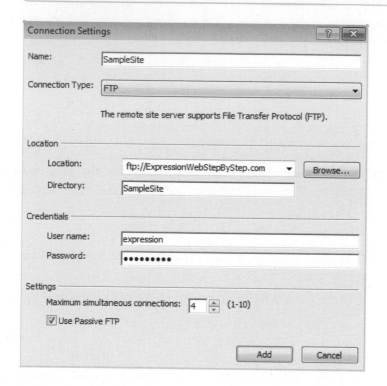

 Important The Connection Settings in this graphic will result in publishing via FTP to *ftp://ExpressionWebStepByStep.com/SampleSite*. Your publishing destination will be different, but make sure that you have at least SampleSite in the Directory field so that you can easily segregate the SampleSite from the rest of your Web site.

7. Click Add.

Expression Web closes the Connection Settings dialog box and returns you to the Publishing tab of the Site Settings dialog box.

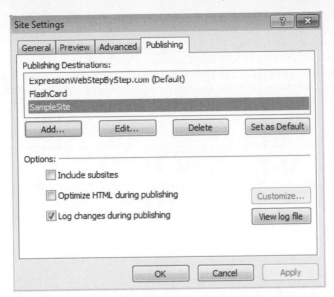

Notice that the Destination Name that you added in the previous steps is now listed in the Publishing Destinations field on the Publishing tab. Besides the Publishing Destinations group, the Publishing tab also contains an Options group that enables you to publish subsites, which you will learn about later in this chapter; Optimize HTML During Publishing, which you learned about in Chapter 2, "Capitalizing on Expression Web 4 Functionality"; and an option to Log Changes During Publishing as well as a button to View Log File.

8. Accept the default settings and click OK to save your new Publishing settings.

> **Tip** The options on this tab are self-explanatory. You might change them from their de-
> faults for issues relating to publishing speed or a publishing strategy. For example, if your
> local site contains subsites, you might choose the option to publish subsites on certain oc-
> casions. In general, the default Publish tab settings are recommended.

9. Click Publishing from the Site menu. Expression Web switches to Publishing view. Click the arrow beside the Connect To field above your workspace and then select the publishing destination you created in the previous steps.

> **Important** If you entered a folder name in the Connection Settings dialog box that
> doesn't exist on the server, Expression Web will open an alert asking if you want to create
> the folder. Click Yes.

Expression Web connects to the publishing destination, and shows you a split pane arrangement with the local site on the left and the remote site on the right. Also notice that the toolbar above your workspace becomes active.

10. Click the Select All button above the Local Site pane.

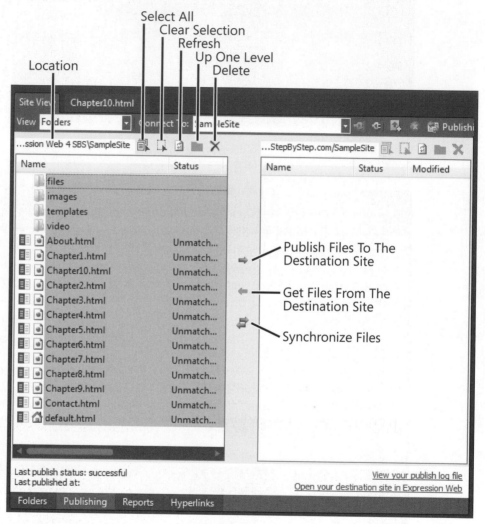

11. Click the Local To Remote arrow between the panes of the Publishing view. The Publishing Status panel opens below the workspace and Expression Web publishes all the files from your local site to the server location.

By selecting all the files and folders and then clicking the Local To Remote arrow, you will publish all the content of your local site to the remote site that you're connected to. You will learn other methods to publish only selected or changed files as well.

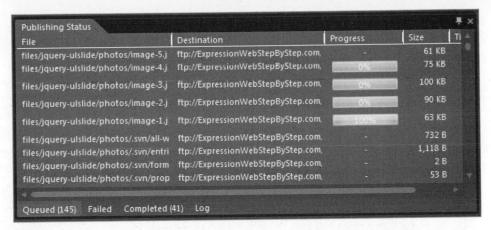

12. When the publishing operation completes, the Queued tab will be empty. Check the Failed, Completed, and Log tabs for additional publishing information.

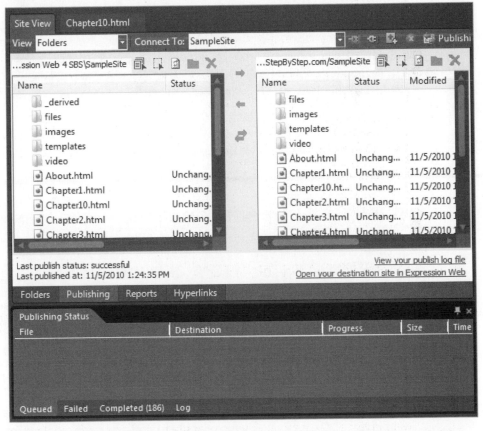

13. Close the Publishing panel and then click the Chapter10.html tab at the top of the workspace.

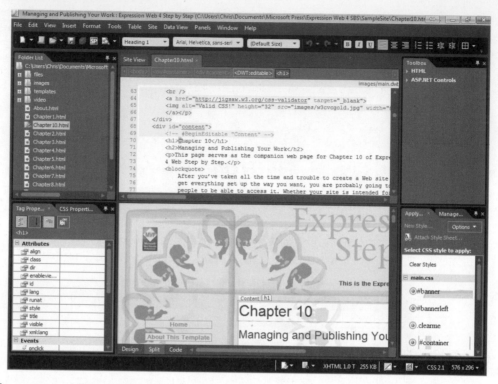

You have now published a local site to a remote server by using FTP in Expression Web. All your local files are now on the server, and you can view them in a browser. Simply open a browser and type your site's domain name followed by */SampleSite* in the address bar to check your work.

Note Leave the Chapter10.html file open for use in the next exercise, but close any open browser windows.

Troubleshooting Sometimes the hosting service places a default file in the root folder of your account. Index.htm, index.html, default.htm, and default.html are common default files for a Web server. If you publish your site and visit the domain in a browser, but you don't see the home page that you published, you will need to delete or rename the default file that the host created. After you do that, your site's home page will take precedence and the server will pass it to the browser as the default file of the domain. You can perform this action in Expression Web in the Remote Web site view by right-clicking the index or default file your hosting company supplied in the Remote Web site pane and then clicking either Delete or Rename.

Important If you intend to publish your Expression Web site using FTP, it's recommended that you use the built-in FTP publishing feature rather than a third-party FTP client. The reason is that Expression Web will skip publishing the hidden folders containing the site's metadata, but a third-party application won't make that distinction, and will publish everything. Publishing the hidden folders can cause publishing to take longer, and also uses unnecessary space on the server.

Publishing Using HTTP (FrontPage Server Extensions)

HTTP publishing is the only publishing method with which you can publish pages containing FrontPage legacy components. HTTP publishing provides the added benefit of encoding the user name and password that you use when publishing and supports publishing through a Secure Sockets Layer (SSL/HTTPS) if you have a Secure Server Certificate installed on your server.

In this exercise, you will see how to use HTTP publishing through Expression Web, and explore the features available with this method.

Publish a site using HTTP

Note Use the Chapter10.html page of the SampleSite site you opened in the previous exercise. Open this book's sample site and Chapter10.html page, if they aren't already open.

1. From the Site menu, select Publishing Settings.

   The Site Settings tab opens with the Publishing tab visible.

2. Click Add. In the Connection Settings dialog box, type **SampleSite-HTTP** into the Name field, and then select FrontPage Server Extensions from the Connection Type drop-down field.

3. Type the HTTP address of your site in the location field, followed by **/SampleSiteHTTP**.

Important Make sure that you have a folder name added to the end of your Web site address. If you don't publish into a specific folder, Expression Web will publish these files into the root of your hosting space and it will be a mess to clean up.

4. Type your user name and password in their respective fields in the Credentials group.

 Tip Notice the option in the Settings group: Use Encrypted Connection (SSL). By selecting that option, you will publish your site to an HTTPS destination. You will need an SSL Certificate installed on your remote Web site to use this option.

5. Click Add in the Connection Settings dialog box.

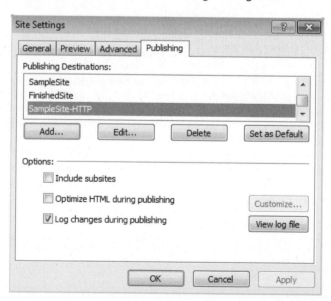

6. Click OK in the Site Settings dialog box, and then from the Site menu select Publishing.

Expression Web opens in Publishing view.

7. Click SampleSite-HTTP (or whatever parameters you used in the previous steps) in the Connect To drop-down field.

Expression Web connects to the publishing destination you set up in the previous steps.

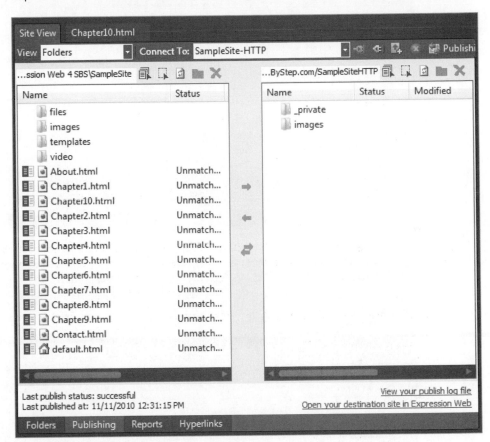

Tip When you log on to your site for the first time, you might see some folders in your site structure. This is generally normal; these folders are put there by your host. Often they're intended to hold server logs, control panel files, and so on.

8. From the Site menu, select Publish Changed Files.

The Publishing Status panel opens beneath the Publishing view and all the files are sent to the destination site.

Troubleshooting You will see an alert window if you don't already have a folder named SampleSiteHTTP on your server. Click Yes to allow Expression Web to create the folder for you.

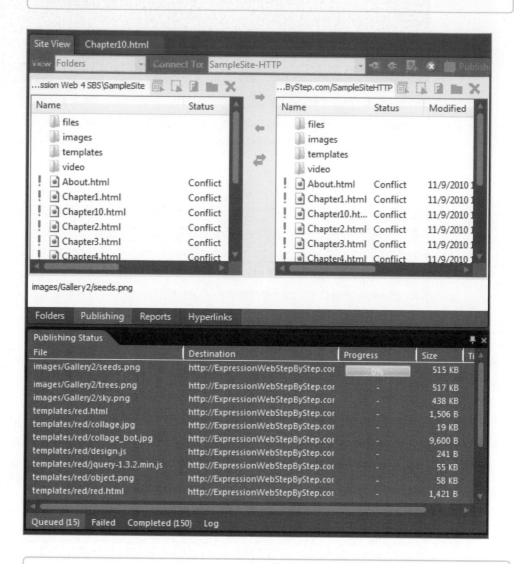

Tip You will find the Publish All Files and Publish Changed Files options in the Site menu as well as on the Standard toolbar.

9. When the publishing operation completes, the Queued tab will be empty. Check the Failed, Completed, and Log tabs for additional publishing information.

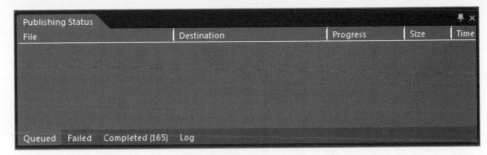

 Important In the exercises in this chapter, you will see references in the graphics to *ExpressionWebStepbyStep.com*. This domain was set up specifically for the publishing operations demonstrated in this book, and used as a support site for its readers. You should have your own site publishing parameters.

10. Close the Publishing Status panel and then click the Chapter10.html tab at the top of your workspace.

11. Open a browser window and type the destination address you just used into the address bar. Then press Enter on your keyboard.

Your /SampleSiteHTTP/ folder opens in the browser.

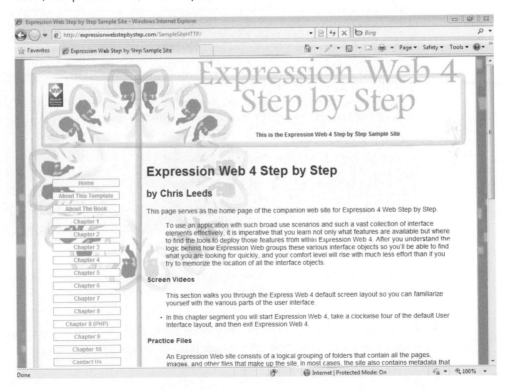

You have now published a local site to a remote server using FrontPage Server Extensions (HTTP) from within Expression Web. All your local files are now on the server, and you have viewed them in a browser.

> **Note** Leave the SampleSite and Chapter10.html file open if you are proceeding directly to the next section.

File System Publishing

File system or disk location publishing is usually used to copy a site from one location on your computer or local network to another. This can be useful when you want to move a site from an "active" folder location where you work on sites to another folder location where you archive finished work, or to move a site from its existing folder location to a network share on your local network.

Publishing from one disk location to another is superior to simply copying and pasting in Windows Explorer, because publishing ensures that all the necessary files are moved, and conversely, that none of the unnecessary ones are moved. It's the best way to move a site to avoid future problems with the metadata that Expression Web uses to manage sites.

In this exercise, you will publish from one folder location to another with Expression Web.

Publish a site to a disk location

> **Note** Use the Chapter10.html page of the SampleSite site you opened in the previous exercise. Open this book's sample site and Chapter10.html page, if they aren't already open.

1. From the Site menu, select Publishing Settings.

   The Site Settings tab opens with the Publishing tab visible.

2. Click Add. In the Connection Settings dialog box, type **SampleSite-FS** into the Name field, and then select File System from the Connection Type drop-down field.

3. Click the Browse button beside the Location field.

4. In the New Publish Location dialog box, browse to this book's installation folder and then click the New Folder button. Name the folder **SampleSiteFS**.

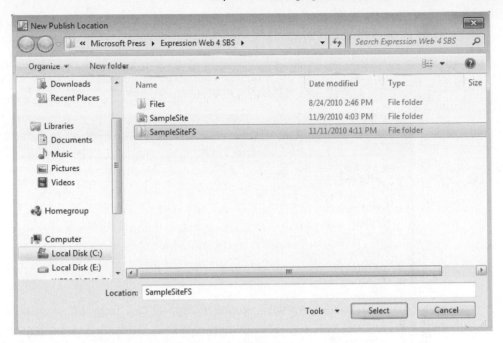

5. Click Select in the New Publish Location dialog box.

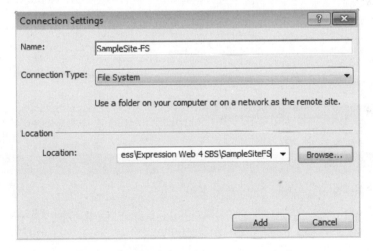

The Connection Settings dialog box is now complete.

6. Click Add in the Connection Settings dialog box, and then click OK in the Site Settings dialog box.

7. From the Site menu, select Publishing.

Expression Web opens in Publishing view.

8. Click SampleSite-FS from the Connect To drop-down field.

Expression Web connects to the publishing destination you set up in the previous steps.

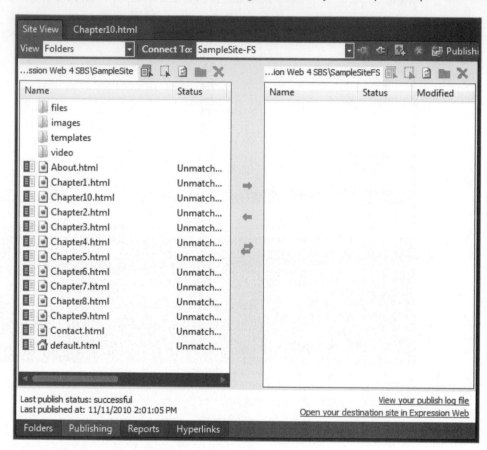

9. From the Site Menu, select Publish All Files.

The Publishing Status panel opens beneath the Publishing view and all the files are sent to the Destination site.

10. When the publishing operation completes, the Queued tab of the Publishing Status panel will be empty and both sides of the Publishing view will be populated.

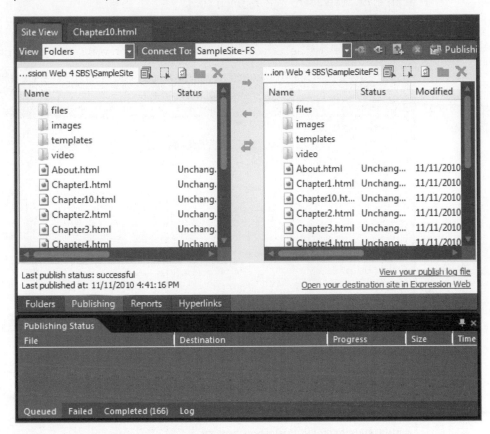

11. Close the Publishing Status panel and then click the Open Your Remote Website In Expression Web link below the Remote pane of the Publishing view.

The newly published SampleSiteFS/ opens in Expression Web.

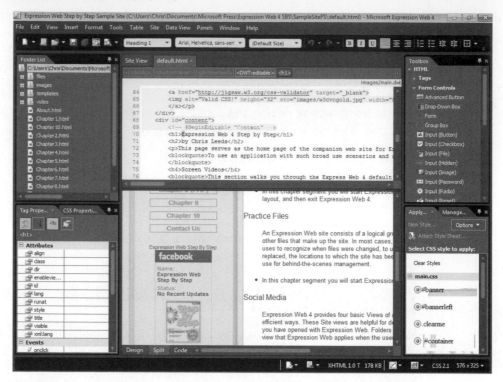

Tip Although the SampleSite opened in Expression Web, something more important has actually taken place—the site opened in another instance of Expression Web. When you open a site from the Site menu, the current site closes and the next site opens, so that only one open instance of Expression Web exists. It's often helpful to have two Web sites open simultaneously.

12. Close the newly opened instance of Expression Web and return to the original SampleSite. Click the Chapter10.html tab at the top of your workspace to close the Publishing view.

You have now published a copy of your local SampleSite to a new disk-based location using File System publishing from within Expression Web. All your Web files are duplicated and the site's metadata has been maintained properly. You've also seen one of the few ways to open multiple instances of Expression Web 4.

Note Leave the SampleSite and the Chapter10.html file open if you are proceeding directly to the next section, but be sure to close the SampleSiteFS instance of Expression Web.

Managing a Web Site

Whether you're the owner of a single site or a professional Web master responsible for a great number of sites, one of the responsibilities you will have is site management. These tasks take many forms and come into play at many points in the life cycle of a Web site.

In addition to being a good editing and publishing tool, Expression Web contains a number of features that offer the user a management system that's truly second to none.

In this section, you will learn to back up and edit server-based sites, use site settings, publish pages selectively, and use subsites.

> **Note** Use the Chapter10.html page of the SampleSite site you opened in the previous exercise. Open this book's sample site and Chapter10.html page, if they aren't already open.

Backing Up Server-Based Sites

Occasionally, the files on a server-based site can actually be newer than the files in the local copy of the same site. For example, if the server-based site contains form data, is a shopping cart, or is a type of dynamic site that takes user input, the server-based site will have more or newer information than the local copy. In this case, making a backup copy of the server-based site is essential.

Another reason to back up a server-based site is that the local copy might become lost, corrupt, or compromised in some way. Still another reason to back up a server-based site is that you might acquire a new customer and need all their online assets to be brought down to your local computer so that you can work on their project.

In all these scenarios and others, Expression Web takes care of everything. To fully exploit its capabilities, all you need is an understanding of how the features work.

Back up a server site to your local computer

> **Note** No practice files are required for this exercise. Use your own published site and server parameters for this exercise. Be sure to start Expression Web and check that you have an active Internet connection before beginning this exercise.

1. From the Site menu, point to Import and then select Import Site Wizard.

2. In the Import Site Wizard, select FTP from the Connection Type drop-down list and type the FTP address of your site into the Location field. Then type the directory name into the Directory field.

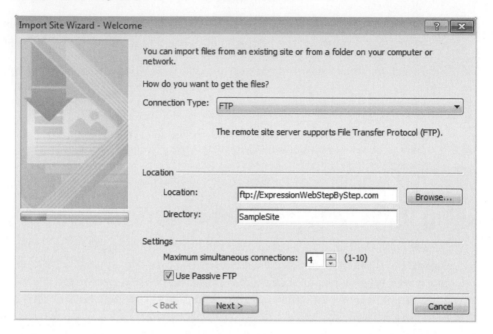

Important The previous graphic uses the FTP location of *ExpressionWebStepByStep.com* and the SampleSite directory that you saw in the preceding exercise. Also note that there's no trailing slash in the Location field and neither a leading nor trailing slash in the Directory field. It's important to let Expression Web work out the path and necessary slashes.

3. Accept the default settings of 4 for Maximum Simultaneous Connections and Use Passive FTP. Click Next.

4. Clear the Add To Current Site check box and then click the Browse button beside the Local Copy Location field.

   The New Publish Location dialog box opens.

5. Browse to this book's installation folder (Documents\Microsoft Press\Expression Web 4 SBS) and then click the New Folder button. Name the new folder **SampleSiteImport**.

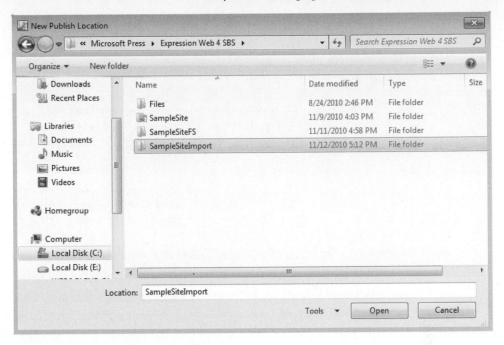

6. Select your new folder and click Open.

The New Publish Location dialog box closes and you return to the Import Site Wizard.

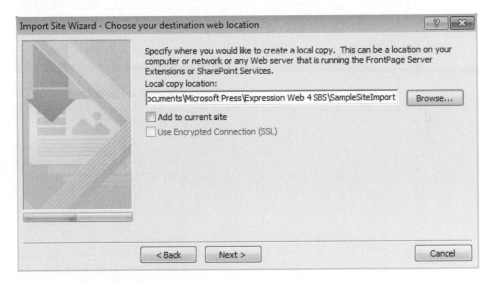

7. Take a moment to examine the Local Copy Location field and ensure that it contains the path you intended. Then click Next.

The final screen of the wizard opens.

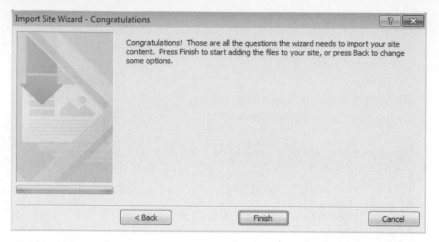

8. Click Finish in the Import Site Wizard. When the server logon dialog box opens, enter your FTP credentials.

When the server accepts your FTP session, Expression Web opens in Publishing view with the site you will be importing in the Remote pane and the new folder location that you set up in the Local pane.

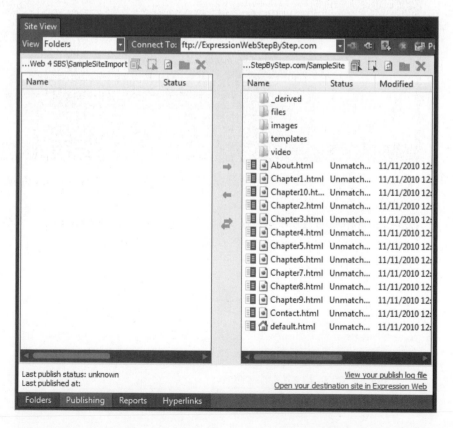

Tip Take this opportunity to ensure that the remote site is the correct location that you intend to import and that the local site is the folder location that you set up during the Import Site Wizard process.

9. Click the Select All button on the toolbar above the Remote pane and then click the Synchronize Files button between the Local and Remote panes.

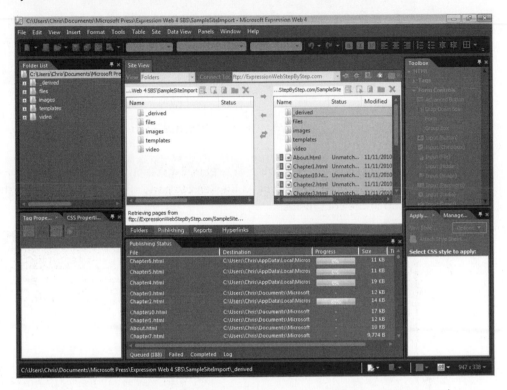

Expression Web begins the publishing process and the Publishing Status panel opens below your workspace.

10. When the publishing process completes, check the results by examining the Failed, Completed, and Log tabs of the Publishing Status panel.

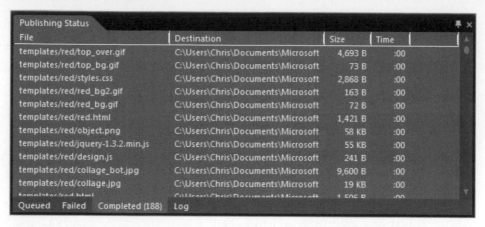

11. Close the Publishing Status panel and then click the Folders tab at the bottom of the Publishing view workspace.

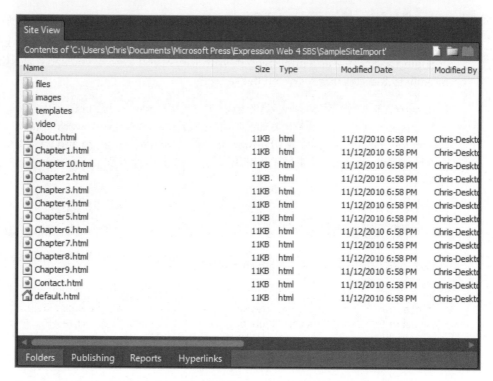

Expression Web displays the contents of your newly imported site in Folders view.

12. From the Site menu, select Close. When your newly imported site closes, point to Recent Sites on the Site menu and then select the original SampleSite (Documents\ Microsoft Press\Expression Web 4 SBS\SampleSite).

The original site you began this exercise with is now open in Expression Web.

> **Note** Leave the SampleSite open if you are proceeding directly to the next section.

You've just used the Import Site Wizard to copy a server-based site to a local folder using FTP. FTP was used in this example because it's the most common publishing protocol, but any of the six publishing types, plus HTTPS, can be used and the experience will be virtually identical.

The more frequently you back up a site, the more synchronized the backed-up data will be, so any restoration operations will potentially lose less data. This method is also necessary for working on a site that has never been stored on your local computer, such as when you need a copy of a new customer's site to work on, if you have a new computer and need your server-based sites on it, or when you need a copy of a site for archival purposes.

Editing Server-Based Sites

Occasionally, you will want to make a change directly to a server-based site, rather than changing a local file and publishing it. With Expression Web 4, you can make the changes directly to the files that reside on the server.

One reason for editing directly on the server is that you might not have access to a computer that contains a local copy of the site. Another common reason to work on a server-based site is that you might be trying to fine-tune some server-side scripting and want to bypass the process of changing a local file, publishing it, and then checking the server-based file with a browser.

By working directly on the server, you can make your change and test it, all from within the Expression Web user interface.

Make changes directly to a server-based site

> **Note** Use your own published sites and server parameters for this exercise. Be sure you have an active Internet connection before beginning this exercise. This exercise will use the server-based site that you published via HTTP (SampleSiteHTTP) and the one you published via FTP (SampleSite) sites that were used in the previous exercises.

1. From the Site menu, select Close. After the site closes, select Open Site from the Site menu. In the Open Site dialog box, type the HTTP address of the server-based site you want to open, and then clear the Add To Managed List check box.

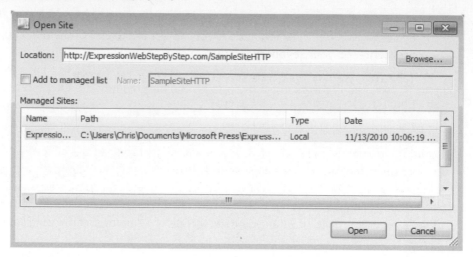

Troubleshooting This step assumes that your site has FrontPage Server Extensions applied. If it does not, skip to step 11 to follow the FTP method for editing a site directly on the server.

2. Click Open in the Open Site dialog box. Type your user name and password in the server logon dialog box if it appears.

The server-based site opens in Expression Web.

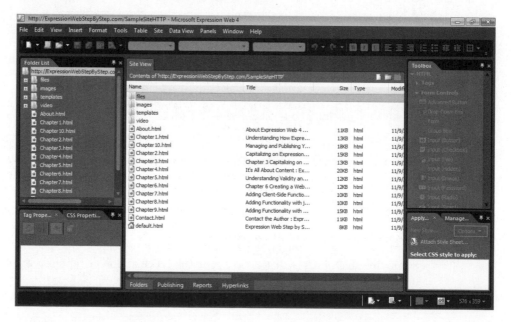

3. Double-click the Chapter10.html file to open it for editing. Scroll down to the "Editing Server-Based Sites" heading and set your cursor at the end of the heading text. Then press Enter on your keyboard to create a new paragraph.

4. Type **This was changed on a server-based site using HTTP**.

5. Click Save and then click the Preview button on the Common toolbar.

   The server-based Web page opens in a browser, and you should see the change that you made.

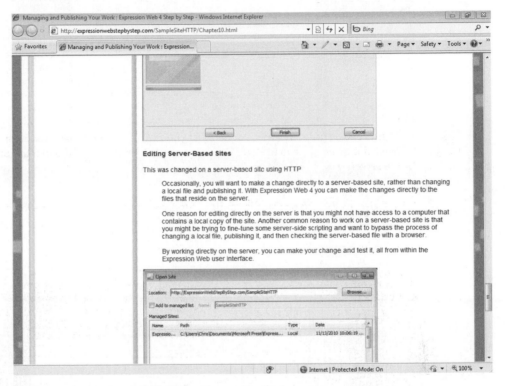

6. Close your browser and return to Expression Web.

7. From the File menu, select New, and then choose Create From Dynamic Web Template.

   The Attach Dynamic Web Template dialog box opens.

8. Click the master.dwt file inside the site's images folder, and then click Open.

   Expression Web creates a new page based on the site's Dynamic Web Template.

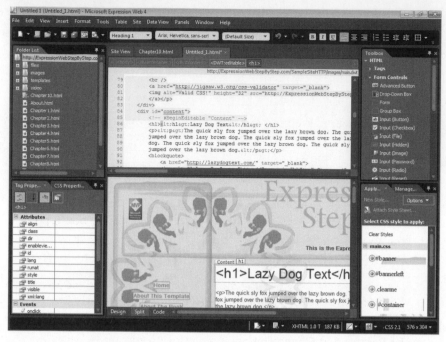

9. Click Save. In the File name box of the Save As dialog box, type **LivePage.html**, and then click Save. Click the Preview button to preview the newly created page in a browser.

10. Close the open browser window, and return to Expression Web. From the Site menu, select Close.

    The site closes, and Expression Web switches to an empty user interface, with no site open.

 Important   It's important that you open a server-based site with *either http://* (FrontPage Server Extensions) *or* FTP. Using FTP on a site with server extensions can cause them to become corrupted. This isn't particular to an entire domain. By using subsites, you can have FrontPage Server Extensions-enabled sites and FTP sites within the same domain and not encounter any conflicts or problems.

11. On the Site menu, click Open Site. In the Open Site dialog box, type the FTP address of your server-based site, and then click Open.

 Important   This example uses the FTP version of the Sample Site you published in the previous exercise: FTP://ExpressionWebStepByStep.com/SampleSite.

    The Remote Site Editing Options dialog box opens.

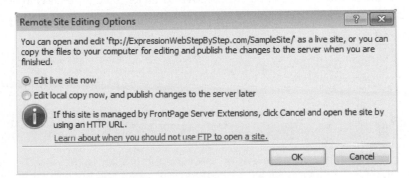

12. Accept the default selection, which is Edit Live Site Now, and then click OK.

 Tip   The Edit Local Copy Now, And Publish Changes To The Server Later option will begin the Import Site Wizard. Also take note of the FrontPage Server Extensions warning that appears when you open a live server-based site with FTP.

13. If the server logon dialog box opens, log on with your FTP credentials.

    The site opens in Expression Web.

14. Double-click the Chapter10.html file to open it for editing. Scroll down to the "Editing Server-Based Sites" heading, set your cursor at the end of the heading text, and then press Enter on your keyboard to create a new paragraph.

15. Type **This was changed on a server-based site using FTP!**

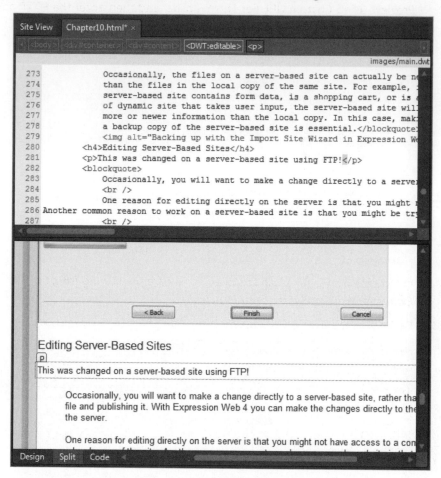

16. Click Save and then click Preview on the Common toolbar to preview the page in a browser.

17. Because you're trying to preview this page through an FTP connection, Expression Web will open an alert prompting you to set up a custom preview URL.

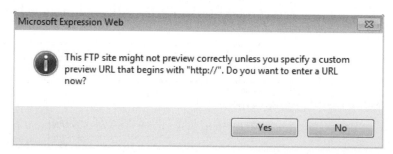

18. Click Yes on the alert. The Preview tab of the Site Settings dialog box opens. Select Preview Using Custom URL For This Website, and then enter the HTTP address that you will use.

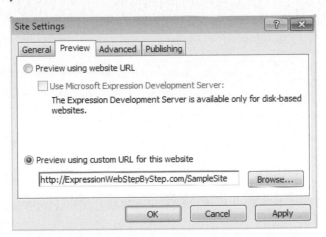

In the case of the images in this exercise, we are previewing from *http://ExpressionWebStepByStep.com/SampleSite*.

19. Click OK in the Site Settings dialog box to set your custom preview URL.

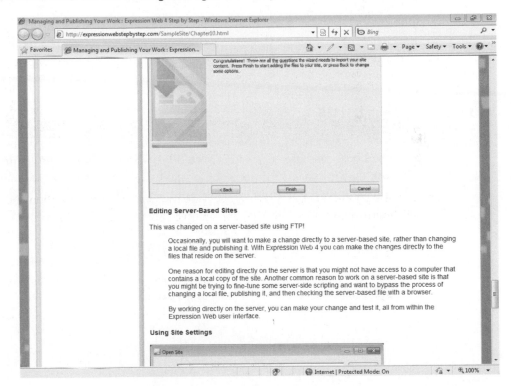

The Chapter10.html file opens in a browser using your custom preview URL as the base URL and folder path. Scroll the page to the line you entered in the previous step to make sure that it appears as it should.

> **Tip** When you add a custom preview URL, add the full domain plus the folder name that the site resides in, if any.

20. Close the browser and return to Expression Web. Select Close from the Site menu.

    Expression Web remains open but without an open site within it.

21. From the Site menu, point to Recent Sites and then select the original SampleSite (Documents\Microsoft Press\Expression Web SBS\SampleSite).

> **Note** Leave the SampleSite open if you're continuing directly to the next segment. Otherwise select Exit from the File menu to close Expression Web.

Microsoft Office FrontPage users have had the ability to edit a live site through HTTP for a long time, but in Expression Web, the ability to open and modify a live site through FTP is truly revolutionary. It's a capability you will not find in any other HTML editor.

The capabilities of live editing and manipulation are more robust through the HTTP protocol, especially with FrontPage features such as Design-time Includes and Dynamic Web Templates, but having the option to work on a live site through FTP is also very useful.

Using Site Settings

Whether you're working with a site that you imported, or a site that you're developing from scratch on your local computer, Expression Web offers some management features that can really help, but they're in a less than obvious location: the Site Settings and Managed Sites List dialog boxes. Using the Site Settings dialog box, you can customize the workflow and certain default settings for a site, on a global basis. You can also do a few things using this dialog box to help troubleshoot a site that isn't functioning properly.

Although you've seen most, if not all, of the Site Settings dialog box tabs in the previous chapters, this section is here to group all the settings together with the specific intent of showing their usefulness from a site management perspective.

Use the Site Settings dialog box to make global changes and troubleshoot problems

 Note Use the SampleSite site located in the Documents\Microsoft Press\Expression Web 4 SBS\ folder. Open the site by selecting Open Site from the Site menu and then open Chapter10.html.

1. On the Site menu, select Site Settings.

The Site Settings dialog box opens. You can change the site name in the Web Name field on the General tab.

 Important Using the Web Name field is the only way that you should change an Expression Web site name. If you change the name in Windows Explorer, issues might arise with the site's metadata.

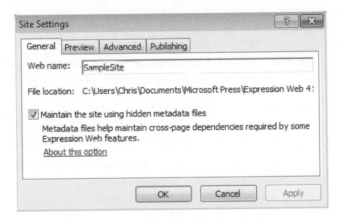

The Maintain The Site Using Hidden Metadata Files check box enables you to selectively use (or not use) the Expression Web metadata.

 Important This is a feature that you will generally leave enabled. The metadata aids Expression Web in such functions as keeping links maintained, keeping the correct Dynamic Web Template attached to the correct pages, and remembering where the site has been published. If you clear the check box, Expression Web will not only stop using metadata, it will also strip it from the site. Stripping the metadata might be purposely done if you were going to compress the site and send it to another developer or designer who publishes with a third-party FTP client, for example.

2. In the Site Settings dialog box, click the Preview tab.

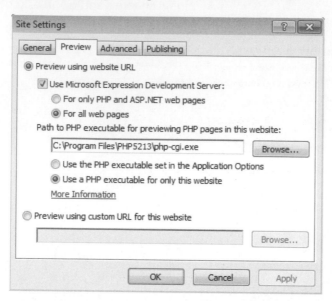

On the Preview tab, the Preview Using Website URL option enables the Expression Web initiated browser view to reflect the URL from which the site was opened.

The Use Microsoft Expression Development Server check box is selected by default, and so is its sub-option, For Only PHP And ASP.NET Web Pages. The For All Web Pages sub-option causes any page, regardless of file type, to be previewed using the Expression Development Server.

Although the ASP.NET Development Server will pass any page to the browser during preview, it only executes server-side scripting for PHP or ASP.NET pages. It will not execute Classic ASP, or any other server-side scripting.

Here's one example that illustrates why you might want to pass all pages through the Development Server: you're designing a static HTML site, but you're setting your links to the folder that contains the page rather than the page itself. Your links will be to, for example, */about/* rather than */about/default.htm*. If you're not using a server when you click a link such as this in browser preview, you will be presented with a Windows Explorer view of the folder, and the browser will not display the default file within that folder. Enabling the Expression Development Server will remedy this situation and pass the default file in a folder to the browser.

If you completed the previous exercise, you have seen how the Preview Using Custom URL For This Website option sets a Custom Preview URL for the site.

3. In the Site Settings dialog box, click the Advanced tab.

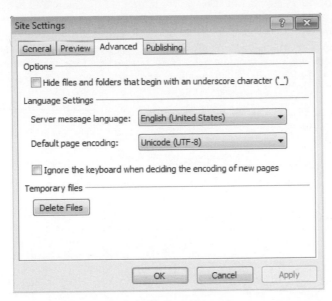

The Hide Files And Folders That Begin With An Underscore Character ('_') check box changes the default behavior of whether Expression Web shows folders beginning with an underscore. For example, if you name a folder _DontShowMe, and select this check box, the folder will not be visible in any of the Expression Web views, such as the Folder List panel or Folders view.

> **Tip** You can use the Hide Files And Folders That Begin With An Underscore Character to gain greater functionality and better management. Here's a scenario: you've built a site, and other users are going to update page content. You've used a Dynamic Web Template to ensure that the other users don't edit outside the editable regions you've set up. If you put the Dynamic Web Template in a hidden folder and check the Hide Files And Folders That Begin With An Underscore Character check box, the users will be much less likely to find the Dynamic Web Template and make unwanted changes to it.

In the Language Settings group, you can set the Server Message Language, when you're connected to the live server as you were in the past exercise, and also set the Default Page Encoding. By default, these settings are English (United States) and Unicode (UTF-8) and rarely need to be changed.

The final item on the Advanced tab, beneath the Temporary Files label, is the Delete Files button, which does just that. It deletes temporary files that Expression Web creates behind the scenes while you're working on a site.

> **Troubleshooting** Remember the Delete Files button. If Expression Web begins to run into problems while publishing a site, or updating Dynamic Web Template–attached pages, one remedy is to use the Delete Files button to delete the temporary files, and then click Recalculate Hyperlinks on the Site menu. This operation almost always resolves the problem. Another great tool that helps correct issues with Expression Web and other HTML editors is the FP Cleaner Utility program, which you can download free of charge at *http://www.95isalive.com/fixes/fpclean.htm*.

4. In the Site Settings dialog box, click the Publishing tab.

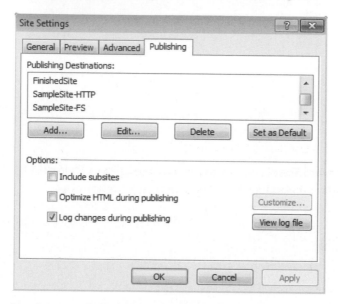

You have used the Publishing tab earlier in this exercise, but from a management perspective, this tab is quite helpful for organizing and maintaining all the locations where a particular site may be published to. There's no limit on how many Publishing Destinations you can enter, so you may want to keep a local back-up location, a public server-based location, a development location, and so on in the Publishing Destinations list. You can also edit the parameters of each of the destinations as well as add and delete locations from this dialog box tab.

Beneath the Options label, you can select whether Expression Web includes subsites during the publishing process, and whether Expression Web optimizes HTML during the publishing process, as well as customize exactly what those optimizations are. You'll also find an option for whether Expression Web logs changes during the publishing process and a button to view the site's log file.

You've now explored all the tabs and functionality available in the Site Settings dialog box. You can use this dialog box on either a local site or on a server-based site that is opened through Expression Web.

5. Click Cancel in the Site Settings dialog box and then, from the Site menu, select Managed Sites List.

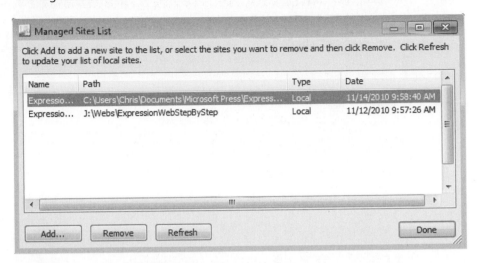

The Managed Sites List dialog box opens.

6. Click Add. In the Add Site dialog box that opens, browse to this book's installation folder and select the SampleSiteImport site you imported previously.

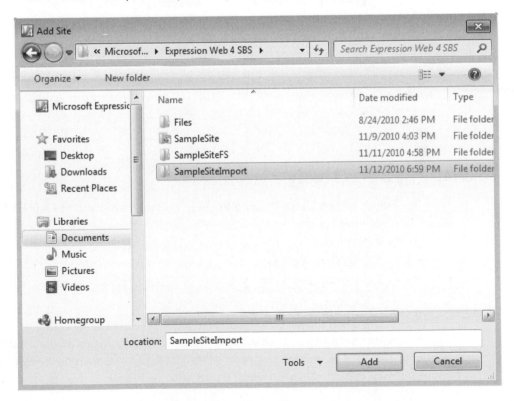

7. Click Add in the Add Site dialog box.

The dialog box closes and you return to the Managed Sites List with your newly added site visible in the list.

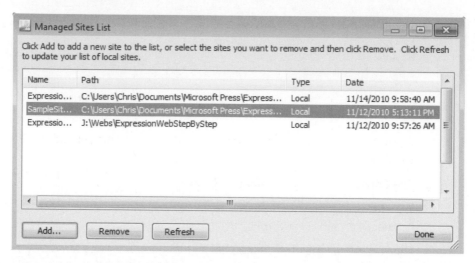

8. Click Done in the Managed Sites List dialog box.

Some developers may have hundreds of sites in the Managed Sites List. There's no limit to how many you add, nor is there a requirement that they be disk based or server based. The more sites you keep in the Managed Sites List, the more important giving them intuitive and meaningful names become.

> **Note** Leave the SampleSite and Chapter 10.html file open if you are proceeding directly to the next section.

Publishing Selectively

From the standpoint of speed during publishing, you might not want to rely on letting Expression Web deduce which pages have changed. For example, if you changed only one file in a site, and you want only that file to be published to the server, you don't have to go through a full publishing operation.

Expression Web provides easy methods for publishing specific files, and provides methods for ensuring that certain files are never published. One reason that you might not want specific files to be published is that if you keep original artwork inside of a local site for management, you don't want the large original files to be published to the server. Another reason is that you might have a configuration file in your local site that is different than the one on the server-based site, or a database file with newer information on the server than is in the local copy.

Publish selected files using File System publishing to prevent specific files from being published

 Note Use the SampleSite that you worked with in the previous exercise. Open the SampleSite and Chapter10.html if they're not already open.

 Tip You can also use these steps to publish to a server-based Expression Web site.

1. From the Site menu, select Publishing Settings. Click Add beneath the Publishing Destinations list.

   The Connection Settings dialog box opens.

2. Type **SelectivePublish** in the Name field and then select File System from the Connection Type drop-down.

3. Click Browse beside the Location field. In the New Site Location dialog box, navigate to the Documents\Microsoft Press\Expression Web 4 SBS folder. Click the New Folder button and name the folder **SelectivePublish**.

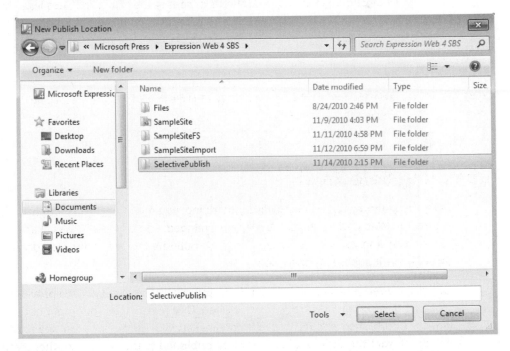

4. Click Select.

5. Take a moment to verify that the Connection Settings dialog box is configured as it should be. Click Add, and then click OK in the Site Settings dialog box.

6. From the Site menu, select Publishing. At the top of the Publishing view, select SelectivePublish from the Connect To drop-down.

Expression Web switches to Publishing view with your new folder location open in the Remote pane.

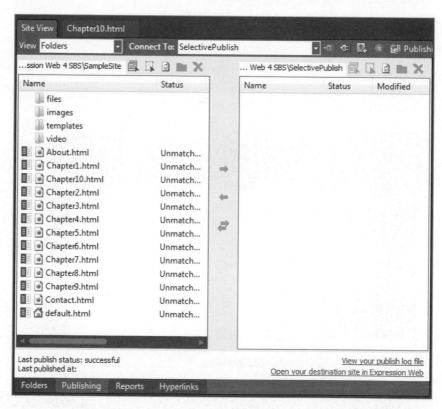

7. In the Folder List panel, expand the site's images folder. Right-click the Document_files folder and in the context menu, click Exclude From Publishing. Expand the \Document_files folder.

Notice that both the Document_files folder and all the images inside of it are marked with the Exclude From Publishing icon.

 Tip The Exclude From Publishing option works on individual files as well as entire folders.

8. In the Local pane of the Publishing view, right-click Chapter10.html and then, in the context menu, select Exclude From Publishing.

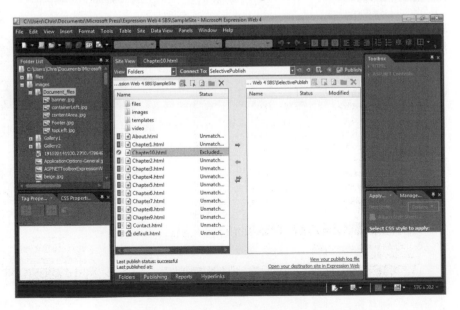

Notice the Exclude From Publishing icon that has been applied to the Chapter10.html file.

9. From the Site menu, select Publish All Files.

Expression Web opens the Publishing Status panel and begins the publishing operation.

10. When the publishing operation completes, close the Publishing Status panel and compare the Local and Remote panes of the Publishing view.

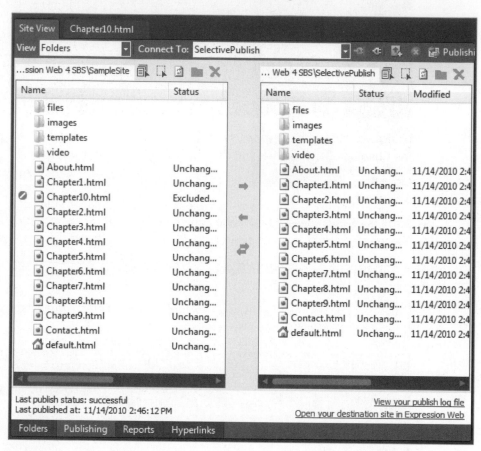

Notice that the images folder in the Remote pane doesn't contain a Document_files folder, and the root of the Remote site contains no Chapter10.html file.

11. Right-click the Chapter10.html file in the Local pane, and in the context menu, click Exclude From Publishing.

The Exclude From Publishing icon is removed from the Chapter10.html file.

12. From the Site menu, select Publish Changed Files.

The Publishing Status panel opens and the Publishing process completes.

13. At the bottom of the Publishing Status panel, click the Completed tab.

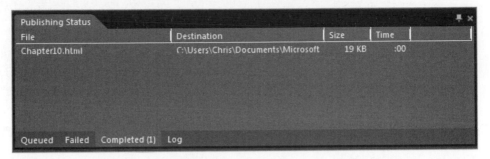

Notice that only one file appears in the Completed tab of the Publishing Status panel—the Chapter10.html file that you cleared the Exclude From Publishing icon from.

14. Close the Publishing Status panel and click the Chapter10.html tab at the top of your workspace.

15. Scroll the Design pane down to the Publishing Selectively heading and make a minor change to the page by putting an exclamation point at the end of the heading.

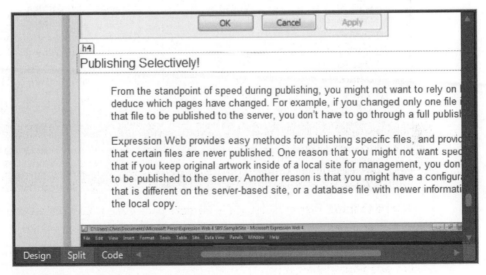

16. Click Save on the Common toolbar and then right-click the Chapter10.html tab at the top of your workspace. In the context menu, select Publish Current File To "SelectivePublish."

The Publishing Status panel opens and the Chapter10.html file is published to the Destination site.

> **Tip** Publish Selected File in the context menu on the page tab is a new feature in Expression Web 4. If you're working on a site with a complex folder structure, it's much faster to use the feature from the page tab on the workspace than it is to hunt for the file in the Folder List panel.

17. In the Folder List panel, expand the site's images folder and right-click the Document_files folder within it. In the context menu, click Exclude From Publishing.

The Exclude From Publishing icon is removed from the Document_files folder and all the files within it.

18. Right click the Document_files folder, and in the context menu, click Publish Selected Files.

The Publishing Status panel opens, and all the files in the folder are published to the Destination site.

19. Click the Completed tab on the Publishing Status panel and check to see which files were published.

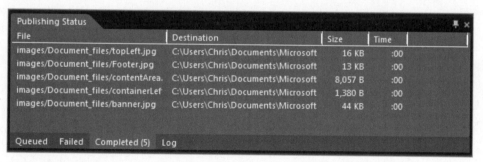

20. Close the Publishing Status panel.

You've now explored methods for publishing specific files, and also for setting files to never publish. These are very useful methods to use when you're working locally on a site that also exists on a server, and you want to publish only a single file that you've changed, or when you want to make sure that a local file never overwrites a server-based site file, such as a Microsoft Access database file (.mdb or .accdb), which often contains more or newer information.

> **Note** Leave the SampleSite open if you are proceeding directly to the next section. Close any open Windows Explorer or Internet Explorer windows.

Using Subsites

Subsites are an important concept for site management. Expression Web treats subsites as though they were completely independent sites regardless of the folder or site that contains them.

One reason that you might want to segregate certain folders in a site as subsites: you might have a large number of files within those folders that don't change as often as the other files in the root of the site. There's no reason to wait for a long file-comparison cycle during an Expression Web publishing session when you know that the files haven't changed. Also, you might want to publish a segment of your site via the Secure Sockets Layer (SSL/HTTPS) if it contains sensitive files such as e-commerce site configuration or database files.

Another good reason to use subsites is when you're developing a replacement site. You can create a subsite in your server-based location, such as *ExpressionWebStepbyStep.com/new-design/*, and then publish your new design directly into the subsite. That way, you can show it to people by providing them with a direct address to it, but the general public wouldn't know it was there, and therefore wouldn't see it.

Subsites are a good way to segregate files for architectural reasons and to gain greater publishing efficiency.

In this next exercise, you will convert a folder to a subsite, publish a subsite, and convert a subsite to a folder.

Convert folders to subsites and subsites to folders

 Note Use the SampleSite that you worked with in the last exercise. Open the SampleSite and Chapter10.html if they're not already open.

1. Click the Site View tab at the top of your workspace. If the Site View opens to Publishing, click the Folders tab at the bottom of the workspace.

2. In the Folder List pane, click the templates folder to display its contents in the workspace.

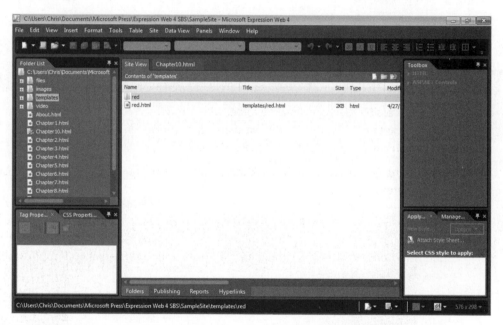

This folder contains a page template that you worked with in a previous chapter. There's really no reason to publish a folder like this to the server or destination site. In the next steps, you will not only prevent it from being published, you will make Expression Web completely ignore it.

3. In the Folder List, right-click the templates folder and then, in the context menu, click Convert To Subsite.

4. You'll see a warning box informing you that Expression Web will consider the folder as a completely separate site. That's your intent here, so click Yes.

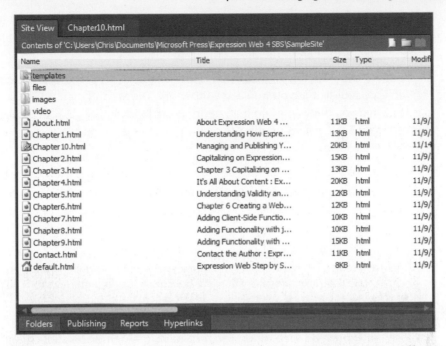

Expression Web converts the folder to a subsite. The folder now has a different icon, and if you select it in the Folder List panel, the workspace displays a notice that Expression Web cannot display the contents of a subsite.

5. In the Folder List, double-click the templates subsite to open it in a new instance of Expression Web.

With the subsite open in Expression Web, you can perform any operation that you could perform on any other Expression Web site. Additionally, you can publish it independently of the parent site that contains it.

There are two ways to publish a subsite. One method is to open the subsite in Expression Web and publish it as you would any other site. The second method is to include subsites when you publish. To do that, perform the following actions: with the parent site open, click Site Settings on the Site menu. On the Publishing tab, select the Include Subsites check box.

Troubleshooting When you publish a subsite by opening it directly in Expression Web, be sure to append the name of the subsite to the publish location of the parent site. For example, if you publish the parent site to *http://example.com*, but you want to publish a subsite named "new_site" only, append */new_site* to the name. The URL would be *http://example.com/new_site*. If you don't append the subsite name, Expression Web will publish all the subsite's files to the root of the parent site. When you publish a subsite for the first time, Expression Web prompts you that a site does not exist at the location you're trying to publish to, and offers to create a site in that location. Click Yes.

6. Close the Expression Web window that contains the \templates subsite, and switch to the Expression Web window that contains the original SampleSite.

7. In the Folder List, right-click the \templates subsite, and then click Convert To Folder.

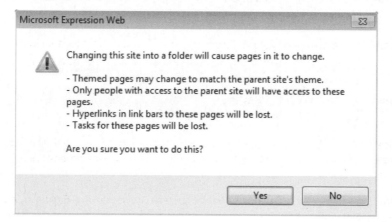

8. Click Yes in the alert dialog box.

The subsite changes back to a conventional folder, and its contents are now displayed in the workspace.

You've now converted a folder to a subsite and back to a folder within Expression Web. Because Expression Web treats subsites as though they were completely independent sites, you'll find they can be advantageous for organizing and for efficiency in publishing. Keep in mind, however, that because Expression Web treats subsites as completely independent sites, you can't use an asset such as a Dynamic Web Template across subsite boundaries.

> **Note** Leave the SampleSite open if you are proceeding directly to the next section. If you are not continuing directly to the next section, exit Expression Web.

Import and Export Web Packages

If you're an experienced site designer, you've probably amassed a collection of files and scripts such as shopping carts or database applications that you tend to use in all or most sites that you create. If you're very new to Web design, you will probably begin to develop this type of collection very soon.

With a Web Package, you can export a collection of scripts or other assets from within a site; and you can save all the data to a single file (an FWP file), which you can save on your local computer or distribute by any method you prefer, such as email or a link on a Web site.

After exporting a collection of files as an .fwp file, any Expression Web user can import it very easily.

Here's a scenario: the \files\validateMyForm folder in the sample site is a jQuery plug-in that you want to save to reuse in other sites. You can export the folder as a Web Package.

Export and import a Web package

> **Note** Use the Chapter10.html page of the SampleSite site you opened in the previous exercise. Open this book's sample site and Chapter10.html page, if they aren't already open.

1. On the Site menu, click Export To Web Package, to open the Export Web Package dialog box.

2. In the Files In Site pane, expand the \files folder, click validateMyForm, and then click Add. When Expression Web asks if you would like to include the contents of the folder in your Web package, click Yes.

   The validateMyForm folder, along with the files folder that contains it, gets copied to the Files In Package list. It is copied because the files within the media folder don't depend on any files outside that folder.

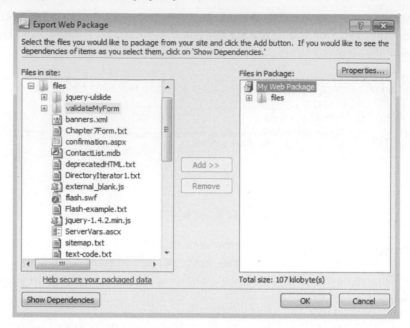

3. In the Files In Package list, expand the files folder.

When Expression Web added the files folder to the package, it added only the contents of the \validateMyForm folder within it. Expand the \validateMyForm folder to verify the contents.

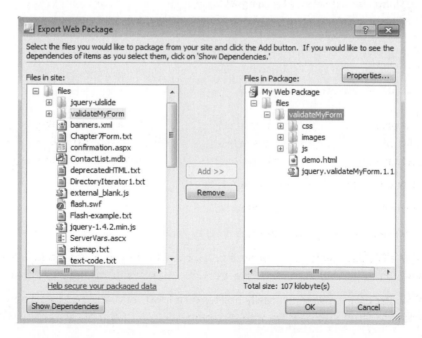

4. Click Properties to open the Web Package Properties dialog box. Change the name from My Web Package to **Media Files**. Add a description, author, and company name if you want.

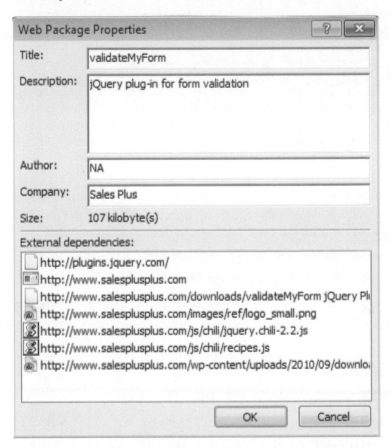

The package will contain this information. In the bottom of the dialog box, you can see a list of external dependencies, which are references to files outside the current site, such as pages that hyperlinks point to or absolute references to images or other files.

5. Click OK to close the Web Package Properties dialog box.

6. In the Export Web Package dialog box, click OK.

   The File Save dialog box opens.

7. In the File Save dialog box, browse to a location where you want to save the exported Web package, and then click Save. Click OK on the Web Package Saved alert.

   Web Package exports can really bolster your long-term asset and workflow building. Imagine setting up your favorite shopping cart, a package of utility-type scripts you use, and a few other items in logical arrangements as Web packages. You'd be able to easily bring them into any project that is open in Expression Web with only a few clicks.

> **Tip** You can use Web Package exports to cull files. If you've been working on a project for awhile, the site probably has become loaded with revisions, old files, and all the other artifacts that a project tends to produce. If you want to pare the project down to the essential pieces—for instance, to send it to a customer or as a preparatory step before publishing to a server—you could select only the files you need to keep and let Expression Web take care of adding the dependent files to your export list.
>
> You can simply export the Web Package and send it off to someone else, or you can create an empty site and import it. Regardless of how you use the Web Package, it's a fast way to isolate only the files you need and leave unnecessary files behind.

8. On the Site menu, point to Import, and then click Import From Web Package to open the File Open dialog box. Browse to the Documents\Microsoft Press\Expression Web 4 SBS\Files folder, click the CH10.fwp file, and then click Open.

   The Import Web Package dialog box opens. In this dialog box, you can select or deselect files and folders and view the properties of the Web package.

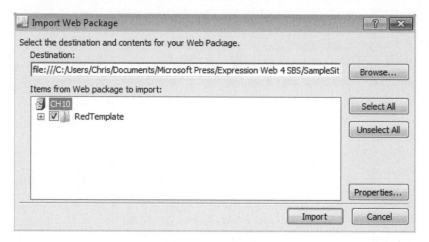

9. Click Import to import the folder and the files it contains to the root of your site.

10. In the security warning dialog box that opens, click Run to continue the process of importing the contents of this Web package.

11. Click OK in the Deployment Complete message box to complete the process.

    A folder named \RedTemplate now exists in your site. Expand the file in the Folders List panel to verify its contents.

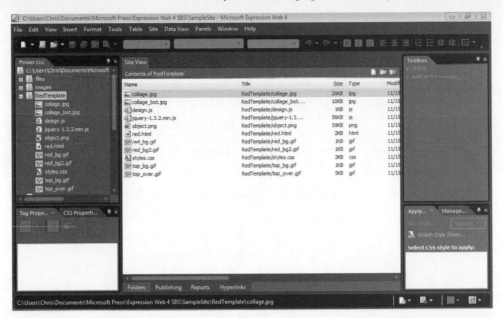

The contents of the newly imported folder will be identical to the contents of the \templates \red folder that already exists in your site.

Note Leave the SampleSite open if you are proceeding directly to the next section.

Personal Web packages make certain functionality, graphics, and other assets portable. In addition to the portability benefit, the export process can be helpful in enabling you to package only files you want to keep and to discard unnecessary files.

Use SEO Reports

It's fitting that the very last segment of this book explains the newest feature in Expression Web 4: Search Engine Optimization (SEO) Reports.

Earlier in this book, you saw several reports that are available in Expression Web 4, but the SEO Reports feature is new and unique among HTML editors.

The SEO Reports feature enables designers and developers to give a sort of "preflight" inspection to their sites and pages from a perspective of attaining the highest possible Search Engine Results Page position (SERP).

Use Search Engine Optimization Reports to analyze the sample site and make changes based on its recommendations

> **Note** Use the Chapter10.html page of the SampleSite site you opened in the previous exercise. Open this book's sample site and Chapter10.html page, if they aren't already open.

1. From the Tools menu, select SEO Reports.

   The SEO Checker dialog box opens. Like many of the other reports, the Check Where options include All Pages, Open Pages, Selected Pages, and Current Page.

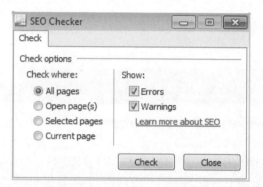

2. In the Check Where group, select Current Page. In the Show group, accept the default selections to show Errors and Warnings.

   Notice the Learn More About SEO link. Clicking this link opens the Expression Web 4 User Guide (F1), which contains detailed information about SEO. (There are more books available about SEO than there are about Expression Web, so that should give you an idea of the depth of information available on this topic.)

3. Click Check.

   The SEO Checker analyzes the Chapter10.html page and the Search Engine Optimization Page appears beneath your workspace.

   Notice the column headers on the Search Engine Optimization panel. Although there are only two issues reported on this particular page, the ability to sort the results is very helpful when you run the reports on multiple pages, or on all the pages in an entire Web site.

4. Double-click the first error in the list.

The Design and Code panes focus on the line of code that Expression Web considers an error.

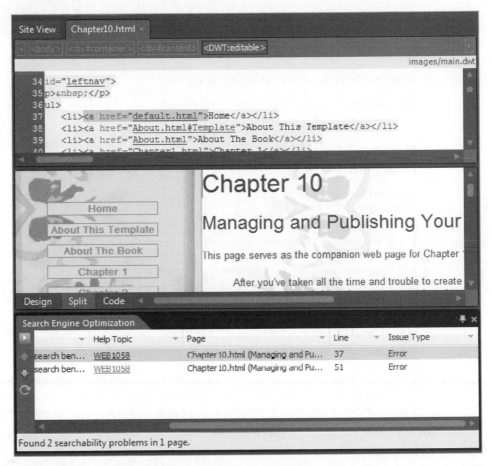

Note that the selected line is part of the site's Dynamic Web Template. With the SEO Reports, as well as other reports based on validity or accessibility, you should run it first against the site's template, whether it's a Dynamic Web Template or a master page.

5. Hold your cursor over the error line to see a tooltip telling you what Expression Web believes the error is.

6. Because we don't want to change the text in the site's navigation, we will ignore these two errors. The reason for the error notification is the same for both reported errors—the text within the link isn't sufficiently descriptive enough to provide any benefit to the search engines.

7. From the Tools menu, click SEO Reports. In the SEO Checker dialog box, select All Pages, accept the default settings (Show Errors and Warnings), and then click Check.

The entire site is analyzed and the Search Engine Optimization panel opens below your workspace.

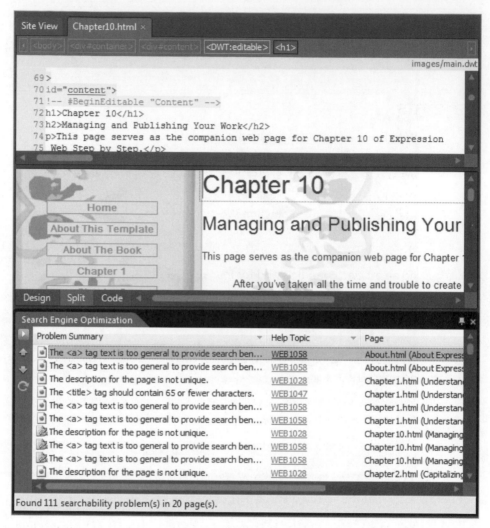

Take a few minutes to examine the results in the Search Engine Optimization panel. The depth and detail that the report analysis does is impressive. Hold your cursor over the individual entries in the list to see the issue that Expression Web uncovered.

> **Tip** Although the report is detailed, not every suggestion is an issue that needs to be dealt with. For instance, there are a few entries about files in the jquery-ulslide folder. That's a folder that contains JavaScript and other assets. It's not something that a user would ever browse to directly, and it's not something that would or should be indexed by a search engine. Issues like this can safely be ignored.

8. Close the Search Engine Optimization panel to return to Split view.

 Note At this point, you can close the SampleSite site, the Chapter10.html file from the File menu, and any open browsers. Exit Expression Web 4.

Key Points

- With Expression Web, publishing is the preferred method of creating a backup. Whether you publish from one file system location to another or from a server-based site to a file system location, the Expression Web publishing operation is the key to success.

- With Expression Web, you can open a site live on the server and edit it as if it were a local site. New features in Expression Web enable you to edit a server-based site by using HTTP or FTP protocols.

- Features in the Expression Web Site Settings dialog box lay the groundwork for setting up an efficient workflow and for managing a site.

- In addition to the Publish Site operation in Expression Web, you can selectively publish individual files or groups of files, and you can also set pages to not be published at all.

- Using subsites can greatly aid in overall site management and publishing efficiency. Subsites can segregate files in a logical way and enhance the basic parent/child folder architecture of a site.

- Expression Web provides six separate publishing methods: FTP, SFTP, FTPS, HTTP (FrontPage Server Extensions), WebDAV, and File System. Each serves a different purpose.

- Publishing by using File System is the most accurate and least error prone way to copy a site from one folder location to another.

- Enhanced security can be attained by using FTPS, SFTP, or HTTPS publishing.

- You can use WebDAV publishing in Expression Web if you have it set up on your server.

- You can set various publishing options through the Remote Website Properties dialog box.

- You can optimize the HTML code of your pages by removing HTML comments, Interactive Button attributes, script comments, and other elements.

- You can import or export Web Packages from within Expression Web.

- Expression Web now contains Search Engine Optimization (SEO) reports.

Index

Symbols

U

About the Author

Chris Leeds is a long-time digital photographer and Web enthusiast who has been a Microsoft Most Valuable Professional (MVP) for Microsoft Office FrontPage and Expression Web for eight years. He is also a Network Partner with Microsoft's Website Spark program (*www.websitespark.com*), commentator at Lockergnome (*www.lockergnome.com*), and a software reviewer on Bright Hub (*www.brighthub.com*).

Chris developed a software product called ContentSeed (*www.contentseed.com*) with which users can create Web pages that they can edit and manage using only a browser.

Chris was a technical reviewer for *FrontPage 2003: The Missing Manual* (O'Reilly), the author of *Microsoft® Expression® Web Step by Step* and *Microsoft® Expression® Web 2 Step by Step* (the previous versions of this book), and co-author for the upcoming book *Microsoft® Expression® Blend 4 Step by Step* (Microsoft Press). He has developed several tutorials about FrontPage, and he hopes to continue helping the user community through the Web site *www.expressionwebstepbystep.com*, from which he'll try to answer questions regarding this book and Microsoft Expression products.